RFID TECHNOLOGY HANDBOOK

Kruger Brentt
Publishers

RFID TECHNOLOGY HANDBOOK

Dimitrie Popescu
Ivana M. Cotabarren

Kruger Brentt
Publishers
2025

Kruger Brentt Publishers UK. LTD.
Company Number 9728962

Regd. Office: 68 St Margarets Road, Edgware, Middlesex HA8 9UU

ISBN: 978-1-78715-319-6

For information on all our publications visit our website at http://krugerbrentt.com/

PREFACE

The "RFID Technology Handbook" serves as a comprehensive guide to understanding the principles, applications, and advancements in Radio Frequency Identification (RFID) technology. This book is designed to be an essential resource for students, researchers, engineers, and industry professionals seeking to explore the diverse and transformative capabilities of RFID technology across various sectors.

RFID technology has revolutionized the way businesses and organizations track and manage assets, inventory, and information. From supply chain management and retail operations to healthcare, logistics, and beyond, RFID systems offer real-time visibility, efficiency, and accuracy in data capture and management, driving operational excellence and innovation.

The primary objective of this handbook is to provide readers with a comprehensive overview of RFID technology, covering key topics such as RFID system architecture, components, operating principles, standards, security considerations, and implementation best practices. Each chapter offers insights, case studies, and practical examples to help readers understand the fundamental principles and applications of RFID technology in real-world scenarios.

Contributions from leading experts in the field explore various aspects of RFID technology, including passive and active RFID systems, RFID tag design and fabrication, RFID reader technology, RFID middleware and software platforms, and emerging trends such as RFID-enabled Internet of Things (IoT) and blockchain integration. Special emphasis is placed on the diverse applications of RFID across different industries and the potential for innovation and growth in the field.

As organizations seek to harness the power of RFID technology to improve efficiency, visibility, and customer experience, it is essential to have a comprehensive understanding of the technology's capabilities, limitations, and implementation considerations. By embracing RFID technology and leveraging its capabilities effectively, businesses and organizations can unlock new opportunities for process optimization, cost reduction, and competitive advantage in today's rapidly evolving digital economy.

We extend our sincere gratitude to the contributors whose expertise and dedication have enriched this handbook. It is our hope that the "RFID Technology Handbook" will serve as a valuable resource and reference guide for readers interested in exploring the transformative potential of RFID technology in their respective industries and applications.

Dimitrie Popescu
Ivana M. Cotabarren

CONTENTS

PART V: CASE STUDIES AND BEST PRACTICES

PART VI: FUTURE TRENDS AND INNOVATIONS

PART I: INTRODUCTION TO RFID

CHAPTER- 1

UNDERSTANDING RFID TECHNOLOGY

At its core, RFID is a technology that uses radio-frequency signals to identify, track, and manage objects, people, or animals. The system comprises two main components: an RFID tag and an RFID reader. The tag, which is affixed to the object of interest, contains a unique identifier and an antenna. The reader, equipped with an antenna as well, emits radio waves, enabling communication with the tag and retrieving the stored information.

RFID operates on the principle of electromagnetic coupling. When an RFID tag enters the electromagnetic field generated by the reader, it draws power from it and transmits its stored data back to the reader. This contactless and wireless communication allows for efficient and rapid data transfer, distinguishing RFID from traditional barcode systems.

Since now we know what the technology is, let's briefly go through some historical background. RFID technology has been around since the dawn of the 20th century, when some brilliant minds first started playing around with radio waves to identify and track objects. However, it wasn't until the 1970s that RFID technology began to take shape in its modern form.

In 1973, the first patent for an RFID system was granted to Mario W. Cardullo. The patent described a system for automatically identifying and tracking articles using radio waves, which marked the beginning of the modern era of RFID.

The 80s and 90s were all about RFID evolution, with the development of various types of RFID systems, including passive and active RFID. During this time, RFID was mainly used in military and industrial applications, such as supply chain management and inventory tracking.

Then came the 2000s, and RFID technology became more widely available and affordable, leading to its increased adoption in various industries, including retail, healthcare, and transportation. The technology continued to grow, and thanks to advancements in it, RFID readers, antennas, and tags became even more advanced.

And now, here we are in the present day, with RFID technology continuing to evolve and expand, with the development of new applications and innovations, such as near-field communication (NFC) and the Internet of Things (IoT). The future of RFID technology looks bright, with many experts predicting that it will play an even greater role in our lives in the years to come.

APPLICATIONS OF RFID TECHNOLOGY

The versatility of RFID technology has led to its widespread adoption across various industries:

- **Supply Chain and Logistics:** RFID streamlines inventory management and enhances supply chain visibility by providing real-time tracking of goods and materials.
- **Retail:** In the retail sector, RFID improves inventory accuracy, reduces theft, and enhances the overall shopping experience through features like contactless payments.
- **Healthcare:** RFID plays a crucial role in patient tracking, medication management, and equipment monitoring, contributing to enhanced efficiency and patient safety.
- **Manufacturing:** RFID optimizes production processes by monitoring and managing the movement of raw materials, work-in-progress, and finished goods.
- **Access Control and Security:** RFID is widely used for access control systems, employee identification, and secure entry systems.
- **Animal Tracking:** in agriculture and wildlife management, RFID is employed for animal identification, tracking, and monitoring.

Advantages of RFID Technology

- **Accuracy:** RFID offers higher accuracy in data capture compared to traditional methods like barcodes.
- **Efficiency:** The speed of RFID data transfer enables quick and seamless processes, improving overall operational efficiency.
- **Automation:** RFID facilitates automation in various processes, reducing the need for manual intervention.

- **Data Security:** RFID systems often include encryption and authentication features, enhancing data security.

Durability: RFID tags are robust and can withstand harsh environmental conditions, making them suitable for a wide range of applications.

Main benefits of RFID

Radio-Frequency Identification (RFID) technology has revolutionized the way organizations manage and track their goods and assets, bringing numerous benefits to the table. RFID technology offers a lot of advantages, including:

- **Improved efficiency:** RFID technology enables fast and efficient data exchange between an RFID reader and an RFID tag, which can result in improved efficiency and accuracy in various applications, such as inventory management, supply chain management, and asset tracking.
- **Increased visibility:** RFID technology provides real-time data and increased visibility into the movement of goods and assets, enabling organizations to make more informed decisions and respond quickly to changes in demand or other conditions.
- **Reduced costs:** By automating processes and reducing manual labor, RFID technology can help organizations to reduce costs and improve their bottom line. For example, RFID can help reduce inventory shrinkage and improve asset utilization, both of which can lead to significant cost savings.
- **Improved security:** RFID technology can be used to enhance security by controlling access to secure areas and facilities and by helping to prevent theft and shrinkage.
- **Improved consumer engagement:** RFID technology can also be applied to create an engaging shopping experience for consumers by providing personalized recommendations, real-time product information, and location-based marketing.

RFID technology offers a range of benefits that make it a popular choice for a variety of industries. It provides a seamless bridge between the physical and digital world through the use of a unique code, or digital twin. With automated and fast non-line-of-sight reading, RFID allows for efficient tracking and tracing without the need to open boxes. Additionally, its advanced security features ensure that data is protected through coding and passwords. RFID also engages customers and enhances sustainability by improving supply chain efficiency and waste management. Its compliance capabilities provide a unique identity to tags, while the aesthetics of the technology keep tags hidden from consumers. Finally, RFID's recycling process stores all data, adding to its environmental benefits.

KEY MARKETS AND APPLICATION AREAS

Now let's explore some of the key markets and application areas where RFID is making a difference. Due to its ability to provide quick and accurate identification and tracking objects, RFID technology has found widespread use in various industries. Some of the most common applications of RFID technology include:

Supply chain management

In supply chain management RFID technology can significantly improve the visibility and efficiency of the supply chain by placing RFID tags on containers, pallets, and other types of packaging, allowing companies to track the movement of goods as they move through the supply chain.

Asset tracking

RFID technology is also used for asset tracking to monitor the location and status of assets, such as equipment, vehicles, and tools. This can help organizations to improve their asset utilization, reduce downtime, and increase efficiency.

Inventory management

RFID is widely used in inventory management to prevent over-stocking or under-stocking of a product or component. Since RFID tags can be attached to products, it enables companies to accurately track inventory levels and to quickly respond to changes in demand. Additionally, RFID allows quality control, particularly for stock items with a limited shelf life.

Healthcare

In the healthcare industry RFID technology improves patient safety, reduces medication errors, and streamlines the delivery of care. RFID tags can be attached to medical equipment, allowing for quick and accurate tracking, and RFID-enabled wristbands can be used to identify patients and track their movement through the healthcare facility.

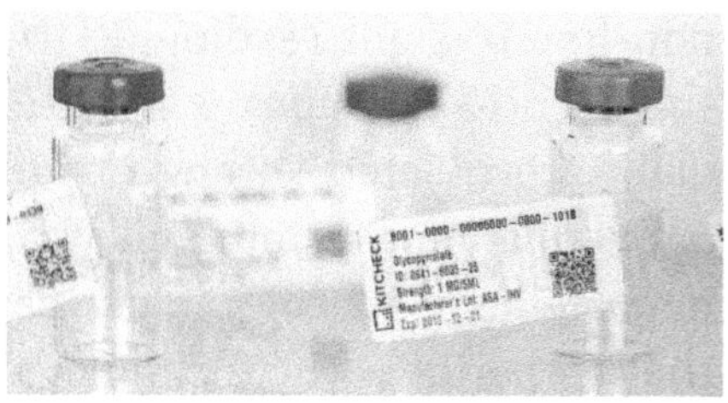

Access control

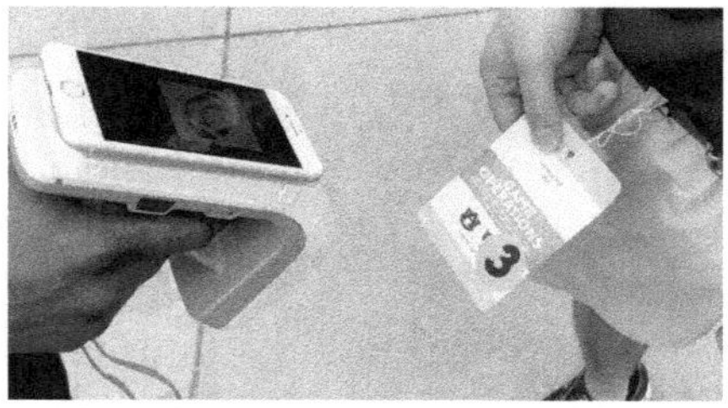

With the use of RFID technology, it is possible to control access to secure areas and facilities. By attaching RFID tags to employee badges, gaining access to restricted areas takes place by simply waving their badge near an RFID reader.

Retail

In retail RFID technology has brought significant improvements to inventory management. It reduces theft and shrinkage, and enhances the shopping experience for customers. By attaching RFID tags to individual items, retailers can efficiently track inventory levels and quickly respond to changes in demand.

Logistics:

RFID is widely applied to optimize logistics processes in a supply chain – tracking goods from one distribution center to another, for inventory accuracy, and for tagging down to the item-level. With the ability to obtain real-time data, logistics companies can quickly respond to changes in demand and provide better customer service, ultimately leading to a more competitive advantage in the market.

Manufacturing

In the manufacturing industry, RFID technology has become an indispensable tool for optimizing production processes, inventory tracking, and equipment monitoring. RFID tags can be attached to components and products to track their movement through the production process, reducing the risk of errors and improving efficiency and overall performance.

Automotive

RFID technology has found numerous applications in the automotive industry including parts tracking, traceability in process automation, especially in production of the vehicle itself, customer safety, authenticating products, brand protection and in manufacturing for improving labor and operational efficiency. In addition, RFID can aid in detecting any leaks in vehicles, thereby enhancing safety and quality.

Product authentication

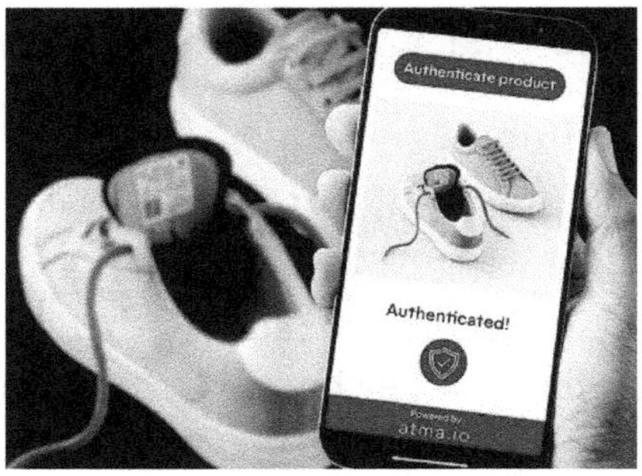

NFC (Near Field Communication) enables the storage of unique and secure information on an NFC tag, which can be attached to a product or its packaging. This information can be retrieved by a smartphone or other NFC-enabled device, providing a way to verify the authenticity of the product. By scanning the NFC tag on a product with their smartphone, customers can access information about the product's origin, manufacturing date, and batch number, which helps them to confirm its genuineness and avoid counterfeit products.

Food

In the food industry, RFID technology is utilized to ensure food safety, track products from their origin to supermarkets, meet legislative demands and needs, and manage waste. It can also be used to monitor the temperature in a cold chain supply, ensuring that products remain fresh and safe for consumption.

Other industries

Besides the mentioned examples, RFID technology has also found its applications in libraries, transportation, animal identification, sports, and events. With the

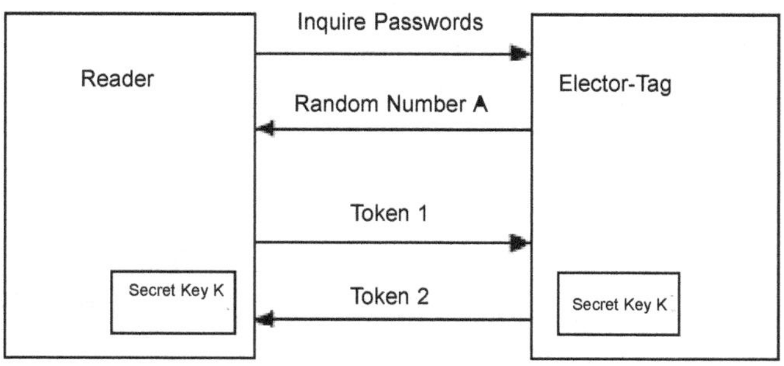

Figure 1. The basic principle of RFID

constant evolution of the technology, it's highly probable that new industries and applications will emerge, presenting organizations with new opportunities to enhance their operations and gain a competitive edge.

DEFINITION AND BASIC PRINCIPLES

Radio frequency identification (RFID) refers to an automated data collection technology that uses radio frequency waves to transfer data between a reader and a tag to identify, track and locate the tagged item. There are two basic categories of tags used for logistics and transportation: passive and battery-enabled. Passive tags collect the necessary energy from the antenna of the reader, which can be fixed or portable. Battery-enabled tags fall into two major groupings: battery-assisted passive (BAP) technology and active RFID tag technology.

Radio Frequency Identification works through a small electronic device, usually a microchip, that has information stored on it. These devices are generally quite small, sometimes the size of a grain of rice, and can hold large amounts of data. While they don't always emit electricity, some can contain a stored power source or batteries. The scanners used to read these devices can also provide enough electricity to allow them to read the microchip. There are many different uses for the technology, but it is commonly used in tracking products, animals, and currency.

RFID and its basic principle

The main principle of RFID is electromagnet theories, and its strongpoint is embodied at the line of sight, which can recognize something in more distance than optical system does. The information in RFID tag can be modified, at the same time, the RFID tag can contain vast data, and it is difficult to fabricate and has the intelligent characteristic. In fact, these characteristics determine its application in wider foreground. Alike the bar card technology, RFID is also an identified technology with non-contact mode, so the RFID tag often be tumbled in related products, even some RFID tags can identify something out of several hundreds meters. Furthermore, because the RFID tag can identify objectives well with non-contact, it can automatically realize the operation with non-effect. So, it is very interested the RFID can identify objectives in moving and can distinguish from multiple RFID tags with convenient and fast operation.

RFID system mainly achieves to identify objectives automatically with the coupling between the radio-frequency signals and the space. Generally, there are two parts to consist of RFID system, the electronic tag and the reader. In application of RFID system, electronic tags often are embedded into the interior or on the surface of objectives, and when objectives with electronic tag are in the active range of the reader, the reader will take away information of objectives automatically with conventional mode. The basic principle of RFID is listed in Fig 1.

Retrospect to the origin of RFID technology, the paper "Communication with echo-power" published by Harry Stockman in 1948 established its theory basis. With the research on theories and technologies about six decades, RFID technology started to enter in the business stage during 1980s, and then the standardization problem of RFID attracted more and more scholars in 1990s with its application widely, especially after Wal-Mart announced that she would apply widely RFID technology to more and more merchandises and actively prompted the research on RFID technology.

Concretely, Wal-Mart requires his main suppliers must set RFID tag into their products, which will be transported to his distributed workshops of Wal-Mart after the end of 2004. At present, because the research and application of RFID in China also be in the stage of exploring, the main contribution of this paper is to wake up more and more managers and scholars in China to pay more attentions to RFID technology and RFID products.

However, these are not also the united standard system accepted by countries, which is a restraint factor to baffle the popularization of RFID. At present, there are two groups for technique standard of RFID. One is the auto-IDCenter in MIT, and the other is Ubiquitous ID Center(UID) in Japan. The former is leaded by the EPC globe association of USA, and he developed the EPC code standard for electronic products This association consists of Wal-Mart, more 100 retail- catenation firms in British, and supported by IBM, Microsoft Corp, Philips, Auto-IDLab, in technology.

The latter consists of firms of Japan, and he presented UID code system. At present, it is in the incandesced stage for firms who are interested in RFID to scramble for the profits from RFID industry. However, in other words, this wrangle maybe take some chance for the developing countries to joint the standardization of RFID technology, especially for China.

HISTORICAL DEVELOPMENT OF RFID

While Walton's patent represented a huge leap forward for radio frequency technology, many smaller steps were required earlier on to make this major development possible. Since then, a great deal of additional progress has taken place. We detail both the past and future of RFID in this timeline:

1940s

World War II and its immediate aftermath produced many technological leaps, including, most notably, the basis for modern RFID. Just a few decades prior, radar had taken a huge step forward as Dr. A. Hoyt Taylor of the U. S. Naval Research Laboratory experimented with high-frequency radio waves at the confluence of the Anacostia and Potomac Rivers.

After that, radar's development progressed rapidly, in part because it was regarded as essential for achieving the security of an aircraft early warning system.

Soon after, the convergence of radar and broadcast technology formed the precursor to RFID, as seen in the 1948 paper "Communication by Means of Reflected Power." Authored by the forward-thinking Harry Stockman, this seminal work highlighted the possibility of point-to-point communication in which radio waves could be called upon.

1950s

Exploration of RFID-adjacent technologies continued during the 1950s. These updates were important, even if Harry Stockman's concept would not come to fruition until far later. For example: the long-range transponder systems known as identification, friend or foe (IFF). This take on radar quickly became essential for the military, as well as in various aerospace initiatives. Some experts regard this as the original RFID application.

1960s

With the 60s came the creation of several companies devoted to RFID technology. Sensormatic and Checkpoint, for example, were founded during this influential decade. In an effort to limit theft, these companies developed tracking solutions we take for granted today — electronic article surveillance (EAS). Featuring tags attached to merchandise, this system can sound the alarm if unpaid merchandise is removed from the store or taken into the restroom.

1970s

The 1970s delivered an explosion of academic progress on RFID, which was studied extensively at this point by several notable universities, government laboratories, and other organizations, such as Sweden's Microwave Institute Foundation. Around this time, RCA (the Radio Corporation of America) began to expand its reach. The company had previously attempted to enter the mainframe computer race in the 1960s in an effort to compete with IBM. It exited this particular market in the early 1970s but continued to hold high standards with satellite communications. In 1975, the company — alongside Fairchild — published "Electronic ID System." RCA's contributions also included F. Sterzer's work on electronic license plates for motor vehicles.

Several noteworthy patents were obtained during the 70s. Inventor Mario W. Cardulla, for example, expressed interest in rewritable active RFID tags. As mentioned previously, this was also an important time for Charles Walton, who sought a passive RFID tag.

1980s

After years of being thought of as a niche technology, RFID began to enter the mainstream during the 1980s. At this time, several commercial entities started taking advantage of RFID solutions. These were used in several sectors and situations, such as:

- Transportation
- Personnel access
- Factory automation
- Animal tagging

Perhaps most notably, it began to take over toll roads in the 1980s. This served as the culmination of earlier research and experimentation, conducted, in part, by the Port Authority of New York and New Jersey. Eventually, this hard work paid off with an effective application for buses using the Lincoln Tunnel.

The Dallas North Turnpike was also an early adopter of RFID, utilizing Amtech systems that had been created by Sandia Labs primarily for the purposes of tracking livestock.

1990s

By the early and mid 90s, RFID was widely used for electronically collecting tolls. This approach quickly became more efficient and effective. In Oklahoma, for example, vehicles were soon able to pass collection points while traveling at highway speeds.

In the Northeast, several agencies joined forces to create the E-Z Pass Interagency Group (IAG), which became a top model for obtaining multiple tolls for a single vehicle-based billing account.

Transportation was by no means the only area in which RFID technology was taking off during the 90s. This application paved the path for RFID-enabled access to campuses, parking lots, and gated communities.

Ongoing research in the 90s was instrumental in enabling later breakthroughs. Perhaps most notably, researchers at IBM developed ultra-high frequency RFID capabilities, allowing for vastly improved read ranges and data transfer. IBM's patents were later sold to bar code company Intermec. For some time, UHF RFID was simply too expensive to be practical for most applications.

Change was afoot, however, especially as the Uniform Code Council (along with familiar names such as Gillette) helped to establish the Auto-ID Center. Based at the Massachusetts Institute of Technology, this initiative focused on low-cost RFID tags, which researchers hoped could be placed on a variety of products and tracked through the entirety of the supply chain.

2000+

The vision of the MIT Auto-ID Center has been achieved, thereby dramatically changing logistics and supply chain management. It should come as no surprise, then, that a variety of companies have expressed enthusiasm for the Auto-ID Center's work.

In the early 2000s, the Electronic Product Code (EPC) numbering system was developed and commercialized, thereby enabling universal identifiers for a vast array of products and other physical objects. These are typically encoded on RFID tags and used for tracking inventory, assets, and personnel.

The Future of RFID

Clearly, RFID technology has come a long way over the last few decades. This is only the beginning, however. The integration of smart-sensing RFID systems could expand the use of the Internet of Things (IoT) within warehouses, thereby enabling more accurate insight into temperature and more. From there, cloud-based systems will produce real-time data to boost stock accuracy and replenishment.

CHAPTER-2

COMPONENTS OF RFID SYSTEMS

RFID technology consists of four components: RFID tags, antenna, RFID receiver (transceiver), and software.

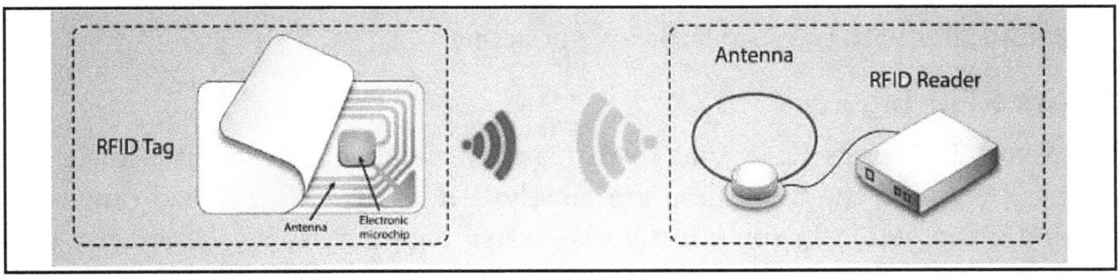

RFID TAG

Low Frequency (LF) RFID

These RFID systems operate in the 30 KHz to 300 KHz range, and have a read range of up to 10 cm. While they have a shorter read range and slower data read rate than other technologies, they perform better in the presence of metal or liquids (which can interfere with other types of RFID tag transmissions). Common standards for LF RFID include ISO 14223 and ISO/IEC 18000-2. LF tags are used in access control, livestock tracking, and other applications where a short read range is acceptable.

High Frequency (HF) RFID

HF systems operate in the 3 MHz to 30 MHz range and provide reading distances of 10 cm to 1 m. Common applications include electronic ticketing and payment and data transfer. Near Field Communication (NFC) technology is based on HF RFID and has been used for payment cards and hotel key card applications. Other types of smart card and proximity card payment and security systems also use HF technology. Standards include ISO 15693, ECMA-340, ISO/IEC 18092 (for NFC), ISO/IEC 14443A and ISO/IEC 14443 (for MIFARE and other smart card solutions).

Ultra-High Frequency (UHF) RFID

These systems have a frequency range between 300 MHz and 3 GHz, offer read ranges up to 12 m, and have faster data transfer rates. They are more sensitive to interference from metals, liquids, and electromagnetic signals, but new design innovations have helped mitigate some of these problems.

UHF tags are much cheaper to manufacture, and as such are commonly used in retail inventory tracking, pharmaceutical anti-counterfeiting, and other applications where large volumes of tags are required. The EPCglobal Gen2/ISO 18000-6C standard is a well-known global standard for item-level tracking applications.

TYPES OF TAGS

There are two other common classifications of tags, depending on how the tag communicates with the reader: passive or active.

Active RFID Tag

Active RFID tags have their own transmitter and power source (usually a battery) onboard the tag. These are mostly UHF solutions, and read ranges can extend up to 100 m in some instances. Active tags are usually larger and more expensive than their passive counterparts and are used to track large assets (like cargo containers, vehicles, and machines). Active RFID tags are also often equipped with sensors that measure and transmit temperature, humidity, light, and shock/vibration data for the objects they are attached to.

There are two types of active tags. Transponders only “wake up” and transmit data when they receive a radio signal from a reader. For example, a transponder attached to a vehicle in a toll payment or checkpoint control location would only be active when passing through a particular gate. This helps conserve battery life.

Beacons, on the other hand, emit a signal at a pre-set interval. This type of active tag is used in real-time location systems (RTLS) for tracking anything from wheelchairs at a hospital to large cargo containers at a shipping dock.

Passive RFID Tag

In passive RFID solutions, the reader and reader antenna send a signal to the tag, and that signal is used to power on the tag and reflect energy back to the reader. There are passive LF, HF, and UHF systems. Read ranges are shorter than with active tags and are limited by the power of the radio signal reflected back to the reader (commonly referred to as tag backscatter).

Passive tags are usually smaller, less expensive, and more flexible than active tags. This means they can be attached or even embedded on a wider variety of objects. Passive UHF tags are commonly used for item-level tracking of consumer goods and pharmaceuticals, for example.

Battery-Assisted Passive (BAP) RFID Tag

A third, hybrid type of RFID tag has also emerged. BAP systems, or semi-passive RFID systems, incorporate a power source into a passive tag configuration. The power source helps ensure that all of the captured energy from the reader can be used to reflect the signal, which improves read distance and data transfer rates. Unlike active RFID transponders, BAP tags do not have their own transmitters.

ANTENNA

RFID antennas are designed to operate at a specific frequency for each application in which it operates. These antennas are often mounted on the RFID reader and easily accessible for tags to tap on it.

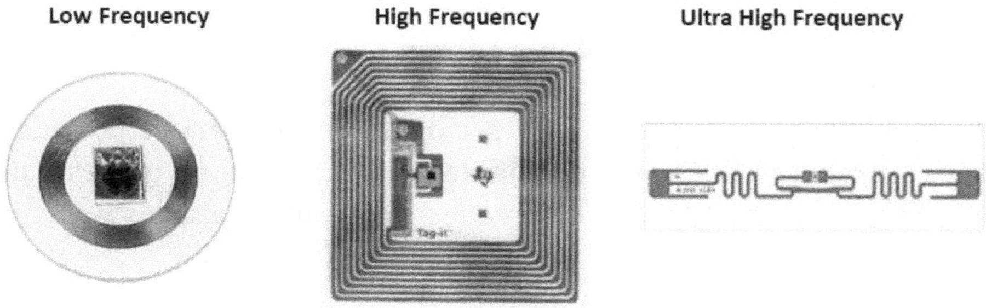

In some handheld devices, the antenna is often attached to the device. The size and shape of the antenna depend on the application and the system's operating frequency.

RFID Smart Reader

An RFID reader is also referred to as an interrogator that communicates with RFID tags to fetch information that is stored within them. It is a type of network-connected device that uses radio waves for transmit signals to activate the tag. After the tag gets activated, it sends back a wave to the antenna where it gets translated into data. The transponder remains within the tag.

An RFID reader uses scanning antenna and a transceiver. Scanning antenna emit rf (rf full form radio frequency) waves and recieve the signal sent back by an RFID tag. Antenna ensures communication between tag and reader. Transceiver generates radio frequency signals that antenna sends out and processes the signal recieved by antenna.

RFID reader or interrogator can read information upto 30 feet from an RFIF tag. This is the read range of an RFID reader. This range depends on several actors including the type of RFID systems, frequency, size and design of an RFID antenna as well as the power output of an RFID reader.

There are two types of RFID readers including fixed and mobile readers.

Specification of RFID Reader

Frequency: Operating frequency is one of the specifications of the RFID reader.

Frequency Band	Range	Data Rate
LF: 120–150 kHz	10 cm	Low
HF: 13.56 MHz	0.1–1 m	Low to moderate
UHF: 433 MHz	1–100 m	Moderate
UHF: 865–868 MHz 902–928 MHz	1–12 m	Moderate to high
microwave: 2450–5800 MHz	1–2 m	High
microwave: 3.1–10 GHz	up to 200 m	High

SOFTWARE

RFID technology uses specific software depending on service providers. This software controls the RFID reader, initiates a scan, retrieves information from the tags, and stores the information on a local computer or sends it to the cloud storage.

RFID tags can be erased and re-used using control software.

How does RFID work?

RFID technology works based on the principle of inductive coupling, including a source and receiver antenna. Each RFID tag will have a microchip that contains a unique identification number, model, manufacturing date, expiry date, access information, etc....

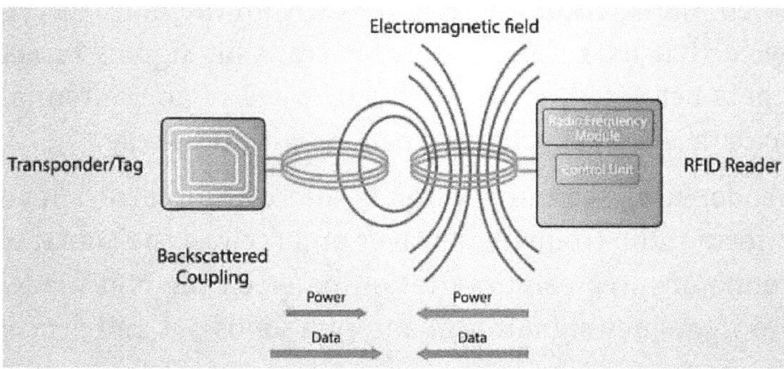

RFID reading is a process of accessing information on a tag using a reader. When the user initiates a scanning, the tags are placed near the RFID reader or vice versa.

RFID reader sends radio frequency signals using its antenna; small coils embedded in the RFID tag pick up the signal from the reader and activate the tag (in passive tags) by powering it.

Once the tag is activated, it starts transmitting data back to the reader using the same antenna coils using the inductive coupling (backscatter coupling) method.

RFID MIDDLEWARE

The middleware refers broadly to software or devices that connect RFID readers and the data they collect, to enterprise information systems. RFID middleware helps making sense of RFID tag reads, applies filtering, formatting and logic to tag data captured by a reader, and provides this processed data to back-end applications (Burnell, 2008). RFID middleware serves in managing the flow of data between tag readers and enterprise applications, and is responsible for the quality, and therefore usability of the information. It provides readers connectivity, context-based filtering and routing, and enterprise / B2B integration. RFID middleware design and components will be discussed further in the next sections.

When designing a RFID middleware solution, the following issues need to be considered:

- Multiple hardware support: The middleware must provide a common interface to access different kinds of hardware offering different features. Synchronization and scheduling: There should be intelligent scheduling and synchronization among all the processes of the middleware. This minimizes the latency and improves the efficiency of the middleware. Real-time handling of incoming data from the RFID readers: The middleware should handle the huge amount of data captured by the connected readers in real time without read misses. Interfacing with multiple applications: The middleware should be capable of interacting with multiple applications simultaneously, by catering to all the requirements of the applications with minimal latency.Device neutral interface to the applications: The application developer should only use the generic set of interfaces provided by the middleware independently of the type of hardware connected to the system. Scalability: The middleware design must allow easy integration of new hardware and data processing features.

RFID middleware components

A RFID middleware is the interface that sits between the RFID hardware and RFID applications. It provides the following advantages:

- It hides the RFID hardware details from the applications;
- It handles and processes the raw RFID data before passing it as aggregated events to the applications;

- It provides an application level interface for managing RFID readers and querying the RFID data.

A layer of the RFID middleware incorporates all the device drivers of different hardware and exposes to the application standard interfaces to access this hardware. If the application was provided with all the device drivers of all connected readers, it will be a hard job to manage and interface each of the devices. The application developer will then need to understand all the hardware specific internals and operations. Also, the application, if provided with the huge amount of raw tag data reported by the readers, will find it very difficult to process the data in real time. A RFID middleware provides a standardized way of dealing with this flood of information, which processes the raw data and provides the application with clean and filtered data.

As shown in Fig. 1 a RFID middleware is generally composed of four major layers:

- Reader Interface
- Data Processor and Storage
- Application Interface
- Middleware Management

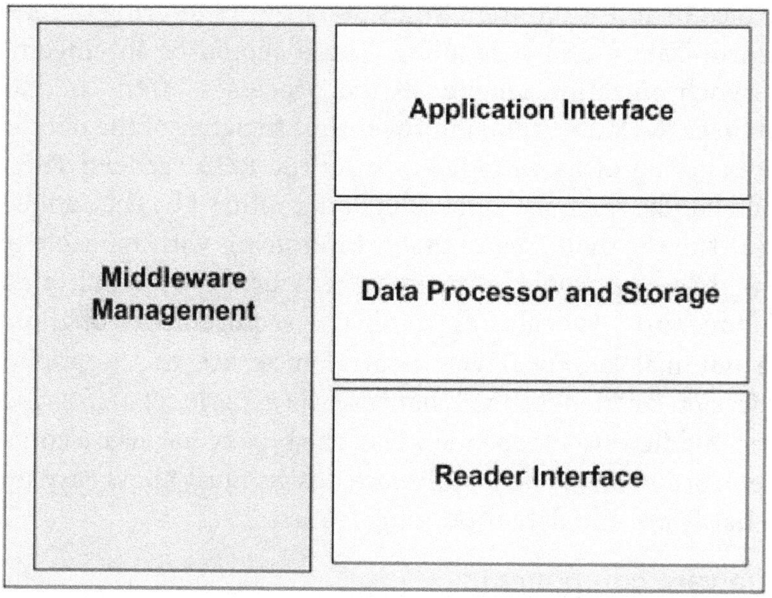

Fig. 1. RFID middleware components

Reader interface

The reader interface is the lowest layer of the RFID middleware which handles the interaction with the RFID hardware. It maintains the device drivers of all the devices supported by the system, and manages all the hardware related parameters like reader protocol, air interface, and host-side communication.

Data processor and storage

The data processor and storage layer is responsible for processing and storing the raw data coming from the readers. Examples of processing logic carried by this layer are data filtering, aggregation, and transformation. This layer also processes the data level events associated with a specific application.

Application interface

The application interface provides the application with an API to access, communicate, and configure the RFID middleware. It integrates the enterprise applications with the RFID middleware by translating the applications' requests to low level middleware commands.

Middleware management

The middleware management layer helps managing the configuration of the RFID middleware, and provides the following capabilities:

- Add, configure, and modify connected RFID readers;
- Modify application level parameters such as filters, and duplicate removal timing window;
- Add and remove services supported by the RFID middleware.

RFID readers are typically abstracted as a logical reader which is either a collection of several readers or a part of the reader. This grouping mechanism is used where there is a need to have a set of readers capturing data from a particular area such as a warehouse with many loading docks. The advantage of this is that the application can query a small number of logical readers rather than having to aggregate events from each of the individual readers.

There are two standardized interaction models used to define the communication between the middleware and the applications. An application can operate at *synchronous mode* when requesting services on demand or *asynchronous mode* when it registers for information to be sent to it when certain conditions are met. RFID middleware usually provide some kind of data filtering, because sometimes it might be required to report only certain type and value of the tag data to the application. The application needs to provide a set of defined patterns to the middleware. The middleware then allows only data that matches the pattern to be reported to the application. E.g. if an application needs to see only tag data that starts with a specific pattern such as "XYZ20", the filter can be set to this value by the application and communicated to the middleware (Al-Mousawi, 2004).

Examples of RFID middleware solutions

The savant middleware

There have been some proposals and research work involving middleware design and RFID data processing. The Auto-ID Center has developed a middleware component called Savant that collects, accumulates, and processes Electronic Product Code (EPC) data obtained from several RF readers. It adjusts multiple readings of a tag, and performs tasks such as archiving data, and inventory control.

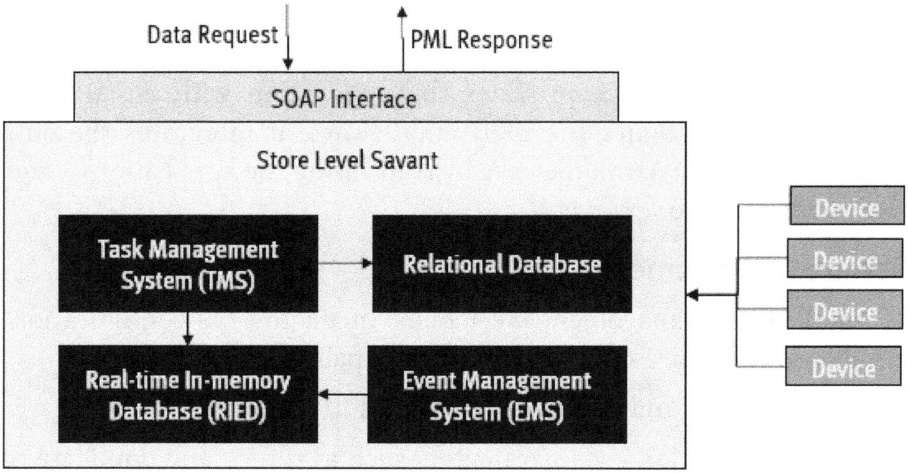

Fig 2. Savant middleware key components

The Savant has a set of *Processing Modules* or *Services* which may be combined to meet the user's application's needs. This modular structure allows innovation to be promoted by independent groups of people, which helps avoiding the creation of a single monolithic specification that attempts to satisfy all needs for everybody. Fig. 2 shows the three key elements of the Savant middleware architecture: Event Management System (EMS), Real-Time in-Memory Data Structure/ Real-Time in-Memory Event Database (RIED) and Task Management System (TMS).

The EMS provides a JAVA API for different types of RF readers and it serves to collect tag read events. The EMS allows adapters to be written for various types of readers, collecting EPC data from readers in a standard format, allowing filters to be written to smooth or clean EPC data, allowing various loggers to be written, and buffering events to enable loggers, filters and adapters to operate without blocking each other.

The EMS is composed of the following elements:

- *Reader Interface*: Allows readers and adapters to communicate events detected by the Auto-ID readers
- *Reader Adapters*: Communicate with readers to capture EPC events

- *Event Loggers (Event Consumers):* Allow for varied processing of events; store the information in the database, store events in a memory data structure, and broadcast the events to remote servers
- *Event Queues (Event Forwarders):* Handle multiple reader event loggers with synchronous implementations

The RIED is an in-memory database that can be used to store event information by Edge Savants. It provides the same interface as a database, but offers much better performance. The RIED should be a high-performance in-memory and a multi-versioned database.

The TMS manages tasks, just as the operating system manages processes, and provides an interface for task management. Task examples include data gathering, remote task scheduling, personnel alerts, and remote upload. The TMS should be a platform-independent system requiring little memory processing power, should automatically upgrade the tasks it executes, and should present a well-defined, interoperable external interface to schedule, monitor, and remove tasks. Tasks should also be written in a platform-independent language using a simple well-defined SDK.

Win RFID middleware

WinRFID developed at the University of California Los Angeles (UCLA), is another middleware architecture that uses web services and enables rapid RFID applications development.

The *physical layer* deals with the hardware consisting of readers, tags and other sensors. This layer abstracts the hardware elements; readers, tags and host I/O interfaces. This abstraction allows extending the middleware capabilities in the advent of introduction of new RFID technology.

The *protocol layer:* The ability to support multiple tag protocols and add new ones is becoming imperative in middleware designs. The protocol layer of the WinRFID middleware allows abstracting the reader-tag protocols. It wraps the command syntax and semantics of a variety of published protocols such as ISO 15693, ISO 14443, ISO 18000–6 A/B, ICode, EPC Class 0 and EPC Class 1.

It also deals with protocol specifics such as byte-based, block or even page reading and writing, structure and length of the command frames, partitioning of the tag memory space, checksums, etc.

The *data processing layer* deals with processing data streams generated by the network of readers. It includes processing rules that deal with problems due to tag density, read/write distance, orientation of tags and material of item that introduce inconsistencies in reading or writing such as multiple reads of the same tag, some tags not being read, erroneous reads, etc. All of these discrepancies are processed as exceptions and a variety of altering systems are available for resolution such as emails, messages, and user defined triggers.

The *XML framework layer* formats the cleaned tag data in a variety of ways to a higher level XML based representation. The purpose of this layer is to provide data in a suitable format to the application layer for decision making.

The WebSphere RFID middleware

The WebSphere RFID middleware solution, designed by IBM, consists of three main components as shown in Fig. 3: *RFID devices*, *WebSphere Premises Server*, and *Websphere Business Integration Server*.

The IBM WebSphere is a sensor enabled product that allows sensor data aggregation and analysis, deriving insights from sensor data and integrating those insights with the SOA business processes. The software provides the use of intelligent business rules that manage complex event identification and processing.

This solution expands device services allowing a single platform to support multiple sensor types, and supports workflow tooling for sensor data integration with business processes. Therefore, it delivers new and enhanced capabilities to create a robust, flexible, and scalable platform for capturing new business value from sensor data.

The Sun JAVA RFID system

Sun Java System RFID software is a Java based commercial middleware platform provided by Sun. It is a critical RFID infrastructure component that allows a safe, secure, and efficient data and device integration from the edge of the enterprise into enterprise application systems. It has a dynamic, service provisioning architecture that enables scaling from small pilots to large deployments with high data volume.

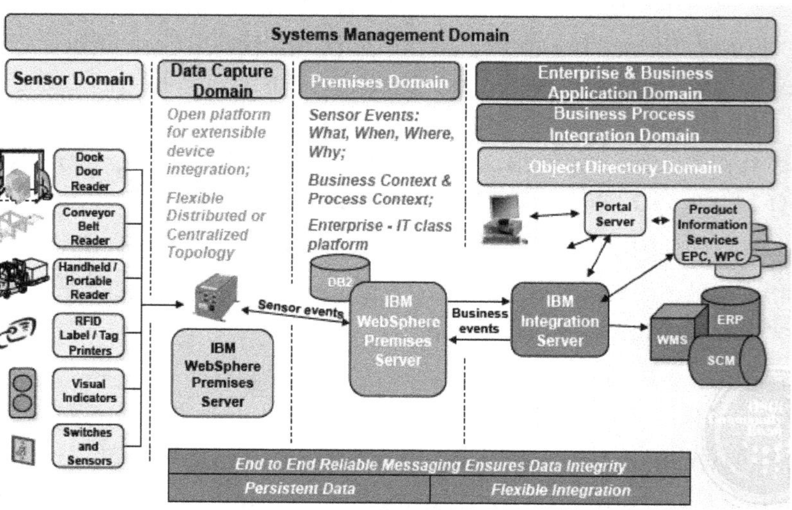

Fig. 3. The IBM sensor and actuator solutions framework (Eisma, 2008)

The Java System RFID Software supports a variety of new and existing standards, such as EPC, ISO, Gen 2, passive and active tags and devices, read/write tags, and commercial and government standards. It is a part of the Java Enterprise System (JES) and has four components: the RFID Event Manager, the RFID Management Console, the RFID Information Server, and a Software Development Kit (SDK). The RFID Event Manager is a Jini-based event management system that facilitates the capture, filtering, and eventual storage of events generated by RFID readers. The RFID Management Console provides a browser based management interface, which allows configuration of various attributes and parameters of the middleware. The RFID Information Server is responsible for storing and querying the EPC related data, it also manages inter Enterprise handling of the data. The SDK provides a development platform to build custom applications.

The Sun middleware exposes to the application, the hardware as logical readers. These logical readers may be a collection of one or more physical readers that the application can select and apply the various processing parameters to the group.

All of these middleware designs aim at providing a scalable solution for gathering, filtering, and providing clean RFID data to the end-user. However, there are still many open issues. The reliability of RFID data needs to be improved since inaccurate data could misguide the application users. The accumulation of RFID data generated in high volumes, may lead to slower queries and updates, therefore efficient RFID data management solutions such as data transformation, aggregation, and dissemination should be investigated.

Raw RFID data is not of significant value until it is aggregated with other data to obtain appropriate inferences, and transformed into a suitable form for application level interaction. Also, the applications with high security requirements are increasingly using RFID; therefore support for data security and confidentiality is needed. However, such support should maintain a desirable system performance. RFID also raises the privacy concerns because of its potential to leak proprietary information and ability to track private information such as the spending history of a consumer. Technical solutions must be implemented to ensure that private data is not compromised with.

While the Savant middleware architecture provides features for cleaning the data and interfacing with different kinds of RF readers, it has limited built-in functionality for addressing business rules management, dealing with all types of sensor devices and providing data dissemination, filtering, and aggregation. Also, none of WinRFID and IBM WebSphere considers the business rules policies implementation, especially the ones concerned with security and privacy.

As compared to the related work described herewith, the distinguishing aspects of our FlexRFID middleware solution are as follows: the FlexRFID design aims to provide the applications with a device neutral interface to communicate simultaneously with many different hardware devices, creating an intelligent RFID network. It also provides an interface to access the hardware for the management and monitoring purposes. The FlexRFID provides all data processing capabilities along with the security and privacy features included in the data processing layer and enforced by a policy based management module for the business events, referred to as the Business Rules layer. The modular and layered design of FlexRFID allows integration of new features with little effort. The design also permits seamless integration of different types of enterprise applications. More detail about the FlexRFID middleware architecture is presented in the next section.

FlexRFID: aflexible middleware for RFID applications development

The FlexRFID middleware architecture takes into account the design issues discussed above. FlexRFID is part of a three-tier architecture consisting of: the backend applications layer, FlexRFID middleware layer, and hardware layer consisting of diverse types of sensors and devices.

The *Diverse Types of Sensors and Devices layer* comprises RFID readers, sensors and other industrial automation devices. Such approach allows incredible flexibility in the selection of devices, lets companies build their enterprise solutions without handling low-level programming, and allows creating an intelligent sensor network, where RFID readers are choreographed with other devices. There are diverse makes and models of devices, which require a middleware layer that monitors, manages, coordinates, and obtains data from the different devices.

In FlexRFID, these functions are taken care of before processing the raw data and applying business logic to them. Our approach is to use a *Device Abstraction Layer* (DAL) that abstracts the interaction with the physical network of devices. The FlexRFID middleware incorporates three other layers which are: *Business Event and Data Processing Layer* (BEDPL), *Business Rules Layer* (BRL), and *Application Abstraction Layer* (AAL).

Device abstraction layer (DAL)

The Device Abstraction Layer of the FlexRFID middleware is responsible for interaction with various devices and data sources independently of their characteristics. The *Data Source Abstraction Module* (DSAM) of the DAL provides a standard view of data regardless of the data source protocol (e.g. EPC Gen2, ISO 15693, and ISO14443A), air interface (e.g. UHF, HF), power supply, type, and memory size of a device. The *Device Abstraction Module* (DAM) of the DAL provides a common interface to access hardware devices with different characteristics such as protocols, air interface, and host-side communication interface (e.g. USB, Serial Port, Ethernet port). The DAM exposes simple functions like open, close, read, write, etc. that trigger the complex operations of the devices. Both, the DSAM and the DAM allow the FlexRFID middleware to be extendable to support various data sources and devices. The *Device Management and Monitoring Module* (DMMM) of the DAL is responsible for dynamic loading and unloading of the driver libraries or device adaptors. This allows the FlexRFID middleware to be light weight as libraries are loaded based upon request. The DMMM configures the devices as specified by the upper layers, and also monitors and reports their status.

Business event and data processing layer (BEDPL)

The BEDPL acts as a mediator between the DAL and the AAL. The services accepted by the BEDPL are first authorized by the *Business Rules Layer* (BRL) and then allowed to issue commands to the DAL in order to get the raw data and process them accordingly. Similarly the raw data are carried from the DAL, processed, and passed on to the AAL by this layer.

Data dissemination

A diverse set of applications across an organization are interested in the captured information. The captured data are therefore broadcasted by the data dissemination service to all the interested entities. In addition, different applications require different latencies. For example, low latency for the notifications is desired by the applications that need to respond immediately to objects' events. In contrast, some legacy applications need to receive batched updates on a daily schedule.

Data aggregation

The fine-grained data has implicit meanings and associated relationships with other data, and need to be aggregated into summaries and/or proper inferences for applications that can not deal with the increased granularity. For example, it is common that an application is only interested in an event when an object enters or leaves a certain area. Other applications may only need a total count of objects belonging to a specific category rather than a serial number of each object detected. The data aggregation service provides such kind of functionality.

Data transformation

Raw data present little value until they are transformed into a form suitable for application-level interactions. So, from an application perspective, it is desirable to provide a mechanism that turns the low-level captured data into the corresponding business event. For example, a detection of a number of tagged books at the exit door of a library can be automatically translated into a books checked out event. This requirement is taken care by the data transformation service.

Data filtering

The volumes of data generated by the different devices require significant data filtering to extract the most important information. Also, different applications are interested in different subsets of data captured. There are filtering policies available in the FlexRFID middleware policy repository of the BRL, therefore the data filtering service filters data depending on the filter characteristics provided by the application. This offers flexibility in handling multiple filtering formats.

Duplicate removal

Multiple devices may generate duplicate readings of the data, for example tags in the vicinity of a RFID reader are read continuously. This results in a large amount of repeated data, and therefore duplicate removal service prevents the reporting of these duplicate data. The application specifies a time window, so that the same data read within it are only reported once.

Data replacement

Usually the rate at which the devices insert data in the channel buffer is slower than the read rate of the applications. However, in case the application is not responsive enough or not executing, the channel buffer gets full, and leads to buffer overflow problem. The data replacement service allows the application to specify the action to be taken in case of channel buffer overflow. The application specifies the data replacement policy stored in the BRL policies repository, which will be executed by the data replacement service.

Data writing

Certain special data sources like RFID tags provision additional memory space for both ID and additional data. The FlexRFID middleware handles both the reading and writing of data to this additional memory.

Privacy

RFID based tracking solutions could trigger RFID tags attached to the personal belongings to reply with their ID and other private information, therefore increasing the potential of unauthorized surveillance mechanism that would pervade large parts of our lives. FlexRFID design supports dedicated privacy enhancing feature through the privacy module. The business rules of this module are stated in the privacy policy of the BRL.

Business rules layer (BRL)

The BRL is a policy-based management engine that defines the rules that grant or deny access to resources and services of the FlexRFID middleware, and enforces different types of policies for filtering, aggregation, duplicate removal, privacy, and different other services. This is achieved by determining the policies to apply when an application requests the use of a service in the BEDPL.

The Middleware Policy Editor (MPE) allows storing, retrieving, and removing policies from the Middleware Policy Repository Database (MPRD). When an application needs to access a service that is protected by the Business Rules Layer, the request passes through the Middleware Policy Enforcement Point (MPEP) which asks the Middleware Policy Decision Point (MPDP) whether to permit or deny access to the service by applying the privacy rule, and how the service will be processed depending on its type.

The MPEP gives the MPDP the authority of decision making; whether or not to grant the application access to the service based on the description of the application attributes, and which policies will be applied to the services used by this application. The MPDP makes its decision based on the applicable policies stored on the system. The returned decision is Permit, Deny, Indeterminate or Not Applicable. Indeterminate is returned when there is an error in processing the request and Not Applicable when no policy that applies to the request could be found.

Policies are operating rules used to maintain order, security, consistency, or other ways of successfully achieving a task. Examples of policies that should be available in the Business Rules Layer are: Access policy, data replacement policy, quality of service policy, and privacy policy.

Different types of applications using the FlexRFID middleware may define rules to detect events and process them using the services provided by the middleware. Primitive events such as observations from readers may lead to actions such as change of location. Sequence events consist of a sequence of primitive events of the same type, defined by the order and closeness of intervals. Composite events are a combination of primitive events and sequence events, and may lead to actions such as aggregation of data. Here we present some examples of rules enforced by their corresponding policies:

- The *filtering rule* filters data according to predefined policies by the applications. For example, multiple readers may generate duplicate readings. To filter this, the filtering policy will scan data within a sliding window to find if there are duplicate RFID tag readings from multiple readers, and delete the duplicate if it exists. A policy for duplicate removal could specify that if readings from reader Rx and Ry have the same tag ID value within time T, then one of them is dropped.
- The *location transformation rule* serves to transform RFID readers' observations into location changes. For example, Reader R1 is mounted at a warehouse departure zone and will scan objects before their departure. A policy for this transformation could state that any observation generated from reader R1 will change the object's location to a value different from its current location.

- The *data aggregation rule* is used to detect a sequence of ordered events and generate an aggregation relationship. For instance when pallets are loaded into a truck to depart, a sequence of readings on the pallets are done, followed by (with a distinctive distance) a separate reading of the truck's EPC. This sequence of events will aggregate as a containment relationship between the pallets and the truck.
- Privacy threats in an RFID application can include covert reading, tracking over time, and individual profiling. The *privacy rule* specifies whether an application has the right to access RFID tag data, can track them over time, and use them to generate events. Applications can load into the FlexRFID middleware's Business Rules Layer privacy policies specifying how to use and configure the RFID technology to maintain the privacy of data and prevent data from tracking and hotlisting.

CHAPTER-3

WORKING PRINCIPLES OF RFID

When the tag enters the magnetic field, it receives the radio frequency signal sent by the reader, and sends out the product information stored in the chip obtained by the induced current or actively sends a signal of a certain frequency. The reader reads and decodes the information and sends it to the management information system for related data processing.

With the progress and development of society, countries and regions such as the European Union, the United States, Japan, and South Korea have successively introduced tire label laws, requiring tires to be labeled to indicate the fuel efficiency, rolling resistance, rolling noise, and wet traction grade of tires. At present, China's tire label system is also vigorously promoting.

Application of RFID labels in tires

Currently, the traceability label identification of tires on the market generally uses the form of "barcode + tire sidewall information" to store various information of the tire. However, both the barcode and sidewall information are located on the surface of the tire body, which will wear off quickly after the tire is used. Once these information cannot be visually observed, it means the loss of tire information, and the identification of tire model, tread, diameter and other information cannot be distinguished. If there are situations, such as illegal or unsafe use of tires (unqualified tires, overloaded use, expired use, etc.), it will directly cause difficulties in the use, maintenance and claims of users, leading to disputes, and even frequent safety accidents, waste of energy resources, and damage to the environment.

However, the application of RFID labels technology can regulate the tire industry for orderly production and sales (preventing counterfeiting, label switching, and counterfeiting), realizing tire life cycle management; regulating the transportation industry to ensure the safety of personal and property; promoting and regulating the tire retreading industry, realizing tire recycling economy. The RFID technology in the tire industry is demonstrated as follows: the electronic tag is implanted into the tire during the tire forming process, and can withstand deformation, high temperature and high pressure during the tire forming and vulcanization process. The finished tire is tested for reliability, such as X-ray detection, air bubble inspection, dynamic balance and uniformity testing, and durability testing.

It can be seen that the combination of RFID technology and tire manufacturing technology can not only solve the problems encountered in the current tire identification and traceability processes but also write tire production data, sales data, usage data, retreading data, etc., by planting RFID labels inside the tire, and the corresponding data can be collected and read at any time through the terminal. In combination with the corresponding management software, the recording and traceability of tire life cycle data can be realized.

FREQUENCY BANDS: LF, HF, UHF, AND MICROWAVE

Radio Frequency Identification (RFID) is a technology that uses electromagnetic fields to automatically identify and track tags attached to objects. These tags contain electronically stored information, which can be transmitted to an RFID reader via radio waves. One key factor to consider when implementing an RFID system is the frequency range in which it operates. In this article, we will delve into the different frequency ranges of RFID systems and their applications.

LF RFID (Low-Frequency RFID)

Frequency range: 125 kHz

Possible read range: up to 10 cm

Standard: ISO/IEC 18000-2

Application area: Low-frequency RFID systems are suitable for reliable detection of tags at short distances. Despite their low data transfer rate compared to HF or UHF systems, LF RFID systems have become firmly established in certain applications due to their low susceptibility to surrounding materials. If, for example, objects with a high water content need to be equipped with RFID tags and recorded, LF RFID systems offer an excellent solution. The same applies to the marking of livestock with subcutaneously implanted RFID tags—here too, low frequency is the range of choice. LF systems are ideal for use in metallic environments, such as identifying workpieces and tools.

Example device: The IPH-L2-V1 RFID read/write device combines the advantages of LF RFID technology with the familiar VariKont L2 design from Pepperl+Fuchs. This makes the device ideal for detecting workpiece carriers in CNC machines. Due to its compact design and variable adjustment capability, this LF RFID read/write device can be easily integrated into machines, even where space is limited.

Fig.. 1. The IPH-L2-V1 RFID read/write device

HF RFID (High-Frequency RFID)

Frequency range: 13.56 MHz

Possible read range: up to 30 cm

Standard: ISO 15693

Application area: High-frequency RFID systems operate at medium-to-high data transfer rates and are therefore ideal for transferring large volumes of data at high speed. HF systems are especially good for guided applications where the tags pass through the read/write devices in a constant position and orientation. The systems are relatively insensitive to humidity and water, but do not offer the same resistance in metallic environments that LF systems offer.

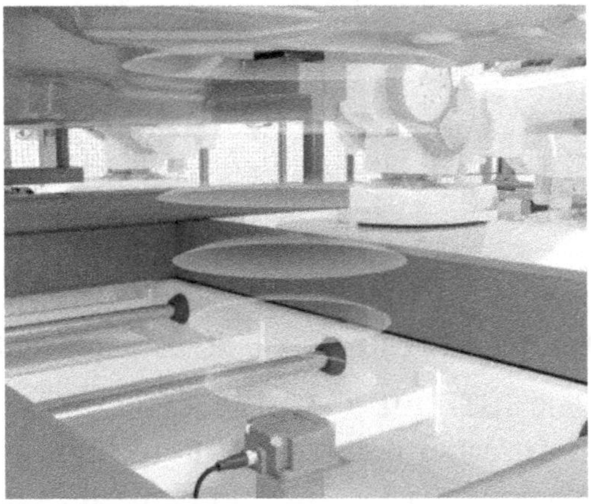

Fig. 2. IQT3-FP-IO-V1 HF RFID read/write device application example

Example device: The IQH3-FP-V1 and IQT3-FP-IO-V1 HF RFID read/write devices have a read range of up to 30 cm (adjustable), which is unique within this class on the market. This gives users maximum flexibility and freedom in adapting the devices to the respective application. In addition, they are among the few HF RFID read/write devices in this class that also support multitag detection. Up to 20 HF RFID tags can be detected simultaneously in a single read operation, thereby achieving fast throughput times and optimized processes.

UHF RFID (Ultra-High-Frequency RFID)

Frequency range: 865 MHz to 928 MHz

Possible read range: up to 6 m

Standard: EPC Gen 2 (ISO/IEC 18000-63)

Application area: Due to their wavelength, ultra-high-frequency RFID systems are less suitable than the other two frequency ranges for use near metallic or liquid surfaces. However, if long distances need to be bridged or large volumes of identifier data need to be sent, UHF RFID is especially suitable due to its high read range, data transfer rate, and multitag capability. These capabilities are responsible, at least in part, for making the UHF range the fastest growing market within the RFID segment. The range of applications in which UHF RFID is used is correspondingly wide. This includes toll and parking systems, loan systems for public libraries, and a large number of production and logistics areas. Whether for monitoring incoming and outgoing goods, picking processes, tracking supply chains, or implementing vehicle guidance systems on the shop floor—UHF RFID is a potentially suitable technology.

Fig. 3. The IUT-F191-IO-V1-FR* RFID read/write device

Example device: The IUT-F191-IO-V1-FR* RFID read/write device combines the advantages of sophisticated industrial UHF technology with a standardized interface for IO-Link communication and can be used as a cost-efficient enabler component for a wide range of standard applications in areas such as intralogistics, automotive, and material handling. The F191 RFID read/write devices are commissioned without time-consuming programming via the future-oriented, integrated IO-Link interface.

Microwave Frequency RFID (MW)

Microwave frequency RFID operates at frequencies above 3 GHz. This range offers the longest reading distances, typically up to several meters. MW RFID is commonly used in applications that require high-speed data transfer, such as toll systems and vehicle identification. However, MW RFID tags are larger and more sensitive to interference from liquids, metals, and other obstacles.

Benefits of Different Frequency Ranges

Each frequency range in RFID systems has its own advantages and applications. Here are some key benefits:

Interference Resistance

LF RFID tags, operating at lower frequencies, are less affected by interference from liquids and metals. This makes them suitable for environments where this interference is common, such as near water or metallic surfaces.

Reading Distance

Higher frequency results in a longer reading distance. UHF RFID offers the longest reading distance, allowing mass reading of tags without the need to scan each tag individually. This makes it highly efficient for supply chain management and inventory tracking.

Tag Size

HF RFID tags, operating at higher frequencies, can be manufactured in smaller sizes. This makes them suitable for embedding in small objects like credit cards and passports, enhancing their security and convenience.

Data Transfer Speed

MW RFID systems, operating at microwave frequencies, offer high-speed data transfer. This makes them ideal for applications that require rapid and efficient data exchange, such as toll systems on busy highways. Understanding the different frequency ranges of RFID systems is crucial when selecting the most suitable technology for specific applications. Whether it's the shorter reading distance of LF RFID, the small tag size of HF RFID, the extensive reading distance of UHF RFID, or the high-speed data transfer of MW RFID, each frequency range offers unique benefits and capabilities. By choosing the right frequency range, companies can optimize their RFID implementations and achieve greater efficiency and enhanced productivity.

RFID COMMUNICATION PROTOCOLS

A communications protocol is a way of organizing the conversation between devices – in the case of RFID, between tags and a reader – to ensure that information actually gets transferred. A protocol defines:

- An **air interface**: what sort of modulation of the reader signal is used to define a binary one? what's a zero? what kind of signal does the tag send? how fast does everything go? is information sent in discrete packets, and if so how are they formed?
- **Medium access control:** who gets to talk when? how are collisions between contending users (tags in this context) resolved?
- **Data definitions**: what sort of data is associated with a tag? what does it mean?

Passive RFID tags face some special problems not encountered in most other digital radio systems. Tags are cheap and dumb, so only changes in amplitude of the reader signal can be used; advanced modulations like phase-shift keying or quadrature-amplitude-modulation (QAM) are not available.

Further, turning off the power from the reader reduces the power available to the tag, so the modulations of choice for the reader are those in which power is on most of the time; such modulations are wasteful users of spectrum, leading to realtively wide channels or low data rates.

The tag reflection can be modulated in phase or amplitude, but the small tag reflection is combined with large reflections from the antenna and ambient, so that the resulting signal at the reader may change amplitude when the tag reflection changes phase, and so on. One can only hope to detect changes in state of the tag antenna, but not the type of change. The reader can count edges from the tag but not the absolute or differential phase or amplitude. Tag and reader symbols must be chosen with these constraints in mind.

There are numerous protocols using different approaches to each of these issues, and all of them work — but the reader and tag need to use the same one! In this discussion we'll briefly examine the UHF tag protocol that has been promulgated by EPCglobal (now part of GS1) for supply-chain tracking using passive RFID tags.

The EPCglobal protocols assume the tag carries a unique identifier, the electronic product code (EPC). EPC's can be either 64 or 96 bits long (longer ID's are available for future use), and are partitioned into a header describing the EPC structure, some information about the 'manager' (typically a company owning some ID space), and other information about the type of object marked and the serial number.

At the time of this writing (2021), the old Class 0 and Class 1 Generation 1 protocols, as well as most other older proprietary and standardized UHF passive protocols, have been substantially displaced by Class 1 Generation 2 (ISO 18000-6C), so the reader short of time may wish to skip their descriptions. However, it is interesting and educational to see alternative methods of solving common problems, so I recommend perusing the older standards if you have the stamina; brief descriptions thereof are found here.

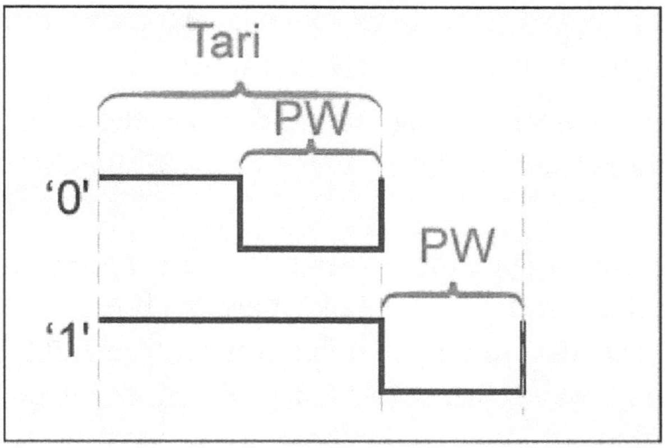

EPCglobal Class 1 Generation 2 (ISO 18000-6C = 18000-63)

First-generation standards had some significant disadvantages. It was awkward to address a specific tag, particularly if you have erased the EPC in the course of assigning a new code to the tag. The use of a 16-bit CRC as the only validation of a tag ID means that on average one in 64,000 reads of random noise would produce an accidentally valid tag read — a phantom or ghost tag. Class 0 tags had problems with large numbers of collocated readers due to the large frequency offset between the tag signal and the reader signal, and had no standard for field writeable tags. Class 1 singulation was relatively slow when a large number of tags are present. Both protocols have problems with late arrivals: tags that enter the read zone when a tag inventory has already started. Finally, class 0 and class 1 were mutually incompatible and approximately equivalent in applications and performance: if the goal is to achieve one global standard, two is one too many.

Realizing these problems, the EPCglobal Hardware Action Group in early 2004 started work on a second-generation standard that would fix the problems in the first-generation standards and provide sufficient performance at sufficiently low cost to become the universal protocol for RFID in supply chain applications. The Class 1 Generation 2 standard was ratified in early 2005, and subsequently ratified by the International Organization for Standardization (ISO) as ISO 18000-6C; the standard has migrated to the new number 18000-63, but is still often referred to as "6C" by practitioners in the field. In order to obtain the aforementioned improvements in performance, the Gen 2 committee started anew in many respects; the Gen 2 standard is completely incompatible with first-generation class 0 and class 1 readers and tags.

The reader symbols are distinct from those older standards. A binary '0' is a short high level pulse followed by low pulse of equal length; a binary '1' is a longer high pulse followed by the same low pulse width. This symbol set provides a high average RF power delivered to the tag. The length of a binary '0' is defined as Tari, and is used as a reference for several other times in the standard. The data rate can vary from 27 to 128 Kbps (Tari from 25 to 6.5 microseconds); the most significant bit of the most significant word is always sent first.

Communication between the tag and reader is packetized. The reader sends a query or command and then transmits continuous (CW) power while a tag hopefully responds.

Two distinct sets of tag symbols are used. The basic approach is FM0: a binary '0' has a transition in the middle of a symbol, whereas a binary '1' does not. However, a second option is provided, Miller-modulated subcarrier (MMS). The FM0 signal is multiplied by a square wave with either 2, 4, or 8 periods for each FM0 symbol. It is important to note that, although in the figure below we show the FM0 symbol time as constant so you can see how the transmitted signal is related to the FM0 signal, in fact it is the time between transitions, or equivalently the link frequency, that is held constant. As a consequence, the data rate for a fixed link frequency is reduced by the MMS multiplier. If we set a link frequency of 100 KHz, FM0 provides a data rate of 100 Kbps, but MMS with a multiplier of M=4 only provides 25 Kbps.

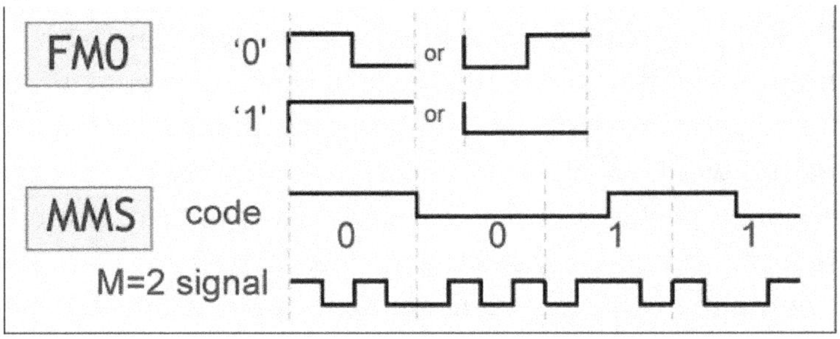

It seems contradictory to intentionally reduce the data rate, but MMS offers some advantages over FM0. In spectral terms, the energy in an MMS signal is concentrated away from the carrier (roughly by the link frequency), making it easier to detect in the presence of phase noise and possible interference from other readers. In the time domain, interpretation of an FM0 symbol depends on a single edge, whereas an MMS symbol provides a number of edges to locate, reducing the likelihood of a bit error.

Inventory operations are based on slotted Aloha collision resolution. The reader issues a QUERY command, and each tag effectively rolls a many-sided die, where the number of sides is set by the reader. A tag that rolls a 0 replies immediately; all tags that roll other numbers record those numbers in a counter and say nothing. The reader, after either receiving a reply or no response, can issue a QUERY REP command, causing all the tags to decrement their counters by 1; any tag reaching a counter value of 0 responds. If the number of sides is chosen properly, one and only one tag will respond to most of the QUERY REP commands.

A tag replies by sending a 16-bit random number RN16. If the reader hears the random number it echoes that number as an acknowledgement, causing the tag to send its electronic product code and error check, along with some protocol control bits (PC). The PC bits provide the length of the EPC stored in the tag, as well as some information pertaining to the numbering system and optionally the type of object to which the tag is attached (the application family identifier (AFI)). The reader can then send commands specific to that tag, or continue to inventory other tags.

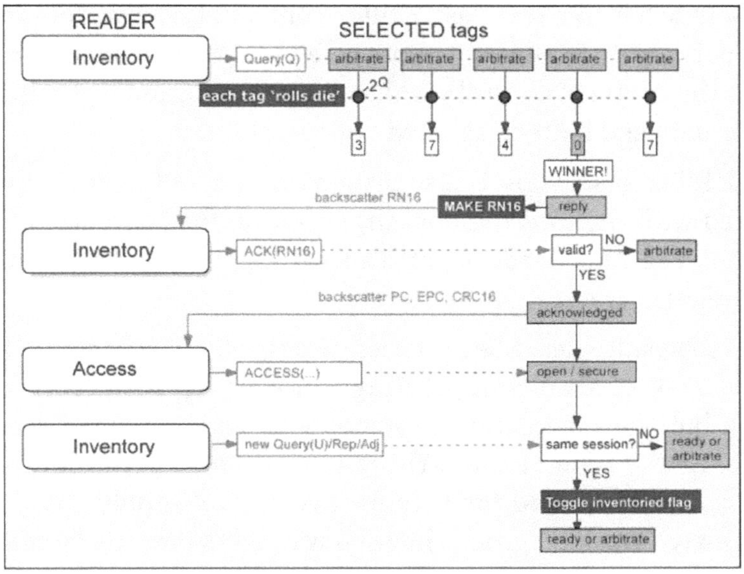

The use of a random number as a handle is an important feature of the Gen 2 protocol. This allows the reader to define a unique session with a particular tag even if that tag has not been identified, or does not have a unique EPC (e.g. if it has just been received from the factory with its EPC initialized to all 0's). A Gen 2 reader can count tags in the field even if all the tags have the same EPC. It can write to a single tag even if that tag has not yet been given a unique identifier. Furthermore, the sequence of exchanging a valid RN16 followed by transmission of the EPC makes it less likely that the reader will see a ghost or phantom tag where none is present.

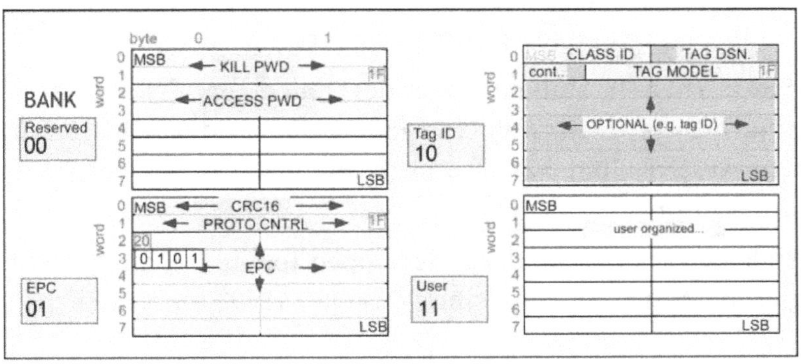

The Gen 2 standard specifies the tag's memory organization. Memory is organized in 4 banks, organized into 32-bit words. Bank 00 is reserved for passwords for the lock and kill functions. Block 1 contains the protocol control bits, the error check, and the unique identifier, normally the EPC. Block 2 contains information about the tag, possibly including a unique tag identifier distinct from the EPC (that is, a number identifying the tag itself and not the object to which it is attached). Block 3 is user memory and may be organized in any fashion. A SELECT command, that works somewhat like the class 1 filter command, is available to choose tags which are to participate in a given inventory session. Recent updates to the standard expand upon the protocol control word to support additional capabilities, such as simple sensor data and battery-assisted tag operation.

A more detailed discussion is also presented in my RFID book, in which you'll get acquainted with the International Organization for Contention (IOC), and the STAR (Slothful Tag And Reader) protocol working group (mis)managed by the illustrious Toulouse Track.

The ISO 18000 suite describes a series of passive tag standards. 18000-6A and 18000-6B = 18000-61,62 are distinct UHF tag protocols. A few aspects of the standards are common, but the modulations, symbol sets, and command sets and mostly incompatible. At the time of this writing (2021), 18000-6C has become the most common worldwide standard for UHF passive tags in supply chain applications. ISO's 18000-related working groups have continued to develop enhancements.

The EPCglobal standards are specifically designed for supply chain applications. There are a number of other RFID protocols applicable to UHF operation, as well as numerous standards for LF and HF ("near-field") tags and readers.

The protocols are called the air-interface protocols, and there are many "standards" for such protocols, depending on the type of RFID system used. Here are a few of the most common air-interface protocol standards ratified by the International Organization for Standardization (ISO):

ISO 14443: This high-frequency (HF) standard is designed to have a short read range and include encryption, since it was created for proximity cards. What that means is that it was created for secure payments.

ISO 15693: This HF standard was developed for vicinity cards. It has no encryption and a longer read range than ISO 14443-based systems. It is used in many access-control systems, but has also been employed for inventory management and other applications.

ISO 18000-3: This HF standard, developed for item management, has never really caught on. Most companies simply use ISO 15693 for item management.

Near Field Communication: While not an official ISO standard, NFC is based on ISO 14443 and adds some additional capabilities, such as the ability of a reader to emulate a tag. NFC will also incorporate ISO 15693 over time, so you will be able to use an NFC-enabled phone to enter a building.

ISO 18000-6C: This ultrahigh-frequency (UHF) standard is based on the EPC Gen 3 air-interface protocol. Although there is an ISO 1800-6A and an ISO 1800-6B, it is ISO 18000-6C that is widely used for passive UHF systems.

ISO 24730: This protocol governs the communication of active RFID transponders operating at 2.45 GHz, and is used in real-time location systems.

PART II: APPLICATIONS OF RFID

CHAPTER-4

RFID IN SUPPLY CHAIN MANAGEMENT

With the development of RFID technology and the internet of things (IOT), RFID technology is widely used in different fields including supply chains and logistics. A supply chain is a system of organizations, people, technology, activities, information, and resources involved in moving a product or service from supplier to customer. Supply chain activities transform natural resources, raw materials, and components into a finished product that is delivered to the end customer.

In sophisticated supply chain systems, used products may re-enter the supply chain at any point where residual value is recyclable. Supply chain applications involve tracking many items (retail item packages, cartons, cases, and pallets) at a relatively slow rate of speed (e.g. fork-lift, conveyor, or items on a storage rack or display shelf) in a protected environment. Oftentimes, the items being tracked in supply chain applications are of relatively low value.

Logistics is the management of the flow of resources between the point of origin and the point of destination in order to meet the requirements of customers or corporations. Logistics involves the integration of information, transportation, inventory, warehousing, material handling, and packaging. Logistics assets that have a circular flow are an essential part of the logistics system.

These assets are often reusable, such as pallets, totes, racks, bins and roll cages, shipping containers, and gas containers that are used to transport goods from one place to another.

Procuring, maintaining, and managing these assets often forms a significant part of a company's annual expenses. Since theft, damage, and replacement erode asset productivity, these assets have to be managed in such a way as to minimize loss as much as possible. It is in this situation that RFID (Radio Frequency Identification Devices) and logistics management comes into effect.

RFID Technologies

Radio-Frequency Identification (RFID) technology is a wireless sensor technology that is based on the detection of electromagnetic signals. A typical RFID system includes three components: an antenna or coil, a transceiver (with decoder), and a transponder (RF tag) that is electronically programmed with unique information. The antenna emits radio signals in order for the tag to be activated and for data to be read and written to it. Antennas establish the communication between the tag and the transceiver, which is responsible for the data acquisition.

The antenna can be packaged with the transceiver and decoder in order to become a reader, which can be configured either as a handheld or a fixed-mount device. The reader emits radio waves in ranges which can reach up to 100 feet or more, depending on its power output and the radio frequency that is used. In the case that an RFID tag is found in the electromagnetic zone that is produced by the antenna, the activation signal of the reader is detected. The reader decodes the data which are encoded in the integrated circuit of the tag and then transfers it to any computer system for processing.

Supply Chain Management Definition and History

The origins of Supply Chain Management date back to the 1950s and 1960s when U.S. manufacturers were employing mass production techniques to reduce costs and improve productivity. During this time-period, there was little focus on creating supplier partnerships, improving process design and flexibility, and/or improving product quality. Development of new products was slow because manufacturers relied on inhouse resources, technologies, and capacities. Sharing of technology and expertise was non-existent in creating strategic relationships and there were large investments made in work in process inventory to keep machinery running and maintain balanced material flows.

In the 1960s and 1970s, material requirements planning systems and manufacturing resource planning systems were developed. The importance of effective materials management was realized and the amount of impact that high levels of inventories had on manufacturing and storage costs. Computer capabilities became more sophisticated resulting in an increase of inventory tracking software, which made it possible to reduce inventory costs. This also created an improvement with internal communication with need for purchased parts and supplies emphasized.

In the 1980s, SCM became increasingly popular as global competition increased, which created a demand for lower-cost, higher quality, and higher levels of customer service. Manufacturers utilized Just-in-time (JIT) inventory and total quality management (TQM) strategies to improve quality, efficiency, and delivery times.

Business process reengineering (BPR) was emphasized and is known now as the radical rethinking and redesigning of business processes to reduce waste and increase performance. In the 1990's managers, consultants, and academics started to see that there was a difference between SCM and logistics; third party service providers (3PL) became more popular, along with the global supply chain. Today we are connecting SCM with ecommerce systems to become more efficient in dealing with suppliers, manufacturers, wholesalers, distributors, retailers, and end customers to provide better service to everyone involved

The origins of Supply Chain Management are important because the concept is a big part of business today and will be an even bigger part of business tomorrow. Companies are still trying to learn and explore ways to create or improve their supply chains. I decided to go into SCM, because it is a field that encompasses many elements of many companies, which supplies me with the foundation to do more with my career. With the evolution of globalization, it has become a career field that has become more in demand and will only get more attention in the years to come.

The four main elements than make up SCM are purchasing, operations, distribution, and integration (Wisner, Tan and Leong).11 As the above historical information showed, supply chain management is not a brand new concept, but it has become more frequently recognized. This is due to the push towards a global economy (trade relations and dependency) and sustainability (efficient operations and waste reduction). There are many definitions of SCM, but they all incorporate the same ideas, below are a few.

No matter the length of the definition or the differences in terminology, my studies have taught me that supply chain management is cutting costs, maintaining efficiency and quality, and providing value-added services from the original equipment manufacturer all the way down to the end consumer. SCM focuses on the customer and making sure that they are fully satisfied with any products or services provided, while building a trusting relationship that can be beneficial for both partners now and in the future. A large part of this today is technology; this is something making a large impact on the supply chain, which is why it is important to discuss its role as supply chain enabler.

Supply Chain Enabler

In order for companies to become successful in the supply chain, they must fully integrate all departments and partners, rather than certain areas. If full integration does not take place, the company will not see full results and will most likely fail due to inadequacies. Full integration is much easier today then it was twenty years ago and this is because of technology. Technology is an "enabler" for supply chain management systems and better efficiency, because of the automation that it creates.

Although technology can solve a problem and identify a need, it should not take over the supply chain completely. A large part of supply chain management is customer service, which is not something technology can provide alone. The systems can provide increased accuracy, better inventory tracking, and a reduction of costs, which are all characteristics that partners and customers enjoy, but speaking with them is a good way to maintain the relationship so they keep coming back. Many consumers are already in fear that technology will take over and yes it enables to do a lot more with a lot less, but companies need to remember communication is the key to all relationships.

INVENTORY TRACKING AND MANAGEMENT

Inventory management is demanded globally by enterprises or manufacturers, and it serves the purpose of satisfying the count audit and management of the existing inventory. Therefore, inventory count management has been emphasized by all enterprises and manufactures. There are quite a lot of enterprises that already use the bar code for inventory management because of these reasons. However, bar codes have numerous disadvantages, and some companies have turned to wireless radio frequency identification (RFID) systems in recent years. This technology has already been classified as one of the most important technologies available. Traditional inventory count requires a lot of manpower, money, and time, and it makes the inventory quantity control of goods considerably inefficient and also influences the time-effect of inventory value.

By using RFID technology and image capture combined with an Oracle back-end database, an inventory management system can be implemented by using the characteristics of instant read-write-enabled RFID tags to carry out the regional inventory count in the warehouse. This inventory management system integrated with a database can be used to identify slow selling items caused by long storing or near over-due-period. Every item of goods has its own serial number, and the first-in-first-out management of goods can be used to keep the product fresh and improve traditional inventory shortcomings.

To effectively manage whether the goods have a flaw or are bad products, all goods can be traced to the original supplier via the tag on the goods and subsequently returned to the original supplier. This entire item tracking system can increase the enterprise's competitiveness, and it is a set of intact product life cycles.

RFID in freight transportation

A well-functioning freight transportation system is an essential element in any successful logistics system. The freight transportation system will face challenges that will require the development of new paradigms of operations and technologies. The impact of information technology such as RFID, EDI, GPS, and GIS on the freight transportation system has been significant and likely will increase sharply in the oncoming years. The steadily declining prices of new technology coupled with an increased awareness among freight operators of the technology's potential benefits will encourage the freight industry to increase its use of information technology.

The industry has already implemented cutting-edge technologies to improve customer service and to reduce expenditures. Information technology also will have varying effects on the different modes of transportation. Carriers in all modes will increasingly rely on continuous updates on the location and status of the vehicles and containers in their system.

Additional growth in the intermodal freight market requires an increase in information sharing across companies. The productivity of integrated freight transportation providers such as Federal Express and United Parcel Service will improve with increased use of information technology.

Transportation RFID tags must be designed for years of continued, reliable use in the harshest of operating environments. Consider, for example, RFID tags affixed to all rail cars used by Class 1 railroads operating in North America. These tags are subjected to every imaginable harsh environmental condition (heat, cold, snow, ice, dirt, rain, oil, and, in certain cases, temperatures over 350°F), yet they are required to be installed once and operate indefinitely with 99%+ reliability.

Also, consider transportation tags used in road tolling applications. These tags are installed on vehicles' windshields where temperatures range from sub-zero to 150°F and must operate for many years or indefinitely with 99%+ accuracy.

RFID technologies can be use to transportation in the following aspects:

Firstly, RFID can be used to automate yard management; In this aspect, the RFID technology can be used to automate workflows and processes while capturing data on tracked assets at multiple sites and to identify shipping bottlenecks in order to quickly adjust delivery schedules within the supply chain. Also, it allows access to historical data on the location and status of assets, eliminating written logs. It provides increased visibility into the supply chain to help meet service level commitments.

Secondly, RFID technology can used for Vehicle Tracking and identification. This will reduce labor costs for vehicle processing and decrease on-site dwell time, enabling better yard throughput and increased responsiveness to dealer and customer demands. It will also enhance quality by ensuring that no process steps are missed and that every vehicle departs in accordance with dealer/customer specifications

Futhermore, RFID can be used to Streamline Break Bulk and General Cargo Operations. It will improve control over the Container Freight Station (CFS) and support for all types of roll-on/roll-off (Ro-Ro) Vehicle Operations. It will reduce labor costs for vehicle processing and decrease on-site dwell time, enabling better yard throughput and increased responsiveness to dealer and customer demands. It will also enhance quality by ensuring that no process steps are missed and that every vehicle departs in accordance with dealer/customer specifications.

SUPPLY CHAIN VISIBILITY AND OPTIMIZATION

Supply chain visibility refers to the ability of companies to maintain transparency in tracking a product from its shipment to its final destination.

- It includes having access to up-to-date data about inventory levels, transportation, the whole production process, and delivery status.
- This is possible only through specialized technology and software that allows every individual involved in the supply chain to access the same information.

Now that we have known about the visibility aspect, let's take a closer look at the intricacies of RFID.

Importance of Supply Chain Visibility

Supply chain visibility enables shippers to reduce costs and improve customer satisfaction through proper management of inventory by limiting disruption and risk mitigation.

The main goal of supply chain visibility RFID systems is to provide advanced insights into how your supply chain works by reducing the risk factor.

- Firstly it is required to mitigate disruptions. Operating a supply chain requires strong data analysis with the help of RFID. Supply chain visibility may reduce these roadblocks and may help in getting exceptional results.
- Warehouse associates may make data-driven decisions related to the supply chain. They may move faster in operation processes when they know what's coming on their way.
- Enhanced visibility helps in aligning supply chain visibility RFID to customer demands. So business must be flexible and adaptable.
- Visibility helps in accessing huge amounts of supply chain data. This helps shippers make decisions. This helps shippers make informed decisions and enhance customer experience.

Improvisation is a crucial factor at every stage of business. So let's understand how we can improve supply chain visibility.

Improving supply chain visibility through RFID

The steps to improve your visibility have been listed below. One should follow these steps to remain ahead of the competition.

Mapping Processes

The first step is to outline procedures to identify disruptions and bottlenecks.

- Mapping product movements from the suppliers to the consumers and tracking communication methods helps in maintaining operational efficiency. This also helps in uncovering reasons for lost items, any delays, or communication gaps.
- Identifying weak areas in supply chain visibility RFID that need attention allows teams to develop strategies for smoother operations and better visibility.

Enhanced Communication

Communication is crucial for enhancing supply chain visibility.

- Clear and consistent communication keeps everybody informed and reduces any kind of confusion. There might be external factors like a spike in demand or weather that may make visibility a challenge.
- Transparent communication helps in building stronger relationships with suppliers and enhances collaboration. Implementation of traceability features aids in real-time shipping of goods. Also seeking timely feedback ensures effective communication.

Data Collection and Analysis

Data analysis and collection are essential parts of supply chain visibility.

- Software system helps in data collection and analytics, and the generation of reports with important matrices like sales numbers and inventory levels.
- It is important to share this data among the distributors, suppliers, and the members of the team to enhance collaboration and unity in the supply chain. Different sectors can provide them inside contributing to informed decision-making.

Using Updated Technology

Outdated systems and disconnected applications may hinder the supply chain visibility RFID mechanisms. Manual data entry reduces accuracy and compatibility with the software.

- Timely Technological upgrades like electronic data interchange and vendor management inventory may improve efficiency and accuracy. These tools facilitate the sharing of real-time data, and provide insight into the inventory levels and the movement of products.

- Upgrading software supports better communication and collaboration with suppliers boosting overall profitability.

Choose the right RFID system

There are different types of RFID systems, such as passive, active, or semi-passive, that vary in their range, cost, and battery life. You need to choose the right system for your specific supply chain needs, considering factors such as the size, shape, and material of your items, the environment and distance of your tracking, and the level of detail and security you require. You also need to select compatible tags and readers that can communicate with each other and your software.

Integrate RFID with your software

RFID data is only useful if you can integrate it with your inventory management software and other systems, such as ERP, WMS, or CRM. This way, you can automate and streamline your processes, such as receiving, picking, packing, shipping, and invoicing. You can also analyze and visualize your data to gain insights into your inventory performance, demand, and trends. You need to ensure that your software can support RFID data formats, standards, and protocols, and that you have reliable and secure data transmission and storage.

Train and educate your staff

RFID can change the way you and your staff manage your inventory, so you need to train and educate them on how to use the technology effectively and efficiently. You need to explain the benefits and challenges of RFID, the best practices and procedures for tagging, scanning, and verifying items, and the common errors and issues that may arise. You also need to provide feedback and support to your staff, and encourage them to share their experiences and suggestions for improvement.

Test and monitor your RFID system

RFID is not a one-time solution, but a continuous process that requires testing and monitoring to ensure its accuracy, reliability, and functionality. You need to test your RFID system before and after deployment, using different scenarios and conditions, to verify its performance and compatibility. You also need to monitor your RFID system regularly, using metrics such as read rates, tag quality, data quality, and system uptime, to identify and resolve any problems or gaps.

Review and optimize your RFID system

RFID is not a static technology, but a dynamic one that can evolve and adapt to your changing supply chain needs and goals. You need to review and optimize your RFID system periodically, using data and feedback from your software, staff, and customers, to measure its impact and value. You also need to explore new opportunities and innovations that can enhance your RFID system, such as new tags, readers, or software features, or new applications or integrations with other technologies.

The Foundation of Real Time Visibility

RFID (Radio Frequency Identification) is a technology that uses radio waves to identify and track objects. RFID tags are attached to objects and can be read by RFID readers. RFID technology utilizes radio waves to identify and track objects equipped with RFID tags. These tags contain electronic information that can be wirelessly captured by RFID readers or scanners. Unlike traditional barcode scanning, RFID allows for simultaneous identification of multiple items without requiring line-of-sight contact. This capability forms the foundation of real-time visibility, enabling businesses to obtain accurate and up-to-date information about their inventory.

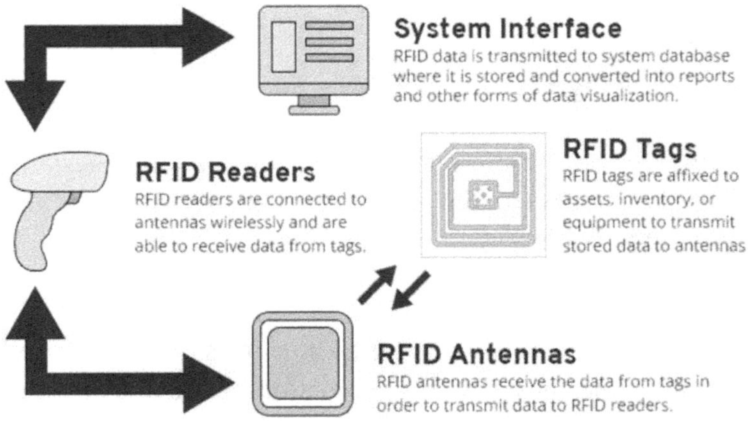

Continuous Monitoring and Tracking

There are two main types of RFID - passive and active. The main difference between the two is that active has a batter built into the tag. This battery allows the tag, and therefore whatever it is affixed to, to continuously send out a location signal. So, for any real time tracking projects, active RFID is really the only way to go. Active RFID facilitates continuous monitoring and tracking of inventory. As tagged items move through the supply chain, RFID readers placed at strategic locations automatically capture data, updating the inventory database in real time. This seamless flow of information provides a comprehensive view of stock levels, locations, and movements. Whether items are in the warehouse, en route to stores, or on retail shelves, businesses can monitor their inventory at any given moment, enabling timely decision-making and efficient stock management.

Improved Product Quality

Visibility tools collect data and deliver it in real time for better decision-making. They help businesses track and monitor the flow of materials or products through a supply chain at the raw material, manufacturing, and shipments stages. Visibility provides companies with a clear view of what they need to fulfill orders, improve production efficiency, and respond to disruptions in the supply chain.

For example, a company with visibility can immediately notify its upstream suppliers when it needs to place an order or receives a shipment. It can also keep tabs on inventory levels, production schedules, transportation routes, and delivery dates. This allows it to proactively address any issues and keep its promise to customers.

In addition, visibility makes it easier to manage logistics partners and 3PL providers. Visibility helps reduce misunderstandings between partners about ETAs or shipping milestones by making all of the information transparent for all stakeholders to see and communicate in one place. This enables companies to cut down on delays and excessive dwell time, which saves money on demurrage and detention fees.

The key to achieving better visibility is not having more eyes and ears on the ground but embracing technology that provides a single, unified data model. This enables automation, predictive analytics and new business models. It also empowers the stakeholders to take control of their network by exercising a high level of visibility into what's going on across the entire value chain.

Better Customer Service

Having real time supply chain visibility improves customer service by giving you the ability to communicate with your customers directly about the status of their orders. This way, if there are any issues with shipping your goods or there's a delay in production, you can resolve it quickly. This will prevent any delays in delivering your products to your customers, which can be an extremely frustrating experience for both parties.

This also gives your business the opportunity to minimize inefficiencies, as you'll have more control over operations. This can lead to savings on both inventory and transportation costs. Additionally, it can help your organization to respond more quickly to disruptions, such as weather or natural disasters.

The best way to improve your company's supply chain visibility is by implementing a unified data model that collects and processes all relevant information in real time. This will give your team a complete overview of all aspects of your operations and allows for collaboration on a single platform. It's important that all stakeholders have access to this information to make informed decisions and reduce the risk of inefficiencies and disruptions.

Reduced Costs

A supply chain is complex and interconnected. Often, one small disruption can cause a domino effect that leads to other problems throughout the system. For example, when a shipment is delayed at one point, it can lead to an increase in the days inventory on hand at the next point of fulfillment or a decrease in customer order fill rate. Having a clear picture of the entire supply chain allows businesses to track and anticipate potential issues, automate processes and make smarter decisions.

Visibility solutions enable businesses to monitor and manage key supply chain metrics, such as perfect order rate (the percentage of orders that are shipped correctly), customer order cycle time and days inventory on hand/inventory turnover. These tools also allow companies to reduce costs by enabling them to optimize transportation routes, predict and avoid unforeseen delays and take advantage of opportunities for reduced rates during pandemic conditions.

The best way to get real-time visibility is through a technology solution that enables businesses to capture and store data from multiple sources, such as GPS devices, ELD telematics networks, mobile apps, and AIS. This data is then analyzed and converted into valuable information to help improve business performance.

Increased Profitability

Supply chain visibility solutions enable companies to see how they are performing at all times and make changes accordingly. This helps businesses to reduce costs, improve quality and increase productivity. This results in greater profitability and overall success.

Visibility solutions allow companies to monitor their supplies and products at a highly granular level, as well as track compliance records, shipping details and other pertinent data in real time. This information is shared with all stakeholders through a unified data platform that ensures transparency, accuracy and speed.

For manufacturers, this means they can easily track their raw materials and components to their manufacturing plants. This also allows them to make better decisions about production schedules and reduce inefficiencies. For logistics vendors, it means they can quickly access key information about cargo batches, consignments and deliveries. This helps them manage their day-to-day operations more efficiently, and it gives customers peace of mind that they're always in the loop about delivery status.

For any business, it's important to be able to keep customers happy and maintain high levels of customer service at all times. This is especially crucial for supply chains, where any issues can result in significant delays or even a complete shutdown of production. With increased visibility, businesses can reduce downtime and lost revenue due to product defects or shipping delays. In addition, they can quickly address problems and recover from any disruptions that occur.

Data Analytics and Business Intelligence

The abundance of real-time inventory data generated by RFID technology presents an opportunity for businesses to leverage data analytics and business intelligence tools. By analyzing the captured data, organizations can gain valuable insights into consumer trends, demand patterns, and inventory performance. This information allows for proactive decision-making, such as optimizing inventory levels, identifying slow-moving items, and aligning supply with demand. Through data-driven strategies, companies can enhance operational efficiency, reduce costs, and improve customer satisfaction.

RFID technology has revolutionized inventory management by providing organizations with unprecedented real-time visibility. Through continuous monitoring, accurate tracking, and streamlined operations, businesses can optimize their supply chains, reduce errors, and make informed.

CHAPTER-5

RFID IN RETAIL

RFID is a wireless technology with two main parts: tags and readers. The reader is a device that has one or more antennas that send and receive electromagnetic signals back from RFID tags.

These tags, which store a serial number or unique identifier, use radio waves to send their data to nearby readers. They contain RFID chips, also known as integrated circuits (IC), which communicate data to the reader.

RFID belongs to a group of technologies called automatic identification and data collection (AIDC). You can use AIDC tools to identify items, collect data about them, and send that data to a computer system, with little human interaction.

For retailers that need to track stock accuracy, an RFID system that integrates with your inventory can increase efficiencies significantly. You can use it to improve inventory accuracy and visibility to create better shopping experiences for today's omnichannel shoppers.

RFID systems have three components that make them work: an antenna, a transceiver, and a transponder (tag). The part of the tag that encodes the data is called the RFID inlay.

When you combine the antenna and the transceiver, you have an RFID reader, also known as an interrogator.

There are two types of RFID readers:

- Fixed readers, when the reader and antenna are installed in a specific place where RFID tag data passes. For example, you can check out at Amazon Go without going to a cashier. You just walk through an RF zone and the reader receives the tag data.
- Mobile readers, which are handheld devices that can be carried anywhere.

- Once you have the equipment, the RFID tracking process can be broken down into four phases:
- Information is stored on a RFID tag and is attached to an item like your product
- An antenna recognizes the signal of a nearby RFID tag
- A reader is connected wirelessly to the antenna and receives the information stored on a tag
- The reader then sends the RFID data to a database, where it is stored and evaluated.

There are two common types of RFID tags:

- **Active RFID tags:** tags that have their own power source and can read in a range of 100+ meters. Active tags are used by companies where asset location or logistics improvements are important.
- **Passive RFID tags:** tags that don't have a power source. Electromagnetic energy from the reader powers a passive RFID tag. This gives them a read distance from close contact to 25 meters.

There are also semi-passive tags, which rely on the same principles as passive tags, but include a battery that helps extend communication range.

However, passive tags are most often used in RFID applications. You can embed them into an adhesive label or into the object itself. Passive tags are low-cost, so they are better in situations where you won't reuse them.

For example, if you receive a case of products, the supplier may attach passive tags to it. When you remove the products and throw out the case, the tags are also scrapped.

The advantages of passive tags include:

- Small size
- Light weight
- Affordability
- Long shelf life (20+ years)

Passive tags are used to scan at a distance from a few inches to a few feet. They operate at the following frequencies:

- Low frequency (LF RFID) 125 MHz to134 kHz
- High frequency (HF RFID) 13.56 MHz
- Ultra-high frequency (UHF RFID) 856 MHz to 960 MHz

- The higher the RFID frequency, the longer range you can scan.

Importance of Inventory Management in Retail?

Inventory management is vital for retailers because the practice helps them increase profits. They are more likely to have enough inventory to capture every possible sale while avoiding overstock and minimizing expenses.

From a strategic point of view, retail inventory management increases efficiency. The practice:

- **Decreases Inventory Costs:** When you know how much stock you have and how much you need, you can pinpoint inventory levels more accurately, thereby reducing storage and carrying costs for excess merchandise. Other savings include shipping, logistics, depreciation and the opportunity cost that comes from not having an alternative product that might sell better.
- **Minimizes Out-of-Stocks:** To avoid disappointing customers and missing sales, retailers want to avoid running out of inventory. Retailers can use inventory management tools to determine how much stock is "just right" to have on hand, neither too much nor too little. This amount will be larger for bestsellers than for unpopular products. Also, with real-time information on sales and stock, retailers can react quickly by reordering, transferring stock from another location or drop shipping to the customer.
- **Improves Profit Margins:** With lower inventory costs and enough supply to fill every order, retailers improve profitability.
- **Prevents Spoilage and Obsolescence:** Inventory management helps retailers address another costly inefficiency that happens when products expire or become obsolete. This phenomenon can apply to perishables that have a limited shelf life, such as milk and meat, or a non-perishable that becomes obsolete because consumer tastes and technology change. For example, season collections or holiday-specific packaging. Or when a piece of consumer technology adds a popular new feature, the old models may face plummeting demand: Consider how the rise of smart televisions sunk demand for models that weren't capable of streaming content.
- **Improves Multi-Channel and Omnichannel Performance and Order Fulfillment:** If you are selling via physical stores, your website and third-party merchants, it can be difficult to keep correct inventory counts across all channels. Having accurate inventory data across selling channels lets you use your inventory more efficiently, ultimately getting the product to consumers faster.

- **Simplifies Processes and Facilitates Growth:** Strong inventory management also reduces friction in your systems as sales grow. Shipping, receiving and order fulfillment run more smoothly, and you minimize errors, customer complaints and staff stress.
- **Reduces Shrinkage:** Shrinkage is inventory loss due to shoplifting, product damage, vendor mistakes or fraud, employee theft and administrative errors. According to a survey by the FMI food industry association, the average supermarket loses up to 3% of sales through shrinkage. A National Retail Federation survey(opens in new tab)puts average shrinkage for its members at 1.4% of sales in 2019. This data suggests that most losses stem from incorrectly recording inventory on intake, miscounting it or misplacing it. Stronger retail inventory management could reduce shrinkage by at least half.
- **Eases Supply Chain Management:** Having a firm grip on inventory and sales trends helps you manage your supply chain better. You can use the replenishment system that works best for you, whether that's just-in-time ordering or fewer, bigger orders. Retail inventory management helps you determine your economic order quantity (EOQ), which is the ideal order size to minimize inventory costs including holding, shortage and ordering expenses. The EOQ formula, which factors in demand in units, ordering costs such as shipping charges and holding costs, works best when these variables remain consistent over time. Learn more about the EOQ formula.
- **Improves Customers Satisfaction:** When customers get the products they want faster with fewer mistakes or out-of-stocks, it increases customer loyalty.
- **Improves Forecasting:** You can use data such as historical sales results and available inventory to project future sales, growth and capital needs. These forecasts are vital to your budgeting and guide spending for marketing, product development and staffing.

ITEM-LEVEL TAGGING AND INVENTORY CONTROL

The conflux of shipping and receiving at distribution centers, as well as the putting away and picking of inventory, make them an ideal place to introduce item-level RFID tagging.

Distribution center management can significantly reduce the travel time lost in picking and putting away inventory, as well as dramatically improve the accuracy of inventory counts, order fulfillment, shipping, delivery, and the verification and proof of delivery. Item-level tagging helps eliminate shortages, disputes, and costly write-downs.

Item-level RFID provides the warehouse with an ideal tool to close the gap to "perfect order" where product delivery is complete, on time, and damage free, and essentially applies a principled philosophy to achieve increased efficiency as manufacturing has with Six Sigma.

The reason manufacturing can achieve such high levels of efficiency is the automation associated with the assembly.

Item-level RFID enables a new set of automation tools to increase efficiency in its primary objective, receiving and shipping products.

The intelligence derived from this new philosophy, enabled by item-level RFID, can improve business processes, reduce workloads, improve decision making, and increase efficiencies that ultimately drive costs and provide a competitive advantage.

Item-level RFID tagging occurs when an RFID tag is placed on each item at a determined point in the supply chain. The earlier in the supply chain an item is tagged indicates an intent for increased and additional tracking and visibility capabilities.

Item-level tagging can be used with new or existing case- and pallet-level tagging operations. The item-level tags can then be associated with the case and pallet tags to provide a heightened level of checks and balances, ensuring that every item in every lot or pallet is what and where it needs to be.

Solving Problems with SmartX HUB RFID

Collapsing the supply chain - shrinking the time it takes for finished products to get from the front end of manufacturing, through distribution and transportation, to the shelves of a store and into the hands of the consumer - impacts the bottom line for all businesses. Master the supply chain and succeed; fall behind and fail.

The supply chain has been affected by various technologies over the years. Few, if any, have had the promise of SmartX HUB RFID. Unlike other technologies that might have provided incremental benefits, SmartX HUB RFID can significantly increase the speed of information and maximize supply chain efficiencies.

Smartx HUB RFID allows users to know the location and status of RFID-tagged containers, pallets, cartons, or individual assets. Unlike a bar code, which must be visually located and scanned for on-demand operation, an "always-on" RFID tag awaits the reader signal to access real-time critical business information at any time.

The SmartX HUB technology has shown that it can increase sales and reduce labor costs, and it also significantly aids in asset protection and counterfeiting. The intelligence it provides can greatly benefit every business within the supply chain as they search for ways to be more efficient, run a leaner operation, grow revenue, and expand profit margins.

Benefits of Item-level Tagging in Distribution and Logistics

Item-level RFID adoption represents perhaps one of the most significant near-term opportunities for businesses to improve operations throughout the supply chain. With many recently documented and achievable use cases, item-level RFID tagging has become widely viewed as a critical competitive advantage and business differentiator

Pros of Using RFID Tags for Inventory Management

Using RFID tags for inventory management offers several benefits, such as reduced labor costs and faster scanning. Here's a look at how RFID tags can be a benefit in the inventory management process.

- **Improved visibility and faster scanning.** Since RFID tags do not require a "line-of-sight" scan like barcodes, it is possible to read them at a distance for fast inventory processing. They can also be read in any orientation and give you **improved visibility** into your inventory with the potential for more frequent updates and scanning locations.
- **Reduced labor costs.** With labor costs accounting for **as much as 50-80% of distribution center costs**, RFID offers potential benefits in this area. Inventory check-in, counting, and shipment verification can be done very quickly and automatically in a few scans without the need for multiple employees to process them. These savings must be weighed against the cost of investing in an RFID inventory solution, which we'll discuss in more detail below.
- **Tracking of returnable assets.** For those companies that utilize a returnable fleet of assets such as containers and pallets, there is often a significant capital investment to protect. Utilizing RFID allows you to track these assets through the entire supply chain loop and provide increased visibility on inventory locations. This has the added benefit of improving returns and reducing theft or neglect.

Cons of Using RFID Tags for Inventory Management

While there are some benefits of using RFID tags for inventory management, the technology also comes with several disadvantages that hinder usability and introduce other concerns, such as security. Here's a look at the distinct disadvantages of using RFID tags for inventory management.

- **Inability to use cell phones as scanners.** Even though there are fixed and remote RFID readers available, it is not possible to use a phone to scan them, as can be done with barcodes. This is especially limiting as it requires drivers or employees in the field to carry specific RFID readers to do any scans, and phones cannot be used as a backup if the provided readers fail.

- **Prohibitive costs when scaling.** RFID tags cost significantly more than barcode labels. In addition, they utilize specific readers that must be purchased from the limited number of RFID equipment manufacturers. This can **add significant costs when scaling** these solutions with the requirement for additional specialized scanners and RFID tags.
- **Demanding infrastructure needs.** Setup for these systems requires the integration of the readers, tags, **inventory management system**, network, and building wiring that can take a significant amount of time and resources to set up. In some cases, companies may need to update their inventory management system entirely, as some software platforms do not support RFID. Also, if real-time asset tracking is required, the RFID-enabled system will need to utilize GPS and cellular data to communicate, which can put a significant burden on your system.
- **Security concerns.** While RFID systems continue to update and improve their data security, they can still be vulnerable to hacking. Remote devices, including cell phones, can sometimes be used to scan tags at close range and copy tag data. This could later be used to create a cloned tag or copy the information to another tag, a risk of particular concern in the retail industry.

While the use of RFID tags in inventory management offers some compelling and tangible benefits, there is a great deal of work to be done to streamline these systems. Much of the challenge involves scaling this solution in a cost-effective way while updating infrastructure enough to be able to capitalize on its greatest benefits.

RFID Tags vs. Barcode Labels: Best for Inventory Management

RFID can be useful for some applications, but for most companies looking for an accurate, user-friendly, and cost-effective solution for inventory management, barcode labels are a proven and trusted solution. Some barcode labels, such as Camcode's Metalphoto® inventory tags, are durable enough to withstand harsh environments in both indoor and outdoor applications and offer excellent resistance to chemicals, solvents, and abrasion.

Compared to RFID tags, barcodes are just as accurate if not better, and they can be affixed to any surface material without impacting accuracy.

In contrast, materials like metal can interfere with an RFID tag's ability to transmit data, and liquid can hinder an RFID tag's signal. While it's possible to use RFID tags on metal surfaces or items, it requires the use of a special type of tag with an RFID block to prevent interference, adding to the overall cost.

Cost to Implement an RFID Inventory Management System

Understanding the total cost of an RFID system implementation can be a complex undertaking as there are many expenses to consider. The largest initial cost is often the equipment, which can include readers, cabling and antennas.

Passive RFID reader systems can run about $1000 per reader and cost as much as $3000 per reader, when you factor in the cabling and other expenses such as power over Ethernet (POE) that are usually required to operate them. In the case of active reader systems, the equipment costs can be about 10 times cheaper than a passive system because they tend to be less sophisticated and complex.

Additional up-front costs can include installation, asset management software, facility modifications which can vary widely for each unique situation.

Ongoing costs for an RFID system include tags, licensing fees, and maintenance.

One of the benefits of operating a passive RFID system over the long term is the low cost of tags. Passive RFID tags only cost about 5 to 15 U.S. cents per chip, though there can be a higher cost for tags with special housings such as those that protect against interference from metal objects.

Active RFID tags generally cost between $5 and $15 each, about 100 times as much as the passive tags, because they require a local power source and more involved housing design.

How Does RFID Work in a Warehouse?

The main difference between an active and passive RFID inventory system is the way in which the inventory tags are powered during operation, but the basic workflow in a warehouse is the same for both configurations.

Before a shipment is sent to the warehouse it will have had an RFID tag, or chip, attached to individual items or an entire pallet. This RFID tag stores important information about the item.

When the shipment arrives at the destination, each RFID tag will transmit its information to readers installed within the warehouse. These readers will have been placed in strategic locations within the receiving and storage areas to pick up the best possible signal.

The data is transmitted via electromagnetic waves and is relayed from the readers to a central warehouse management system. From there, information can be modified and sent back to the RFID tags for later recall at any time.

This gives warehouse operators the ability to perform tasks such as real-time asset counts and advanced inventory transactions.

RFID Increase Inventory Accuracy

Using an RFID inventory system has been shown to improve inventory accuracy by up to 13% compared to traditional inventory tracking methods and manual inventory checks in some situations. Particularly in the retail industry, where maintaining inventory accuracy is an ongoing challenge, there are some benefits to implementing a more automated system.

In a warehouse environment, the implementation costs may outweigh the benefits in some cases. It can be beneficial in situations where a very high inventory accuracy rate is required, but there is always a balance between hardware and labor costs that should be considered.

For companies looking to adopt an inventory tracking solution, it's important to conduct a thorough analysis of the differences between established technologies such as barcode labels and tags designed for inventory control and newer solutions like RFID to ensure that you will achieve a desirable ROI for your investment.

Industrial Automation

Tool Identification

As well as its metal cutting tool industry, Germany's woodworking industry also plays a dominant role in the world market. The modern woodworking and furniture manufacturing industry is dominated by CNC technology because this enables manufacturers to manufacture at a low cost and remain competitive.

CNC machines equipped with tool holders and automatic tool changers fulfil tasks that are increasingly associated with small batch production. This increases the proportion of manufacturing costs incurred by retooling and tool-change times. Another consideration is the fact that a CNC woodworking machine differs from a metalworking machine because of its higher rotation and path speeds. Rotation speeds from 1000 min^{-1} to more than 20 000 min^{-1} (!) are attained in wood and plastic processing. The risk of accidents for worker and machine is therefore very high during the tool-change operation; for example, hazards may be caused by the wrong fitting of the CNC machine's chain magazine.

This potential hazard can be eliminated by fitting a transponder in the taper shaft or in the retention bolts of the toolholder. All relevant tool data are preprogrammed into the transponder by the tool manufacturer. The machine operator fits the transponder tools into the CNC machine's toolholder in any order.

Then the CNC machine initiates an automatic read sequence of all tools in the toolholder, during which the tools are first ordered into toolholder positions and then all geometric and technical data for the tools is transmitted correctly to the tool management system of the CNC control unit. There is no manual data entry, which eliminates the possibility of human error. The danger of accidents due to excessive speeds, the selection of the wrong rotation direction or the incorrect positioning of the tool in relation to the workpiece is thus eliminated.

Inductively coupled transponders operating in the frequency range < 135 kHz are used. The transponder coil is mounted on a ferrite core to shield it from the metal surface. The transponder must have a minimum of 256 bytes of memory, which is written with an ASCII string containing the required tool data. An example of a data record is illustrated in Table 1.

Table 1 Example of a data record for a tool transponder

Customer	Furniture production plant XY
LEITZ ID number	130004711 D25x60
Manufacturing reference	Y21
Place of manufacture	UHE
Rotation direction	3
Maximum rotation speed	24 000
Min. rotation speed (min^{-1})	18 000
Ideal rotation speed (min^{-1})	20 000
Radius correction	25 011
Longitudinal correction	145 893
Greatest radius	25 500
Greatest length	145 893
Maximum travel	3000
Current travel	875
Tool number	14
Tool type	1
Number of sharpenings	2
Angle of clearance (degrees)	20
Cutting rake (degrees)	15
Free text	Finishing cutter HM Z = 3

Industrial Production

Production processes underwent a process of continuous rationalisation during the development of industrial mass production. This soon led to production line assembly ('conveyor belt production'), with the same stage of production being performed at a certain position on the assembly line time after time. For the present, a production process of this type is only able to produce objects that are identical in function and appearance. However, the days are numbered for machines that produce large quantities of a single product with no variants.

If different variants of a product are to be produced at the same time on an assembly line in an automated procedure, the object must be identified and its status clearly recognised at every work station, so that the correct processes can be performed.

Originally, this was achieved by objects being accompanied by process cards, which gave the operating personnel all the information required at a particular workstation – the desired paint colour, for example.

This was first achieved in electronic form using coding pegs affixed to the revolving palettes so that palette numbers could be read by the electronic control system. The position of these coding pegs could be sensed by inductive proximity switches. This procedure has recently been improved by the use of barcode labels, which can simply be stuck onto the individual objects.

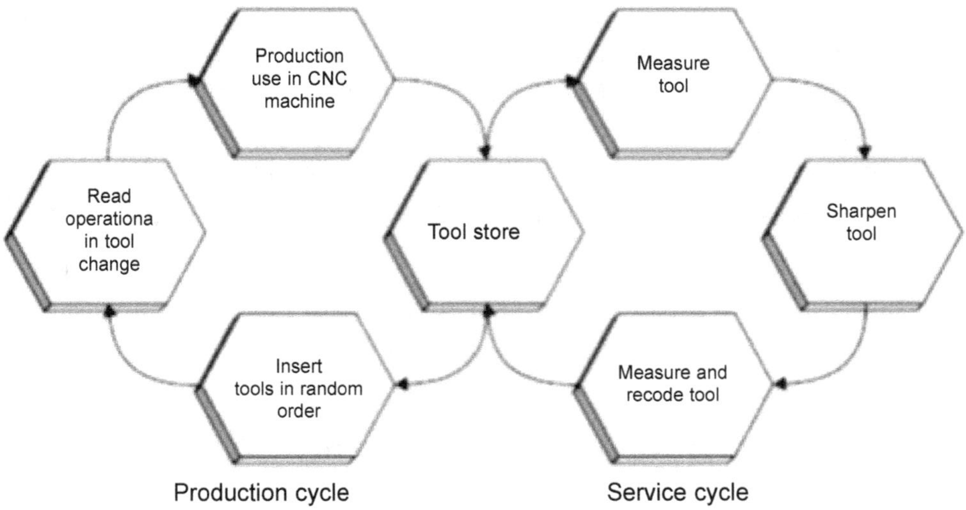

Fig Representation of the tool cycle when using transponder-coded CNC tools

RFID technology now provides an additional option – data carriers that can not only be read, but also written. Now, in addition to recording the identity of an object, it is also possible to document its current status (e.g. processing level, quality data) and the past and future (desired end state) of the object.

Using modern identification techniques, production systems can now be realised which can produce variants of a product, or even different products, down to a batch size of one. The automotive industry is a good example: since vehicles are predominantly produced to order and it is rare for two identical vehicles to be ordered, automatic material flow tracking is crucial to smooth operation.

A vehicle must be clearly identified at the individual manufacturing stages to avoid, for example, an unwanted air conditioning system from being fitted, or the wrong paint colour being applied during painting. There are two possible methods of controlling a system based upon object data: centralised and decentralised control.

Centralised Control

In this approach, material flow and object status are continuously monitored during the process and are stored in a database on a central computer. This builds up an image of the current process data and system status in the process control system of the central computer. It makes no difference whether the status of objects in the process is determined using barcodes, radio, optical character recognition, RFID or any other type of information coding and transmission. The monitoring of the process must be completely infallible, otherwise there is a danger that an object will become out of control.

Restarting the system after a fault or the crashing of the control software can be a particularly critical moment. Centralised control systems based upon a powerful central database are particularly common when it is necessary to access the information from different locations simultaneously, when a transparent image of process data must be available continuously for other purposes, or if important data needs to be stored permanently (Homburg, 1996). Apart from production, typical applications include stores technology, logistics or the collection of operating data.

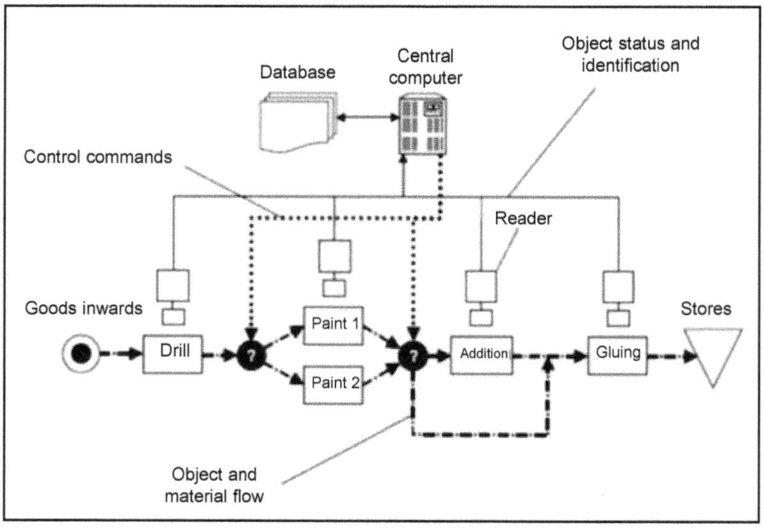

Fig. The object and data flow in a central control system is performed using completely separate routes. The central computer has a powerful database in which all process data is stored

Decentralised Control

The use of readable and writable data carriers opens up the possibility of controlling a system locally, i.e. completely independently of the central process computer. Each object carries a complete data record with it that contains information about its identity, its current status, its history and its future – material and data flow are thus interlinked. For this to be successful, it must be possible not only to read the relevant data from the object at each processing station, but also to change and update this information. Of all known identification technologies, this can only be achieved with the necessary reliability using writable RFID transponders.

The option of changing the object data in the transponder at each processing station means that it is possible to create an information flow between the individual processing stations, which takes the pressure off the control system. Production and processing operations are becoming faster all the time, so the fact that information can be carried with the object and is available in the right place can become a decisive factor in speeding processes up. Due to possible overheads associated with accessing a remote database, readers in systems that operate at a rate of seconds are becoming increasingly unable to keep pace with the process, for example in the setting of points or the initiation of the correct processing operation.

ENHANCING CUSTOMER EXPERIENCE WITH RFID

RFID technology, or radio frequency identification, is a system that uses tags and readers to track and identify items remotely. It can help retail buyers optimize their inventory management, reduce costs, and improve customer satisfaction. However, it also poses some challenges, such as privacy concerns, security risks, and high initial investment. In this article, we will explore the benefits and challenges of implementing RFID technology in retail buying, and how to overcome some of the obstacles.

Staying ahead of the competition requires embracing innovative technologies. One such technology that has gained significant attention is Radio-Frequency Identification (RFID). As a leading technology service provider for the retail industry, we are excited to explore the transformative power of RFID and its potential to revolutionize operations. In this blog post, we delve into the benefits and applications of RFID technology, highlighting how it can enhance efficiency and streamline processes for retailers.

- **Tracking Inventory with Precision:** RFID tags offer a game-changing solution for inventory management. By utilizing radio-frequency signals, RFID tags track items in real-time, providing accurate data on their location and status. With RFID technology, retailers gain unparalleled visibility into their inventory, enabling them to optimize stock levels, minimize out-of-stock situations, and reduce excess inventory. This level of precision empowers retailers to make data-driven decisions, resulting in improved operational efficiency and customer satisfaction.

- **Streamlining Operations and Reducing Costs:** RFID technology simplifies various retail processes, leading to significant time and cost savings. Unlike traditional barcode scanning, RFID tags can be read simultaneously and from a distance, allowing for rapid inventory counts and stock replenishment. This automation eliminates manual counting and minimizes errors, enabling employees to focus on high-value tasks such as customer engagement and sales. By streamlining operations and reducing manual work, retailers can maximize productivity, reduce labor costs, and enhance overall efficiency.
- **Enhancing Loss Prevention and Security**: The ability of RFID tags to track and monitor merchandise throughout the supply chain plays a vital role in minimizing theft and unauthorized activities. By tagging products with RFID technology, retailers can detect any unauthorized movement, triggering alerts in real-time. This proactive approach to loss prevention deters potential theft, reduces shrinkage, and enhances security. With improved inventory visibility, retailers can identify and address security gaps, protecting their assets and enhancing the overall shopping experience.
- **Elevating the Customer Experience**: RFID technology has the potential to transform the customer experience. By utilizing RFID tags, retailers can enable self-checkout options, allowing customers to seamlessly purchase items without waiting in long queues. Additionally, RFID can facilitate personalized shopping experiences by providing real-time product recommendations and targeted promotions based on customers' preferences and purchase history. These personalized interactions enhance customer engagement, foster loyalty, and drive repeat business.

CHAPTER-6

RFID IN HEALTHCARE

Today, the most important challenges for healthcare professionals are minimizing the impact of adverse events and improving patient safety. An adverse event is defined as any complication that arises during the patient's stay in hospital and is not directly related to the underlying disease or reason for hospitalization. These events can have serious consequences for the patient, her / his family and even the health system. The concept of traceability can provide many benefits to these processes. Traceability means the identification of all information relating to a product from origin to delivery and/ or consumption.

In the context of health services, this can be translated as the exact identification of the patient, the drug and the patient/drug relationship administered, which can significantly reduce the incidence of adverse events, thus increasing safety. Healthcare is currently facing the challenges of improving this aspect and reducing operating costs, which unfortunately are often caused by human and systematic errors. The American Institute of Medicine (IOM), recently renamed as the National Academy of Medicine (NAM), estimated that between 44,000 and 98,000 deaths per year are related to medical errors occurring in hospitals, thus showing the desperate need to improve patient safety and well-being in hospitals. It is possible to identify common phenomena that lead to serious healthcare operation failures in addition to medical mistakes, such as theft loss, and drug counterfeiting.

RFID technology is becoming more prevalent across a variety of industries, with the healthcare sector being a growing area. Indeed, the maturation of applications such as real-time locating system (RTLS) for patient tracking, medical personnel, and asset tracking will most certainly contribute to rapid expansion in the RFID industry in the future years.

The use of Radio Frequency Identification (RFID) technology in the healthcare industry has been growing rapidly over the past few years. RFID technology allows for the automated tracking and monitoring of medical devices, supplies, and even patients. This technology has the potential to improve patient safety, increase efficiency, and reduce costs in healthcare facilities.

RFID technology is widely used in hospitals for tracking and monitoring medical devices and supplies. It allows healthcare facilities to keep track of inventory levels, prevent loss or theft of supplies, and reduce waste. RFID tags can be attached to medical equipment and supplies, allowing them to be easily located and tracked throughout the hospital.

RFID technology is also used for patient tracking and monitoring. RFID tags can be attached to patient wristbands, allowing healthcare providers to easily identify and locate patients within the hospital. This can help prevent medical errors and improve patient safety.

RFID technology, alone or together with other technologies, has been considered as a possible solution to reduce problems that endanger public health or for improving the management of the latter. For example, the problems related to medical waste recycling, if not managed in a safe and conscious way can cause the spread of diseases and environmental pollution, that traditional methods often fail to prevent. There are some studies aimed at finding a solution to this type of problems; some of these aim to design methods that apply reverse logistics based on RFID technology.

Leading Companies in the RFID in Healthcare Market

- Alien Technology Corp.
- Awarepoint
- Honeywell Scanning and Mobility
- Gao RFID
- Impinj Inc.
- Mobile Aspects
- Radianse
- RF Technologies
- STiD RFID
- Stanley Healthcare
- Solstice Medical

RFID in Healthcare Market Dynamics

The RFID in Healthcare Market is poised for exceptional growth in the coming years, and this technology is increasingly being adopted in the healthcare sector.

One of the primary drivers of this growth is the need for effective inventory management in pharmacies, hospitals, and biotechnology companies, as well as enhanced patient security by healthcare providers. Additionally, the high efficiency and low cost of RFID systems and the implementation of automated processes in pharmacies and hospitals are contributing to the market's demand.

The market growth is also being fueled by the increasing research and development operations by non-profit organizations and the rigorous strategies adopted by top participants in the market, such as expansion, mergers, and partnerships. These efforts are aimed at developing new technologies to reinforce RFID in healthcare. For example, Harland Simon, a leading provider of location tracking solutions, recently partnered with PervasID to introduce novel RFID reader technology to the market. This Cambridge-based and award-winning technology firm is expected to make significant contributions to the growth of the RFID in Healthcare Market.

Another factor contributing to the growth of the RFID in Healthcare Market is the growing need to prevent the expiry, spoilage, and counterfeiting of products in the market, as well as the increasing demand for adherence to regulatory standards such as the FDA's Drug Supply Chain Security Act, MHRA, and other regulatory establishments. The market growth is further driven by the snowballing installation of RFID in manufacturing units for efficiency enhancement, the increasing use of access and security control applications, and swelling government initiatives.

Furthermore, the extensive implementation of RFID technology in the retail sector and the development in the RFID ecosystem via organic growth strategies such as acquisitions, mergers, and collaborations are aiding in the progression of the market. Overall, the RFID in Healthcare Market is expected to experience substantial growth in the coming years, and this technology is poised to revolutionize the healthcare industry.

Global RFID in Healthcare Market Segmentation

By Product

- RFID tags
- RFID systems

By Application

- Tracking prescription drugs
- Infection control
- Injection safety
- Others

Overview of RFID in Healthcare

RFID (Radio Frequency Identification) is a technology that uses radio waves to identify and track objects, animals, or people. In healthcare, RFID technology has various applications, including inventory management, asset tracking, and patient tracking:

- **Inventory Management:** RFID technology is widely used in healthcare for inventory management. RFID tags can be attached to medical supplies, equipment, and devices, allowing healthcare facilities to keep track of inventory levels in real-time, prevent loss or theft of supplies, and reduce waste.
- **Asset Tracking:** RFID technology is also used for asset tracking in healthcare. RFID tags can be attached to medical equipment and devices, allowing healthcare providers to easily locate and track them throughout the hospital. This can help prevent loss or theft of equipment, reduce equipment downtime, and improve maintenance schedules.
- **Patient Tracking:** RFID technology is also used for patient tracking in healthcare. RFID tags can be attached to patient wristbands, allowing healthcare providers to easily identify and locate patients within the hospital. This can help prevent medical errors, improve patient safety, and reduce wait times.

Overall, RFID technology has the potential to improve patient outcomes, reduce costs, and increase efficiency in healthcare. As such, the RFID in healthcare market is expected to continue to grow in the coming years as healthcare providers seek to adopt new technologies to improve patient care.

Benefits of RFID in Healthcare

By monitoring assets and people, RFID in healthcare may cut costs and enhance efficiency while also improving patient safety and saving lives. There are several benefits to RFIDenabled health reform. RFID might have a significant impact on healthcare quality, efficiency, and administration if it is used properly. Efficiency benefits encompass investment as well as stock reductions; operational costs; labour cost reductions; individual care enhancements; as well as workforce cost savings.

For example, eradicating errors such as prescribing the incorrect medicine to the wrong person or performing the wrong technique should be included as should all other benefits associated with improving quality of patient care, improve patient satisfaction, strengthening infection prevention and control capabilities, as well as trying to improve the capacity to inhibit as well as appropriate equity inadequacies.

Main benefits

Patients Safety

Patient safety must be prioritised since, medical and human mistakes in hospitals result in about 42.7 million adverse events each year. Healthcare quality may be improved for patients by eliminating human mistakes in interactions between patients and healthcare workers using RFID. One of the most common causes of medical mistakes in hospitals is the misidentification of patients. An RFID-enabled smart bracelet might be used to identify patients and expose personal data such as birth date, name, insurance information, allergies, blood type, and prescription needs as part of a positive patient identification system.

Plethora of research suggests medical facilities must endeavour to avoid these mistakes by improving hospital safety processes by creating an adequate patient identification system. Similarly, smart RFID technology might help to reduce the number of patient identification mistakes. Patients are identified by RFID, which might be used to search and collect relevant medical data from a variety of current healthcare information systems, possibly reducing the number of mistakes in patient management. RFID may also be used to identify surgical patients to verify that the treatment is carried out on the correct person.

RFID is currently being considered as a technology that may improve medical care and safety by monitoring vulnerable patients, rather than an asset tracker. Tracking the movements of long-term old or confused patients, as well as youngsters to prevent infant snatching, is an example of this.

To immediately detect and identify patients in the ER, RFID monitoring of patients has also been utilised to promptly begin delivering medical help. This means that RFID patient monitoring technologies have the ability to cut waiting times by automatically displaying what stage a patient is in as well as providing transparency for patients and staff in the surgical trajectory and improving patient flow. Identifying patients who are ready to be discharged from the hospital may also be done via RFID tagging. This helps to reduce unnecessary hospital stays and better allocate resources.

For patients with chronic illnesses, it may also be used to monitor them from their own homes. Persons who have been in touch with people who are infected may be tracked down by following the movements of visitors, employees, and patients. Several Asian hospitals used RFID during the Severe Acute Respiratory Syndrome (SARS) outbreak to track infected patients.

When SARS broke out in Taiwan, the Show Chan Hospital employed active RFID tags to track patient temperatures as well as identify those who were at risk of infection. After that, it was put to use at an elderly citizen's residence to transmit cognitive and psychosocial data from residents who were unable to leave their beds.

Medical Reporting

Healthcare information systems (HIS) may help doctors make better decisions and diagnose patients faster by providing them with quick access to the accurate data about the patient. Case studies in Saudi Arabia have shown that RFID wristband sensors for monitoring and wirelessly ECG monitors for taking vital signs and delivering devices electronically may be used for elderly patients with chronic diseases.

Also, it's possible that RFID could be used to improve drug adherence. With the use of wristbands as well as bar codes, the Wisely Aware RFID Dosage (WARD) system would help hospitals create an effective and safe medical healthcare system by lowering the possibility of medication mistakes. RFID tags may be used to find a patient at a specific area and determine the correct amount of prescribed medication. It is possible for doctors to monitor patient adherence to medicine using RFID data that is connected to a centralised database.

Prototypes such as an RFID-tagged pill dispenser that monitors medication usage as well as human facial recognition were on display at the CES trade show. As soon as a medication's use-by date approached, the system alerts healthcare practitioners. RFID-enabled smart bandages may potentially be utilized to direct the distribution of postsurgical medications to patients.

Scientists in Greece conducted another research in which the usage of RFID technology was used for the intention of tracking and controlling blood samples. RFID as well as barcode technologies may be used to reduce the risk of blood production waste and inaccurate identification. Transfusion department could also benefit from RFID technology, which might also help them to better organise samples of blood as well as ensure that the correct blood donations are being supplied to the correct patient.

Expense Mitigation

The rising expenses of healthcare may be mitigated in several ways. As an example, an RFIDbased asset tracking and monitoring system may assist avoid the theft of expensive assets and equipment. Improved worker productivity, reduced equipment rental costs and improved regulatory compliance are just some of the other advantages. Employee in the healthcare may save a great deal of time and energy by using the RFID to find medical supplies in their everyday work. Small-scale hospitals may save as much as $1 million a year because to these changes.

In order to reduce money and increase patient happiness, hospitals are looking to optimise patient throughput and operational processes. The laborious methods that are generally used to record data may be automated using RFID's automatic data capture and storing capabilities. The active monitoring of asset and patient movement through the hospital by RFID does have the potential to greatly enhance operations.

The captured data may be examined in order to increase hospital efficiency. In addition, RFID technology has additional advantages, such as preserving medicine supplies and increasing resource usage.

Avoiding ongoing capital expenditures, operating as well as maintenance cost reductions, and higher throughput all lead to new income opportunities as well as enhanced patient safety. Patients and caregivers will be happier and more productive, allowing for more attention at the bed as well as a higher standard of care. The define-measure-analyse-improve-control paradigm was used in conjunction with the Six Sigma technique, which discovered that RFID technology improves healthcare efficiency, as well as safety. Resource allocation and utilisation may be improved through RFID.

For example, the inventory database is updated in real time using data acquired via auto-ID. Tracking the number of products received from suppliers, sent to hospitals, and the real inventory level, things no longer available, back-ordered item identification and number, and physical conditions, locations, and ages may all be accomplished using RFID.

In order to decrease inventory-related expenses, managers must be aware of disparities in physical flows and be able to identify the variables that contribute to mistakes. Inventory shortages, underutilization, and inflated inventory may all be reduced via the use of real-time location-based services (RTLS). Using RFID, employees may be alerted to theft and asset loss in real time, eliminating the gap between predicted inventory levels and actual physical counts.

There is a risk to people when pharmaceuticals and medical equipment are kept over their expiry dates, mishandled temperature conditions as well as short life cycles are not properly managed. Patient lives are at jeopardy if faulty medical equipment is not identified and repaired as soon as possible. Information on the date, time, batch number, and other aspects of manufacturing may be used to create recall systems.

Researcher conducted a case study at the UC San Diego Health System involving an emergency recall of medical equipment by the Food and Drug Administration (FDA).

Managers may discover unnecessary replacement inventory as well as rental expenditures by tracking and evaluating equipment utilisation rates. In order to determine whether assets need an extra safety stock, idle equipment monitoring, and equipment utilisation patterns are critical.

High service levels, high shortfall costs per item, high demand, quick delivery times, and cheap ordering costs per order placed in an environment all contribute to the Real-Time Locationbased Service (RTLS) benefits.

PATIENT TRACKING AND IDENTIFICATION

It's possible that RFID technology may make it easier for equipment to track the movement of people or objects. As a result, RFID-enabled monitoring is required to show the location and activities of a person in real time at key points, such as entrance and exit points. This feature is particularly important for individuals with dementia, requiring healthcare providers to disclose their destinations with their families.

RFID may also be used to locate patients and staff in an emergency with pinpoint accuracy. Patients, doctors, paramedics and other bureaucratic, security, and social workers are all included in the scope of person monitoring. Throughout the pharmaceutical industry, the production process is closely regulated before the products reaches its destination in order to prevent drug money laundering, smuggling, and the misuse of medical commodities. RFID tags are attached to drug flasks in order to identify fake injections of narcotics. In practice, Purdue Pharma and OxyContin use these strategies to assure the safety of pharmaceuticals.

Devices like breathing apparatuses, wheelchairs, blood bags, etc. can be easily monitored using RFID systems. Hartford Hospital in the United States uses passive RFID tags to detect telemetry transmitters, while RFID active tags, together with bar code technology, are employed throughout the hospital facility for critical care to identify prefilled syringes, beds, and other moving objects. The results show that surgical tools can be located quickly and easily, improving patient safety and reducing repair time.

- A medical facility's inventory control will be improved when RFID is used in conjunction with stock management software.
- Improving expenditure accuracy and streamlining the way money is managed.
- In order to ensure patient safety or staff safety, it is important to quickly locate and retrieve any equipment that may be a threat.
- The complete delivery of health instrument operations, from acquisition and termination, will be improved by RFID technology in real time.

Identification and Verification

RFID is useful for patient identification and verification. A common cause of medical mistakes that may be reduced by RFID is misdiagnosis. In some institutions, the principal type of medical record depends on hand wristbands, which might lead to indecipherable or rotographing problems, or both, in the patient's identification. The wristbands would help hospital staff by allowing them to share patient information, such as gender, birth date, input of instructions, remuneration, and the location of operation, using RFID labels.

Patient safety may be improved using RFID by reducing the medical errors, or even operating on a fake patient which can be a major source of deadly situations. As a result, medical experts were able to get precise information about each patient via the use of RFID. Detection has also benefited from improved verification and identification among patients, as well as between mothers and neonates.

Sensing

Another fascinating, well defined RFID characteristic is the ability to read and respond to signals in order to acquire or compute sensor-derived information. A number of studies have shown that RFID sensors may aid in the assessment of a patient's clinical state. These e-health apps allow hospitals and other important healthcare systems to remotely operate equipment using RFID technology. Sensors may also be used in managing systems, maintenance processes, and general machine patching speeds.

Studies have demonstrated that RFID sensing may be used for a variety of purposes outside patient monitoring, such as compliance monitoring. For example, it may be printed on employee ID cards to remind them to practice good hygiene, such as washing their hands after using the restroom. Employees may enter and depart an organization based on their degree of protection using RFID sensing features like device access protection intent.

RFID adoption in health care

RFID is adopted in healthcare for authentication, safety, tracking patients, and blood transfusion medicines.

Authentication

Authenticating a patient's identity in the age of electronic health records is a common and timeconsuming task. Adoption rates can only rise if a compromise can be made between the two competing demands of convenience and privacy.

Safety

Preventing privacy and security breaches during inpatient drug delivery is a top priority in the healthcare industry. There are several instances of RFID technology deployments for increasing medicine safety. RFID-aided drug delivery is seldom explored in terms of data protection. In the end, the evidence was discovered to be vulnerable to DDoS and replay assaults.

After that, a lightweight binding proof technique for RFID and medicine authentication and verification provided enhanced security. Low-cost RFID tags may be used in conjunction with increased security mechanisms in the new protocol. Additional methods for privacy, security, and anonymity are available.

With a one-way hash and encrypted data, the RFID reader and tags are authenticated. In addition, a challenge-response system is used to prevent replay assaults. A secure RFID protocol is needed in this area because of pharmaceutical safety, privacy and security issues.

Tracking patients

It is feasible to use passive RFID patient monitoring in an outpatient clinic. As a result of noise and missing readings in raw data, tag location cannot be determined at a rate of 60–70 percent that would be optimal. False positives and false negatives may be reduced by using a fuzzy logic approach. Tracking a patient's medical history isn't very useful if the data isn't reliable. Tracking patients entering the incorrect operation room and alerting medical staff is shown.

Asset monitoring in operating rooms has been studied by others in a similar fashion. Using an automated RFID system, Patients were quickly reassigned after the RFID technology correctly identified all of the events that had occurred in the incorrect operating room. Patients in multidisciplinary health care organisations might benefit greatly from RFID, but there are several challenges to solve.

Blood transfusion medicine

Transfusion medicine uses RFID technology effectively. International Blood Transfusion (ISBT) and Food and Drug Administration (FDA) have accepted RFID for use in integrating and augmenting barcode data on blood supplies. Described technique is the first FDA-approved implementation of all blood transfusion stages, from donor to transfusion.

If database access isn't possible due to a catastrophe or conflict, all pertinent information about the blood product may be found on its label, according to an established concept in blood transfusion medicine described by the authors. As a passive system, it adheres to ISBT Code 128 for blood product labelling, which was established in the year 2000. A checksum is also kept on the RFID tag to ensure the accuracy of the data.

Radio frequency exposure was shown to have no negative impact on blood products prior to deployment. This information (such as the patient's name and date of birth) is kept on an RFID tag after it has been read and validated to match a patient order. In the event of a failed transfusion, the patient's data is either cleaned or destroyed by the nurse at the completion of the procedure.

Furthermore, no privacy or security safeguards are described when RFID technology is used in blood bank medication. However, they may claim that bar codes do not provide privacy protection, since RFID technology is supposed to enhance bar codes. RFID data, on the other hand, may be eavesdropped on from a considerably greater distance without the need for a direct line of sight.

After the blood product is matched to the patient's blood type and clinical transfusion order, recipient patient details are saved on a unique RFID tag. Using a fake blood product tag or listening in on an eavesdropper would raise serious privacy and safety issues.

ASSET MANAGEMENT IN HEALTHCARE SETTINGS

RFID technology enables hospitals to track and manage medical equipment and supplies more efficiently. RFID tags can be attached to equipment such as wheelchairs, infusion pumps, and monitors, allowing staff to locate them quickly. RFID tags can also be used to track the inventory of medical supplies, such as surgical instruments, gloves, and gowns. This ensures that the hospital has the necessary supplies on hand when needed, reducing delays in patient care.

RFID Asset Tracking in Hospitals

Hospitals and healthcare facilities can handle a variety of equipment and gadgets with the use of asset-tracking systems. However, many systems are antiquated, unstable, and prone to errors, which adds time and money to what should be a quick procedure.

RFID asset tracking allows you to collect asset data in a fraction of the time it would take to locate your assets manually. RFID offers a fully automated and significantly more reliable method of tracking medical equipment. By utilizing it, hospitals can improve data collection, lower personnel expenses, and streamline mission-critical activities.

Recent years have seen a significant uptake of RFID technology, which employs wireless communication to identify and monitor people and equipment. In addition to asset management, other RFID use cases include enhancing patient workflow by automating previously manual processes for monitoring and scheduling operations and providing real-time information about the location of medical equipment.

Hospitals and healthcare facilities can handle a variety of equipment and gadgets with the use of asset-tracking systems. However, many systems are antiquated, unstable, and prone to errors, which adds time and money to what should be a quick procedure.

RFID asset tracking allows you to collect asset data in a fraction of the time it would take to locate your assets manually. RFID offers a fully automated and significantly more reliable method of tracking medical equipment. By utilizing it, hospitals can improve data collection, lower personnel expenses, and streamline mission-critical activities.

Recent years have seen a significant uptake of RFID technology, which employs wireless communication to identify and monitor people and equipment. In addition to asset management, other RFID use cases include enhancing patient workflow by automating previously manual processes for monitoring and scheduling operations and providing real-time information about the location of medical equipment.

While RFID functions similarly to a barcode, it has certain additional advantages. Numerous tags can be read simultaneously, no direct line of sight is required for the reader to read the tag, and RFID enables each item to be identified and tallied as a separate unit.

The scanner immediately communicates to local networks or cloud-hosted software when it finds an RFID tag. That information, updated in real-time for all users, may now be shared around the firm by individuals with the required permissions. When combined with other applications such as electronic patient records and bed availability databases, the RFID-tagged patient, device, or asset can be tracked continuously, automatically, and correctly.

You can enhance patient care, prevent employee dissatisfaction, and cut capital expenses with the aid of RAIN RFID asset management systems. For instance, 10,000 pieces of portable equipment, including everything from gurneys and wheelchairs to infusion pumps and portable monitors, are generally present at a hospital with more than 500 beds. Except when it is being maintained or cleaned, each item should ideally be in use most of the time. Because clinical departments care about keeping equipment available when needed, things are sometimes lost, put away for maintenance, or even hidden.

With a RAIN RFID-enabled solution, minute, robust tags alert readers positioned all over your hospital to the location of every piece of equipment. It enables you to determine whether something was accidentally put in the laundry, lost, or left outside the door. A comprehensive solution built on the RAIN RFID platform allows you to create a hospital-wide requisitioning system to use every asset you have when and where it is required, plan and track items for maintenance and cleaning, and more.

RFID Solutions Improve Patient Safety and Hospital Workflow

Although radio frequency identification (RFID) is a well-established technology, new developments, and the potential to use RFID in conjunction with other technologies, such as cloud computing, have increased its usefulness. Clinical and administrative procedures in healthcare can be transformed by RFID technology in hospitals and other locations. Let's see how RFID solutions improve hospital workflows and improve patient safety,

- RFID patient monitoring systems provide real-time visibility and control over occupancy, patient distribution, and space availability, enabling institutions to track down specific patients and safeguard those most vulnerable. As a result, patient paths and workflows are significantly more effective.
- RFID helps to avoid misunderstandings and updates/exchanges of data in real time, especially when coupled with electronic patient and administrative information. It improves planning, continuing communication, and follow-up and decreases delays and non-compliance at every stage of the patient route.
- When combined with an electronic record, RFID tags create a single shared source of truth for all clinicians and managers that can be updated at the bedside/treatment site and keeps everyone informed throughout the patient's care and at all other points the way.
- RFID makes the automation of formerly laborious operations simple, including note transcription and conveyance, bed availability evaluation and communication, and discharge information. It reduces human mistakes and delays and dramatically improves workflow efficiency.
- Medical device traceability is completely provided via the RFID tagging of equipment. In just a few seconds, gadgets may be detected, and patients who need devices can be recognized.
- Instantaneous stock information, including use-by dates and the amount of time since purchase, is provided by RFID tagging and reading of devices and pharmaceuticals. Utilizing this will improve ordering, inventory management, and availability. Compare this to the high expense and imprecision of manually auditing and accounting for each item with RFID, which can read hundreds of tags in only a few seconds.

Benefits of RFID asset tracking in hospitals

RFID is a useful tool for automating the tracking of essential objects in hospitals. More crucially, facilities that have adopted RFID technology can gain from:

Enhanced Patient Safety and Equipment Tracking

Improving patient safety through accurate tracking is one of the most critical advantages that RFID technology can offer hospitals. It comprises:

- Keeping a reliable record to ensure the proper patient receives the right medication.

- Assuring the proper cleaning and autoclaving procedures were followed with the tools.
- Directing the patients to the appropriate hospital location.
- Confirming that each patient's room has the appropriate equipment.

Automatic and Precise Inventory Management

Hospitals can automate inventory counts by carefully placing fixed RFID readers at dock entrances and entry points. With a passive system like this, your asset management software automatically updates inventory counts when tags are scanned as people pass through checkpoints or portals. Due to eliminating inventory receiving and shipping errors, hospital staff can spend less time scanning products. Additionally, it gives managers a simple method to check what the hospital received in each shipment and spot any shortfalls. However, you won't experience those issues if your warehouse uses the same system.

Locate Critical Assets Quickly

The healthcare sector cannot afford to lose time on inefficient supply and equipment searches. Additionally, hospitals do not have the financial resources to replace lost equipment continually. Installing a passive RFID system allows hospital staff to track the movement of assets across a facility and ensure their current positions. With RFID checkpoints placed at entrances, rooms, and laundry chutes, you will always have access to information about an item's most recent location, preventing crucial supplies from going missing or ending up in the trash or waste.

Lower operating expenses

RFID technology aids in automated inventory management, enabling front-line healthcare staff to access real-time inventory data, track trends, and place orders before supplies run low. It improves the patient experience by giving them more time to concentrate on patient care. Hospitals can better identify which medical equipment is underused thanks to RFID technology. It decreases the need to buy additional inventory by increasing the use rates of the present equipment.

The global usage of asset tracking solutions has reached a pinnacle in the past 20 years among businesses. It's hardly surprising that the Manufacturing, Logistics, Retail, and Healthcare sectors are leading the way in the worldwide asset tracking market share.

RFID asset monitoring has established itself as a "go-to" solution as businesses continue to strive for total management of their assets that are essential to their income streams.

More than ever, businesses with a high asset concentration must implement efficient asset monitoring solutions in response to growing stakeholder and consumer demands. No matter what category your business falls under—business size, kind, or industry—all goals for asset management are essentially the same.

Implementing a Passive UHF Mobile RFID Asset Tracking System: A Step-by-Step Guide

Although passive RFID systems for hospitals are useful, there is a bit of a process to implementing them. By following the steps below, your hospital will be on its way to a speedy and efficient mobile tracking system.

Preliminary Steps:

- **What Are Your Needs?:** Figure out what assets you'll be tracking, where they're going to be stored in the facility and any asset management related problems your hospital might face.
- **Consult with RFID Experts:** Identification experts such as the ones at Metalcraft can help you to find the right product to fit your medical facility's needs.

Implementation Steps:

- **Apply RFID Tags to Your Assets:** The medical assets and equipment you'll be tracking will need passive RFID tags. Using these tags will let you store data on the assets like their locations, names and maintenance history.
- **Employee Training on Handheld Readers:** These devices are what are used to scan assets and update information within the Grey Trunk RFID asset tracking system. Employees will need to be trained on their proper use to ensure that the inventory status updates and maintenance reports are going smoothly.
- **Setting Up Asset Tracking Rules:** From maintenance to scanning assets and doing inventory assets, your hospital will want to create procedures for how these processes will be done.
- **Make Changes as Needed:** Hospital workers will want to analyze how the RFID system is working for them. Things can be moved around or adjusted to make the asset tracking process run like a well-oiled machine.

Real-World Examples of Improving Patient Care with Passive RFID

Passive RFID technology in healthcare environments makes the asset tracking process simple while greatly improving the lives of patients. There are some real-world examples below about how the combination of RFID tags, readers and software can change hospitals for the better.

- **Quickly Find Essential Equipment:** Passive RFID asset tracking systems let hospitals find things like defibrillators and ventilators quickly. When you're trying to save a life, time is of the essence. With RFID tracking, staff can quickly find life-saving items and use them on the patient. An example of this is finding a defibrillator when a patient is under cardiac arrest.

- **Equipment That's Ready When You Need It:** Finding equipment is important, but if biomedical equipment isn't working, it's not going to be effective. The combination of RFID readers with passive RFID tags lets workers properly maintain their equipment and see how often it's checked in/out for use. By taking the initiative with equipment maintenance, it'll reduce the risk of malfunctions with equipment like a dialysis machine.
- **Take Inventory Without Disturbing Patients:** When you use a passive RFID system in a medical facility, the fixed assets don't have to be right in front of the scanner (unlike with barcodes). This means that taking inventory won't interrupt the patients while they're trying to rest.
- **Scenario: Taking Routine Inventory in a Hospital Room:** In this scenario, there's a hospital with a multitude of different equipment pieces. From monitors and infusion pumps to patient beds, there are all sorts of things in patient rooms to keep track of. With a method like barcode, hospital employees have to enter every room, find the assets and then scan the barcode with a direct line of sight. This is cumbersome and it has the potential to interfere with patient care. Passive UHF RFID systems make this process faster and less intrusive.

RFID tags and handheld RFID readers allow the hospital to take inventory from a distance. This can be from the doorway to a patient's room or even just within the hall. Being face-to-face with the tags isn't required with RFID. The tags can be scanned from a distance. Each one has a unique code that allows you to assign inventory or status info/descriptions to the hospital's assets.

RFID Inventorying Benefits:

- **Provide a Calmer Patient Environment:** When workers don't need to physically find and scan each item, the patients will have less interruptions during their stay. RFID brings peace of mind the workers and patients alike.
- **A More Efficient Process:** When inventories can be taken at a faster pace, it leaves more time for staff to look after patients. RFID can make this dream a reality.
- **Know Asset Locations:** It's easier to manage and maintain equipment when you know where it's at. This lets hospitals only purchase necessary equipment while doing routine check ups and maintenance on the inventory they already have.

Passive RFID systems like Grey Trunk RFID allow hospitals to put their patients first. Through this technology, a hospital can properly manage its inventory without needing to go directly into the patient's room. When it's used in the healthcare industry, RFID makes for a smoother workflow. This allows for an increased devotion to serving patients.

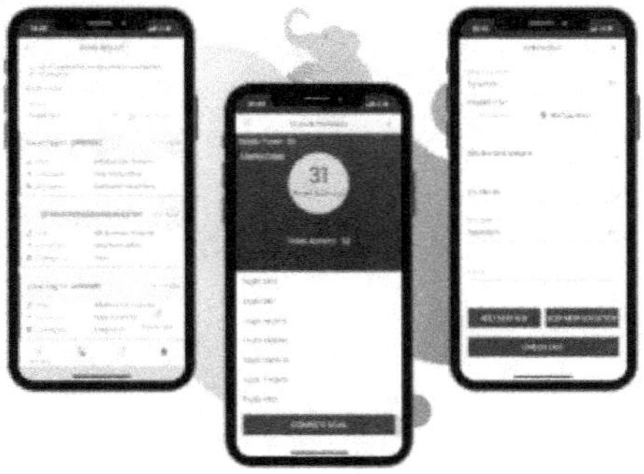

Mobile Asset Tracking App

Keep track and manage your assets all in the palms of your hands.

Check in and Check out

Check in and check out tools and equipment to employees or locations using RFID or Barcode.

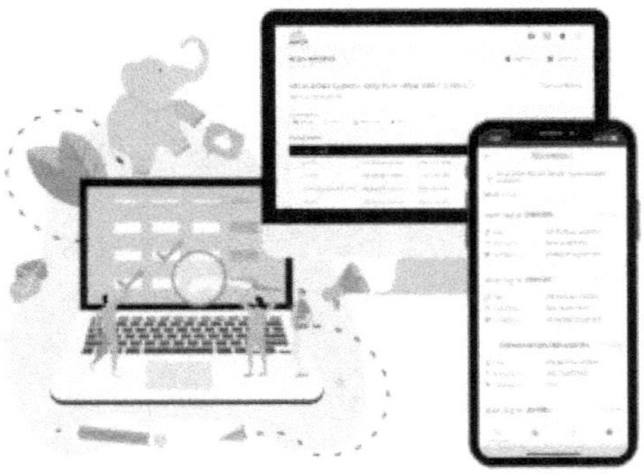

Fully Customizable Asset Tracking Solution

Grey Trunk asset tracking software is fully customizable to fit any industry.

CHAPTER-7

RFID IN TRANSPORTATION AND LOGISTICS

One common reason you'll find businesses implementing RFID is to make labor-intensive tasks automated. Therefore, saving them money on wages and staffing requirements. Whilst also devising all of their practices more streamlined. It's also a very popular way for achieving a better insight into the status of tasks. Now we have a better understanding of RFID solutions for transportation and logistics.

Radio-Frequency Identification (RFID), a technology that enables data to be transmitted from a micro silicon chip at very fast speeds and without the need for line of sight, as required by barcodes, is an established data-carrying and automatic identification technology used throughout industry.

Data relating to an item is stored on an RFID tag, which is attached to the item. Like a bar code, a tag is a data carrier. A bar code carries data in a visible symbol and is read by a bar code scanner using optical or infrared wavelengths. An RFID tag carries data programmed into a small computer chip and operates at a wide range of radio frequencies.

The tag is activated by radio waves emitted from an RFID reader. The reader communicates wirelessly with the tag across what is known as the air-interface. Once activated, the tag sends data stored in its memory relating to the item back to the reader. This data can then be used within and between organisations and trading partners in a secure manner via the EPCglobal Network.

The use of RFID enables businesses to manage their supply chains with unprecedented levels of automation and a vastly improved degree of control.

Vehicle identification used on entry to site, plus also confirmation of load: Various transportation companies are using tags on vehicles to identify them when arriving at sites. This information is then fed into the IT systems, including yard management and WMS in order to facilitate quicker planning/association to a loading bay and subsequent unloading by pre-emptive resource & putaway planning by the WMS.

RFID is also used to identify if vehicles have actually gone to the right loading bay or filling station (e.g. cement silos to check their loading of the correct grade). Visual feedback to the driver can be given in addition to IT systems.

Tractor/Trailer identification/association

RFID is used to check the correct association of tractors and trailers. At Tag on the trailer is used to identify to the driver (possibly linked with a telematics system), that he has hitched up to the correct trailer. The association information is sent via GPRS to the vehicle's telematics system. This system ensures the correct trailer is collected and despatched.

Trailer load identification at Gatehouses

Where curtain sided vehicles are used, there is the possibility to read passive, UHF-Tagged pallets or stillages, without the need to fold back the curtain itself. So, when a vehicles stops at the gatehouse, the pallet/stillage contents can be verified as the vehicle slowly goes through. When relayed back to the ERP/WMS system, this could form an ASN (outbound), or manifest check (inbound).

Wheelie Bin identification, for environment charges, also skips

Already in use, where identification of wheelie bins for domestic refuse charges is legislated. Coupled with a vehicle telematics system linked to an RFID reader and load-cell (weight), this solution can record a loaded and tare weight of a bin and the associated user.

For commercial waste an RFID tag on skips for identification at the refuse sites can associate charges to the skip owner.

Fig. 1 Uses of RFID Transportaion

Road pricing (e.g. Singapore or tunnels)

Overhead gantries tags in cars give access/payment to toll roads, tunnels and other pricing schemes including 'pay-as-you-go'.

Plant Hire – identification at site, reduction of loses/theft

Active tagging of plant equipment to provide security (illegal removal), location and hire-rate charges (when it was removed and hire ends).

OYSTERCARDS, TRANSPORT PAYMENTS

Used by Transport for London on the underground and bus network. Enables both pay as you go and season ticket applications to be operated. Currently being expanded to include payments options on the card in order to facilitate cashless payments within shops.

Identification of fixed roadside furniture for uses in surveys/repairs

Local authorities/highway agency can identify assets (lamp-posts, etc) as they pass them (x-reference with GPS positioning) to allow quick surveys. Where required, the tag can also record 'last serviced/surveyed' dates, etc.

Identification of temporary road assets (barriers, cones)

Contractors have to remove/account for all assets left on repair sites, otherwise they could be liable to fines (H&S).

Enabling the vehicles with a RFID 'portal' and tagging the assets could enable automatic checking in/out assets from the vehicle with an electronic manifest automatically updated – could also form proof for the CC.

Baggage handling, boarding card (late boarding issues)

RFID has a proven better read rate than barcodes in baggage handling applications. RFID in boarding cards to allow detection of passengers late to the boarding gate; reduce plane delays.

H&S – entry into hazardous areas (e.g. tanker loading, etc), vehicle alerts near walkways

Active tags (esp. Real Time Location Systems (RTLS)) can be used on personnel for muster station confirmation. Also man-down (with tilt/orientation sensors). RTLS systems can also provide alerts when people enter dangerous or unauthorised areas of plants, etc.

Trailer location in yards (RTLS)

Locate specific trailers required for vehicle planning/yard management applications; interface directly from the RTLS into such a application will provide a real-time feed that will significantly improve the planning capability in terms of time and accuracy.

The above gives an insight into the breadth of opportunities the technology offers in terms of delivering improvements within transport applications. While some application areas are in their infancy and additional development is required to enable business to realise the business benefits of the technology, many companies are already deploying the technology and achieving real benefits.

Radio Frequency Identification Explained

Radio-Frequency Identification (RFID), a technology that enables data to be transmitted from a micro silicon chip at very fast speeds and without the need for line of sight, as required by barcodes, is an established data-carrying and automatic identification technology used throughout industry.

Data relating to an item is stored on an RFID tag, which is attached to the item. Like a bar code, a tag is a data carrier. A bar code carries data in a visible symbol and is read by a bar code scanner using optical or infrared wavelengths. An RFID tag carries data programmed into a small computer chip and operates at a wide range of radio frequencies.

The tag is activated by radio waves emitted from an RFID reader. The reader communicates wirelessly with the tag across what is known as the air-interface. Once activated, the tag sends data stored in its memory relating to the item back to the reader. This data can then be used within and between organisations and trading partners in a secure manner via the EPCglobal Network.

Automated Ticketing for Public Transport

This clever implementation of RFID is not only great for speeding up the process of issuing tickets for the transport company themselves. However, it is also benefiting their consumers. How so? Since RFID technology is not requiring a line of sight to be used and so it is hugely versatile and quick to use. This is helping to reduce queuing times and human errors which in turn will maximize customer satisfaction!

RFID tags on vehicles

This approach is often used to track when vehicles arrive back at the depot. This is accurately keeping a record of the available vehicles at any given time! Other applications involve vehicle identification when arriving at a site. These two ways of implementing RFID is greatly contributing to faster business processes, planning, and in turn the overall success of the whole transportation company.

Shipping Containment Tracking

Perhaps one of the most general uses of RFID technology is tracking shipping containers as they move along the shipping process. A container can be scanned at the port and then again once it arrives at the right destination, providing a live feed of where the container is up to in its journey. Hence, this is giving you more control and a more detailed view of your assets.

Here are five ways in which RFID is useful in transportation:

- **RFID-based toll collection: FasTAG:** Although India is a developing nation, the use of AIDC technology is catching on fast here. A few years back, keeping up with its 'Digital India' initiatives, the Indian road and transport ministry made it compulsory to use FasTAG, an RFID tag/sticker that is attached to vehicle windshields that are used for automatic toll collection, without having to stop at the tolling stations, on highways.
- RFID toll collection has been a success in many countries that employ RFID readers, and antennae at toll booths and vehicles are equipped with an RFID tag that is linked to the vehicle owner's digital wallet. It saves valuable time for people and allows smooth movement of traffic.
- **RFID at Airports:** Airports often witness some of the worst congestion and taxis and personal vehicles of flyers also make for congestion outside. RFID-enabled solutions can be used to grant smooth access to flyers at the airport premises and can help manage congestion outside as well.
- RFID-enabled tickets will allow flyers to enter and exit the airport without having to go through security checks which will facilitate easy movement of passengers and will enhance customer experience as well.
- RFID tags can also be used for luggage tracking and processing as well as enabling real-time updates on passenger luggage and easy baggage claim post travel.
- **RFID in Railways:** RFID-based solutions can also be used to mitigate crowds at congested railway platforms and to allow easy access to passengers without long security queues. RFID on rail coaches can provide a greater degree of visibility as well. RFID-based smart cards are also being used as tickets in various metro rail services across the world providing easy access and extremely efficient ticketing systems, for example, UK's Oyster cards and Oyster visitor cards.
- **RFID in shipping:** It is worth mentioning that the shipping industry is the last to adopt RFID given the obvious unfavorable circumstances as to where RFID tags should be used. Cargo ships are loaded with metal containers

and handled by an overhead crane, so where one should use **an RFID tag** so that it can be read by an RFID reader? Notwithstanding this particular problem, RFID can still be used to grant access to people on cruise ships and the various sections of the ships as per the ticketing rules. RFID-based access control will also increase the safety of passengers onboard.

- **RFID at transport repair and maintenance stations:** Repair and maintenance of transport vehicles, rail engines, or planes at regular intervals is an extremely important part of the transportation industry. It is of utmost importance to keep in mind the safety of passengers and the proper functioning of the transport unit as well.
- RFID system can be used to monitor which transport units have been to the maintenance station/ hanger, and which haven't. This results in proper upkeep of the transport unit and ensures passenger safety at large.

To conclude, RFID as an IoT technology has the power to streamline transportation and various issues the transportation department faces whether it is traffi c management, real-time tracking of vehicles, scheduling or maintenance, and repairs of vehicles. RFID baggage tags can be attached to passenger luggage at airports and real-time tracking can be provided to flyers, enabling enhanced air travel experience as well.

RFID-based smart cards are being used in various rail and metro transport services across the globe, the UK's Oyster cards being a primary example.

Transport Systems

Eurobalise S21

Although Europe is moving towards standardisation, cross-border transport still presents an obstacle to Europe's railways. Different signals and train security systems force trains to incur the cost of carrying multiple sets of equipment on locomotives and traction units. It is often necessary to expend precious time changing traction vehicles at the border, burdening trains with a disadvantage compared with flying or travelling by road.

For this reason, the European Union is backing the purchase of a unified European train security and control system, the *ETCS* (European Train Control System). The ETCS will facilitate interoperable cross-border traffic and improve the competitiveness of railways by implementing the latest train control technology.

The ETCS comprises four main systems:

- *EURO-Cab.* A vehicle device, in which all connected elements are linked to the secure vehicle computer EVC (European Vital Computer) by a special ETCS bus system.

- *EURO-Radio.* A GSM radio link between the vehicles and a radio centre by the track, the RBC (Radio Block Center).
- *EURO-Loop.* A system for linear data transfer over distances up to several hundred metres. The system is based upon so-called leakage cables, i.e. coaxial cables for which the sheathing is designed to be partially permeable to the electromagnetic field. The frequency ranges of this application lie between around 80MHz and 1 GHz (Ernst, 1996). EURO-Loop is primarily used to transfer information for the evaluation of discretely transmitted data.
- *Eurobalise.* A system for the discrete transmission of data. Depending upon design, local data (location marking, gradient profiles, speed limits) or signal-related data for the route are transmitted to the vehicle (Lehmann, 1996).

The *Eurobalise* subsystem is particularly important, because it is a crucial prerequisite for the full introduction of the ETCS. In January 1995, after lengthy experiments, the technical framework data for Eurobalise were determined. It is an inductively coupled RFID system with anharmonic feedback frequency. The power supply to the system is taken from a passing traction unit by inductive coupling at the ISM frequency 27.115 MHz. Data is transferred to the tractive unit at 4.24 MHz, and the system is designed to reliably read the data telegram at train speeds of up to 500 km/h.

Four different balise types have been developed by Siemens:

- Type 1 transmits a permanently programmed telegram.
- Type 2 transmits a telegram that can be programmed by the user via the contactless interface. For example, this may be line data such as gradient and speed profiles.
- Type 3 transmits a telegram generated by a line device (transparent balise). Type 3 is primarily used in connection with signals.
- Type 4 makes it possible to download data as vehicles drive past.

Table 1. Basic data for Eurobalise

Coupling	Inductive
Power transmission frequency, vehicle ® balise	27.115 MHz
Data transmission frequency, balise ® vehicle	4.24 MHz
Modulation type	FSK
Modulation index	1
Data rate	565 Kbit/s
Telegram length	1023 or 341 bit

Coupling	Inductive
Useful data size	863 or 216 bit
Read distance	230–450mm
Maximum sideways offset	180mm
Coverage with snow, water, ore	Noncritical

RFID in Logistics

RFID is providing logistics managers with multiple ways to track and manage products and assets in the supply chain. Also, RFID tags and scanners are potentially improving product and materials handling inside and outside the warehouse environment, with applications ranging from inventory management to automation.

Improving product tracking through WMS integration

Warehouse management systems (WMSes) is helping in tracking the receipt, storage, and distribution of goods. A WMS stores data which are relevant to inventory levels, product locations, reordering details, and other information that users may require for the logistics.

Improving product handling efficiency

RFID tags are also helping in route planning and goods handling within and between supply chain locations. Warehouse employees are putting RFID tags on logistics assets like trucks, containers, forklifts, and other material-handling equipment. So, workers know the location of equipment at all times and can rapidly retrieve it to transport products.

Increasing inventory counting speed

RFID tags and scanners are helping in speeding up inventory counting and reconciliation. Because warehouse employees can then be using handheld RFID devices to easily and accurately scan RFID tags. Some scanners can count tags one-by-one for every individual item. While others can near-simultaneously count all the tags in a specific location.

International Container Transport

International freight transport containers have been identified using the alphanumeric identification procedure specified in the international standard ISO 6346 since the end of the 1960s. This identification mark consists of four letters, the owner's code, a six-digit numeric serial number and a test digit, and is painted onto the outside of the container at a specified position.

Almost all of the 7 million containers in use worldwide employ the identification procedures specified in this standard and thus have their own, unmistakable identification number. The process of manually recording the container identification number and entering it into the computer of a transhipment plant is extremely susceptible to errors. Up to 30% of identifications have been falsely recorded at some point. Automatic data transmission can help to solve this problem by the reading of a transponder attached to the container. In 1991 the international standard ISO 10374 was drawn up to provide a basis for the worldwide use of this technology.

The bands 888–889MHz and 902–928MHz (North America) and 2.4–2.5 GHz (Europe) are used as the operating frequencies for the transponders. The transponders must respond on all three of the frequency ranges used. Backscatter modulation (modulated reflection cross-section) with an FSK modulated subcarrier is the procedure used for the data transfer from the container to the reader. The subcarrier frequencies are 20 and 40 kHz. A total of 128 bits (16 bytes) are transmitted within just 2ms.

The reader's signal is not modulated (read-only transponder). The specified maximum reader distance is 13 m.

ABZU 001234 **3**

Fig. 2 Container identification mark, consisting of owner's code, serial number and a test digit

ISO 10374 specifies the following information that can be stored in the transponder:

- owner's code, serial number and test digit;
- container length, height and width;
- container type, i.e. suitcase container, tank container, open top container and others;
- laden and tare weight.

A battery provides the power supply to the electronic data carrier in the transponder (active transponder). The lifetime of the battery corresponds to the lifetime of the container itself, i.e. around 10–15 years.

The same technology is used in the identification of goods wagons in North American and European railway transport. A European standard is in preparation for the automatic identification of European interchangeable containers

The benefits of applying RFID technology in logistics

- Better parcel control by knowing the status of the products in real time
- Control and traceability of high value shipments. Unknown loss reduction

- Enhanced visibility throughout the supply chain, including alternative warehouses and logistics companies
- Total control of shipments
- Cost reduction and error elimination
- Shorter times in the registration processes of distribution centers and warehouses
- Management of the transit of goods from remote centers
- Optimization of internal processes such as batch, date and property management
- Quick tagging and packaging
- Lower operating costs
- Real-time reports with guaranteed traceability information

This technology will allow carriers to perform the following operations more efficiently

- getting access to information in real time;
- monitoring the operation and movement of transport;
- identifying goods that cannot be transported together on board a vehicle;
- Reducing the time for transmitting information.

In warehouse complexes, it becomes possible to facilitate the process of preparing, processing, and sending orders, as well as increase the accuracy of inventory control. The main goal of implementing the RFID technology in a warehouse is to reduce costs through automatic data collection. Fig. 3 shows the scheme of implementing the RFID technology in a warehouse.

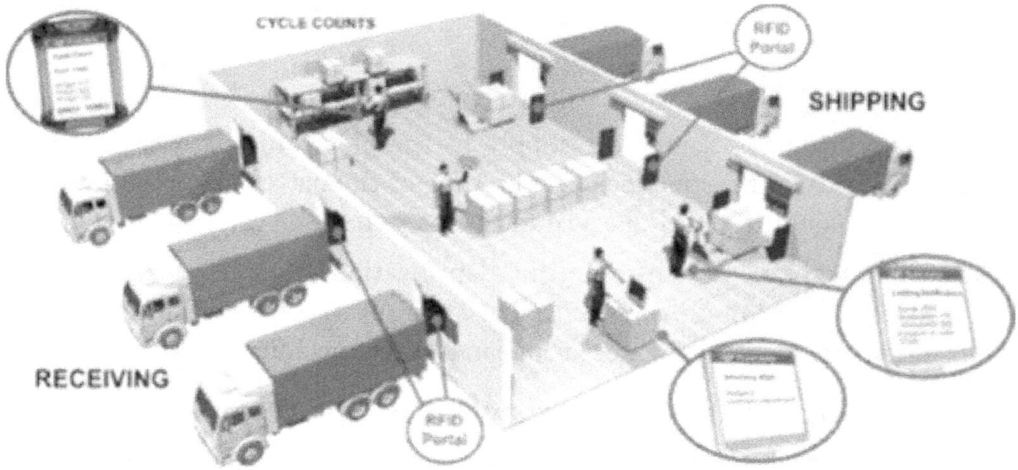

Fig. 3. Implementation of the RFID technology in a warehouse

Basic elements of intermodal transport system overview

Intermodal transport is a complex system of the transport chain with the freight unit in its center that consists of smaller units connected in an entirety of certain dimensions that do not change during the transportation. Intermodal transport unit represents a container, a changeable truck chest and a semi-trailer. Its use enables transportation cost reduction, freight homogeneity and massiveness. In Figure 4 the flow of goods in intermodal transport is demonstrated.

In Fig. 5 the flow of the product in the development of the intermodal transport unit is presented.

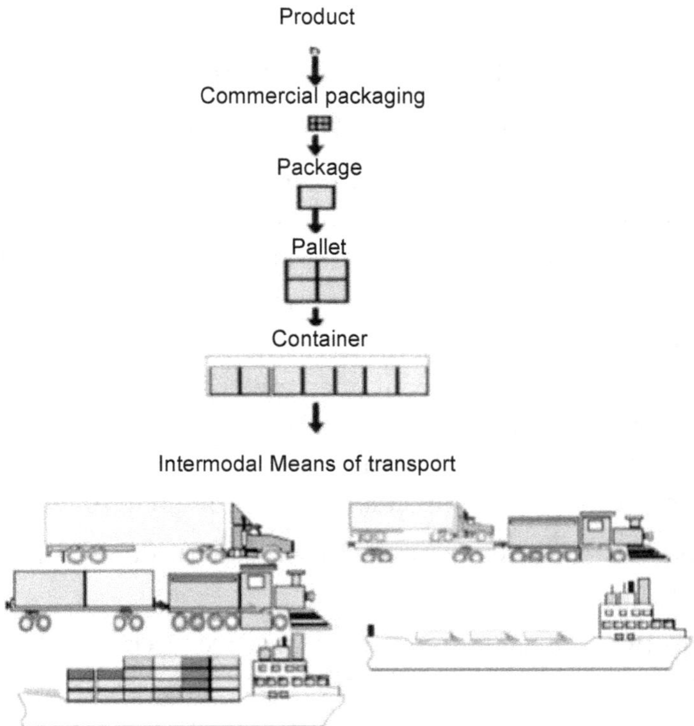

Fig. 4: Flow of goods in intermodal transport

RFID technology in intermodal transport

Intermodal transport unit holds a unique identification number. Manually written numbers as well as their control during the transport are subject to errors. With the introduction of RFID technology, container identification number, as the main freight unit in intermodal transport, is stored on an RFID tag not leaving any room for error. The tag holds a unique identification numbers named Electronic Product Codes (EPC) - the code that resides on an RFID tag that is unique to each product. The code contains manufacturer and product information as well as an individualized serial number which is shown in Fig. 6. EPCs are maintained by EPC global.

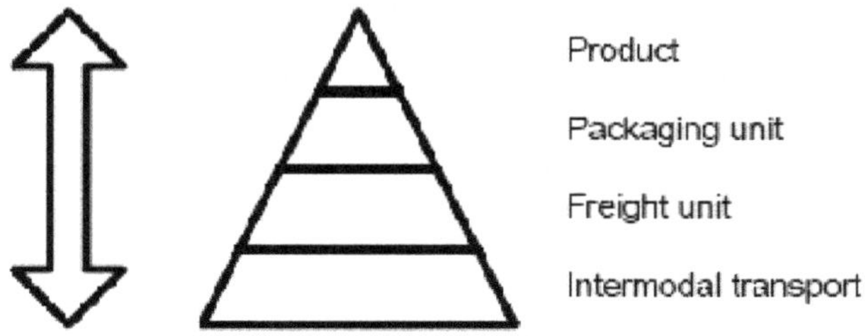

Fig. 5: Intermodal unit development system

Fig. 6: EPC code example

Header EPC Manager Number Object Class Number Serial

When implementing RFID technology in each segment of intermodal transport, all manipulative devices have to be equipped with RFID readers, thus enabling automatic container identification as well as all manipulative activities performed with it. RFID readers can be placed on cranes, vehicles etc.

With the implementation of active transponders with sensors and GPS, instant supervision of key information in container transport is enabled. Sensors analyze given data boundaries and the change that is not within given boundaries can be automatically sent to authorized organization. Some of the basics magnitudes whose value is measured when implementing sensors in RFID technology are:

- **Position** – using the GPS system it is possible to determine the momentary position of the containers;
- **Temperature** – if measured, it can be discovered whether the container was opened, the presence of fire, electronic devices, person;
- **Chemicals** – the presence of poison, explosives and radioactive material is tested;
- **Air pressure** – in the case the container is hermetically closed, its damaged condition or opening are automatically discovered;
- **Sound** – whose measuring can reveal whether the device is used inside and is a person talking inside;
- **Movement** – if something is moving in the container etc. Basic costs of RFID technology implementation

RFID technology architecture intermodal transport

With a suitable way of implementing RFID technology in intermodal transport, an intermodal transport company is enabled to monitor the product in the entire transport chain, from its packaging in intermodal unit to its arrival to the destination. If damage, breaking in the container or any opening happens, data base will automatically be uploaded and each dysfunction that occurs will be pointed out. Except for the investment problems at the beginning, there is also the problem of piling data that constantly upload the server (data base), however this is solved by an advanced version of middleware which filtrate gathered data.

RFID influence on automatization of transport process in intermodal nodes

It is a fact that the longest possible freight hold-up or loss of time happens during loading/unloading of the ship or land vehicles (wagons or trucks), i.e. intermodal node (place where two branches of transport are intertwined or certain freight manipulative actions take place). In Fig. 7. an intermodal node is shown.

Using RFID technology, we have the possibility to monitor the freight in ports or goods and port terminals and consequently the possibility to influence the delivery. Monitoring the flow of freight is significant in order to optimize port transport process for instance and, consequently, to ensure market supply in due time, i.e. planning the course of production process in production companies (e.g. car industry, shipyards etc.), especially organizations that deal with transport (different transporters). Introducing RFID technology to the mentioned freight processes, we have the possibility to directly influence trans-shipment time reduction in intermodal node with the following consequences: reduced cost, higher efficiency, bigger profit etc.

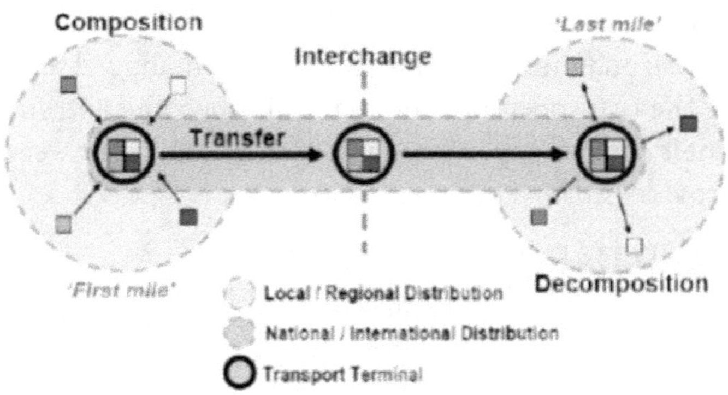

Fig. 7: Intermodal node

One of the most interesting intermodal nodes is surely the seaport. RFID technology enables the reduction of total amount of time of port occupancy. Total amount of time of port moorings occupancy can be demonstrated with the following equation (1):

$$T_{uvzv} = T_{var} + T_{vib} + T_{vpob} + T_{vni} \text{ [hours]} \quad (1)$$

where:

T_{uvzv} – total amount of time of moorings occupancy;

T_{var} – administrative action time upon ship´s arrival to the berth;

T_{vib} – time needed to unload the ship;

T_{vpob} – time needed to prepare the ship to leave the berth;

T_{vni} – time when there is no unloading.

In the previously mentioned relation, the use of RFID technology can directly influence the T_{vib} variable accelerating the time needed to unload the ship because of the automatic identification of the intermodal unit.

Testing RFID in actual working conditions

One of the first world companies to introduce and test RFID technology in intermodal transport was the shipping company Horizon Lines in September 2006. The integration of RFID together with WEB management system enabled an incomparable visibility of the containers from the loading time until they reached the final destination. The test was performed during transport under extreme conditions in the area of Alaska on 40 degrees Celsius below zero. This experiment eliminated the fear that a certain company upon introducing this technology would become and has proven the functionality and cost effectiveness of RFID technology. With regard to the positive test results, in January 2007, the company introduced an active RFID solution, enabling their clients to monitor the freight movement in any transport phase. Precisely because of the investment in the research and development in intermodal transport and because of constant efforts to improve the technology, Horizon Lines, Inc. have successfully managed to reduce total costs when processing the transport data and have also become extremely popular and appreciated in their area of expertise. On March 7, 2008 they were selected in top 100 logistic IT providers.

CONTAINER AND CARGO TRACKING

RFID Container Tracking is a technology that uses Radio Frequency Identification (RFID) tags to track the movement of shipping containers.

These RFID tags are attached to containers and communicate with an RFID reader, allowing businesses to quickly and accurately identify the contents of each container. This technology helps businesses track and monitor their shipments, ensuring accurate and timely delivery of goods. RFID Container Tracking works by capturing the data stored on the RFID tags, which is then sent to a central server. This data can be used to determine the exact location of the container, its contents, and its estimated arrival time. Businesses can then use this information to optimize their supply chain management, resulting in more efficient operations. In addition to tracking the movement of containers, RFID Container Tracking can also be used to monitor environmental conditions inside the container.

For example, it can detect temperature, humidity, and other conditions that could potentially affect the quality of goods inside. This helps businesses ensure that their shipments are always in optimal conditions. Overall, RFID Container Tracking is an invaluable tool for businesses that need to accurately track their shipments. It is a cost-effective and efficient way to ensure that goods are delivered on time and in the best possible conditions.

Implementing an RFID Container Tracking System

Implementing an RFID container tracking system is a relatively straightforward process, as long as you have the right equipment. The basic components of an RFID system include a reader or scanner, tags or labels attached to each container, and software to manage the data.

The reader or scanner is responsible for reading the data stored on the tags or labels. It transmits the data to the software which then stores it in the cloud. This allows users to access the data remotely from anywhere in the world. The tags or labels are affixed to the containers and contain information such as the container's ID number, its origin and destination, its contents, and other relevant data.

The tags or labels must be durable enough to withstand harsh conditions and extreme temperatures. The tags or labels also have to be secure enough to prevent unauthorized access or tampering. The software used to manage the data is typically web-based. It allows users to track shipments in real-time, view detailed reports, generate alerts, and more. The software should also be secure and able to integrate with other systems such as ERP and WMS. Finally, training for staff and stakeholders is essential for successful implementation of an RFID container tracking system. Employees should be trained on how to use the system correctly and efficiently, as well as any safety protocols that need to be followed when dealing with RFID technology.

Types of RFID Container Tracking Technologies

RFID container tracking is a highly versatile technology. There are several types of RFID tracking systems available, each with its own advantages and disadvantages.

The most common types of RFID container tracking technologies include active, passive, semi-passive, and hybrid tracking systems.

- **Active RFID Tracking Systems** – Active RFID tracking systems use radio frequency signals to transmit data from a tag or beacon to a reader. This type of system requires an external power source, such as a battery, to power the RFID tags. These systems are ideal for long-range tracking and have a longer read range than other types of systems.

- **Passive RFID Tracking Systems** – Passive RFID tracking systems use the same radio frequency signals as active systems but without an external power source. Instead, the tag is energized by the reader's signal. These systems are typically used for short-range tracking due to their limited read range.
- **Semi-Passive RFID Tracking Systems** – Semi-passive RFID tracking systems are a combination of active and passive systems.

These systems use both an external power source and the reader's signal to power the tag. These systems are usually used for medium-range tracking and have a longer read range than passive systems.

Hybrid RFID Tracking Systems – Hybrid RFID tracking systems are a combination of active and semi-passive systems. These systems use both an external power source and the reader's signal to power the tag, but the tag also includes additional sensors to provide more detailed data about the shipment.

This type of system can be used for long-range tracking and provides more detailed data than other types of systems. In conclusion, RFID container tracking technology is a powerful tool that can help businesses better monitor their shipments and reduce costs. It offers numerous benefits over traditional methods of tracking, such as improved accuracy and efficiency. However, it is important to consider potential challenges associated with implementing an RFID container tracking system before committing to it.

Imagine millions of shipping containers constantly on the move. RFID container tracking tackles this exact challenge. This system uses rugged RFID tags attached to thee containers and strategically placed readers to pinpoint their location.

An RFID container tracking system employs wireless communication technology to identify objects within a designated rage. This is particularly done for specific industries that require efficient inventory management, like cargo logistics or equipment rental.

It functions as an advanced iteration of traditional barcode por QR code scanning. Operating within the ecectromagnetic spectrum, RFID utilizes radio waves and microwaves via antennas for transmission.

For oinstance, clothing tags in sores, equipped with RFID capabilities, trigger coupling at exit gates. Modern RFID systems offer enhanced capabilities for data identification and system updates, thus optimizing operational efficiency.

RFID Container Tracking Benefits

Let's explore how this technology can enhance your processes and the benefits of RFID. Among the numerous advantages of RFID tracking, consider these benefits that can significantly streamline your warehouse operations:

- **Minimized time spent on item tracking:** RFID tracking drastically reduces time consumption. It effortlessly scans items within a designated range, eliminating the need for line-of-sight. Moreover, it accomplishes this task within seconds. When multiplied across various projects, it translates to saving several hours every week.
- **Reduced operational expenditures:** Without RFID tracking, companies often rely on manual labor, incurring substantial fixed costs. Implementing RFID systems diminishes this reliance, freeing up workers to focus on tasks requiring specialized skills, thereby enhancing cost-effectiveness.
- **Enhanced asset visibility and traceability:** This advantage is paramount for industries dealing with extensive stock volumes (e.g., cargo logistics, shipping, event management). Maintaining constant awareness of item locations and comprehending their movement within the operational chain is crucial.
- **Improved management of lost items:** Occasionally, items go missing due to human errors or bottlenecks, especially in industries handling large stock volumes. While RFID tracking cannot miraculously retrieve lost items, it facilitates identification of lost items and pinpoints the stage within the operational chain where the loss occurred, leveraging its visibility and traceability capabilities.

RFID and Shipping

RFID has been a transformational introduction to warehouses in many ways, but one of its main functions is shipping. All the aboved-mentioned advantages also apply perfectly to shipping. Having instant, real-time information about where your inventory is, how much you have, its history, and where it's going is crucial for running a really smooth logistics operation.

In the shipping and receiving context, this translates to:

- **Asset and Container Tracking:** Integrating RFID tags into shipping containers and other reusable assets and incorporating them into an automated closed circuit significantly accelerates turnaround times for logistics companies like Hollingsworth. Each stage of the process, from initiation to completion, is expedited with pinpoint accuracy.
- **Real-time Tracking of Goods Movement:** Having precise, real-time data removes uncertainties and empowers informed decision-making. With remote access to your database, you can execute this seamlessly from any location.
- **Tracking Traffic:** Accurately tracking traffic patterns enables streamlined planning of loading and unloading operations, such as cross-docking or efficiently managing double-stacked forklift loads on regular circuits to distribute items to various locations within one lap.

- **Ensuring Perfect Accuracy:** By scanning the tags of each individual item, containers, and pallets always carry the correct goods, in the precise quantity, aboard the correct truck. A straightforward checklist program enables cross-referencing of the manifest with the RFID-scanned cargo, providing an immediate confirmation of load accuracy.

RFID and Container Tracking in the Port

Productivity concerns not only terminal operators but ship owners, shippers and consignees. Ensuring the most efficient loading and offloading of container ships is critical to profitability. Certainly time spent looking for containers that have not been placed where they should have been is a waste of time and in the case of perishable goods this may result in the loss of the entire shipment.

With the help of proper management software, containers can be tracked efficiently with the help of the Radio Frequency Identification (RFID) technology. RFID provides the ability to automatically collect real-time data without burdening employees. RFID is one of the technologies that would dramatically change the capabilities of an organization to acquire a vast array of data about the location and properties of any entity that can be physically tagged and wirelessly scanned within certain technical limitations.

This provides managers with an up-to-the-minute picture of activities and that, in turn, allows them to respond to promptly to critical situations in a timely manner. Tags can be buried at regular intervals in the passageways to serve as location markers. These tags can be read by readers in the yard and provide information on the exact location of the container and also capture the identification number of the container being transported.

In spite of the potential advantages of RFID the capabilities this new technology has also engendered anxiety from certain segments of the society where concerns about personal privacy are significant. As a result of extending the use of RFID tags to as many port applications as possible, containers with RFID container seals will enable shippers and carriers to:

- Consistently monitor container security and integrity.
- Speed shipments through the supply chain.
- Verify that a container was loaded at a secure loading point.
- Significantly reduce the likelihood a tamper event may happen during container transit.
- Gather enough data to conduct a 'virtual inspection' in advance of arrival.
- Guarantee that shipping containers meet governmental security regulations.

- Receive fast track or 'green lane' handling through customs at the point of dispatch and/or the point of receipt.
- Avoid extensive delays in the shipment and receipt

Components of container tracking

There are two key things you need to track a container, a tracking number which could be your container number or booking number or Bill of Lading number and access to an intelligent container tracking system.

Numbers that could be used for container tracking

- **Tracking sea shipment by booking number:** A booking number is a value assigned to the reservation of space or a particular service. This number is used to identify and often trace the status of the shipment. In case of shipping, it is issued by a carrier or freight forwarder to the shipper.
- It is usually found on the receipts or invoices, etc. generated after making a reservation. A shipper can use this number to track his shipments on online container tracking systems.
- **Sea cargo tracking with Bill of Lading number:** A Bill of Lading is a legally binding agreement issued by the carrier to the shipper. A Bill of Lading number is a unique number that appears on this document. It is given at the time the cargo is accepted for shipment by the carrier. Shipment tracking with BL number is a widely used method of tracking containers. Several tools available in the market today allow you to track shipments by BL number instantly.

Types of container tracking systems:

- **GPS container tracking system:** Most of the container tracking systems available in the market today use GPS location that is sent either via satellite or via cellular (typically GSM).
- Here's how GPS container tracking works: A GPS based tracking device is attached to the outside of the shipping container. The working of two of the most commonly used GPS based tracking devices is explained below:
- **Magnetic devices:** These devices are placed on the sides of the container, in between the structural ribs. The structural ribs are an ideal place to attach these devices as they cannot be fixed on top as containers are stacked on one another while in transit.
- **Locking mechanisms:** A locking mechanism that seals the container is yet another way of tracking the movement of shipments. These mechanisms are designed to include a tracking device. It's added usually by a first party, once the goods are stuffed in the container.

- Via accelerometer, the device is engineered to sense the movement of the ship or else switch on at regular intervals and get a GPS fix. The tool then sends a location update to the concerned party; it gets added to their backend system and then becomes available to the customer.

Some of the benefits of GPS container tracking systems are as follows:

- These systems are available off-the-shelf, and self-contained.
- GPS container tracking systems offer an accurate location of the shipping container.
- **Shorter range wireless container tracking system:** In the case of shorter range wireless container tracking systems, the tracking system doesn't communicate to cellular or satellite directly. Thus, it involves a range of ways that could be used to trace and trace a container. This type of Internet of Things (IoT) system can be customised to meet the needs of an organisation.
- While these systems can be more complicated vas compared to a GPS based tracking system, they are more cost-effective. Yet another plus point of a shorter range wireless container tracking system is that its battery life is better than those of GPS-based systems.
- Some of the terms/acronyms associated with container tracking are as follows:
  - ETD (Estimated Time of Departure): It refers to the day the container is estimated to leave the Port of Loading (POL)
  - ETA (Estimated Time of Arrival): It refers to the day the container is estimated to arrive at the Port of Discharge (POD)
  - POL (Port of Loading): Refers to the port of origin where the container was first loaded
  - POD (Port of Destination): Refers to the port where the container is unloaded for delivery to the importer

Today a wide range of software/systems that enable easy, instant container tracking are available in the market. These systems have made container tracking extremely convenient for businesses across the globe.

Steps for Container Tracking

More the visibility you have over your shipments, more scope you have to minimise risks and unpleasant surprises. Thus, how to track shipping containers online has become a commonly asked question. To track your containers instantly, in real-time using GoComet's container tracking tool , you can follow the following steps:

- First of all, you need to go to the GoComet container tracking tool page. It is a lite version of the GoComet container tracking software.
- Once you open the page, you can enter either your booking number or Bill of Lading number or container number and the name of the carrier in the 'track now' field.
- On entering the information, the container tracking system will immediately display the real-time location of your container. Besides, the containers that you search for will show at the bottom of the 'track now' field so that you don't have to enter the details of your shipments every time you want to track your container.
- By choosing the option to get notified, you can even get automated updates every time your shipment achieves an important journey milestone straight to your inbox and Whatsapp.

You can use the container tracking tool for sea shipment tracking by vessel name and track your international shipments with different shipping line companies on a single dashboard.

Real-time tracking of shipment

To keep pace with the rapidly changing global supply chain industry and have the edge over your competitors, real-time visibility over your shipments is a must. Till the time digital technology-based solutions emerged in the supply chain space, tracking shipments was a laborious process.

In order to keep track of all the shipments, logistics managers had to manually visit websites of shipping lines or make calls to their freight forwarders, key in the booking number for each container and check the status. To make matters worse, the intervals at which the data would get updated were not known which created scope for misleading information.

But present-day advancements in technology, have simplified the process and made it easier for companies to track sea shipments in real-time. The emergence of state-of-the-art container tracking systems can give timely, live updates on the different stages in the movement of your freight. These software enable you to deal with any rerouting or delays proactively.

Software and tools used is container tracking

With companies increasingly turning towards automated container tracking systems, the market has witnessed an explosion of such software. This has made it difficult for companies to separate the wheat from the chaff and choose the system that meets the requirements of their business.

We have done our due diligence and compiled a list of some of the well-known container tracking software available in the market today. While the list may not be exhaustive, it will help you get started with your research regarding the container tracking systems available.

Any intelligent container tracking system should be able to provide information such as the name of the port where your containers might be stored, live location of your containers, status and exact delivery times and more. Here are some of the container tracking systems that have helped several companies streamline their freight transportation processes and gain visibility over the movement of their freight:

- **GoComet Container Tracking Software:** GoComet's container tracking software allows you to track all your international shipments in real-time on a single dashboard. The module is engineered to auto-capture every movement of your freight, assess your carrier performance and automatically notify you each time your shipment achieves an important journey milestone.
- The system has the edge over other platforms as it offers extensive, actionable insights based on historical data. The software helps you enhance customer experience by allowing you to share the tracking data with your customers, making way for unprecedented transparency.
- **Kuebix container tracking solution:** Kuebix's International Container Management technology enables you to save time and money via increased visibility over the movement of your ocean freight. You can track and trace shipments in real-time, get up to date arrival information and much more with this software.
- **Project44**: You can experience global multimodal visibility with project44's predictive tracking platform. The platform makes it possible to gain actionable insights on the location of your orders, how they are being shipped and other real-time shipment tracking metrics. The system provides live updates in case of any disruption and thus, helps you proactively plan and collaborate with stakeholders. Project44's system also provides accurate ETAs along with detailed container status updates.
- **Infor Nexus:** Infor Nexus has come up with a single networking system that offers live track & trace feature with mapping visualisation and location-driven ETAs for the ocean, truckload, and air modes. The system makes available all the information regarding your shipment on a single dashboard including data on multiple carriers, multi-piece shipment tracking details, alerts and notifications on delivery delays, shipment returns, tracking etc.

- **FourKites:** FourKites container tracking solution is equipped with AI and machine learning algorithms, that provide end-to-end live shipment visibility across various modes of transportation. In case of any delays/ emergencies, the system sends out proactive alerts to logistics managers and documents detailed predictive analytics for analysing and improving performance.
- **Ocean Insights:** Ocean Insights enables you to build efficient risk mitigation strategies with the help of their container tracking software. You can track and monitor all of your shipments in real-time on a unified dashboard using the software.
- Their container track and trace solution promises to offer comprehensive data from 55+ shipping lines, 700 seaports, and 5k+ vessels. The system has smart filter options which allow you to quickly and easily identify shipments that require immediate attention. The system also gives auto alerts and notifications on delays, discharge, rollovers or lengthy wait times, on-the-go.
- **Cogoport:** Cogoport offers convenient, live container tracking and facilitates better customer relationships via increased transparency. The system continually displays detailed shipment information like addresses and carrier details, comprehensive tracking history such as location, time and status of the shipment, and original as well as up-to-date ETA of the shipment, etc.
- The system also allows you to track packages that are shipped using applications other than Cogoport, enabling you to monitor all your shipments, from a single dashboard.
- **Alpega:** Alpega offers a cloud-based solution that enables real-time container visibility. Alpega's Reusable Package Management Software assists in the transportation process, right from scheduling a shipment to tracking arrivals to automated fee settlements.

The software helps you gain full visibility over your shipping containers at all times. The solution equips you to monitor the movement of your containers closely. Identification technologies such as barcode or RFID distinguish every container clearly, making them easily locatable and their movements traceable.

RFID APPLICATIONS IN FLEET MANAGEMENT

RFID technology is a technology that identifies and reads information stored in RFID tags through radio waves. RFID tags can be passive or active. Passive RFID tags do not require power. They use an RFID reader to send electromagnetic waves to the tag, which activates the circuit in the tag, and the tag can send a signal to store information. Active RFID tags have an independent power source and can send signals by themselves. The characteristics of RFID technology are that it can read and write the information inside the tag non-contactly, it is fast, it can identify multiple targets at the same time, it is non-visual, it has high reliability, it has low cost, and it is easy to integrate into the system.

RFID technology is widely used in vehicle management and is mainly used in the following aspects:

- **Vehicle entry and exit management**: By installing RFID tags on vehicles, vehicle entry and exit management can be realized. An RFID reader is installed at the entrance. When the vehicle enters, the information of the RFID tag is read to realize automatic access control. Install a reader at the exit to cancel access control when the vehicle is allowed to leave to ensure safe management.
- **Vehicle location monitoring**: By installing GPS devices and RFID tags on vehicles, vehicle location monitoring can be achieved. By reading the information of the RFID tag, the location of the vehicle can be determined, and the trajectory of the vehicle can be monitored in a timely manner, which facilitates vehicle scheduling and management.
- **Vehicle maintenance management**: By installing RFID tags on vehicles, vehicle maintenance management can be achieved. When a vehicle needs maintenance, technicians can use an RFID handheld device to read the information in the tag and make maintenance records for the vehicle. During vehicle maintenance, the maintenance record of the vehicle is recorded in the RFID tag so that the maintenance status of the vehicle can be viewed in the future.

RFID technology has the following advantages in vehicle management:

- **High degree of automation**: Through the application of RFID technology, vehicle management can be automated. All operations are automatic without human intervention, which not only improves work efficiency but also reduces labor costs.
- **All-weather real-time monitoring of vehicle conditions**: Through the application of RFID technology, the status of vehicles can be monitored in real time, including vehicle location, maintenance status, etc. It is conducive to vehicle dispatching and management, and timely detection and solution of problems.
- **High data accuracy**: RFID technology can guarantee the accuracy of data. When reading RFID tags, the information in the tags can be accurately read to avoid problems caused by human error.

- **High security:** RFID technology can improve the safety of vehicle management. Through the installation of RFID tags and the configuration of RFID readers, vehicle access control can be achieved to avoid illegal intrusion.

Fleet Management

Fleet management refers to the process of managing and maintaining a fleet of vehicles. This involves activities such as monitoring vehicle usage, scheduling maintenance, and monitoring the availability of vehicles. Effective fleet management is essential for ensuring that vehicles are well-maintained, available for use when needed, and that costs are minimized. One of the key challenges of fleet management is keeping track of the vehicles in the fleet, and this is where RFID technology comes in.

Advantages of Using RFID in Fleet Management for Car Rentals

- **Real-time Vehicle Tracking:** RFID technology enables real-time vehicle tracking, allowing fleet managers to monitor the location of their vehicles at all times. This means that they can quickly identify the location of a particular vehicle, which is crucial for managing rental bookings effectively. RFID asset tracking provides the exact location of each vehicle in real-time, allowing managers to assign rentals more efficiently and reducing the time and costs associated with searching for vehicles.
- **Improved Asset Management:** RFID technology enables more efficient asset management, making it easier for fleet managers to track and manage their assets. RFID asset tracking tags can be attached to vehicles, allowing fleet managers to monitor their location and condition. This ensures that vehicles are properly maintained, reducing the likelihood of breakdowns and increasing their lifespan. By using RFID asset management software, fleet managers can easily track vehicle maintenance schedules, ensuring that vehicles are serviced on time, reducing the likelihood of costly breakdowns.
- **Increased Efficiency:** RFID technology enables increased efficiency in fleet management. By automating many of the manual processes involved in fleet management, RFID technology reduces the time and costs associated with managing a fleet of vehicles. With RFID asset tracking, managers can quickly locate vehicles, reducing the time and costs associated with searching for missing vehicles.
- **Reduced Labor Costs:** RFID technology reduces labor costs associated with fleet management. By automating many of the manual processes involved in managing a fleet of vehicles, RFID technology reduces the need

for manual labor. This means that fleet managers can reduce the number of staff required to manage their fleet, reducing labor costs and increasing profitability. RFID asset management software also streamlines the process of managing maintenance schedules, reducing the need for staff to manually track maintenance.

Components of RFID based Fleet Management System

The RFID-based fleet management system has several components that come together to not only collect data automatically but to provide valuable information about the fleet. These components include:

- RFID windshield tags, RFID tire tags
- RFID fixed readers and handheld readers.
- RFID antennas
- RFID Software system
- RFID printers for printing on RFID tags and for encoding purposes.

Benefits of RFID based Fleet Management System

The RFID-based fleet management system benefits businesses in trucking and car fleet management in several ways, allowing them to monitor fleet, keep record of all the drivers and associates associated with each vehicle. It ensures vehicle security and to some extent, security of goods and individuals on the vehicle.

Following are prominent benefits of RFID based fleet management system:

- Accurate records of total no. of vehicles
- Accurate data on total vehicles present in the compound at any time of the day
- Records of vehicles on road
- RFID based fleet management system also provides data on vehicle drivers and their attendance throughout the month
- Streamlined vehicle rental activities
- Security of vehicles, goods and individuals with RFID data collection
- Accurate record on vehicles coming in and going out of vehicle repair shops for maintenance.
- Data on vehicle utilization and maintenance scheduling
- Accurate data on vehicle lifecycle
- Real-time visibility into the fleet
- Reduced losses due to minimized human errors

- Reduced labor force needed maintain the fleet
- With streamlined fleet management, higher customer satisfaction and growth.

Applications in Used Cars and Fleet Management

Vehicle Tracking and Location

RFID technology enables real-time tracking and location identification of vehicles within a fleet. This is particularly valuable for tracking the movement of used cars, ensuring accurate inventory management, and enhancing overall visibility into the fleet's status.

Maintenance and Service Scheduling

Each vehicle equipped with an RFID tag can store maintenance history and service schedules. RFID readers can access this information, enabling proactive maintenance scheduling based on usage patterns, mileage, and historical data.

Automated Check-in and Check-out

RFID facilitates automated check-in and check-out processes for vehicles in a fleet. As vehicles enter or exit a facility, the RFID reader captures the tag information, updating the system in real-time. This automation streamlines the management of vehicle movements.

Enhanced Security and Access Control

RFID enhances security by providing access control to vehicles within the fleet. Only authorized personnel with the corresponding RFID credentials can access specific vehicles, reducing the risk of unauthorized use, theft, or tampering.

Driver Identification

RFID tags can be linked to driver profiles, enabling driver identification when entering or using a vehicle. This feature is valuable for monitoring driver behavior, tracking individual usage, and ensuring that only authorized drivers operate specific vehicles.

Inventory Management

For dealerships and businesses dealing with used cars, RFID technology streamlines inventory management. Each used car can be equipped with an RFID tag, allowing for efficient tracking, location identification, and inventory control. concerns and comply with privacy.

PART III: IMPLEMENTATION AND DEPLOYMENT

CHAPTER-8

PLANNING AND DESIGNING AN RFID SYSTEM

Several factors should be carefully considered as you develop your road map. How will your company absorb and deploy the technology, and will the market be able to support these activities? Is the project based on customer-driven demand? Consider your supply network ? how do you bring products to the marketplace and how would you deploy the technology based on your topology? What about transaction volumes and infrastructure?

The road map you build for RFID deployment will be very similar to those for other technology deployments. However, make sure you include time and any necessary support for unique RFID issues such as tag placement, reader/antennae placement, orientation and attenuation, and environmental testing. In most cases, expertise in these disciplines will not reside within your company.

Before mounting a full-scale RFID implementation, it is critically important to conduct meticulous product tests in a real-world environment. Companies must define optimal technology combinations during product testing (i.e., various types of tags, readers, and business software). A complicating factor is the changing vendor and technology landscape. Make sure your technology selections will still be appropriate at time of deployment. Design contingency plans to deal with potential changes.

Choosing System Components

Once you know what you need for your RFID tracking system, you can start browsing for components. There are several components in a functional RFID system:

- **Tag:** Every RFID system starts with the tag. Each RFID tag contains a microchip and an antenna. The microchip contains the information, while the antenna boosts the radio signal.

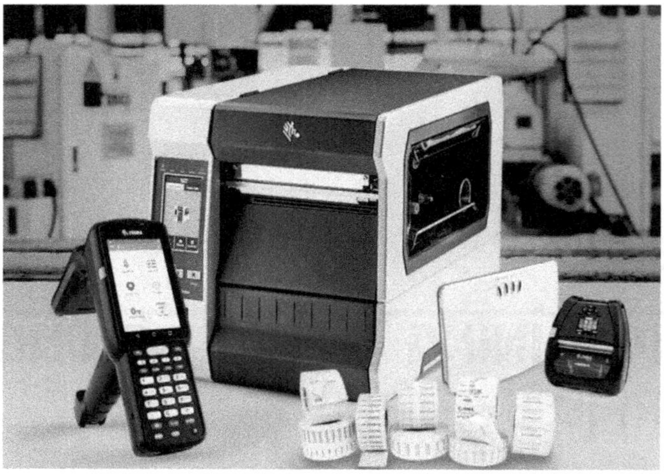

Fig. 1 System Components

- **Antenna:** Even with the antenna connected to the tag, RFID systems need several external antennas to function. These antennas serve as communication points that direct the signals from the tags to the nearest RFID reader.
- **Reader:** The RFID reader converts the radio signal from the tag back into readable data. There are two main reader types: fixed and mobile. A fixed reader is wired directly to an antenna and can read signals automatically, while mobile readers are usually handheld mobile computers with RFID-reading software.
- **Printer:** In order to replenish your stock of RFID tags, you'll need a printer. Make sure that your printer has RFID encoding capabilities and isn't a standard thermal printer before purchasing.
- **Software:** Similar to how barcode scanners need software to process the information they scan, an RFID system needs software to process the information it receives. The type of software you need depends on what you wanted out of your system, so be sure to browse carefully.

SUCCESSFUL DEPLOYMENT OF RFID SYSTEM

Select the Right RFID System for your Business

Installing an RFID system is a big decision for any business. There are a lot of different vendors and solutions out there, and it can be tough to know which one is right for your company. Here are a few things to keep in mind when choosing an RFID system:

- **What is the scope of your project?** RFID systems can be used for simple tasks like inventory management, or for more complex applications like tracking people or assets. Be clear about the goals of your project, and select a system that is well suited to your needs.

- **What is your budget?** RFID systems can vary widely in price, depending on features and functionality. Work with your team to determine how much you are willing to spend on an RFID system, and look for vendors that offer solutions within your budget.
- **What do you need to track?** RFID tags can be used to track just about anything – people, assets, inventory, etc. Decide what you need to track before you start looking at RFID systems, as this will help narrow down your hardware and software options.
- **Do you need real-time data?** Some RFID systems offer real-time data tracking, while others only provide offline data. Think about whether you need real-time data tracking for your application, and select a system accordingly.

By taking the time to choose the right RFID system for your business, you can set yourself up for success. Work with your team to consider all of the factors above, and find a solution that meets your needs and budget.

With the right RFID system in place, you'll be able to streamline your operations and take advantage of all that RFID technology has to offer.

Develop an RFID Implementation Project Plan

Once you have selected the right RFID system, you need to develop a clear understanding of how you plan to use it.

This will involve working with your RFID provider, conducting a site survey, mapping out your business processes, and determining where the RFID system can be used to improve efficiency or accuracy.

Once you have developed a clear plan, you need to commit the necessary resources to make sure the implementation is successful. This includes ensuring that you have the right staff in place to manage the project, as well as adequate funding to cover the costs of the RFID system and its deployment.

By taking the time to carefully plan for your RFID implementation, you can improve your chances of achieving a successful outcome.

Consider Implementing Your RFID System Gradually

Any business looking to deploy an RFID system needs to take care to do so gradually.

A hasty or haphazard deployment is likely to lead to technical difficulties and user resistance, both of which can hamper the success of the system. Instead, businesses should take a phased approach, starting with a pilot project in order to work out any kinks before expanding the system.

This will give employees time to get used to the new technology and help ensure that the RFID system is deployed smoothly and successfully.

Provide Proper Training on your RFID System to Employees

When it comes to RFID system implementation, one of the most important factors for success is employee training.

A poorly trained workforce can quickly lead to an RFID system that is not being used to its full potential, or even worse, not used at all.

Your RFID system champion and the project manager must work together to ensure that employees are properly trained on how to use the system. This includes everything from understanding how the system works to be able to find and correct errors.

Without proper training, an RFID system will likely not be deployed successfully.

Expect the Unexpected when Rolling Out your RFID System

No matter how well you plan, there's always a chance that something will go wrong when implementing an RFID system.

The RFID system is a complex piece of technology, and there are a number of potential issues that can occur during deployment. For example, RFID tags can become detached from objects, making them difficult to track. In addition, RFID readers can experience interference from metal objects or other electronic devices.

As a result, it is essential to have a plan in place for dealing with these and other issues that may arise. By being prepared for problems, businesses can help to minimize their impact and ensure their RFID deployment is successful.

Be Sure to Monitor the Performance of your RFID System

Another critical aspect of successfully deploying an RFID system is performance monitoring.

Performance monitoring involves tracking the RFID system's effectiveness in meeting its intended goals. This data can then be used to make adjustments to the system, ensuring that it is operating at peak efficiency.

Without performance monitoring, it can be difficult to troubleshoot problems with an RFID system. In addition, performance data can be used to justify the cost of an RFID system to upper management.

As such, performance monitoring is essential for any business considering deploying an RFID system.

Don't Overlook Ongoing Maintenance and Post-Implementation Support

Deploying an RFID system is a big investment and one that can pay off handsomely in terms of increased efficiency and accuracy. But as with any complex system, ongoing maintenance and support are essential for ensuring that the RFID system continues to operate at peak performance.

RFID systems are constantly evolving, and new software updates and firmware releases are released on a regular basis. In addition, RFID tags and readers are subject to wear and tear and may need to be replaced or repaired over time.

By investing in ongoing maintenance and support, businesses can ensure that their RFID system remains up-to-date and runs smoothly.

Have Patience While Managing the Transition to RFID

Any business considering RFID deployment must be patient in order to be successful. RFID is typically and most effectively rolled out in phases, with each phase building on the previous one.

To properly manage the transition to RFID, businesses must have a clear understanding of their goals and objectives, as well as a realistic timeline for implementation. They must also be prepared to invest in training and support for employees and to work closely with their RFID partner to ensure smooth deployment.

With careful planning and a commitment to patience, businesses can successfully deploy an RFID system and realize the many benefits it offers.

PLANNING AND DESIGNING AN RFID SYSTEM

Define your objectives and scope

The first step in designing an RFID pilot project is to define your objectives and scope. What are the problems or opportunities that you want to address with RFID? What are the expected benefits and outcomes of using RFID? How will you measure the success of the pilot project? What are the key performance indicators (KPIs) that you will use to evaluate the results? You also need to define the scope of the pilot project, such as the location, duration, budget, resources, and stakeholders involved. The scope should be realistic and manageable, but also representative of the full-scale implementation.

Select your RFID hardware and software

The next step is to select the RFID hardware and software that best suit your objectives and scope. RFID hardware includes tags, readers, antennas, and printers, while RFID software includes middleware, applications, and integration tools. Make sure to consider the characteristics and requirements of your objects, environment, processes, and systems when choosing your RFID hardware and software. For example, select the appropriate tag frequency, type, size, memory, and durability for your objects, and the suitable reader configuration, placement, and connectivity for your environment. Also ensure that your RFID software can collect, process, and transmit the data from the tags to your existing systems and applications.

Test and optimize your RFID system

The third step is to test and optimize your RFID system before deploying it in the pilot project. Verify that your RFID hardware and software work as expected and meet your performance and quality standards. Also, identify and resolve any issues or interferences that may affect the reliability and accuracy of your RFID system.

For example, you need to test the readability and range of your tags and readers, the compatibility and integration of your software and systems, and the impact of environmental factors, such as metal, liquids, or other RF sources. To do this, use various tools and methods to test and optimize your RFID system, such as simulation software, tag placement analysis, reader tuning, and field testing.

Deploy and monitor your RFID pilot project

The fourth step is to deploy and monitor your RFID pilot project in the selected location and duration. Install and configure your RFID hardware and software according to your design and testing results. Train and support your staff and stakeholders on how to use and maintain the RFID system.

Monitor the performance and results of your RFID pilot project using the KPIs that you defined in the first step. Collect and analyze the data from your RFID system and compare it with your baseline data or benchmarks. Finally, evaluate the benefits and challenges of using RFID and identify any gaps or areas for improvement.

Review and report your RFID pilot project

The fifth step is to review and report your RFID pilot project after it is completed. You need to summarize and communicate the findings and outcomes of your RFID pilot project to your stakeholders and decision-makers. Highlight the successes and lessons learned from using RFID and provide recommendations and feedback for the full-scale implementation. Document and share your best practices and tips for using RFID and address any questions or concerns that may arise from your audience. Make sure to demonstrate the value and feasibility of RFID for your business and persuade your stakeholders and decision-makers to support the scale-up of the RFID project.

Scale up your RFID project

The final step is to scale up your RFID project from the pilot to the full-scale implementation. Plan and execute the scale-up of your RFID project based on your review and report from the previous step. Consider the resources, timeline, scope, and risks involved in scaling up your RFID project. You also need to ensure the continuity and consistency of your RFID system and processes across different locations, departments, or functions. It's also important to maintain and update your RFID hardware and software as needed and monitor and measure the performance and results of your RFID project. You need to continuously improve and optimize your RFID system and processes to achieve your business goals and objectives.

ASSESSING BUSINESS NEEDS AND OBJECTIVES

Project Scoping

The typical tasks in this step are to understand the potential and the limitations of RFID systems and to define a given project's objectives. These are critical tasks that need to be completed during the planning stage. Understanding the potential and limitations of an RFID system can help to avoid unrealistic expectations towards RFID's deployment. Defining the project objectives can give a clear direction to the implementation team.

Understand the Potential and the Limitations of RFID Technology

RFID technology will bring a lot of benefits when it is successfully implemented, but this does not mean that it is a perfect solution that does not have limitations. Organizations should understand what RFID both can and cannot do before the making the decision to implement a system. As discussed by Hardgrave and Miller (2006), organizations tend to create unrealistic expectations and have incorrect perceptions towards the system. Misunderstandings and false expectations about the technology could lead to the formulation of unachievable goals or else the premature rejection of a project.

Grasping the technology's limitations would also allow managers to reflect upon the suitability of implementing the solution in their own organizations. For example, data accuracy is one of the common false expectations encountered by the public. Indeed, RFID cannot work properly with metals and liquids; thus, in the case on placing RFID tags directly on a metal surface (such as a truck) for vehicle in under the container terminal environment, managers need to be aware of the risk of getting poor readability results, as metal will reflect radio waves. To avoid poor reading performance, managers are required to take into consideration the limitations of RFID; they will ultimately adjust the tag's location by placing it away from metal surfaces (i.e., affixing the tag on a windshield). As a result, a better understanding of the technology could assist in formulating a clearer goal and gaining most of the potential benefits.

Define the Project Objectives

After gaining a clear picture about what RFID technology can bring to an organization, it should attempt to identify the areas that need to be improved in the current process. It is essential for the organization to know the reasons and expected outcomes of the implementation. A clear scope and objectives in implementing the system will guide the organization towards a productive programme.

Establishing the scope of the project could assist decision makers to develop well-defined boundaries for the implementation of the project. The project objectives to be established must be achievable and sensible, and sometimes short-term goals may also be set at this stage. Take a wine cellar as an example - the objectives of its RFID system are identified as functions with regard to:

- (i) the prevention of counterfeiting,
- (ii) avoiding the mixing of customer's wines,
- (iii) enhancing the stock-take accuracy and process, (iv) avoiding theft in shops, and
- (v) mapping wine products with location information automatically.

Concerning the scope of the work for these objectives, wine cellar managers should divide the project into different phases (i.e., objectives (ii), (iii) and (v) are achieved in first phase, whereas objectives (i) and (iv) are achieved in the second phase). In this way, achievable goals and objectives will encourage an organization to improve the system continuously and to gain the most benefits from the project. Furthermore, these objectives should also align with the organization's strategies. To earn the support of all stakeholders, the project objectives should be communicated across the whole organization.

The organization should focus on those RFID solutions that will have a significant impact upon the business performance of the company. Setting long-term goals and major milestones is also important. Members of the project team will have a sense of fulfilment when the milestones are met, one by one.

Analysis of the Existing System

During this step, various methods are used to collect information on the existing system which is analysed to evaluate the current system. This helps to identify the vital procedures in the process – i.e., the vital inputs to the subsequent redesign stage.

Collect information

The details of the current process will be collected by various methods, such as conducting interviews with the key individuals and front-line staff who use the present system, collecting comments from stakeholders, and eliciting experts' opinions. Observations should also be made through site visits in order to understand the physical flow of items that may be tagged in the new process. Information about the current process that needs to be collected would include data on the operation, equipment, related documents and forms, as well as the activities performed in the process. It is stressed that only information relevant to the RFID implementation process should be collected. Making reference to the project's scope will help to achieve this. Apart from the physical flow of the process, the information flow of the process should also be studied.

It is important to collect information about the daily decision-making processes. For example, Sonoco - a global manufacturer of packaging products - invested in a RFID system upon their customers' request (RFID News, 2008). Sonoco's customers requested better visibility into the company's supply chain. Sonoco and its customers were able to improve inventory management and track their goods in real-time. The company tagged the goods when they were manufactured.

Thus, the traceability of product quality could be improved, as the source of defects could be precisely identified. This could help Sonoco to reduce the frequency of lost shipments and reduce waste. More importantly, it increases customers' satisfaction. This example illustrates the implications of collecting information from different kinds of people.

Information Analysis

After collecting information about the operation process, the analysis and evaluation of the current process will follow. This could be performed by using the diagramming techniques and tools that have been agreed upon by the key individuals who are currently using the system. By examining the current process with the aid of workflow diagrams, areas for improvement can be identified. When multiple candidates for improvement exist, they should be prioritized according to their impact upon the organization's business performance. Those candidates that will bring about more potential benefits to the organization will be given higher priority in implementation.

For example, in the case of the wine cellar again, the stock-take accuracy and process can be significantly improved, with a 60% time reduction (when compared with manual operation). Therefore, managers will decide to develop the system with this objective first, as it is the most direct and worthwhile benefits of RFID implementation.

System Design

After analysing the current situation and the operation process, the organization should design a new process that is most suitable to matching its needs and requirements. The system design stage should include requirement analysis, hardware and software selection, and the development of the new process.

Requirement Analysis

This task is the follow-up step of information analysis. Upon the completion of information analysis, the major problems and potential steps that need to be modified are identified. The purpose of performing requirement analysis is to thoroughly understand the ways in which RFID technology can address the problems identified.

Sometimes, this may suggest a complete redesign of the process in order to optimize the process flow. However, a complete redesign is not always necessary; very often, minor modifications that meet the system's requirements can remarkably improve the process flow. For example, in the case of warehouse operations, the company has developed its own Enterprise Resources Planning (ERP) system to enhance day-to-day management; however, the company would like to adopt RFID technology in its forklift for automating the product flow within the warehouse (e.g., from Location A in G/F to Location C in 1/F).

Therefore, it is suggested that the operator drive slowly when passing through the RFID gate door for the better capture of RFID signals; this is constitutes a minor change of operation. However, according to the findings of the detailed analysis of twenty-four businesses conducted by the Grocery Manufacturers of America (GMA), one of the major issues of RFID deployment lies in defining the process that requires changes. Such an analysis can help to pin-point the specific supply chain management issues that need to be addressed.

Hardware/Software Selection

The performance of an RFID system is easily influenced by the operating environment. Therefore, the careful selection and testing of hardware and software is crucial to the successful implementation of the system. An RFID system comprises hardware items such as RFID tags, antenna and readers; these hardware items should be selected by taking into consideration the environmental factors which are identified in the requirement analysis step. One of the factors to be considered is the material of the tagged object, because it will have a significant effect on the performance of the RFID system.

For example, metal absorbs and degrades radio frequency signals; to avoid such problems, the RFID tag attached to such objects should be coated with an insulator (Ngai, et al., 2010). In developing the software, one should study the radio frequency signals that might exist in the environment in which the system is going to be deployed; such signals may have the potential to interfere with the RFID system.

Therefore, a suitable radio frequency should be selected to avoid the interference problem. The organization should design the way in which the readers are connected to the network and the software architecture, including the RFID middleware and the application level software.

The selection of hardware and software also involves the process of testing them; this is to understand the characteristics of each element of hardware and software and to decide which option is more suitable for the current environment. The testing of the hardware would give decision-makers a clearer picture of how the hardware and software items function in an integrated system, as well as providing data for measuring the reliability of the system.

One should also select the appropriate means of mounting the antenna and the orientation of the tags so as to optimize the readability of the tags. The proper selection of the software could also assist in meeting the data requirements - some software might perform better in handling a special kind of data and some might not; therefore, an organization should select the software that meets its requirements.

Develop the New Process

After information and requirement analysis, the organization should be familiar with the process's needs and the improvements that need to be made. At this stage, the organization should be able to modify the existing process or else develop a brand new one to enhance its performance and meet any project objectives. The new process should be designed based upon the knowledge of the current process and any potential changes so as to avoid surprises when the system is implemented.

Apart from designing the hardware and software systems, the decision-making and operation processes may also need to be redesigned. The RFID system's implementation may involve the simplification or elimination of existing procedures. For example, the stock in and out process can be automated by capturing the RFID signals when the RFID-tagged objects passed through the reading device (e.g., a RFID gate way). As a result, one should ensure that the decision-making process and the operation process are aligned with the new procedures to be implemented. It could avoid tag collisions and the duplication of efforts, thereby reducing confusions in the early stage of system implementation.

Prototype Testing

Before the actual implementation of the RFID system, it is very important to conduct demo testing so as to ensure that the workflow developed together with the RFID technology will work and that it is ready for deployment. This will also help users to understand the systems. On the successful completion of prototype testing, the implementation of the system in the actual environment can start. Prototype testing may be conducted in the laboratory or in the actual environment. Conducting on-site testing is more reliable, because all the environmental factors can be considered and tested. When it is impossible to conduct the test in the actual environment, demo testing in the laboratory could be an alternative. The simulated environment should be as similar to the actual environment as possible, to ensure that the test results will be useful. Apart from debugging the technical system and eliminating the mistakes in the analyses, this step also includes collecting feedback from users after the demo testing. This is designed as such in order to elicit comments on the various user interfaces and in order to fine tune their design.

Debug

The prototype testing covers both software and hardware tests. Thus, bugs and the collision of systems may be detected. Technical staff should be involved so as to support the testing and in order to resolve (debug) any technical problems detected in the test. Tests under different foreseeable scenarios are conducted to assess the flexibility and capability of the system. For example, proof-of-concept testing on several scenarios is conducted to simulate all the situations to be encountered by the RFID system. As with the case of vehicle tracking, tests on various speed levels (e.g., normal speeds, fast speeds, and over the limit speeds) should be taken into consideration to capture the reading performance of different levels so as to see how to debug the system and help it fit with all situations.

System Adaptation

The adaptation of processes may be necessary to ensure that the RFID system will deliver the expected performance results. Problems found during the demo testing should be recorded and reviewed so as to fine-tune the system and resolve these problems. Consider the case of Mississippi Blood Services, a non-profit organization that collects more than 60,000 units of blood annually. It faced problems in managing the inventory of blood products that have a short shelf life. The organization would like to know if RFID would help to solve this problem. After consulting some experts, the organization conducted a pilot test on 1,000 units of blood products. The process being tested involved transferring specific blood products from the tray to the cooler.

Problems of interference caused by the metal trays and other electronic devices in the operating environment are yet to be addressed. However, after the pilot test, it was found that the high water contents of the blood products together with the metal tray exacerbated the readability problem presented to the auto-identification system. This case shows that, without the actual on-site testing of the system, it would be difficult to identify the full extent of potential problems in a given environment. Therefore, prototype testing is an essential step of any RFID implementation project.

Implementation

Implementation follows the adaptation of the system; it is more than just the installation and commissioning of hardware and software systems. Typically, it also involves change management, training and system deployment. All if the tasks in the implementation step are vital, as they will affect the success of the implementation. Sometimes, implementation might not involve a clean changeover to the new system; the new RFID system may run side-by-side with the original system, and the latter will phase out only when the performance of the new system is assured.

System Deployment

System deployment will include installation and commissioning of hardware and software systems, as well as developing the new procedures. During the process of installing hardware items, care must be given to the placement of the antenna as well as that of the tag on the object to be tracked, because such factors will affect the readability of the tags. The placement of hardware items should have been tested earlier - what needs to be done at this stage is to install these items according to the optimal design determined during the earlier test. Software configuration is the other issue that goes hand-in-hand with hardware installation.

Software configuration involves middleware configuration and deployment. Middleware is used to control the readers' ability to read from and write to the tags; it also filters the tags' data and forwards useful information to other functional applications. It is important to configure the middleware properly to achieve the seamless integration of the current applications and database with the new RFID system. For example, a data interface layer for an application may need to be developed - the database may need to be modified in order to make it possible to accept data collected from the new system. A security system should be set up at this stage as well. RFID applications can be high risk systems when there is no control to protect their security. Therefore, at this stage, it is important to establish control measures for assuring the security of the system, such as formulation and enforcement of access controls that apply to data collected by the system.

In addition, policies and procedures that support the implementation of the new system would be established at this stage. Current policies and procedures may need to be modified to facilitate the adoption of the new system. Sometimes, management practices may need to be changed. However, people tend to resist change because familiar practices will become obsolete - there is anxiety about unknown factors such as the impact of the new system.

Management should be sensitive to those problems that threaten the successful implementation of the new system. Myths should be broken before they become perceived truths. New management practices that accompany the implementation of the RFID system may involve new divisions of labour or coordination and communication with multiple stakeholders.

Training

Users need to receive training on technical operations of the system and basic information about the system. The training should include courses that introduce the system and basic knowledge of its operation and shatter the myths about it.

It is also essential to provide users with practical training so that they will have hands-on experience in using the new system and the changed process. This will also provide users with opportunities to understand the guidelines and precautions as to system usage.

At the same time, the organization should listen to users' comments on the changes, as well as their acceptance of these changes. This will reduce conflicts between users and managers and speed up implementation, thereby turning successful deployment into a reality.

Continuous Improvement

The last step for implementation is continuous improvement. Since no system is perfect upon its introduction, there is always room for improvement. The organization should continuously evaluate the system's performance and compare it with the preset objectives, enhance the system with emergent technologies, or else adapt it to match the changing needs of the market. This step includes the tasks of system monitoring and the collection of user feedback.

Monitoring

After system deployment, the performance of the RFID solution needs to be closely monitored - especially in the early stage of implementation - so that the project team can quickly respond to the problems encountered. The actual performance of the system should be compared with the targets set during the system design stage.

For example, a multi-frequency tag readability test was conducted at United Airline's ticket counter in Tokyo. In that test, an average of fifteen pieces of dummy baggage per day were tagged with randomly generated numbers that simulated passenger names.

The dummy bags would then be dispatched to flights for different destinations via different routes and then sent back to Tokyo flights in the reverse direction. The readability of the tags on these bags was recorded and the results were analysed to monitor the performance of the baggage tagging system.

Collecting Feedback from Users

Feedback from the different stakeholders of the RFID system should be collected and analysed so as to spot potential problems and issues in the newly deployed system. Both technical and operational issues should be covered when comments from users are elicited through interviews.

Apart from monitoring system performance and collecting user feedback, the project team should also keep track of the development of new technology and be sensitive to potential any problems revealed by the findings of the interviews.

Implementation Considerations

A systematic and holistic framework for the implementation of RFID systems has been proposed above. Specific issues that need to be considered before and during the implementation of RFID have also been discussed briefly and they are further elaborated upon below.

Scoping

Fontanella (2004) states that there are four types of RFID implementation, namely discrete processes, intra-company processes, inter-company processes and information synchronization. They represent different scales of implementation scenarios. Some might only involve the entities of a company; others may need to create links across the whole supply chain. Before launching the implementation project, the organization should decide upon the boundaries of it so that appropriate objectives and performance targets can be established for the project. For any type of RFID project, consultation and assistance from internal or external RFID experts will be crucial.

Privacy and Security

One of the factors that needs to be considered is privacy, while the security issues associated with the deployment of RFID technology are another important factor to be considered. Concern has been raised about access rights to information and the related privacy problems across the supply chain. Unauthorized users may intercept communications between the tags and RFID readers in order to capture private or sensitive information that is not supposed to be made available to a third party).

For example, there is concern about tagging items or patients who do not wish to share their personal information without their prior consent. There are a number of ways to address these problems, including "kill tags", password locks, a cage approach and active-jamming. This is a very important issue that organizations must address so as to ensure that the information written on the tags are securely protected.

Lack of Standards

Unlike barcodes, RFID technology is still evolving. Thus, the standards related to the technology are not yet well-developed, presenting a major obstacle to the implementation of the technology. According to researchers, there is no standard related to RFID technology that meets the needs of all users. The development of standards has progressed through the formation of the Electronic Product Code (EPC) network, while EPC's operation itself must be backed up by the International Organization of Standards (ISO) to develop a widely accepted standard. Since common standards for the radio frequency and other technical aspects are yet to emerge, it is difficult to develop RFID solutions that will cover the whole supply chain. People tend to stick to the existing barcode system and refuse to get involved in deploying RFID systems. Therefore, the lack of clear standards and policies for RFID technology is an intangible barrier to the deployment of such systems (Floerkemeier and Lampe, 2004).

Interference Issues

RFID technology uses radio frequencies to transmit data. This creates interference problems in a number of environments. It is common to encounter objects and equipment that are covered with metal or have liquid contents in a supply chain. These items will adversely affect the readability performance of the RFID tags; they will disrupt the RFID signals generated, making it challenging to track the tagged objects. Electronic devices will also affect the read rate of RFID signals.

Therefore, RFID readers are not always 100% successful in reading all the tagged items. Objects with metal components, glass fibres or nylon may also create noise in the RFID signal, creating an environment that is unfriendly to RF. It is challenging to implement RFID systems in an RF-unfriendly environment, even with precise prototype testing, because the interference problem cannot be completely eliminated in such an environment.

Cost Control

Deploying an RFID system to enhance the performance of a process involves significant investment. This constitutes the common roadblock to the implementation of the technology. Investment includes the costs of tagging objects, acquiring and installing hardware devices and application software, system integration, staff training and other expenses, all of which must be taken into consideration before making the decision to implement the technology across the system.

During the initial stage of deployment, the cost of infrastructure is high because, given the current state of technology, RFID tags are much more expensive than barcodes and the testing of the new system requires a considerable amount of time. Thus, before the adoption of any new technology, the organization should determine the ROI. The ROI of deploying RFID technology is often slow - being aware of the slow return rate will help organizations to be realistic in estimating the benefits of deploying such systems.

For example, a book store that has implemented RFID system will result in savings from faster and more accurate stock receiving operations and better inventory management (Bansode and Desale, 2009). The system also reduced the out-of-stock rate and improved re-ordering effectiveness, producing the potential for increasing sales by five percent.

Motivation of Adoption

The organization should have the appropriate motivation and expectations of RFID systems. As RFID technology is still evolving, it is not as powerful as commonly perceived; decision-makers should gain more knowledge about RFID technology so that they will not have excessive expectations about it. It is advisable to consult the experts to acquire knowledge about the technical issues. If the organization wishes to apply the technology to streamline an inter-company process or to achieve data synchronization, it should note that many supply chain players may be reluctant to invest in RFID. Moreover, front-line users of the system usually tend to resist changing their practices when necessitated by the deployment of new technology. This is a critical issue because the success of the implementation will depend upon acceptance of users. The organization should make efforts to eliminate users' concerns and earn their support. It is important not to have unrealistic expectations, because in the end it will lead to disappointment.

SYSTEM ARCHITECTURE AND INTEGRATION CONSIDERATIONS

Proposed middleware architecture (UMIUR Middleware)

Preliminaries

In this work, we have explored the gaps in RFID middleware architectures for new applications such as IoT applications. By analysing different constraints associated with this kind of applications, a large part of them is related to the processing and storage of large amounts of RFID data in real-time, as well as to security and interoperability. This wide variety of applications and their specific constraints has prompted us to propose a new architecture that, based on a set of technologies, fills this set of gaps by ensuring.

Interoperability

The volume of RFID data is constantly growing in modern applications. This (big data) reality means that data transformation is more important than ever for back-end applications, as they do not have the capacity to understand and process raw RFID data without it being transformed so that they can make the right decisions. From the existing literature on RFID middleware architectures, most middleware architectures use XML as an exchange format.

Nevertheless, this can be understood given that, by far, XML has been the single option to share and transfer of data for a long time. Although this exchange format has its benefits, it is not adequate for big RFID data sets, is significantly more verbose, relatively more difficult to read and interpret, and has a much more complex syntax that does not directly correspond with data structures in today's coding languages, it is becoming unsuitable for use in modern systems. Over the last decade, the debate between XML *versus* JSON has been one of the most prominent topics in developer circles. However, based on the literature comparing these two formats, we find that JSON has several advantages over XML.

For instance, data processing with JSON is easier than with XML, and JSON is independent of the languages that use it and easy for machines to parse, allowing JSON to rapidly replace XML in last few years. This set of advantages allowed us to consider adding the functionality of formatting raw RFID data in JSON format as well.

Big data storage

The term Big Data is used when traditional data management tools are not able to store or process such massive data sets, and this is the case with RFID data in modern applications. Big Data is often defined based on three concepts called the 3 Vs.:

- **Volume:** the data volume is already large and is constantly increasing. This can generate storage and analysis difficulties -which is one of the characteristics of RFID data-. For example, the use of RFID technology as a traceability system by a medium-sized retail chain will produce 300 million RFID scans a day and getting the relevant information out of this vast data stream will not be easy.
- **Variety:** the data come from different sources, disciplines, formats. This can lead to difficulties in understanding and integration; and this is the case for RFID applications, as RFID data often comes from heterogeneous data sources.
- **Velocity:** large volumes of data are collected very frequently (this can be in real-time). This can generate difficulties in data processing.

Thus, the development of autonomous objects equipped with RFID tags produces large amounts of data that challenge many traditional approaches in Information Systems. The latter have to deal with huge amounts of disparate RFID data, i.e., highly variable, structured or unstructured, sometimes imperfect.

A set of data characterized by these notions must therefore be managed using dedicated Big Data tools. Today only the NoSQL systems can manage the huge volumes of big data which is generated very fast. The term NoSQL covers database systems that are not relational. These databases offer an alternative to traditional databases for processing large volumes of data. They do not present the properties of a relational database [ACID properties (atomicity, consistency, isolation and durability)] and are not, in general, interrogable with SQL language.

They have been designed to manage large volumes of data (for this they have the "horizontal scalability" properties, because the data can be distributed over several databases) and unstructured data (their data model is more flexible than that of RDBMSs (Relational Database Management Systems).

NoSQL databases can be classified into four categories: key-value databases (Dynamo, Reddis, Voldemort, etc.), document-type databases (MongoDB, CouchDb, etc.), column-type databases (Hbase, Cassandra, BigTable ...) and graph type databases (Neo4J, InfoGrid ...).

For our architecture, we chose the MongoDB database (belongs to the document-oriented model databases) for its multiple advantages and functionalities. MongoDB is a system that stores data in BJSON (binary JSON), it is optimized for loading from JSON files (which makes it perfect for our Middleware that uses this type of data formatting), that's why we have coupled for our Middleware the JSON format for data presentation and the MongoDB database for storing large amounts of data.

Real time RFID data processing

In a general context, modern RFID applications require continuous processing of streaming data detected at different locations, at different times and at different rates, in order to achieve added value in their business and service areas. Real-time analysis is now a central concern for companies. It is an essential practice to significantly increase turnover but also to remain competitive. The science that examines raw data in real-time with the aim of drawing conclusions–without delay-is called real-time analysis. Analytical tools are adopted to empower organizations and businesses to make better decisions, and data analysis is considered among the most essential tasks behind success in several fields of services and business. Some examples of these areas include the RFID technology application areas where they rely on timely and rapid analysis based on available data to make quality decisions.

Recently, CEP has proven to work as a basic tool for processing RFID data in real time to identify all circumstances on demand and act instantly (Aftab et al., 2018), as it was designed specifically to solve issues related to real-time event processing in distributed systems. The CEP is characterized by scalability, efficiency, speed, robustness, and heterogeneity.

It inputs an endless and infinite stream of events from different sources to facilitate real-time data management and detects a massive number of events with low latency. Furthermore, CEP can be used for a wide range of applications, from simple surveillance to very complex applications such as fraud detection and algorithmic trading. Thus, CEP can handle massive unpredictable RFID data, which is generated by RFID networks from multiple sources.

Security

With the rapid developments in the RFID technology field, there has been a growing trend toward the adoption of this technology and even in critical sectors. This raised the important security issue of how to control and prevent unauthorized access to RFID data.

- **RBAC:** One approach to protect the privacy of stored data is to use access controls. Many access control models have been proposed over the years in the literature. In this context, there are two well-known models, RBAC and ABAC, and according to researchers the RBAC is most trustworthy instead of ABAC. Role-based access control (RBAC) is a well-known access control model that can help simplify security management, especially in large-scale systems. Since its first formalisation in the 1990s, RBAC has been widely used in many systems to provide users with flexible controls over access to their data. The RBAC model was extended and updated in 1996, and the RBAC standard was proposed in 2000. This model makes it possible to establish, within a company's information system, an efficient access control to the services and applications and of this IS. It is mainly based on the definition of roles to be attributed resources and users. RBAC has become the most widely used management model because it can be easily applied to different structures. Each role is a simple collection of permissions and users are granted permissions only through the roles to which they are assigned.

When defining an RBAC model, the following conventions are useful.

- U: users
- R: roles
- P: permissions
- S: sessions

- OPS: Operations
- OBS: Objects
- UA: User Assignment
- PA: Permission assignment

The role is the core of the RBAC model and is seen as an intermediate entity between users and permissions as it groups a set of privileges and then assigns them to users according to their role.

As shown in Figure 2A, role assignment in the RBAC model follows a mutual relationship where a User (person, computer process, machine, etc.) can play multiple roles in a single session and a role can be assigned to multiple users.

UA Í U x R

Assigning a role will grant multiple permissions to the user and a permission can be assigned to multiple roles.

PA Í R x PRMSPA Í R x PRMS

The nature of a permission describes the type of operations (OPS) (e.g., read, write, update, etc.) allowed on OBS objects (data resources: documents, computer processes, machines, etc.). The relationship between these objects and the assigned operations is also mutual; an operation can be allowed on several objects and an object can be assigned different permissions.

PRM Í OPS x OBSPRM Í OPS x OBS

- **Blowfish**; As mentioned before, in the current era of RFID applications, with terabytes of data generated daily, securing information is a challenge. Crypto-graphy is a process of making information unintelligible to an unauthorised person, thus providing confidentiality to genuine users which can make the RFID data environment more secure. In general, there are two main families of cryptographic encryption algorithms: Symmetric or private key algorithms and Asymmetric or public key algorithms.

Symmetric key algorithms

A symmetric key algorithm consists of using the same key (a secret key) to encrypt plaintext and decrypt ciphertext data.

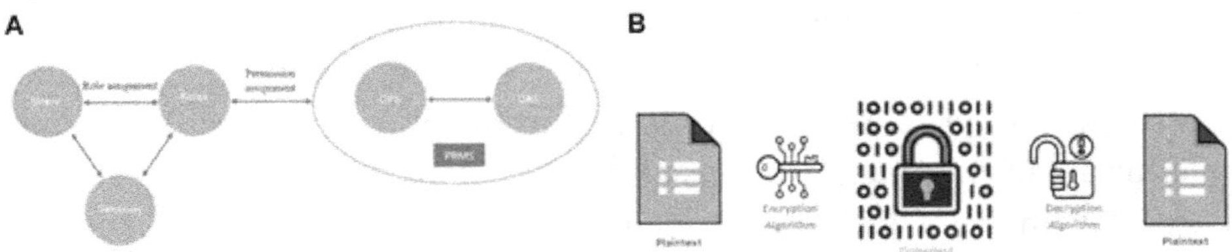

Fig 2. (A) RBAC mechanism. (B) Blowfish algorithm process.

Principle

- Symmetric encryption involves applying an operation (algorithm) to the data to be encrypted using the private key, in order to make it unintelligible.
- Exchange and the private key between entities, so that it can be used in the decryption process.

Asymmetric encryption (or public key encryption)

Consists in using a public key for encryption and a private key for decryption.

Principle:

- The users choose a random key that only they know (this is the private key).
- They each automatically deduce an algorithm (this is the public key).
- The users exchange this public key through an unsecured channel.

The task of choosing the best algorithm to integrate in our architecture was not simple due to the number of existing encryption algorithms. In order to choose we relied on researchers, which implemented and analysed in detail the costs and performance of the commonly used cryptographic algorithms DES, 3DES, AES, RSA and blowfish. Researchers showed in an overall performance analysis in contrast to theoretical comparisons. The paper states that each of the encryption techniques has its own strengths and weaknesses, which showed that of all the cryptographic algorithms, Blowfish algorithm is the best in terms of execution time, memory usage, throughput, power consumption, security and thus blowfish algorithm is well suited for RFID applications.

This algorithm was designed by Bruce Schneier in 1993 as an alternative to existing algorithms. It can take a key length ranging from 32 bits to 448 bits. Since its conception, it has been extensively analysed and is now considered to be a robust encryption algorithm. It is also present in many solutions (OpenVPN). Among its benefits, it consumes the least time among DES, 3DES, AES and RSA and in Blowfish, the memory required for implementation is the smallest. Therefore, since time and memory are major factors four our case, Blowfish is the best option. Figure 2B outlines the Blowfish algorithm process.

UMIUR middleware description

To highlight the contribution of this article, we point out that, firstly, it suggests a new approach which fills a set of known gaps in existing RFID middleware architectures, The proposed design of our architecture represents a framework suitable for a variety of applications and is based on the already developed RFID standards. Secondly, it declares the coupling of the RBAC model and the Blowfish encryption algorithm as a tool regulating the access and display of decrypted data between the AAL and DPL layers, solving the security problem occurring in previous RFID middleware.

And, to tackle the problem of processing a very large number of extremely complex queries, our architecture is based on the paradigm of real-time event processing based on the CEP. Moreover, in order to improve interoperability, the proposed middleware provides RFID data formatting in JSON which has become a popular alternative to XML for its various advantages. Finally, the proposed architecture is also based on NoSQL technology to ensure the storage of large volumes of RFID data. Figure 3 shows the different layers and sublayers of our Middleware architecture.

Application layer

This layer is responsible for providing the various services and functions to the end users of the IS. This layer can be composed of one or many backend applications, such as WMS, ERP, user applications (website, mobile application).

Hardware abstraction layer (HAL)

HAL is in charge of interfacing with the physical RFID infrastructure. It represents the abstraction of the physical parts of the system and supports different devices (read-only, read/write, passive, active tags.) working with multiple frequency bands (HF, LF or UHF). The device abstraction is done in a different way in RF^2ID, it is based on the notion of virtual readers so that each virtual reader manages a set of physical readers in the same neighbourhood.

The diversity of RFID devices constituting the Physical Layer in our case makes the RFID network heterogeneous, and this requires the integration of an abstraction layer of RFID devices into the middleware that interacts with the physical RFID network. Such an approach allows companies to adopt RFID solutions without managing the low-level programming. Furthermore, this approach improves the flexibility of the middleware in terms of hardware selection, as it provides a unified communication gateway to the physical RFID infrastructure, i.e., heterogeneous RFID devices, regardless of the employed frequency range (HF, UHF or LF), or the adopted communication protocol (e.g. LLRP or other), the manufacturer or the communication interface. So, in our case, the Hardware Abstraction Layer will ensure the interfacing with the hardware independently of its characteristics. The HAL is structured in three different sub-layers.

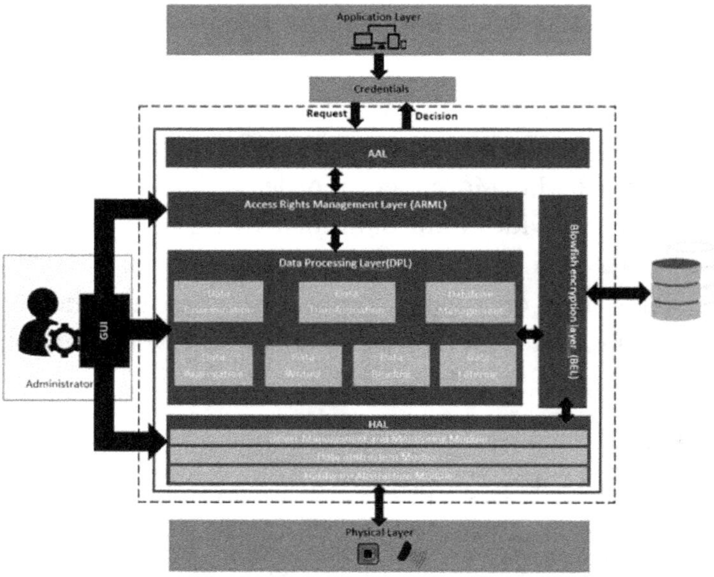

Fig. 3. UMIUR Middleware architecture.

Hardware Abstraction Module

As mentioned before, there are many readers of different brands and of course with different characteristics and protocols. Thanks to the functionalities offered by this module, our middleware architecture will be able to communicate with a heterogeneous RFID physical RFID infrastructure no matter which communication protocol is employed (USB, Ethernet or RS232), the brand, or the frequency range, because this module acts as a unified interface of communication with the physical RFID infrastructure. In addition, via HAM, all basic RFID reader parameters are under the control of the system administrator, this set of parameters includes Stop/Start, Activation/Deactivation, and Read/Write.

Device Management and Monitoring Module

This module offers the user the possibility to select from a broad range of RFID devices depending on their requirements and allows him to replace equipment directly without influencing the insurance software solution. Thanks to DMMM the RFID reader driver libraries are called dynamically which makes the architecture more flexible.

Data abstraction Module

Still with the aim of guaranteeing a unified interfacing with heterogeneous RFID devices, this module ensures that the RFID data will be communicated with the RTDP layer in a common format regardless of the characteristics of the hardware RFID components, in addition DAM handles middleware requests such as ACKs and inventory results.

Data Processing layer

Equivalent to the "data management layer" for WinRFID, it fills a set of inconsistencies (read errors, unread tag, tag read several times), defines management rules for checking the data read, aggregation and redundant data filtering.

Gathered at the layer named Middleware for the Fosstrak middleware, which is in charge of filtering, aggregating and distributing data, this layer also allows applications to define a subscription in which each application defines the readers to be used, the type of data it is interested in, their formats, etc.

For the AspireRFID middleware this layer is called the Hardware Abstraction Layer, it provides a hardware abstraction to unify the way the middleware interacts with readers from different manufacturers, and which use different communication protocols.

It is the "RFID Event Manager" layer in the Sun Java System middleware, its main purpose is to interface with readers, collect EPC events, filter redundant data and feed important EPC events to the RFID information server or other ERP application. This layer is based on Jini technology.

The Data Processing Layer (DPL) layer for our case, which lies between AAL and HAL, is the core of the Middleware. Because any kind of middleware service or functionality is provided through it. The lower HAL layer communicates with the RTPL by providing it with the raw collected RFID stream.

Subsequently the different modules of the RTPL layer will be responsible of storing, formatting, filtering, and the exchange of formatted RFID data with the appropriate back-end applications.

The CEP module is required to apply complex queries to several data streams simultaneously to detect specified conditions (events), thus triggering appropriate actions in real time. This enables the middleware to track, analyse and process large RFID data streams when an event is detected. This layer consists of.

- **Data Dissemination:** Normally, client applications have to exploit the RFID data. DD module is implemented in order to transmit this data to any interested application. When a back-end application requests RFID information and if it has the required authorisations, this module ensures the transfer of the data it is interested in.
- **Data Aggregation**: The DA component is tasked with grouping RFID data according to specific criteria so that each back-end application receives only the data relevant to it, and to reduce the increased granularity. For instance, "grouping data coming from the same RFID reader".

- **Database Management:** DM is responsible for all database organization e.g., deletion, storing and sharing data. As discussed in Section 5.1, among the things that characterize new areas of application of RFID technology is the flow of RFID data, which is really very important, and in order to ensure the storage of this huge volume of RFID data our approach relies on the SQL solution for big data storage, and more specifically the MongoDB database.
- **Data Reading:** For our approach the Data Reading component represents the same thing for most proposed middleware architectures, it is in charge of collecting data from the RFID tags.
- **Data Transformation:** The raw data has no meaning for the applications, that's why "Data transformation" in our architecture transforms it into business events. For instance, in the scenario of deploying RFID technology in the baggage handling process, a bag's location can be expressed as: the bag was in this location at this hour. According to the literature, it has been observed that middleware architectures are mainly based on the representation of data in the XML form, certainly, this format offers a number of significant benefits in terms of data presentation and exchange, but it has a set of limitations which has led us to think of other data presentation formats to ensure better interoperability. As mentioned in (Lanthaler and Gütl, 2012), today the lighter approach of JSON has proven to be popular and is rapidly replacing XML, which led us to consider including the option to format raw RFID data in JSON as well, according to the need of the IS applications.
- **Data Filter:** The RFID data stream generated is always huge in the case of a network of mobile RFID objects. The task of extracting useful data from this vast selection requires data filtering mechanisms. So, it is the role of the module DF to eliminate the undesired data, especially the duplicates.
- **Data Writing:** As mentioned in the "RFID System Components" section, we find read/write tags, which enable the insertion of information on the RFID tag chips. This proposed middleware architecture provides this functionality by calling the DW module.
- **CEP Module:** As mentioned in the introduction, RFID enhances the presence of data that evolves regularly over time and needs to be processed continuously, due to the massive presence of RFID tags. Such exponential data growth causes the 3V in Big Data nature with extreme data streaming speed. This poses significant challenges to overcome the problems of Big Data analysis and real-time decision-making issues. To this end, it is realistic to consider the representation of data as streams and to use processing models corresponding to this information. To tackle the

problem, our architecture is based on the paradigm of real-time complex event processing via the CEP Module which solves the Big Data velocity problem. CEP Module will be responsible for tracking RFID data streams from multiple sources to analyse events in real time in order to respond as quickly as possible, providing organisations with greater situational awareness and business agility.

Application abstraction layer

Equivalent to the data presentation layer in the WINRFD architecture, which provides data and functionality to users. In order to hide the complexity of the RFID system, this module aims to provide a common interface for the application layer to give them the option to access the different functionalities of the middleware if they are granted the necessary authorisations.

Access rights management layer (ARML)

One of the aims of this work is to secure RFID data, as security is the major problem facing every user. This prompted us to include the Access Rights Management Layer (ARML) in our proposed middleware design. This layer based on the RBAC module limits the system against unauthorized access, as there are a number of restrictions to access RFID data with each user. ARML will therefore help to regularize access to RFID data so that only authorized users to access, will have the right to use the decrypted RFID data. Its operating principle is firstly based on authentication to certify the identity of the user, and then, depending on the authorizations granted to this user, the Access Control Decision module (ACD) shares the decision. In the case that it has appropriate authorisation, ACD will identify the resources he can access and the operations he can perform; if the user is not authorized, their requests will be denied.

- **Authentication Management:** Each time the Middleware receives an authentication request, it delegates it to the Authentication Management Module, which is in charge of analysing the credentials provided by the user during the Login phase and then saves the authentication results to the Authentication History module.
- **Authorization Management:** After communication with the Decision Module, it determines the permissions granted to an authenticated user.
- **AC Decision Module:** This is the element that evaluates incoming requests ("who" wants to do "what" on "what") against registered rules ("who" can do "what" on "what"), the Allow/Deny decision will depend on the roles and permissions assigned to users.

- **Policy Definition**: Policy Definition contains statements that collect roles and permissions to express what can and cannot be accessed. Policies in ARML can grant or deny actions on the middleware. In this layer, roles are used to associate users with permissions on resources. Users are assigned roles, and permissions are assigned to roles rather than to individual users; only users who have been granted role membership can access the permissions associated with the roles and can therefore access resources. The ARML consists of:
    - **Permissions Assignment**: The administrator is the only actor who can assign permissions to roles. Permissions represent statements describing the behaviour, i.e., the set of operations that can be performed on the middleware.
    - **Roles Assignment**: The administrator is the only actor who can assign roles to users, a role contains one or more permissions, roles are assigned to users and, therefore, users will have the right to access permissions assigned to roles.
- **Authentication History Module**: This module records historical information about the use of the middleware by storing all successful and failed authentications.

Blowfish encryption layer (BEL)

This layer is responsible for data encryption, upon arrival of RFID events, BEL encrypts all RFID tag data collected by the reader based on the Blowfish encryption algorithm.

UMIURMiddleware implementation

Architecture

RFID has been used in many sectors for many years, but due to the evolution of RFID equipment, its application has broadened in recent years to include critical areas. As these kinds of domains face a variety of new challenges, especially in gathering, processing, analysing and securing big RFID data in real-time, that is why our middleware must support interoperability by ensuring the dissemination of RFID data according to the format requested by the IS, while supporting the heterogeneity of RFID devices, the security of RFID data, and the processing and storage of real-time RFID big data.

Aviation is one of these areas; today airlines face many challenges that have an impact on customer retention, and therefore on profitability. SITA (Société Internationale de Télécommunications Aéronautiques) reports that both the number of travellers and the volume of luggage are constantly rising. International Air Transport Association (IATA) and SITA estimates, lost baggage costs airlines worldwide \$2.1 billion annually! And according to traveller surveys, baggage disputes and delays are the major causes of traveller dissatisfaction, and baggage reclaim is the main stressor for travellers. The aviation industry is one of the areas that has great opportunity to profit from RFID and IoT.

To provide a better and secure system for the aviation industry and travellers, we have proposed a design for an RFID-based baggage tracking system. This project aims to build a baggage tracking system for Moroccan airports. To our knowledge, this is the first innovative academic research study on this topic in Morocco. The implementation of this system will provide an efficient tool for Moroccan airports to recover lost luggage. architecture.

One of the ways in which airlines can become more efficient is to adopt and leverage technological advances in their overall offering. RFID has demonstrated strong benefits in many areas, so it can contribute to the improvement of the baggage handling process, with the aim of solving the problem of lost baggage or at least minimising the number of lost bags, which can be reflected in customer satisfaction. The implementation of an RFID-based IoT system (in which labelled suitcases are considered the "objects" of RFID infrastructure) will offer real-time monitoring of baggage location, with accurate checking stages carried out at different phases of the travel process and without manual handling. Streamlining luggage handling using RFID technology by implementing a system that performs following our proposed middleware architecture specifications outlined previously, will benefit Moroccan airports and airlines in several ways, and by exploiting an approach such as the one described in this paper, airports will benefit from the widespread connectivity and availability of RFID data, which will be integrated into the IS. Figure 25B show some of the interfaces of our middleware, namely: Authentication interface, Dashboard, Reader configuration, Encrypted RFID data.

Interoperability evaluation

The functionality metric of the ISO/IEC 9126 standard was used to assess the interoperability of our middleware. Interoperability was identified as the most important alternative factor of functionality. Until formatting is applied, back-end applications cannot process the raw RFID events stream. In our proposed architecture the task of receiving and transforming the raw RFID data into business events exploitable by applications is guaranteed by the data transformation module.

Currently, XML and JSON are the two most frequently used data exchange formats. However, JSON is generally preferred over XML, and has quickly come to replace it, which motivated us to add the option to use the JSON format. The added value of our architecture is that it allows the user to choose between XML or JSON depending on the specifications of the company's IS.

In addition to these essential functionalities, our proposed architecture also supports other services that are specific to the newer areas of application of RFID technology. For example, this kind of application is characterised by a high volume of data, and in some sectors, it is not only necessary to manage very large quantities of data but also data with a very large size, although the relational DBMS are limited for use with very high data flows.

Our database management module enables the storage of big data due to the integration of the NoSQL MongoDB database. There is also the real-time analysis service, which extracts relevant real-time content from huge raw RFID data stream via the CEP module, which captures information from real-time data streams.

Security and privacy assessment

The security and privacy assessment are intended to evaluate the security and privacy of the RFID middleware, and how it protects sensitive application data where necessary through the use of policies. This is achieved by generating a scenario in which access to decrypted data is restricted to specific parts and by testing how the middleware handles this access control policy. This policy maps an airport business rule that says that only the admin can access decrypted traveller information after the authentication phase. This policy restricts access to this information.

Integration

Since the RFID reader may not manage independently, to integrate with other systems or embedded in an existed applications becomes an important issue. First, the application designer has to know that the integration of the application is based on the software, hardware, or both. If the application is a new system, the RFID system can be embedded in initially. However, if the RFID system is integrated with the existed system, to define and decide the interface for integration is important. In this section, the integration mentioned is based on the existed systems or applications though the new applications also applicable.

According to the communication interface of the RFID reader, hardware and software communication is available. Even the microprocessor of the RFID reader is not powerful, general logic computing based on electric circuit can be implemented. By controlling the voltage of the circuit, the primary circuit can implement the On/Off action or signal. After receiving the signal from the circuit combined with the RFID reader, mechanical action can be realized such as door locking or opening.

In addition to the simple On/Off signal, further information may be required for the applications. Corresponding to the RFID reader selected, simple circuit, RS-232, USB, or RJ45 Internet access can be used.

Simple circuit for RFID system integration

Most hardware for simple mechanical control or action is based on the designed circuit. According to the requirement or action of the machine, some mechanical actions are triggered when receiving an On/Off signal. The reader of the RFID system equips the control circuit such as the MOSFET of simple IC control circuit. Sometimes the undercontrolled applications or systems only need a trigger signal. In other words, the reader of the RFID system provides only an electric wire for signal transmission

In this type of integration, the RFID system acts as a signal sender. When the reader of RFID system inducts the RFID tags, the reader determines that the inducted RFID tag is the predefined (Ex: legal, valid, permitted, etc.) tag or not. If the inducted RFID tag is the predefined RFID tag, the RFID reader sends the control signal to trigger the hardware or mechanical action such as unfasten the lock of door, open a lock gate, etc. In other words, the RFID system is the active controller of the integrated system. The integrated system will act based on the decision of the RFID system.

RS-232 for RFID system integration

RS-232 serial port is the general communication interface. Most appliances or computers support the communication based on RS-232 (D-sub). The RS-232 (EIA232) consists of DTE device (Data Terminal Equipment, usually a computer or terminal) and DCE device (Data Circuit-terminating Equipment, usually a terminal or receiver such as a modem). By sending the control signal, two devices can connect each other vial RS-232 connection. In addition, according to the standard of the RS-232 communication, the reader of RFID system can 1) send the pre-defined command via RS-232 to drive the machine or systems, or 2) send the emulated signal as the command to drive the systems.

In this type of integration, to implement the RS-232 interface of the RFID reader, the RFID system has to equip at least one of the two functions: a simple electric wire for simple action of driven systems or a simple computing unit (or IC chip) for serial port control and command ordering.

Sometimes, the connection between RFID system and the controlled machine will add the middleware (or hardware). The command from the RFID system via RS-232 connection can be translated to the digital signal.

USB and internet access for RFID system integration

For most integration with the existed applications or systems, a host PC (Computer) is the main platform for all information management. Due to the computing ability and the easy maintenance, many applications provide service and control other systems based on PCs. In addition, most applications today consist of different software, applications and database. To integrate the RFID system with the existed applications or systems, a main platform for dealing with all requirements and messages are needed. According to the hardware of the computer, the RFID reader can connect to the PC via USB port or RJ45 Internet connection. When the RFID reader connects to the PC via the USB connection, the information from the RFID tag can be transmitted to the PC directly.

Since the computing ability and processing performance are better than the RFID reader, the applications which gain the information from the RFID reader can enhance the functions or capabilities of the services. The control signal, function executing, or further information management can be done by the applications.

If the RFID system communicates with the integrated systems via Internet, the RFID reader has at least the network component and sufficient centre processing unit for information computing. The RFID system works as a network device belongs to the platform. In other words, the RFID system works independently. The Internet access is only for data and information transmission.

No matter communication based on USB port or network connection, the RFID system is just the role of information gathering. The main platform which manages all information, defines the corresponding actions, and gaining service from the third party applications, is independent from the RFID system. In this case, the RFID system is selected for replacing some identification procedure of the existed systems.

Example of RFID system integration

The characteristic of the RFID system is to identify the RFID tag and exchange the information with the RFID tag. If an application needs no identification, to integrate the RFID system becomes useless. Therefore, to recognize whether an application or a system needs for RFID system integration or not is the first important thing. Then, considering the object served by the applications, to select the suitable RFID system is an important issue. The object can be the human, animals or goods. Most objects follow pre-defined action functions or fixed procedures when served by applications. Only the procedure which is used to identify and differentiate the objects can be replaced by the RFID system. Therefore, based on different frequency of RFID system, different size of RFID tags, and different way for integrations, there are different integrated systems and applications. In this section, some integrated systems are introduced.

- **Guard system**: In opposition to creating new execution or service environment, there were many existed systems or applications such as guard system or application deployed. Since these existed systems or applications run for a long time and present the stability themselves, to include the original systems or applications can reduce the time for stability testing and cost of new infrastructure establishment.

- In this section, a realistic application for parking guarding is presented.
- Via using the proposed system, the main contributions are:
  - the efficiency of management can be improved,
  - the is modular and can be embedded in other similar parking system and hardware without additional re-modification,
  - the procedure of passing the Inlet & Outlet can be simplified via using RFID,
  - the costs of the real construction for the proposed system can be decreased and estimated.
- The RFID System, original gate hardware, and other business management system colored blue in the framework are independent.
- These independent systems are the already existed systems. Each existed systems can independently and individually work. For example, the lane gate management can be controlled by the manual operation or parking ticket machine without RFID. It means that these independent sub-systems can be substituted. The gate hardware can be the product of any possible company.
- There are also many RFID hardware providers. Moreover, to suitably manage and monitor the parking place, the manager may need the attendance information of different users according to each business application. Hence, different type hardware or products need the general interface to communicate with the main management system. In this example, the Main System provides the middleware software and hardware for the interaction.
- In the presented system, the RFID antennas and reader are deployed at the gate. In addition, the RFID tags are placed in the car. Considering the practicability, the RFID System should overcome the accuracy affection of weather and sunshade-paster of car, and the RFID tag type. To increase the usability of the proposed system, the UHF type of RFID tag in this paper is selected. When a user's car approaches the gate, the induction and communication between RFID tag inside the car and antenna of RFID System is automatically established.
- Then the reader of RFID System translates the signal information to the digital content. If there is no further action or information required, the RFID system can send a signal to the gate directly. In other words, even without the Main System, the RFID system can communicate and control the gate (Ex. Via wire, simple circuit integration) directly.

- If the information from the RFID tag is required by other systems or applications such as database, the information will be sent to the Main System first. In this case, the Main System communicates with the hardware of gate via RS-232 link (RS-232 for RFID Integration). The ADAM digital I/O module as the middleware to construct the computing_commands / voltage_signal module is selected. ADAM-4520 is the RS-232/RS-485 converter module that communicates with host PC via RS-232 link. The digital computing command from the host PC is converted into the RS-485 type data stream. Then, the converted data is inputted to the module ADAM-4050. The output DATA+ of ADAM-4520 is connected to the DATA+ of ADAM-4050 and also is the DATA-. In addition to hardware, a software program is executed. This program is designed corresponding to ADAM. The program sends the commands from host PC to the ADAM via RS-232. Then, to command the gate hardware, the voltage_signals are sent from the data output, DO0, DO1, DO4, and DO5 of ADAM-4050 to the gate hardware.
- To really replace/join the original control hardware, four states of the lane gate should be known first: 1. Inlet gate open, 2. Inlet gate close, 3. Outlet gate open, and 4. Outlet gate close. Hence, to match the control requests of these four states, four individual voltagecontrolled IO hardware such as: 1) InletGate_open, 2) OutletGate_open, 3) Expansion_1, and 4) Expansion_2 are defined. The InletGate_open is used to transmit a voltage signal to open the inlet gate. The OutletGate_open is used to transmit a voltage signal to open the outlet gate. Considering the real gate controller, most gates are closed after counting down an on demand time period. In other words, the control IO for closing the gate can be needless.
- To control the original and existed gate hardware, the four individual voltage-controlled IO hardware are linked. If the InletGate_open which connected to the DO0 of the ADAM-4050 is set a signal with the voltage 12V, the inlet fence of the gate is opened. After 6 seconds counting down the inlet fence of the gate closes automatically. The OutletGate_open which connected to the DO4 of the ADAM-4050 controls the outlet fence of the gate and opens it when is set a signal with voltage 12V. In addition, the Expansion_1 and Expansion_2 are connected to the DO1 and DO5 of the ADAM-4050 individually. If the Expansion_1 is set a signal with voltage 12V once, the counter which counts and presents the total number of current available parking space subtract 1. In opposition to Expansion_1, the Expansion_2 is set a signal with voltage 12V once to add 1 from the current total number of available parking space. When a valid car approaches the inlet gate, the Main System sends commands to set the DO0 and DO1 a signal with voltage 12V.

- In addition, the communication between the database (other business management system) and Main System is based on Ethernet or Java server socket. The connection between ADAM and Main System on server PC is RS-232.

CHAPTER-9

RFID TAGGING AND LABELLING

Radio-frequency identification (RFID) is a powerful tool used by hospitals, histopathology labs, research facilities, and IVF labs for record keeping, access control, inventory tracking, sample and patient management, and much more. Our RFID solutions are outfitted with flexible NFC, HF, and UHF inlays that allow them to be applied to various surfaces or our durable, resistant labels, creating RFID labels suited to harsh environments.

The basic function of an RFID tag is to store data and transmit data to the interrogator. At its most basic, a tag consists of an electronics chip and an antenna (see Fig. 1) encapsulated in a package to form a usable tag, such as a packing label that might be attached to a box. Generally, the chip contains memory where data may be stored and read from and sometimes written, too, in addition to other important circuitry. Some tags also contain batteries, and this is what differentiates active tags from passive tags.

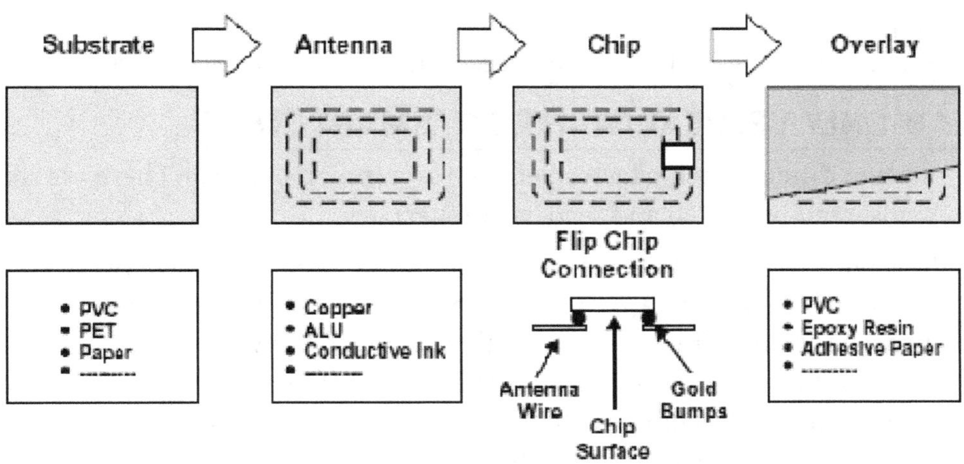

Fig. 1 RFID Tag Components.

Active vs. Passive Tags

RFID tags are said to be active if they contain an on-board power source, such as a battery. When the tag needs to transmit data to the interrogator, it uses this source to derive the power for the transmission, much the way a cell phone uses a battery. Because of this, active tags can communicate with less powerful interrogators and can transmit information over much longer ranges, up to hundreds of feet. Furthermore, these types of tags typically have larger memories, up to 128 Kbytes.

However, they are much larger and more complex than their passive counterparts too, making them more expensive to produce. The batteries in active tags can last from two to seven years.

Passive RFID tags have no on-board power source. Instead, they derive power to transmit data from the signal sent by the interrogator, though much less than if a battery-were on-board. As a result of this, passive tags are typically smaller and less expensive to produce than active tags. However, the effective range of passive tags is much shorter than that of active tags, sometimes under two feet. (Compare a battery-powered megaphone to an oldfashioned plastic cone.) Furthermore, they require more powerful interrogators and have less memory capacity, on the order of a few kilobytes.

Some passive tags do have batteries on-board but do not use these batteries to assist in radio signal transmission. These types of passive tags are called battery-assisted tags and they use the battery only to power on-board electronics.

For example, a food producer may apply RFID tags equipped with temperature sensors to pallets in order to monitor the temperature of their product during shipment and storage. Were the temperature of the product to rise above a certain level, that occurrence could be marked on the tag automatically by the sensor. Later, at the time of delivery or sale, the tag could be checked to verify proper shipment or storage. Passive tags equipped with this type of peripheral sensor would need an on-board battery to operate during shipment or storage.

READ-ONLY VS. READ/WRITE OR "SMART" TAGS

Another differentiating factor between tags is memory type. There are roughly two kinds: read-only (RO) and read/write (RW).

RO memory is just that; memory that can be read only. RO tags are similar to bar codes in that they are programmed once, by a product manufacturer for instance, and from thereon cannot be altered, much the way a CD-ROM cannot be altered after it's burned at the factory. These types of tags are usually programmed with a very limited amount of data that is intended to be static, such as serial and part numbers, and are easily integrated into existing bar code systems.

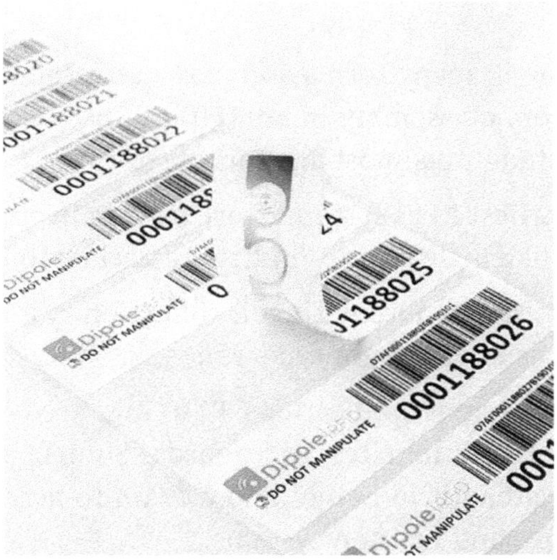

Fig. 2. "Smart" Tag

RW tags are often called "smart" tags. Smart tags present the user with much more fl exibility than RO tags. They can store large amounts of data and have an addressable memory that is easily changed. Data on an RW tag can be erased and re-written thousands of times, much the same way a fl oppy disk can be erased and re-written at will. Because of this, the tag can act as a "traveling" database of sorts, in which important dynamic information is carried by the tag, rather than centralized at the controller. The application possibilities for smart tags are seemingly endless. This, in addition to recent advances in smart tag technology that have driven production costs down to under $1 per tag, accounts for much of the present interest in RFID systems.

There are a few variations on these two types of memory that need mentioning. First, there is another memory type called write-once-read-many (WORM). It is similar to RO in that it is intended to be programmed with static information. Drawing on the analogy above, if RO is similar to a CDROM, then WORM would be akin to CDRW, in which an end-user, a PC owner for instance, gets one chance only to write in its own information, i.e., burn a blank CD. This type of memory could be used on an assembly line to stamp the manufacturing date or location onto a tag after the production process is complete.

In addition, some tags could contain both RO and RW memory at the same time. For example, an RFID tag attached to a pallet could be marked with a serial number for the pallet in the RO section of the memory, which would remain static for the life of the pallet. The RW section could then be used to indicate the contents of the pallet at any given time, and when a pallet is cleared and reloaded with new merchandise, the RW section of the memory could be re-written to refl ect the change.

Tag Form Factors

RFID tags can come in many forms and may not resemble an actual tag at all. Because the chip/antenna assembly in an RFID tag has been made so small, they can now be incorporated into almost any form factor:

- Some of the earliest RFID systems were used in livestock management, and the tags were like little plastic "bullets" attached to the ears of livestock.
- The RFID tags used in automatic toll collection systems are not really tags but plastic cards or key chain type wands.
- In prison management applications, RFID tags are being incorporated into wristbands worn by inmates and guards. Similarly, some FedEx drivers carry RFID wristbands in lieu of a key chain to access their vans through keyless entrance and ignition systems.
- The pharmaceutical industry is incorporating RFID tags into the walls of injection-moulded plastic containers, thus blurring the line between tag and packaging.

In short, the form a tag takes is highly dependent upon the application. Some tags need to be made to withstand high heat, moisture, and caustic chemicals, and so are encased in protective materials. Others are made to be cheap and disposable, such as "smart" labels. A "smart" label is just one form of a "smart" tag, in which an RFID tag is incorporated into a paper packing label. While there are many applications in which RFID tags are anything but, the overall trend in the industry is towards this small, fl at label that can be applied quickly and cheaply to a box or pallet.

BENEFITS OF RFID LABELS & RFID TAGS

- **Wide Scanning Radius:** RFID smart labels can be scanned and read in batches, simultaneously, from a few inches to a few feet in range and without full visibility/direct line of sight. As such, RFID tags will emit their signal within a wide omnidirectional read range, even when covered or embedded within a container. This provides RFID labeling greater freedom in tag placement, reducing the label's risk of falling off or being removed.
- **Printed & Encoded:** RFID labels and tags can be encoded with far more information than barcodes, and the technology protects your data with encryption and physical shielding. Moreover, thermal RFID labels are compatible with most thermal-transfer printers, allowing them to be printed with serialized text and barcodes. This combination of barcodes and RFID makes it possible to fully integrate RFID tag and labels into a laboratory management system, speeding up routine processes such as sample gatekeeping, inventorying, and tracking.

- **Flexible inlays:** Our RFID smart labels are equipped with a passive inlay that does not require a battery to function. This permits the labels to be made in much smaller sizes, while the inlay's flexible nature allows the labels to be applied to various surfaces, including curved surfaces. Passive RFID labels and RFID tags do, however, require an integrator system that will store and process the encoded information.
- **Applications:** The primary benefit of RFID labeling for the healthcare industry is the reduction of misidentification errors. Perfect for use in the clinic and by research facilities, RFID tags allow patient samples to be tracked in real-time, from collection to testing. They also make supply chain management more efficient, improving your inventory's accuracy, can be programmed to send medical alerts to staff, and be used to locate valuable samples. In the lab, RFID thermal labels make tracking and monitoring workflows easier.

RFID Tags for Retail

The benefits of RFID for retail are proven. Improved inventory accuracy enables retailers to leverage inventory across store locations, enact omni-channel initiatives, improve sales, and increase margins by selling fewer merchandise at markdown.

Fig. 3 RFID Tags for Retail

FineLine Technologies has leveraged our core capabilities into integrated RFID tagging solutions to print and encode RFID tickets in 36 hours on average – just as fast as we print standard retail tickets.

RFID tags and labels are developed to meet customers' total ticketing requirements: read performance, visual appearance, and application to merchandise.

Product features include: data transformations, global and regional print formats, color variable printing of logo, size bar, or product image, material, adhesive, and construction options.

Global retailers and brand owners use FineLine produced RFID hangtags and labels, including Macy's, Target, Matalan, and Inditex.

]RFID Tags for Tires

Automotive, industrial and aviation tire manufacturers, fleet managers and re-treaders have tagging options with FineLine. Our patent pending products are designed in compliance with worldwide tire safety regulations and guidelines. With emphasis on:

Fig. 4 RFID Tags for Tires

- **Durability.** Tested under real world manufacturing and operating conditions, our solutions are proven to function under the most extreme conditions.
- **Data management.** FineLine's RFID tagging products provide tire supply chain owners with tracking, tracing and validating functionality through the tire life cycle.
- **Quality Management.** With RFID tagging solutions, inventory and stock taking operations and accuracy are improved exponentially.

FineLine's tire tagging solutions provide full process transparency, to quickly identify and trace process inefficiency or quality issues within the tire manufacturing or re-treading process.

RFID Tags for Events & Entertainment

Ensuring guest satisfaction should be the No. 1 objective for event organizers, museum and stadium management and corporate conference organizers. Guest satisfaction starts with the minute the ticket is received. FineLine uses RFID or NFC technology to encode passes with guest data to provide that personalized and engaging experience. RFID integrated wristband, badges help to track patrons and guests that the venue or event, validate access, and speed up entry processes.

Fig. 5. RFID Tags for Events & Entertainment

TAG SELECTION CRITERIA

Some of the factors considered during tag selection are tag type, operating frequency, materials to be tagged, tag mounting method, read range, read rate, tag size, environmental conditions, cost, and mandated requirements.

Tag Frequency

Selection of tag frequency depends on factors such as read range requirements, material to be tagged, and data rate. Applications such as access control and payment systems require a very small read range. In these types of applications, reading tags beyond a few inches creates a security risk, and therefore the read range must not extend beyond a few inches. LF and HF tags with shorter read ranges are ideally suited for such applications. In tagging pallets used in a supply chain, a read range of 5 to 10 feet is required. UHF tags are well suited for this application.

Items with aqueous content require separation between the item and UHF or microwave tag. At the item level, few choices for tag placement are available and less opportunity exists to create an air gap between the tag and the object. In this type of situation, an HF tag with 2 to 3 feet of read range is an ideal choice. HF and LF tags are well suited for tracking humans and animals because living bodies have a high water content. The FDA has approved LF tags for human and animal implantation.

Objects with metals pose a special problem to tagging. Tags directly attached to metal objects are detuned and cannot work well regardless of the tag frequency. If UHF and microwave tags are attached to metal with a small air gap between the tag and the object, they can be easily read.

Tag Type

The factors affecting tag type selection are read range requirements, sensor requirement, cost, size, weight, and the type of application. Passive tags are cheaper than semi-passive or active tags. Tag cost should be considered relative to the cost of the items being tagged. For example, a $100 active tag attached to a container is economical, while a 25 cent tag attached to a box of cereals may not be.

Passive UHF RFID tag in form of a smart label is often used for case and pallet tracking of inventory.

Passive UHF RFID Tag

Some applications dictate the type of tags used. For example, to monitor temperature within a refrigerated truck, you would need semi-passive or active tags with temperature sensors.

Environmental Factors

The environmental conditions that the tag may encounter during its lifetime are major considerations in tag selection. A tag embedded within the product may encounter high temperatures and pressures during product manufacturing, and it must be able to survive those conditions. Evaluate environmental conditions not only within your own facility but also in any environment the tag will travel through during its entire lifetime. These environmental conditions may affect the tag's read range or read rate:

- • The substrate may absorb moisture or may become brittle and crack.
- • The adhesive may not hold the tag due to moisture or chemicals and the tag may fall off the item.
- • The interconnection between the antenna and the IC may break due to vibration or due to repeated flexing of the tag.
- • The antenna may be weakened due to corrosive effects of the chemicals in the environment.

You may need to use encapsulated tags that are protected from abrasion or chemicals in the environment.

RFID Standards Compliance

Tags may be selected for compliance with certain standards. The standards may be open, such as ISO, or they may be proprietary. It is a good practice to follow the open and popular standards, because more companies manufacturing products use these standards than proprietary ones, providing a wider choice of products. In addition, these products may be cheaper due to higher volume, and support for them may be available for a longer period. With the wide acceptance of EPC Gen 2 standards (now also ISO 18000-6c), it is best to use Gen 2–compliant products if you are going to use UHF.

Fig. 6. Identec Solutions Active RFID tag with Temperature Sensor

Compliance Requirements

Many large organizations and government agencies have mandated that their suppliers provide goods with RFID tags. These published mandates may specify tag type, frequency, amount of memory, read range, read rate and speed, and protocol. In addition, the mandates may specify how the goods should be tagged. If you are supplying goods to one of the mandating companies, you have little choice in tag selection. The frequency and tag types are specified in the mandates. You may select tag manufacturer and tag model depending on the materials being tagged and the location of the tag on the goods.

Tag Orientation and Location

Tag performance is affected by the orientation of the tag relative to the interrogator antenna. The best tag orientation occurs when the tag plane and the antenna plane are parallel to each other. At this orientation, the tags receive the maximum power. As the tag is rotated, it presents a smaller effective area to the incoming radio waves and thus collects less power. The tag read range decreases as the collected power decreases.

Most passive UHF tags have a single dipole antenna that has nulls along its north and south poles. This type of tag cannot be read when the axis of the poles on the tag antenna is perpendicular to the plane of the interrogator antenna. Two options are available to remedy this situation: install two interrogator antennas—one perpendicular to the other—so the tag antenna axis is not perpendicular to the plane of at least one of the interrogator antennas. Or, use tags with two dipole antennas (a dual dipole tag), with one antenna perpendicular to the other. The axis of at least one of the two antennas on this tag will never be perpendicular to the interrogator antenna plane.

The location of the tag within the IZ also affects the tag's performance. As the tag moves away from the interrogator antenna, it receives less and less power. The reflected signals mixing with the original signal further reduces the power available to the tag. At the outer edges of the IZ, signal strength may decrease in pockets to such a low degree that the tag may not be powered and the consistency of the tag read decreases.

Placement of the Tag

Placement of the tag on an object affects the tag's performance. Placement is an important consideration for passive UHF and microwave tags used for the products containing aqueous liquids, such as wine bottles, shampoo bottles, many drugs in liquid form, and most food items. Radio waves at UHF and microwave frequencies are absorbed by the water. To read UHF tags attached to packaging containing aqueous liquids, the tag must be placed so that an air gap exists between the tag and the aqueous liquid. You can design the tag so that its antenna is always pointed away from the liquids, or you can take advantage of the way the liquids are packaged so that the tag is attached to the container away from the liquids in the container. At case-level tagging, as opposed to item-level tagging, the tag is attached to the case. The best place to attach passive UHF tag on cases is where the item packaging provides the most separation from the liquids inside. This may require a very precise tag placement, with a tolerance of only a few millimeters. The best way to determine the best tag location is to experiment with various tags.

Selecting the Right RFID Labels or Tags:

- **Understanding RFID Technology:** Before diving into the selection process, it's crucial to grasp the fundamental principles of RFID technology. RFID systems consist of RFID tags or labels, RFID readers, and backend software systems. The RFID tags, equipped with an integrated circuit (chip) and an antenna, communicate with RFID readers via radio waves to transmit and receive data, facilitating seamless asset tracking and management.

- **Application-Specific Requirements:** One of the first steps in choosing the right RFID label or tag is understanding the unique requirements of your application. Consider factors such as the type of items or assets you need to track, the operating environment (e.g., indoor, outdoor, temperature fluctuations), the required read range, and any industry-specific regulations or compliance standards that need to be met.
  - **Unique Identifiers:** If you need to track items with unique identifiers or encode specific information on the tags, choose tags that support these requirements.
  - **Customization:** Some applications may require customized RFID tags with specific features or capabilities. Work with tag vendors to develop customized solutions tailored to your needs.
- **RFID Frequency Bands:** RFID tags operate at different frequency bands, each offering distinct advantages suited for specific applications. Low Frequency (LF), High Frequency (HF), and Ultra-High Frequency (UHF) are the primary RFID frequency bands. LF tags are ideal for short-range applications, HF tags offer better penetration of materials, and UHF tags provide long-range capabilities suitable for inventory management and logistics.
  - **Low Frequency (LF):** Typically operates at 125 kHz and is suitable for short-range applications such as access control, animal tracking, and proximity cards.
  - **High Frequency (HF):** Operates at 13.56 MHz and offers a good balance between read range and tag size. HF RFID is commonly used in applications like payment cards, public transportation, and library book tracking.
  - **Ultra-High Frequency (UHF):** Operates at frequencies ranging from 860 MHz to 960 MHz and provides longer read ranges, making it ideal for inventory tracking, supply chain management, and asset tracking in large warehouses.
- **Tag Form Factors and Mounting Options:** RFID tags come in various form factors and mounting options to accommodate diverse application needs. From adhesive labels and hang tags to rugged hard tags and specialty form factors, choose a tag design that aligns with the size, shape, and material of the items being tracked. Additionally, consider mounting options such as surface mounting, embedding, or attaching to ensure optimal tag placement for reliable performance.

- **Material Compatibility:** Different materials can affect RFID tag performance. For example, metal and liquid can interfere with RFID signals, so special RFID tags designed for these environments may be required.
- **Item Size:** Choose tags that are suitable for the items you need to tag. For example, small and flexible tags are suitable for tagging clothing and other soft goods, while larger tags may be required for tracking pallets or containers.
- **Mounting Options:** Consider how the tags will be mounted on items. Some tags come with adhesive backing for easy attachment to surfaces, while others may require special mounting hardware or enclosures.

- **Read Range and Performance:** The read range of RFID tags refers to the distance at which they can be detected and read by RFID readers. Factors such as tag frequency, antenna design, and environmental conditions influence the read range and performance of RFID tags. Conduct thorough testing to determine the optimal tag configuration and positioning to achieve the desired read range while minimizing interference and signal attenuation.
- **Durability and Environmental Resistance:** For applications in challenging environments or outdoor settings, durability and environmental resistance are critical considerations. Choose RFID tags with robust construction and ingress protection (IP) ratings to withstand exposure to moisture, dust, temperature extremes, and physical impact. Additionally, opt for tags with UV-resistant materials for prolonged outdoor use without degradation.
  - **Environmental Conditions:** If tags will be exposed to harsh conditions such as extreme temperatures, moisture, or chemicals, choose tags that are designed to withstand these conditions.
  - **Durability:** Select tags that are durable enough to withstand handling, transportation, and storage without degradation in performance.
- **Data Storage and Encoding Options:** RFID tags can store varying amounts of data, ranging from a unique identifier (Electronic Product Code - EPC) to additional information such as product details, batch numbers, and expiration dates. Evaluate your data storage and encoding requirements to select RFID tags with sufficient memory capacity and encoding options to accommodate your data storage needs.
- **Regulatory Compliance and Standards:** Ensure that the RFID tags you choose comply with relevant regulatory standards and industry specifications to avoid potential compliance issues. Depending on your

industry and geographic location, there may be regulations governing RFID frequency bands, transmission power levels, and data encryption requirements. Choose RFID tags that adhere to applicable standards to ensure interoperability and compliance with regulatory requirements.

- **Integration with Existing Systems:** Consider the compatibility and ease of integration of RFID tags with your existing RFID infrastructure, including RFID readers, middleware, and backend software systems. Choose RFID tags that support common communication protocols and data formats to facilitate seamless integration with your existing systems and workflows. Additionally, ensure that the chosen RFID tags are compatible with your chosen RFID reader technology to maximize system interoperability and performance.
- **Total Cost of Ownership (TCO) Considerations:** While upfront costs are a significant factor in selecting RFID tags, it's essential to consider the total cost of ownership (TCO) over the tag's lifecycle. Evaluate factors such as tag durability, reliability, maintenance requirements, and scalability to determine the long-term value and return on investment (ROI) of RFID tags. A comprehensive cost-benefit analysis will help you make informed decisions and choose RFID tags that offer the best balance of performance and affordability.

Main elements

RFID tags are composed of 3 main elements, which must be of very high quality to ensure the functionality of the components:

Material or substrate

This is the component that binds the rest of the parts of the tag. It is usually made of a thin and flexible polymer or plastic material. It must be able to withstand the various environmental conditions the tag will be subjected to during its life cycle, so the substrate can be of various types (metal, plastic, cardboard, etc.). It is important to consider that the requirements for proper functioning will not be the same for a tag intended for logistics as for one to be used inside freezers. A protective layer made of materials such as PVC, epoxy resin, or adhesive paper is usually added. This allows the tag to be attached to an object.

Antenna

This is the largest part of the tag and is connected to the chip. Its shape will determine the frequency at which it operates. It is usually composed of a strip of a conductive material (copper or aluminum), and its mission is to receive signals emitted by RFID antennas and, depending on the type of tag, transmit or reflect the received signal (in an active tag, the signal is transmitted back, and in a passive tag, it is reflected). To choose the best antenna, we will have to consider the reading processes that the product in question will be subjected to during the supply chain.

RFID chip

This is an integrated circuit (IC) that has a memory store and a microprocessor for decision-making. It needs energy to function, so in passive tags, the chip is designed as a passive power device. It obtains energy from radio waves radiated by the RFID system's antenna. In active tags, this energy usually comes from a battery in the tag itself. There are many options for memory capacity and security. For most applications, a low-capacity chip (from 128 bits) is more than sufficient.

Types of RFID labels

It is essential to select an appropriate RFID tag for the product and the environment in which it will be used. That's why there are different types of tags based on their application. At Dipole, we work with the necessary standards to ensure that all needs are covered with our RFID tags.

That's why we have a wide variety of materials (standard paper, polyethylene, polyamide, cardboard, etc.) to manufacture the tags, as well as multiple delivery formats (in rolls, zig-zag, loose, etc.). The types of RFID tags we have available at Dipole are:

- **Standard RFID labels:** The customization of materials, dimensions, integrated circuits, or memory, among other features, make them perfect for various applications. They comply with international standards and are printable on any standard printer in the market. Dipole designs and manufactures standard RFID tags in different sizes and materials, in addition to having numerous internal circuits (IC) and memories depending on each need. They can be used in logistics, industrial processes, plastic containers, etc.
- **Rugged RFID labels:** As the name suggests, these tags can withstand complex conditions and both internal and external environments. Their design is intended for long-lasting products such as boxes, pallets, or automotive components exposed to high temperatures, chemicals, or water.
- **RFID timing labels:** Their ability to resist moisture makes this tag the best choice for sports timing, whether for the bib or the shoe. Dipole's RFID timing tags are designed with optimal materials such as foam or plastic and use adhesives resistant to moisture and conditions found in these types of events. Dipole's timing RFID tags stand out not only for their resistance and reliability but also for being the thinnest and most precise on the market,

with thicknesses ranging from 0.25 to 5 mm. They can all be encoded on any RFID printer in the market.

- **RFID labels for metals:** RFID tags for metals are designed to optimally identify and be easily detected on any metal element, avoiding the interference this material causes in radiofrequency waves. At Dipole, we have this type of RFID tags, specially designed for the metallurgical, automotive, aviation sectors, etc.
- **RFID labels for retail:** At Dipole, we have heat-sealed tags, textile tags, hang tags, etc., to cover different needs for footwear, clothing, or accessory manufacturers. Retail tags are among the most used thanks to the great benefits they bring to the sector. Our customization services in printing and encoding RFID tags enable the brand identity to be conveyed to the consumer and product information to be collected.
- **RFID labels for vehicles:** These tags are used in access control, presence control, vehicle verification, tailor-made logistics identification, etc. Identifying vehicles with RFID tags can help streamline logistics processes and passage through gates. It ensures reliable traceability and detection. It is necessary to ensure that RFID tags are designed for all types of vehicles, from cars or trucks to buses. Also, the materials used must not leave residues and must withstand external environments.
- **RFID labels for laundry:** Although it may seem a bit strange, RFID tags in laundries can save a lot of work. At Dipole, we design them with textile products and the industrial washing process in mind. That's why we have created resistant and flexible tags that can adapt to all garments.
- **RFID labels for laboratories:** Laboratory tags must meet very strict requirements. They must be designed to withstand the chemicals that may be present in a laboratory, freezing temperatures, and high temperatures to identify materials, samples, and products that require specific features. RFID identification ensures identification and tracking without the need for direct vision and in an automated way.

How are RFID tags printed?

RFID tags are printed on a specialized printer for RFID label printing. This printer can be a thermal or inkjet printer, and it is necessary to have access to specialized software for designing and customizing the tags. To print, the label is placed in the printer, and the printing process is followed using the software. The software is responsible for writing the information on the RFID tag, as well as printing the design and necessary information on the label's surface.

It is important to follow the instructions and recommendations of the printer and label manufacturer to ensure high-quality printing and proper functionality of the RFID tag.

There are many printer models, capable of adapting to industrial, desktop, portable environments, and more:

- **Industrial:** These printers have a high-performance capacity, as they are designed for industrial environments where they will be in operation for long periods (manufacturing, industry, warehouses, logistics processes, asset tracking, shipping, and receiving). At Dipole, we have printers capable of encoding all types of labels and sizes with great flexibility.
- **Desktop:** The perfect printer for medium or low volume printing. Its use is generally focused on encoding RFID tags and wristbands for hospitals, retail, entertainment, inventory, etc. Its compact form makes it ideal for indoor areas.
- **Card printers:** These RFID card printers with identification can provide easy and reliable personnel, user, or customer tracking. They feature plastic printing on one or both sides to create gift cards, financial cards, or personal credentials with excellent photographic quality. Their ideal applications would be for medium or high volume environments (sports events, concerts, building security, healthcare, etc.).
- **Portable:** The best option if you want to increase process productivity since workers can take them anywhere. They are designed for low-volume mobile printing solutions, thanks to their lightweight and compact design. They are mainly used in retail for labeling boxes or pallets, shipping and receiving, transportation management, or document traceability.
- **Color:** Perfect for printing and encoding RFID tags at high speed and with maximum resolution. They are considered industrial or desktop printers and are mainly used in warehouses, logistics, order picking, and/or packaging, etc.

How long does an RFID tag last?

RFID tags and technology, like any other electronic system, can malfunction due to equipment failures, software defects, environmental influences, or the natural aging of components. The tag, being the most delicate element, is usually the most affected by all these circumstances. To analyze their performance, duration, and the differences that may exist between them, it is necessary to investigate the most common failure modes:

- High electrical resistance between the chip and the antenna, caused by corrosion or oxidation of the conductive adhesive that connects them.

- A break in the integrated circuit.
- The breakage of the connection between the chip and the antenna.
- The antenna may fail due to metal fatigue.

To estimate the approximate duration of RFID tags, manufacturers perform various aging tests. These tests allow them to predict degradation and response levels over long periods. These experiments are monitored and accurately reproduced, so they can be compared with each other.

BEST PRACTICES FOR TAG PLACEMENT

RFID tag performance analysis is a crucial step in ensuring the efficiency and accuracy of your inventory management system. RFID tags are small devices that store and transmit data using radio waves, and they can be attached to various types of products, such as clothing, books, or electronics. However, not all RFID tags work equally well on different materials and surfaces, and some factors can affect their readability and range. In this article, we will show you how to optimize RFID tag placement for different types of products, and what to consider when choosing the right RFID tags for your needs.

RFID technology can be used in a wide variety of processes and sectors. More and more industries are adopting this identification system. Here are some examples of RFID technology and its potential applications:

Supply Chain Management

One of the fundamental applications is improving the overall supply chain by automating, simplifying, or even eliminating identification and data capture tasks at various points in the chain, ensuring traceability. RFID tags are placed on all products to be tracked, providing information about them at each stage of the process. This simplification leads to benefits such as increased productivity and efficiency and reduced operational costs.

Industry

To be competitive today, it is essential to improve production times, reduce direct labor in non-value-added processes, and increase overall company productivity. The industrial sector has found RFID technology to be a great ally, offering advantages such as data capture in procedures where it is impossible or costly to do manually. It has streamlined and optimized all processes within industrial activity, with many sectors incorporating it into their systems.

One example is the automotive industry: many car manufacturers and component suppliers use this technology for a comprehensive view and control of the supply chain, managing assembly lines more easily, detecting errors, and storing important information about each piece (such as serial number or manufacturing date) thanks to RFID tags. This ensures complete traceability of their products and simplifies interactions between various supply chain actors, from material suppliers to dealership agents.

Logistics

Logistics processes have experienced positive change due to RFID systems: the interaction between manufacturing, distribution centers, and stores is much more agile and effective. Goods can be identified massively and reliably, avoiding manual information verification. Warehouse management is improved, allowing automated loading and unloading of goods. Order preparation, packing, and collection times are reduced, and errors are easily detected.

By applying radiofrequency to logistics, businesses gain a global view, ensuring good service and increasing productivity by 20-30% more than using barcodes.

Retail

Retail is one of the sectors that has benefited the most. Adhesive RFID tags placed on products allow the exact location of each item to be known at all times, as well as storing relevant information about them.

This greatly simplifies inventory management, preventing stockouts. These tags can also be used as anti-theft systems, only deactivated when passing through the checkout; a detection gate will sound an alarm if someone tries to take a product without paying.

In addition, this technology can offer customers a new shopping experience through interactive screens and fitting rooms, which allow for product identification and information, purchase recommendations, or requests for different sizes and colors, among other options.

Overall, RFID is a useful tool for improving customer satisfaction and increasing sales volume. Fashion, jewelry, and cosmetics are some of the sectors where this technology has become indispensable.

Today, RFID technology is the best system for tagging clothing and other retail products in an easy, fast, and effective way.

Hospitals / Pharmaceutical

Industry Hospitals also collect large amounts of data daily, essential for the proper functioning of all treatments performed there (patient admissions and discharges, medical supplies, medications, access data to restricted areas for hospital staff, etc.). Collecting all this data requires a system capable of storing and updating it immediately, simply, and securely. Thus, the benefits and tools of RFID technology:

- Patients are identified at all times, thanks to RFID wristbands and other systems such as RFID tags in their medical records.
- The hospital itself is more secure, as it has constant control over both product inventory and facility users.
- Search and manual note-taking times are eliminated.

Food and Drinks

One of the primary concerns of the food industry is the sanitary safety of products. RFID technology offers numerous advantages in ensuring food traceability at any stage of the production process:

It allows product entries from the field with alerts for ripening time or other associated processes; temperature control in the cold chain; movement registration between drying chambers/curing zones; and even controlling turnovers in cheese curing processes and similar products. We can also create alerts to prevent obsolete or expired stock.

In addition, with RFID tags, we can store all the information that must be included about the products (entries, sizes, varieties, etc.), ensuring compliance with current legal regulations.

Libraries / Documents

RFID tags provide books and/or documents with a unique identification number, allowing for more accurate and effective tracking since the system can read the identification of multiple units simultaneously and avoid manual identification. Additionally, this technology is used for the authentication of official documents, preventing forgery. Implementing RFID technology in a library enables real-time registration of book loans and returns and control of due dates. Users can access the information they need at any time. With this system, a library user could check from home if a book or CD is available at the library or not.

Sports Timing

RFID technology allows for better management and control of participants times in races and other sports events. The RFID tag assigned to each participant enables tracking of their course and timing. These disposable tags allow for accurate timing without causing any discomfort to the athlete. They can be attached to the bib, sports shoes, or other clothing worn by the runner.

Identification and Location of Assets

We can record asset movements in real-time, enabling control and management on-site or from a remote location. By identifying assets with appropriate tags, we can easily locate them even if they have been moved and placed where they do not belong. We can even record changes in environmental conditions for critical products.

These systems help prevent asset loss or misplacement while simplifying management and reducing operational costs.

Inventory Management

Proper inventory management is essential for the smooth operation of any business.

With RFID technology, we can manage the inventory process in real-time, automatically: we can assign a unique identifier to each stored product, avoiding duplicates and discrepancies; we can easily obtain relevant information about stored products and their location; and we can maintain a more accurate and constantly updated stock.

This way, we can save time and reduce costs while increasing productivity, avoiding errors, and preventing unnecessary expenses.

Access Control

This is one of the most common uses of this technology. With an RFID tag, real-time and rapid control of products entering and leaving a warehouse or people participating in an event can be achieved. To do this, RFID portals can be placed at access points, capable of identifying the number of tags passing through them and their carrier.

Companies can obtain a wealth of information for the management and control of activities. Examples include, but are not limited to, goods entries and exits, order distribution (the entire process), worker identification and access, event entry supervision, door locking in hotels, and many more.

RFID Label Construction

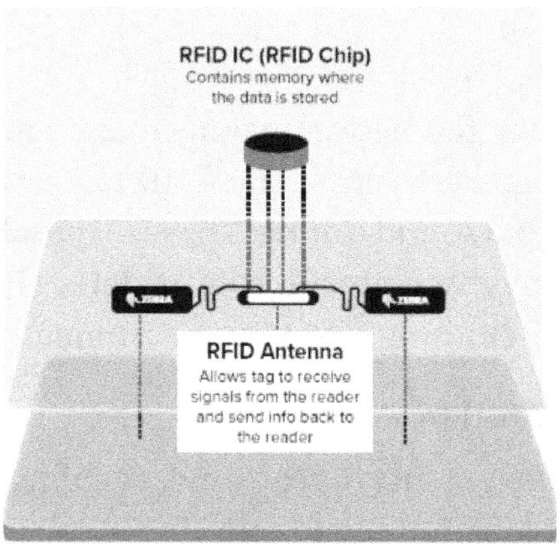

Fig. 7 RFID Tag Label or non-adhesive tag with inlay

Testing Capabilities

Voyantic testing equipment can help you identify the optimal inlay for the surface being labeled. The Zebra RFID team will test any combination of labels and inlays for specific use cases that may arise.

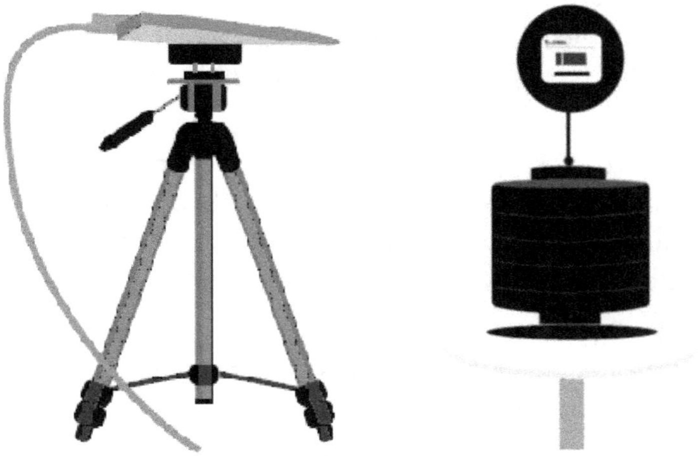

Fig. 8 Voyantic testing equipment

In-House RFID Label Manufacturing

With our manufacturing equipment and wide range of raw materials and inlays, Zebra can add almost any inlay to almost any label material.

RFID Tag Designs

A passive RFID tag is divided into two main sections: the analog front-end and the digital section. The front-end tasks include all analog processing for DC power, incoming signal detection and information extraction (called demodulation) and the transmission of the modulation signal. The digital section decodes incoming data, responds to commands from the reader, reads and writes to internal EEPROM (electrically erasable programmable read-only memory) memory, and encodes and transmit data to the modulator.

A backscatter modulator is a device used to modulate the impedance (the measure of the opposition that a circuit presents to a current when a voltage is applied) seen by the transponder's antenna when transmitting, which decides the overall performance of the tag. The analog front-end is the key block of a passive RFID transponder.

It provides a regulated voltage supply for the digital core and other circuits by correcting the incoming radio-frequency signal. While in transmitting mode, the analog front-end also works to ensure its communication method of backscatter modulation will function properly.

Passive RFID devices obtain their operating power from the radio-frequency waves transmitted from the RFID reader. This wireless link is classified into two groups based on the wireless link coupling mechanism: near-field coupling and far-field coupling. Near-field coupling is essentially an inductive coupling with frequencies up to a few MHz which forces the reader to be near, so the coupling coils of near-field coupled RFIDs will have a large voltage at its terminals and is not that severely affected by nearby devices. This is not the case for far-field coupling.

The efficiency in power harvesting is one of the key factors in determining the range of the tag. UHF RFID tags work on far-field coupling, thus their efficiency of power harvesting is an important factor in their design. This efficiency is determined by different factors such as the efficiency of the antenna, accuracy of the matching between the antenna and the circuitry, and the efficiency of the voltage multiplier.

In the case of near-field passive wireless systems, a diode bridge rectifier can be used to convert the carrier signal to DC.

Far-field RFID tags, on the other hand, require an efficient way to convert RF to DC. Voltage multipliers that increase voltage levels whilst performing the conversion are used, due to the low voltage of the antenna.

Antennas are a critical part of designing the reader, as they are required to efficiently carry a signal to and from the tag. PCB tracks are commonly used to form a loop. The range of a tag is affected by various factors, such as:

- The tag's antenna size. A larger antenna is better at being detected.
- The reader's antenna size. A larger antenna results in increased read range, but a noisy environment may cause a worse signal-to-noise ratio and decrease the reading distance
- The orientation of the antenna
- Environmental noise
- The antenna's Q factor. Generally, a Q between 30 and 40 is needed.

Most designs aim for an antenna between 0.8 and 1.6 μH, as values below 0.8 μH become increasingly more difficult to sync. Maximum energy transfer occurs when the antenna and associated components are in resonance.

For the tag and reader to communicate, the impedance presented to the transponder's antenna has to be varied to modulate the reflected power. To achieve this change, a transistor is inserted between the two antenna terminals which when turned on will short the antenna terminal, effectively presenting a short circuit that cuts off power and signal from flowing. When the transistor is off, it has no effect on the antenna and the rest of the modules. The process of varying the impedance is a type of modulation based on backscattering.

Modulation is the process of modifying the characteristics of a signal, called a carrier wave, to convey information. These characteristics include amplitude, phase, and frequency. For example, Amplitude Shift Keying (ASK) modifies the amplitude of the signal as the name implies. A protocol standard chooses the amplitude modulation used to convey data from the reader to tag. From that point, the signal will need to be demodulated for the information to be extracted.

In passive UHF RFID tags, the demodulator block receives the incoming encoded radio-frequency signal and converts the shifted waveform back to baseband '1's and '0's. The components of the demodulator block depend on the modified characteristic and the system design topology.

RFID Tag Substrates

This is the layer that holds all the other components together. A substrate is usually made from a flexible material such as thin plastic but can also be made from a rigid material. Most passive tags use substrates of flexible material. The material is selected to withstand various expected environmental conditions that the tag is to encounter in its lifecycle. Some materials include polymers, PVC (polyvinyl chloride), polyesters, styrene, and paper. The material used must provide a smooth printing surface for antenna layout, durability, and stability under various conditions, dissipation of static buildup, and mechanical protection for the components and their interconnections. The substrate is designed to withstand conditions such as sunlight, chemicals, heat, moisture, vibration, impact and corrosion.

The substrate material may affect the design frequency of the antenna, which must be considered during the proper tuning of the antenna. Adhesive material designed to withstand the appropriate environmental conditions is used on one side of the substrate to attach the tag to an object. A protective overlay made from materials such as PVC lamination, epoxy resin or adhesive paper is sometimes added to provide additional protection.

RFID Tag Packaging

Inlay

An inlay or insert is a complete tag that is ready to be embedded in a label or encapsulated and consists of all the components already attached to the substrate. During this stage, adhesives are typically not yet added. Furthermore, during the production of the inlays, RFID functions are embedded into the labels by converters or label makers.

Inlays are classified as either wet or dry. Wet inlays have adhesive applied to the inlay, while dry inlays are attached without the use of an adhesive, such as by bolting the tag to the inlay.

Smart Labels

Smart labels, or labels as they are typically called, are composed of thin sheets of various materials in layers with an embedded inlay in the layers. The material used for these layers usually include the linear or carrier sheet, inlay, inlay adhesive, face stock adhesive, label material, linear release coating, and label top coat. Barcodes and textual information are typically printed on the label material.

Labels come in various sizes and different types of tags depending on the material to be tagged. They provide logistical information for shipping and handling of products and allow RFID encoding to be used in parallel to any current barcode and human readable systems. These labels are designed to provide an easy way to implement RFID systems within supply chains, particularly for companies that want both RFID and ongoing barcoding systems. This kind of packaging tends to be more affordable.

Encapsulated Tags

RFID inlays are sometimes contained inside a hard case. This case is made of materials such as PET (polyethylene terephthalate), polypropylene, and Elastomere. These cases are used to protect the tags within from harsh environments during usage, such as extreme temperatures or pressure. For example, these tags are used for containers in closed-loop systems and returnable assets in the supply chain. The size and shape of the case may be designed to provide isolation from the object so the tag may be attached to metal objects, and some case designs provide other methods of tag attachment, such as bolting or riveting.

Antennas are typically designed to work in certain environments, thus an unexpected environmental condition can affect the tag's read range or read rate. Encapsulation not only allows the tag to endure harsh environments but can also ensure desired specifications when these unwanted conditions are encountered. For example, the antenna may be weakened due to corrosive chemicals in the environment. Therefore, environmental conditions should be evaluated in any environment the tag will travel through in its entire life to ensure proper encapsulation for optimal performance and longevity.

CHAPTER-10

RFID READERS AND INFRASTRUCTURE

RFID readers are composed of an antenna and an electronics module. The antenna is used for communicating with RFID tags wirelessly. The electronics module is most often networked to the host computer through cables and relays messages between the host computer and all the tags within the antenna's read range. The electronics module also performs a number of security functions such as encryption/decryption and user authentication, and another critical function called *anti-collision*, which enables one reader to communicate with hundreds of tags simultaneously.

Figure 1 depicts a distribution center. When the shipment arrives in the unloading area, RFID readers at the doors examine its contents and update inventories accordingly. The manufacturer can be notified automatically that the shipment has been received and the pallet can quickly be routed to the appropriate delivery truck or to its proper place in the warehouse, all without the need to open packages or examine their contents.

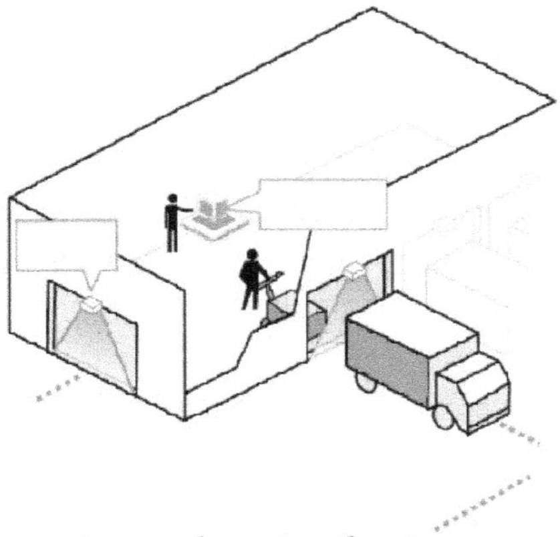

Fig. 1: The Distribution Center

RFID readers installed at the exits will automatically identify the contents of a customer's basket. Payment could be made without an employee ever having checked the basket, and, in fact, with RFID enabled payment systems, payment could be rendered without the customer even having to break stride on the way to the parking lot. All of this will ultimately lower costs for both customers and retailers.

Low-Level Reader Protocol

The Low-Level Reader Protocol (LLRP) (EPCglobal) defines a protocol to provide control of RFID air protocol operation timing and access to air protocol command parameters, and is the second generation of the Reader Protocol defined earlier. The LLRP features provide the following:

- A means to command an RFID reader to inventory tags, read tags, write to tags, and execute other protocol-dependent access commands (such as "kill" and "lock" in C1G2).
- A means for robust status reporting and error handling during tag access operations.
- A means for conveying tag passwords necessary to effect commands that may require them, such as the "kill" command in C1G2.
- A means to control the forward and reverse RF link operation to manage RF power levels and spectrum utilization, and assess RF interference, among RFID readers in a system. A means to control aspects of Tag Protocol operation, including protocol parameters and singulation parameters
- A means to facilitate the addition of support for new air protocols
- A means for the retrieval of reader device capabilities
- A means for vendors of reader devices to define vendor-specific extensions to the protocol in a manner that is noninterfering among vendors, and which, to the extent possible, is vendor-administered

While LLRP is component of the second-generation Reader Protocol, the other component will be the High-Level Reader Protocol (HLRP). Reader devices may implement HLRP, LLRP, or both. LLRP is air-protocol-aware (V1.0 is C1G2 protocol aware), whereas HLRP will be air-protocol-unaware, and will incorporate only those commands and facilities that are generic across air protocols.

RFID Infrastructure

USTRANSCOM will ensure that designated strategic CONUS and OCONUS aerial ports and seaports (including commercial ports) supporting Operation Plans (OPLANs) and military operations have RFID equipment (interrogators, write stations, tags, brackets) with read and/or write capability to meet Combatant Commander requirements for asset visibility. Military and commercial ports will be instrumented with fixed or mobile RFID capability based on volume of activity and duration of the requirement at the port. Military Departments and Combat Support Agencies will ensure sufficient RFID infrastructure and equipment (interrogators, write stations, tags, and brackets) are appropriately positioned to support Combatant Commander requirements for asset visibility. As above, military and commercial ports will be instrumented with fixed or mobile RFID capability based on volume of activity and duration of the requirement at the port.

To ensure that users take maximum advantage of inherent efficiencies provided by this technology, RFID capability will be operational at logistic nodes and integrated into existing and future logistics automated information systems. RFID recorded events will become automatic transactions of record. Geographical Combatant Commanders may direct Service Components/ Combat Support Agencies to acquire, operate, and maintain additional theater supporting RFID infrastructure to meet changing theater operations. As a general rule, an organization responsible for port or logistics node operation is also responsible for installing, operating, and maintaining appropriate RFID capability. Additionally, when responsibility for operating a specific port or node changes (e.g., aerial port operations change from strategic to operational), the losing activity is responsible for coordinating with the gaining activity to ensure RFID capability continues without interruption.

CHOOSING THE RIGHT RFID READERS

The software-defined RFID reader, from here on referred to as SDLR, was developed to solve this interoperability problem. Traditional radios use hardware circuits, fixed at the time of manufacture, to perform the high-speed signal-processing tasks that convert back and forth between user data and the radio waveform. SDLR exploits advances in components such as digital signal processors (DSPs) and field-programmable gate arrays to make the hardware generic, and move all of the waveform-specific tasks into software.

One SDLR device can support a variety of communications standards, just as one PC can run a variety of software applications. SDLR has a number of benefits in addition to improving interoperability.

SDLR has significant advantages over traditional RFID readers, that is why many Auto-ID labs are supporting its development.

Desirable characteristics include:

- Receive and transmit various modulation methods using a common set of hardware.

- Alter functionality of the system by downloading and running new software.
- Possibility of adaptively choosing an operating frequency and a mode best suite to prevailing conditions.
- Opportunity to recognize and avoid interference with other RFID readers and communication devices in a high-density reader environment.
- Elimination of analog hardware and its cost, resulting in simplification of data logging reader architectures and improved performance.
- Chance for new experimentation and development of new RFID protocols.
- Support of multiple modulation formats.
- System can be simulated Exactly.
- Flexible bandwidth selection and management.
- Ability to dynamically join or leave an ad hoc network formed by other readers in proximity.
- Ability to transmit neighbor information to other readers or a server along with a request to transmit.
- Ability to scan the status of its neighbours and respond accordingly.
- On collision with other readers, reducing its power level by a predefined factor.

Although SDLR offers benefits as outlined above, a few obstacles remain to its universal acceptance. Those include:

- Difficulty of writing software for various target systems
- Need for interfaces to digital signals and algorithms
- Poor dynamic range in some of the designs

Novel Properties of SDLR

SDLR is capable of adjusting its software to suit the particular RFID environment in use.

The following sections give an overview of two novel applications that can be used to demonstrate the advantages of integrating the software radio into an RFID reader.

Automatic Change of Modulation Scheme

In this case, the modulation scheme is determined by a packet header that identifies the modulation scheme. With proper signal processing it is possible to determine the modulation scheme used at the transmitter. A novel approach would be for an RFID reader to detect the modulation scheme of the incoming signal and then reconfigure its signal-processing stack accordingly. This powerful feature can be used to provide flexibility to readers not only in a multitag environment but also in a high-density reader environment. An FPGA device could dynamically load a new modulation scheme and become part of a new reader network without changing the hardware.

A layer in the communication stack can be used to act as a modulation detector and load the appropriate op-code into the FPGA device to demodulate the incoming signal. The modulation detection layer must perform analysis of the incoming signal to determine the modulation scheme used. This information can be added to attributes of the message block as it is passed to the next layer in the stack. The DSP, then, makes sure that the appropriate demodulation scheme is available to demodulate the incoming signal. If it does not have the appropriate demodulation scheme then, it raises an alarm, notifying the operator. Or alternatively it can send a request to the host computer asking for the latest demodulation scheme.

Choosing the Right Commercial RFID Reader for Your Business

RFID (Radio Frequency Identification) technology is becoming more and more popular in various industries due to its accuracy, efficiency, and cost-effectiveness. This technology can be used for inventory management, asset tracking, supply chain management, and many other applications. If you're planning to implement an RFID system in your business, the first thing you need to consider is choosing the right commercial RFID reader. In this guide, we'll give you five factors to consider when buying a commercial rfid reader to help you make an informed decision.

Frequency Range

RFID systems operate at different frequencies, such as low frequency (LF), high frequency (HF), and ultra-high frequency (UHF). The frequency range of the RFID reader you choose should be compatible with the frequency of the RFID tags you plan to use. For example, if you intend to use UHF tags, you should choose a UHF RFID reader. Each frequency range has its advantages and limitations, so you should choose the one that best suits your business needs.

Antenna Type

The antenna type of an RFID reader can affect its range, accuracy, and performance. There are two main antenna types, linear and circular. Linear antennas are suitable for reading tags at short distances and in a straight line. Circular antennas have a wider reading range and can read tags in different orientations. Based on your business needs and the environment you will be using the RFID reader in, you should choose the appropriate antenna type.

Reading Distance

The reading distance of an RFID reader refers to the maximum distance at which it can read the RFID tags. This range can vary depending on the antenna type, frequency range, and power output of the reader. If you need to read tags from a long distance, you should choose a reader with a higher power output and a suitable antenna type.

Connectivity

An RFID reader can have various connectivity options such as Wi-Fi, Ethernet, USB, and RS-232. The connectivity option you choose can affect how you integrate the reader with your existing systems. For example, if you have a centralized system that uses Wi-Fi, you should choose an RFID reader with Wi-Fi connectivity. If you have older systems that use RS-232, you should choose a reader with this connectivity option.

Brand and Quality

Choosing a reputable brand such as Invengo can ensure that you get a high-quality commercial RFID reader that's reliable and long-lasting. The brand you choose should also offer excellent customer support and after-sales service to address any issues you may have with the reader. You can check online reviews and ratings of different brands to find the one that best meets your business needs.

In conclusion, choosing the right commercial RFID reader is essential to ensure the success of your RFID system implementation. By considering the frequency range, antenna type, reading distance, connectivity, and brand/quality, you can select a reader that's suitable for your business needs and is capable of delivering accurate and reliable RFID data. With Invengo as your partner, you can be confident in the performance of your RFID system, ensuring your business operations run smoothly, accurately, and efficiently.

Types of Reader

Commonly on the market you can find:

- **Desktop readers:** they are set up to create a fixed ID control place.
- **Mobile readers:** they are generally used by staff to identify marked items or commit inventory counts. Mobile readers are a versatile tracking identification tool.

Reading Distance

Radio frequency identification (RFID) technology uses radiated and reflected RF power to identify and track a variety of objects. A typical RFID system consists of a reader and a tag. The RFID reader has the task of requesting and receiving information from each tag. An RFID reader contains an RF transmitter, one or more antennas and an RF receiver. The power level is the amount of RF energy emitted from an RFID reader. Read distance is related to the transmitted RF power from the reader. In layman's terms, the higher transmitted power, the higher read distance. Of course, even the kind and the size of the used tag, especially its antenna, affect the reading range.

Power Consumption

Since many readers use a battery, you make sure the reader has a good one. But how? You need to know how much energy is consumed when transmitting at full power and how it saves energy when it is at the minimum setting. There are many options available that can help preserve the battery, including a sleep mode.

RF Receiver Sensitivity

Each RFID reader has a maximum receive sensitivity indicated as a dBm value, below which it is not able to "hear" the tag response signal. This sensitivity value contributes, together with the other characteristics, to determine the quality of an RFID reader.

Communication Interfaces

RFID readers can connect to host devices (computers, smartphone, tablet,..) or networks and communicate data in various ways. The main interfaces are:

- **LAN**: uses an Ethernet cable to join a network. Once on the network, the reader can interact with programs and other connected devices;
- **Wi-Fi**: together Bluetooth, provides a cordless, flexible option for RFID solutions;
- **Bluetooth**: allows the reader to connect to a host computer while remaining wireless. Bluetooth options are generally available on mobile for connecting to smart devices like pc, phones and tablets;
- **Serial port**: RS232, TTL and USB are some of the most common serial interface for direct connection with host computer. Serial connection is optimal for simple solution with one reader and computer, with no need to use additional network functions.

Country of Operation:

There are three different frequency ranges popular all over the world:

- LF (120-145 KHz);
- HF (13,56MHz);
- UHF (860-960 MHz).

Low and high frequency RF bands are mostly standardized and used uniformly from country to country. As for UHF things get more interesting. In fact, different areas still use different frequency ranges for UHF; European Union uses 865-868 MHz, while North America sends at 902-928 MHz, and China has chosen 920.5-924.5 MHz.

Environment Conditions

Among the factors to be considered is certainly the temperature of the working environment. As a rule, most RFID readers on the market are commercialized and guaranteed to operate at certain temperature ranges. However, if the working environment is extreme, it is always a good idea to check the data sheet before purchasing the reader (What temperature range can TERTIUM readers work?). Metals and liquids can also cause problems, since metals reflect the signal emitted by the reader, while liquids absorve it. This involves interference with the communication between the tag and the reader, significantly degrading performance. Luckily now, on the market there are readers with special antennas (find out TERTIUM readers dedicated for metal) that are suitable for reading tags on metal or into a liquid. Among the type of transponders suitable to be used in these cases there are embedded tags.

User Interface

RFID readers usually offer some type of programming options for configuring the MMI (Man Machine Interfaces) like LED and beeper for feedback. These interfaces provide users a visual, aural, or both indicator of when a reader is powered and usable, and to notify after interrogation if the tag has been read or not, the battery level, and wireless interface connection status.

Make sure the reader is future proof

The ability to upgrade the reader can considerably reduce the system cost in the long run. Because you don't want to buy a new reader next year due to the current reader's obsolescence.

API

The availability of APIs (Application Programming Interface) is an important facet to consider before purchasing an RFID reader, especially before developing software, because they make application development easier and faster. So it is important to investigate, if the APIs provided fit your needs.

Compliance

The manufacturing and operation of RFID devices has been regulated by international standards. In Europe, The European Telecommunications Standards Institute better known as ETSI, sets the standards for the European Union for all Information and Communication Technologies which includes RFID. ETSI's standards ensure that compliant devices will be both safe and won't interfere with other radio communication, e.g. broadcasting or emergency services. In U.S, the Federal Communications Commission or the FCC, is the governing body that oversees these standards for the United States in accordance with the Federal Communications Act.

DESIGNING AND INSTALLING RFID INFRASTRUCTURE

The concept of Auto Identification has been a major concern in the past century. People and objects were traveling all over the globe without any means of security taken, thus the prospect of Auto Identification become more and more demanded.

Various types of identification procedures have been created, these procedures became a major element in our life, and it is seen every where, in stores, malls, airports, etc. Some of the most important and widely spread Auto Identification (Auto ID) techniques that are being used nowadays are Barcode Systems, Smart Cards and Radio Frequency Identification (RFID).

RFID is an Auto ID procedure that is similar to smart cards and was created to replace barcodes. RFID is a technology that enables the electronic labeling and wireless identification of an object using digital communication. RFID tags can hold up to 32 Mega Bytes of data making the information more difficult to counterfeit than barcodes, they offer the possibility for reading, writing, transmitting, storing and updating information. Theses benefits were considered a major advantage over barcodes along with the huge capacity of storing information that the RFID tags offer in comparison to the barcode tags.

Information is exchanged over radio waves where no contact or line of sight is needed for the identification process. This makes RFID more secured since readers could be designed to locate tags in a distance of several meters where no other Auto ID technology can offer this kind of distant identification. Over the past five years the information technology industry has seen a surge towards development of an affordable RFID tag. These developments have lead to larger reading ranges, more memory capacity and faster processing of radio frequency operating systems.

Today RFID tags can be found almost everywhere they were embedded in money, pasted on food cans and even implanted in the human body. RFID technique is characterized by the following features:

Support for non-static data as an RFID tag data can be rewritten many times. An RFID reader does not need a line of sight to read an RFID tag's data. Also An RFID tag can have a much longer read range than other Identification techniques. Depending on several factors, this can range from several meters to a few hundred of meters. It is also characterized by larger data capacity and multiple reads, where a suitable reader can read several RFID tags within a very short period of time, automatically, using a feature called anti-collision. Finally RFID can be programmed in order to perform intelligent tasks besides simply being a data carrier and transporter.

The design and implementation of the hardware and software system related to the RFID are well performed and synchronized. The final system results are satisfactory and data was transferred successfully between the three RFID system components, the computer, the RFID reader and Tag, and radio frequency identification was realized.

RFID System Design

A full system design for an RFID system will be presented with the design algorithms and electronics circuits. The hardware design and a complete analysis of the software application and the programs for both Tag and Reader will be explained . The electronic circuits as well as the program flow charts concerning the reader and tag circuits will be designed and implemented in order to produce a complete RFID system.

The block diagram of the RFID system is given in Fig. 2

While the block diagrams of the Reader and Tag devices are given in Fig. 3 and figure 4 respectively.

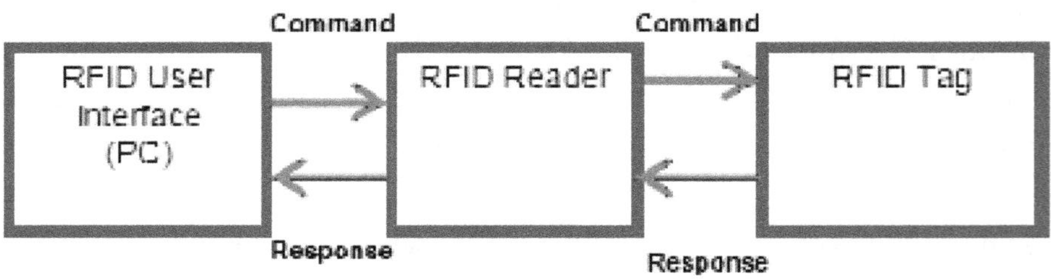

Fig. 2 The block diagram of the RFID system

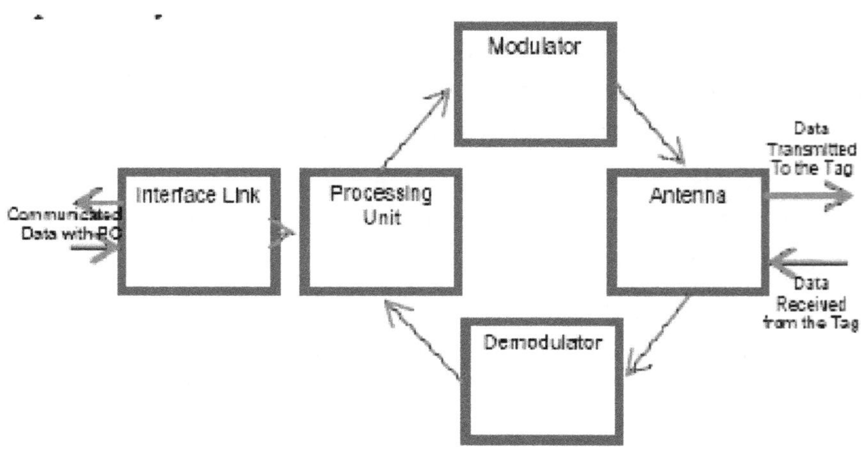

Fig. 3 The block diagram of the RFID Reader

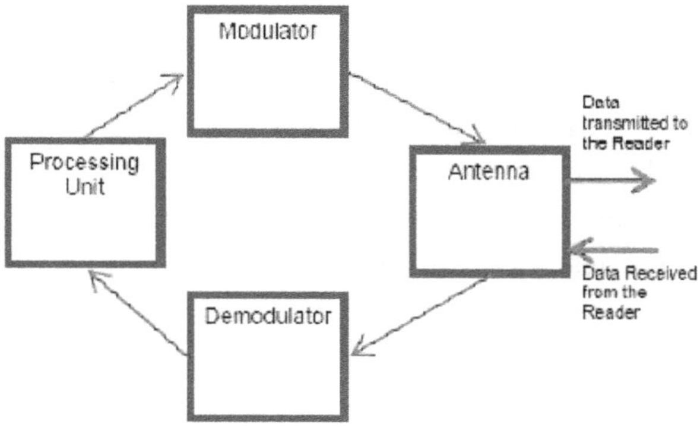

Fig. 4 The block diagram of the RFID Tag

Hardware Design

In this section there will be a full system analysis for the RFID system circuits. First there will be a design explanation for both the modulator and the demodulator being the most important part of an RFID system. The simplest form of an RFID system was taken as a design basis for the device. The RFID system is based on the sequential procedure (SEQ) with no voltage induction. This means that the Reader and the Tag work on independent power supplies.

The Modulator

The modulation technique used in this RFID system is FSK modulation. This method of modulation is widely used nowadays in various systems and therefore is easy to implement. The modulator works on two discrete frequencies that were chosen to create a carrier signal as close as possible to the widely used HF carrier of 13.56 MHz. The two carrier frequencies are 14 MHz and 6 MHz. the modulator block diagram is shown in Fig. 5.

The digital signal is inverted using an (7406) inverter, this is to invert the signal so as the zeros (spaces) will also be modulated and then sent the mixer.

The first mixers level shown in Fig. 5 is replaced by an analog switch, a (CD4016) to be precise. This switch has a switching response of 40 MHz which is far beyond the need of this design, The digital signal works as the switching trigger, for example if a “1” is sent from the microcontroller to the switch it will be modulated by the first carrier signal as the analog switch will turn on and pass the signal. However, in the second switch the signal is inverted thus becoming a “0” keeping the switch off so as not to pass the second carriers signal. The third mixer is used for merging both signals obtained from the analog switch, one for the (1’s) and the other for the (0’s). This technique was used as the analog switch is bi-directional which means that same pins that are used to input a signal can be used to fetch one.

RF Amplifier Circuits

In RF devices power amplifiers are crucial; they are mostly used to raise the voltage level of an RF signal to a desired level and to provide impedance matching between the modulator circuit and external antenna. These amplifier circuits were used in the demodulator circuit shown later in this section. Thus a two stage direct coupled amplifier was designed to raise the voltage of the VCXO to 5Vp-p, and act as a buffer circuit for this oscillator. This amplifier is shown in Fig. 6 above.

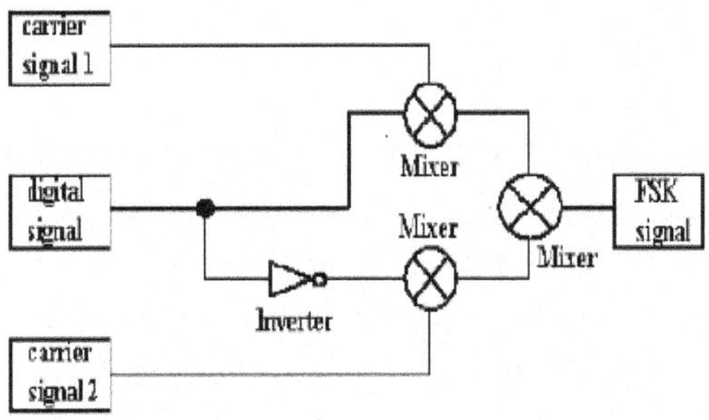

Fig. 5 FSK modulator block diagram

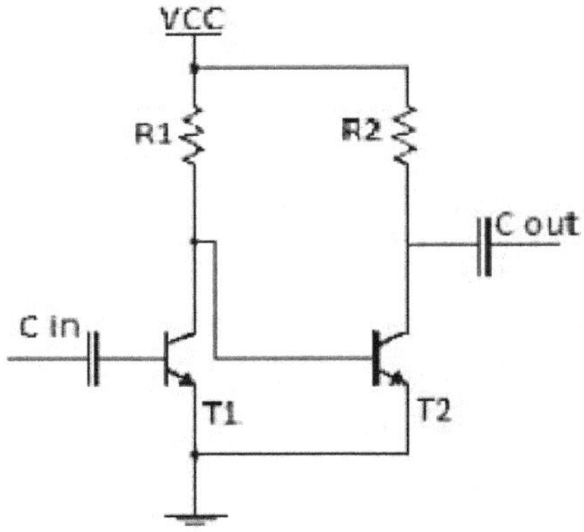

Fig. 6 Direct Coupled Amplifier

The digital signal voltage was raised to a 10VDC which was needed to control the analog switch, which is realized using the same design. Although they were not used to amplify any signal but two BJT gates were used to merge the two RF signals coming out of the analog switch. Such a circuit is designed in order to prevent the signal from going back into the analog switch and creating noise, as it is mentioned earlier that the analog switch is a bidirectional device. Such a circuit is shown in Fig. 7.

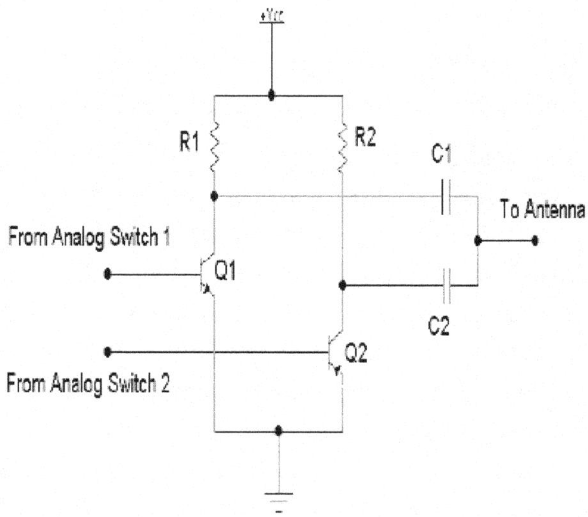

Fig. 7 The two BJT gates used to combine the two modulated signals

The Demodulator Circuit

The demodulator part of the RFID system was designed using two basic elements, passive High Pass Filter and envelope detector followed by voltage level shifter, as shown in Fig. 8.

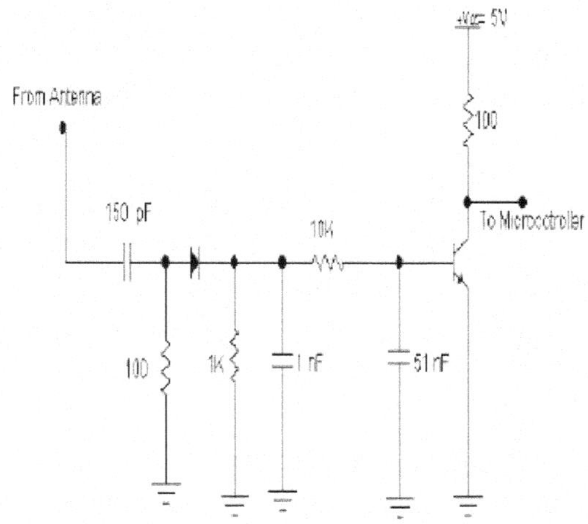

Fig. 8 Demodulator circuit with level shifter

Choosing the size and type of antenna circuit depends on the system design topology. For the RFID system a parallel resonant circuit antenna is designed, it consist of a multi turn coil in parallel with variable capacitance a parallel resonant circuit results in maximum impedance at the resonance frequency. Therefore, maximum voltage is available at the resonance frequency.

Technology basics

A passive tag harvests the energy it needs from an electromagnetic field created by the reader. As illustrated in Figure 9, the reader feeds the "antenna" (really more of a coil than a conventional antenna) an oscillating signal – thanks to Maxwell's Laws that field couples to the tag's antenna (again a coil). The signal is rectified and charges a small capacitor which powers the tag.

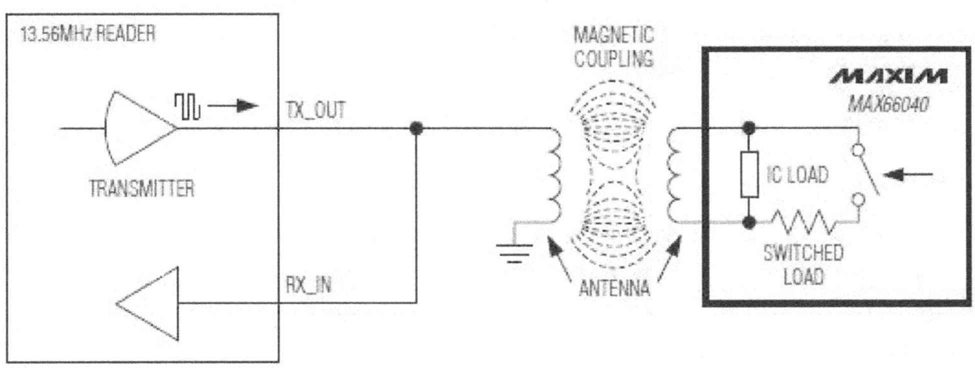

Fig. 9: Typical arrangement between reader and tag

Tags are usually dead – totally unpowered and not in any sort of sleep mode unless interacting with a reader. When the reader initiates a data exchange it first drives the antenna for, typically, 15 to 50 msec. That excites the resonant circuit on the tag and charges the capacitor.

Data is exchanged using backscatter modulation. As the tag switches a load on and off, the reader's antenna experiences a change in voltage. Think of the two coupled antennas as a transformer: drop a load on the secondary and that affects the primary winding.

Either frequency-shift or phase-shift keying it used, and on 13.56 MHz devices two or more subcarriers may be employed. The details are surprisingly complex for such low-cost devices, but happily they are completely managed by the tag and reader ICs; the design engineer will not be exposed to those aspects.

Antennas

A critical part of designing the reader is creating an antenna which will most efficiently carry a signal to/from the tag. While commercial antennas can be used, they are expensive. It is common to build one using PCB tracks to form a loop.

The range of a tag is influenced by:

- The size of a tag's antenna. The larger the tag's antenna the stronger the response and the better the tag can be detected above the background noise.
- The size of the reader's antenna. A larger reader antenna increases the read range, but in a noisy environment it may have a worse signal-to-noise ratio and cause the reading distance to go down.
- The orientation of antenna.
- The match of the LC formed by the antenna and stray (or intended) capacitances.
- Environmental noise. The tag has to have a 6 dB stronger signal so that the reader can distinguish it from the background noise. As noise increases the tag has to move closer and closer to the reader's antenna to be detected.
- The antenna's Q factor. Generally a Q between 30 and 40 is needed.

Readers

A reader can be a pretty complex device depending on its intended application. One might just simply push data from RFID tags to another computer for inventory management; another may require a display and keyboard with a wireless connection to an accounting computer.

All modern RFID reader ICs take care of the entire RF front-end (excepting the antenna) and handle all of the modulation and message passing. The IC's interface is entirely digital using a conventional parallel or serial bus.

Texas Instruments' TRF7970ARHBT, whose block diagram is shown in Figure 10, is a typical reader IC.

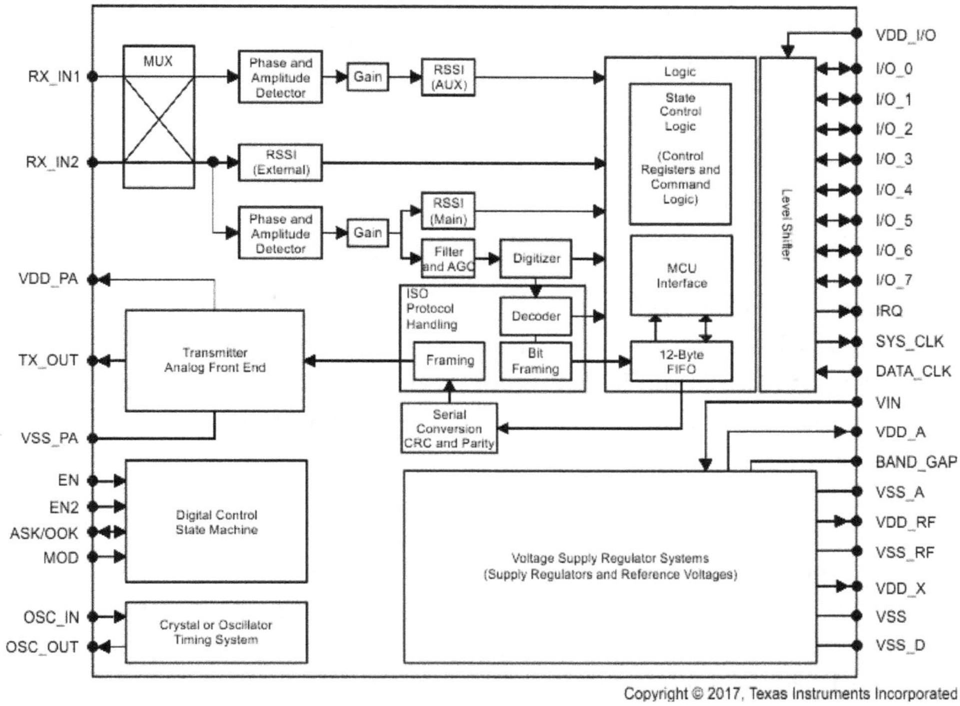

Fig. 10: Texas Instruments TRF7970ARHBT block diagram

Unlike some other devices, the TRF7979ARHBT does provide access to analog/ RF front end (via digital command sets) letting the user create custom, non-standard, communications protocols.

The part includes signal strength measurements as well as a programmable power level to the RF front-end. An application can use these features to communicate at low power to maximize battery life in portable applications, but it can dynamically boost the RF levels if the tag's signal is weak.

That brings up an important point. The power level into the antenna of a reader is highly dependent on supply voltage. In the case of this part, a five volt supply supports levels up to 200 mW; at three volts that is reduced to 70 mW, shortening the reader's range.

NXP Semiconductor's HTRC11001T is another reader IC. At 14 pins it is smaller than the previously-mentioned Texas Instrument's part, as well as cheaper; the pin-count reduction is driven in part by the use of an SPI interface to the rest of the system.

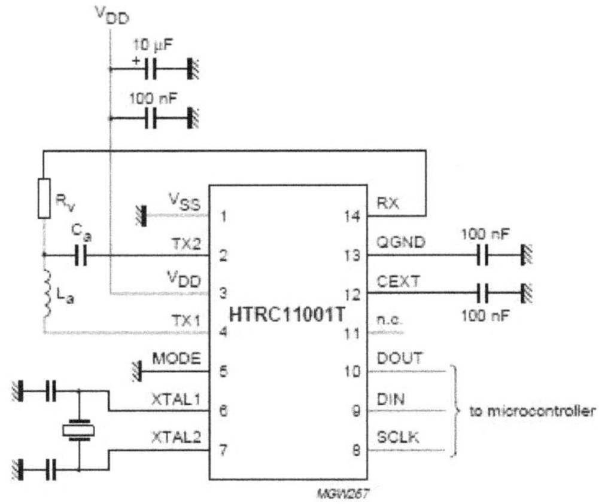

Fig. 11 shows a typical application.

Like many of these devices, it will automatically detect a short-circuited or open antenna. It is checked every cycle of a transmission; it is up to the code in the processor that is controlling it to shut down transmission to keep the device from failing. Idle and power-down modes can drop quiescent current to under 20 µA. This is a very simple device to use.

Tags

Tags are most often used as simple data storage devices. The reader extracts a tag's unique ID to track packages and the like. Or it could write information (in a read/write tag, of course). The EZ-Path® toll transponders are sometimes used this way; authorities can have the toll booth write where a car entered a highway to compute tariffs based on distance traveled. All tags used just for data storage come as assembled units rather than as ICs. An example is the cylindrical glass unit described earlier.

The critical specification for any tag is the memory size. Read-only devices typically can store a 64- or 80-bit unique number that is written by the factory. Read/write versions will have anywhere from 256 bits of user-memory up to tens of thousands of bytes.

Read/write transponders will always have a command set used to control store and read data. Generally the command set is very simple: read, write, and announce your ID. Some include a kill, which causes the tag to go inactive forever as a security precaution.

TI has an entire line of "inlays" – tags that are complete with an antenna on a flexible sheet of plastic. The Tag-it™ series has several hundred different devices with varying physical configurations (round, square and rectangular) and memory of 256 or 2 kbits. An example is Texas Instruments' RI-I16-114A-S1, a circular unit as shown in Fig. 12.

But there is another use for RFID transponders. Consider a tire pressure monitor. Though the IC is the reader half of the system, there is also a tag in each wheel. This is an example of an application where the tag IC is tied to a microprocessor that reads a sensor. A typical block diagram for this sort of application is shown in Fig. 13.

But wait! What powers the CPU?

The RF field does. Figure 13 shows Texas Instruments' TMS37157 transponder IC supplying power to the attached controller. This part can be used in battery-powered systems, of course, but it has a V_{BAT} output that sends power harvested from the field to the MCU. Not much is available – no more than 16 mA, and then only in a strong field. Also the processor will be dead when there is no active reader nearby, so the code has to deal with a sudden wake up and just as quick death; RAM contents will be lost. But the TMS37157 has 121 bytes of EEPROM in which the CPU can store state data.

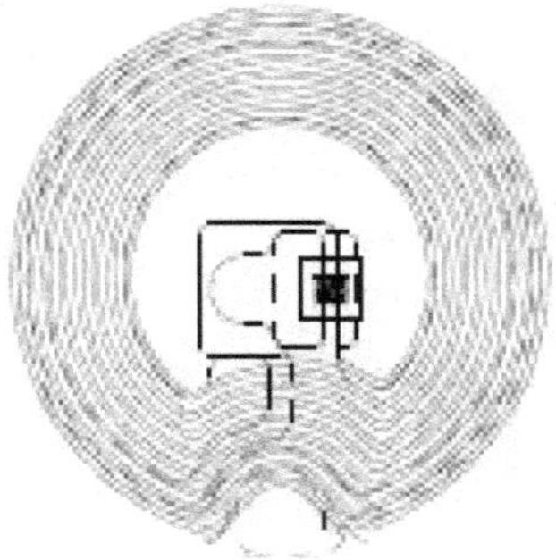

Fig 12: One member of Texas Instruments' Tag-it family

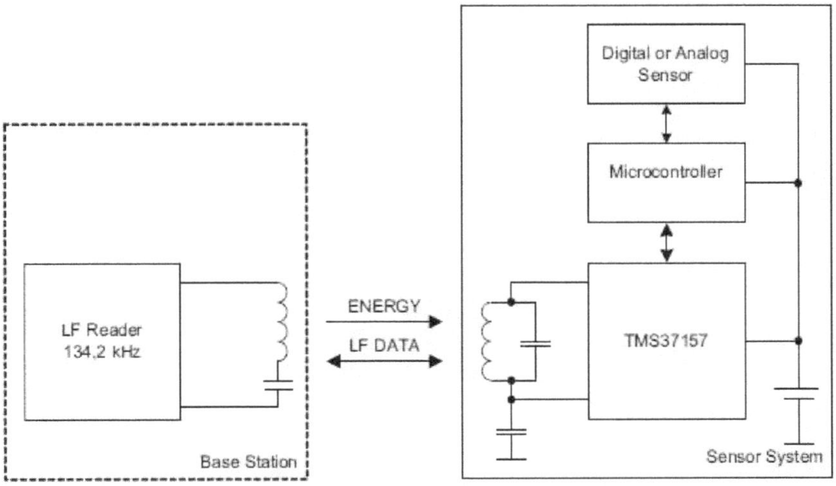

Figure 13: A tag that talks to a local microprocessor

STMicroelectronics sells transponder ICs but calls them EEPROMs. An example is the M24LR16E-R, which is sort of a hermaphrodite. It can be used as a conventional RFID tag, but it also has an I²C output that connects to a processor; in the latter mode it will need power from a battery or other source. Its 2 KB of memory can be password-protected in 512 byte blocks.

Development support

Most vendors have development kits and boards to support prototyping. Texas Instruments' TRF7970A evaluation module, shown in Fig. 14, lets the user experiment with all of the TRF7970A's commands.

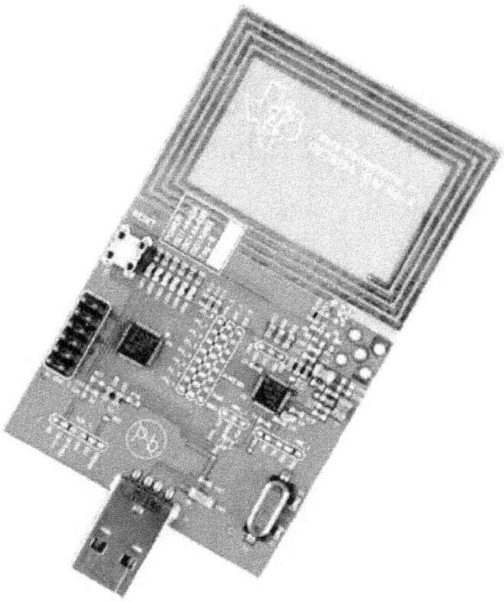

Fig. 14: TRF7970A evaluation module

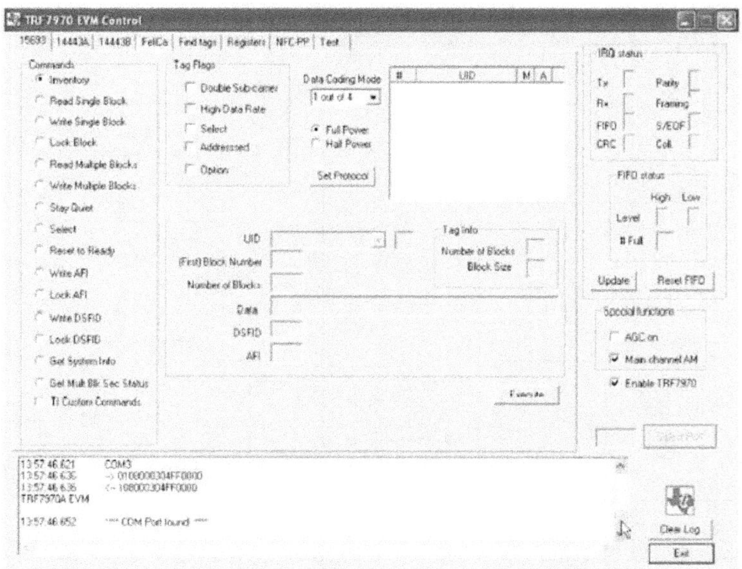

Fig. 15: TRF7970A GUI.

It connects to the PC via USB and has a custom GUI to control the board, as shown in Figure 15.

For low-volume products, readers are available as subassemblies. Texas Instruments' RI-RFM-003 is a reasonably-priced module that communicates with a host computer using a proprietary interface (Fig. 16).

DLP Design makes a similar reader, the DFP-RFID1 which communicates via USB (see Figure 17).

Fig. 16: Texas Instruments' RI-RFM-003C

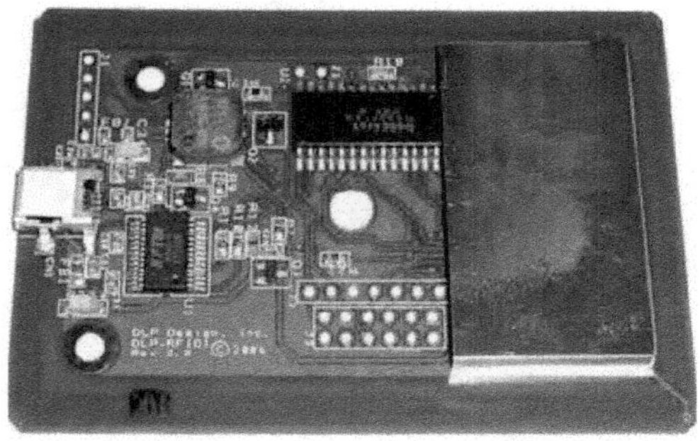

Figure 17: DLP Design's DLP-RFID1 reader

CHAPTER-11

DATA SECURITY AND PRIVACY IN RFID

INTRODUCTION

Radio Frequency Identification, also known as RFID, is a technology that was created by Léon Theremin in1945 and later patented by Mario Cardullo in 1973. It was first developed by Léon Theremin as a spy device for the Soviet Union government. The device itself could transmit a sound within a radiowave. The device itself was an early example of RFID technology, even though it worked as a passive spy device and not as an ID.

Radio Frequency Identification (RFID) is a new technology for automated object identification. An RFID tag is an electronic device that consists of an antenna and an inexpensive chip, often smaller than a grain of rice, that can be read from distance by a nearby reader. This device is typically attached to an object and upon request it can return information related to the tagged item, such as product characteristics, date of manufacture, date of purchase, and so on.

RFID tags can be passive or active. Passive or semiactive tags get their power directly from the signal broadcasted by a reader. This ability to draw power from a nearby reader is what makes passive tags attractive; they do not need batteries, so they can be smaller and cheaper opening a new way of interesting applications. Active tags, on the other hand, have their own power source but are typically more expensive and are used only in specialized applications.

Tags, of the "passive" variety, are often envisioned as a next-generation bar-code technology, automating inventory procedures, thus cutting costs for manufacturers and retailers. Their two most important characteristics are small size, which allows them to be implanted within objects, and their ability to be read inside boxes, pallets, etc. which does not require line-of-sight. Passive tags are consequently less expensive and offer an unlimited operational lifetime. The tradeoff is that they have shorter read ranges and memory capable of holding a very small amount of information

Despite these limitations, however, RFID tagged items can have remarkable applications. One can imagine a future where passive RFID tags are in every humanmade object and even in some natural ones (such are animals or even people). This would allow better tracking of items in complex automated chains and revolutionize distribution networks, thus permitting goods to be traced from manufacturers to retail stores. This may help companies combat theft or improve management of stock and inventories in shops or warehouses (many industries and government agencies in the US, including the Department of Defense, already mandate the use of RFID tags by all of their suppliers.

To see how this new technology can be (ab)used, under today's bar-code technology, an ABC wrist watch sold in Athens has the same bar-code as a watch sold in Paris. With RFID, however, each watch carries a unique identification number which could be tied to a particular person, the buyer of that watch. The person could then be tracked if he/she ever entered the same store, or if they entered any other store with an RFID reader at the premises. Eventually, the reader may be able to identify that wrist watch, the time and date it was bought, where it was bought, and how frequently one visits a particular store.

RFID PIA (Privacy and Impact Assessment) process aims to reach several objectives:

- To favor "privacy by design" by helping data controllers to address privacy and data protection before a product or service is deployed,
- To help data controllers to address privacy and data protection risks in a comprehensive manner, an opportunity to reduce legal uncertainty and avoid loss of trust from consumers,
- To help data controllers and data protection authorities to gain more insight into the privacy and data protection aspects of RFID applications.

The industry has proposed a RFID PIA framework which classifies a RFID application into 4 possible levels:

- **Level 0:** applications that do not process personal data and where tags are only manipulated by users, and which are rightly excluded from conducting a PIA.
- **Level 1:** applications where no personal data is processed, yet tags are carried by individuals.
- **Level 2:** applications which process personal data but where tags themselves do not contain personal data.

- **Level 3:** applications where tags contain personal data.

If the RFID application level is determined to be 1 or above, the RFID operator is required to conduct a four part analysis of the application, with a level of detail that is proportionate to identified privacy and data protection implications. The first part is used to describe the RFID application. The second part allows highlighting control and security measures. The third part addresses user information and rights. The final part of the proposed PIA framework requires the RFID operator to conclude whether or not the RFID application is ready for deployment. As a result of the PIA process, the RFID operator will produce a PIA report that will be made available to the competent authority.

For the industry, only levels 2 and 3 are to be submitted to a PIA because it considers that information contained in a level 0 tag are not personal. However level 1 rises concerns of Article 29 Working Party because tagged items carried by a person contain unique identifiers that could be read remotely. In turn, these unique identifiers could be used to recognize that particular person who will be tracked by a third party without her knowledge. When a unique (or multiple identifiers) is associated to a person, it falls in the definition of personal data set forth in Directive 95/46/EC, regardless of the fact that the "social identity" (name, address, etc.) of the person remains unknown (i.e. she is "identifiable" but not necessarily "identified").

Additionally, the unique number contained in a tag can also serve as a means to remotely identify items carried by a person, which in turn may reveal information about social status, health, or more. Even in those cases where a tag contains solely a number that is unique within a particular context and without additional personal data, care must be taken to address potential privacy and security issues if this tag is going to be carried by persons.

The Working Party has urged the industry to fully address this issue, by clearly mentioning it as part of a revised risk assessment approach for level 1.

RFID tags come in a wide variety of shapes and sizes. While some tags are easy to spot, others can be very small (the μ-chip by Hitachi measures 0.4 mm including the antenna) or they can be embedded inside boxes, clothes, etc. and thus be invisible to the human eye. Since tags can be interrogated by hidden readers, the data transmitted by the tag may provide identification and/or location information as well as specifics about the tagged product, such as price, color, date of purchase, etc.

This threat to privacy is magnified further by the fact that readers can scan multiple tags at the same time. This means that if a person enters an area carrying several tagged items, it takes just one RFID reader to collect the information emitted by all the tags! This information can then be used in numerous ways. For one, retailers can use RFID readers to build complete profiles and target specific individuals. For another, even if tag responses do not make sense because they are encrypted, a collection of fixed identifiers may still help identify the whereabouts of a person by matching these identifiers either through some form of payment that reveals the person's identity (e.g. credit card) or through a snapshot taken by a hidden camera.

Although our focus here is personal privacy, RFID tags can also pose a threat to corporate security because many different entities can read the tags. For example, competitors can remotely gather confidential supply chain data or more frighteningly deny this information to the company by performing radio frequency jamming attacks. For a more complete list of threats, the authors offer a taxonomy of attacks across the different stages of a typical industrial supply chain. Finally, several interesting books (other than the current one) have already been published: which is dedicated to RFID security and privacy that focuses on consumer privacy violations.

Thus incorporating security to RFID technology is not only in the interest of individuals but companies as well. In the remainder of this section, we will list in more details the various threat and security requirements we expect from secure RFID protocols and then present an overview of existing privacy enhancing techniques.

SECURITY MEASURES IN RFID SYSTEMS

Radio-Frequency Identification (RFID) tags were initially developed as very small electronic hardware components having as their main function to broadcast a unique identifying number upon request. The simplest types of RFID tags are passive devices that not have an internal power source and are incapable of autonomous activity. They are powered by the reader's radio waves, with their antenna doubling as a source of inductive power.

While admittedly a new technology, the low-cost and high convenience value of RFID tags gives them the potential for massive deployment, for business automation applications and as smart, mass-market, embedded devices that support ubiquitous applications. However, current RFID protocols are designed to optimize performance, with lesser attention paid to resilience and security. Consequently, most RFID systems are inherently insecure. In this paper, we discuss four common types of RFID tag attacks that are particularly threatening.

Unauthorized tag disabling. These are Denial-of-Service (DoS) attacks in which an attacker causes RFID tags to assume a state from which they can no longer function properly. This results in the tags becoming either temporarily or permanently incapacitated. Such attacks are often exacerbated by the mobile nature of the tags, allowing them to be manipulated at a distance by covert readers.

Tag disabling can be a serious threat to the integrity of automated inventory and shipping applications. Any RFID system vulnerable to such attacks could become a serious organizational weakness. Consider for instance the use of RFIDs to prevent shoplifting; in this case, the disabling activity might be performed covertly, avoiding detection through secondary mechanisms such as monitoring by cameras. If RFIDs are being used for automated inventory and/or shipping, it could again be a target of sabotage by competitors, paramilitary organizations (in the case of military shipments), militant activists, and/or terrorists.

Unauthorized tag cloning. These are integrity attacks in which an attacker succeeds in capturing a tag's identifying information. Again these attacks are exacerbated by the fact that the tags can be manipulated by rogue readers. The ability to create clones of tags can be used as a means to overcome counterfeit protection (e.g., in passports and drug labels) and as a preparatory step in a (largescale) theft scheme. Again, it exposes corporations to new vulnerabilities if RFIDs are used to automate verification steps to streamline security procedures.

Unauthorized tag tracking. These are privacy attacks in which the attacker can trace tags through rogue readers. We distinguish these attacks from "Big Brother" concerns that corporate entities managing the back-end server might leverage RFID capabilities to infringe on the privacy of consumers. An analysis of consumer privacy concerns, addressing policies, standards, and checks to protect consumer interests. In this paper we concentrate instead on the prospect of rogue readers, controlled by hackers or adversarial organizations, being used to monitor tags. This issue is more difficult to address, since hackers cannot be presumed to adhere to policies or standards, or to follow specified protocols.

Replay attacks. These are integrity attacks in which the attacker uses a tag's response to a rogue reader's challenge to impersonate the tag. The main concern here is in the context of RFIDs being used as contactless identification cards (in substitution of magnetic swipe cards) to provide access to secured areas and/or resources. In such applications, RFIDs can be more vulnerable than other mechanisms, again due to their ability to be read at a distance by covert readers.

Security issues

- *spoofing:* Spoofing is when a fake tag takes unlawful advantage of valid tag by pretending as the valid tag.Tag cloning is a form of spoofing attack that takes the data from a valid tag and duplicates it into another tag.
- *Man in the middle attack:* An attacker can obstruct the communication between the RFID tag and the RFID reader and manipulate or change the information before it reaches the intended device.

- *Snooping:* Snooping takes place when a tag is being scanned by the approved RFID reader, an attacker blocks the data with any compliant reader for the right tag frequency. Due to tag memory capability and cost limits, most RFID systems use pure text messages. This makes snooping simple and effective way for the attackers to get data which is kept in the transponder.
- *Denial of services:* The purpose of Denial of Service (DOS) is not to leak or modify data but to hinder or weaken the RFID systems so that it cannot be used. This can be done by flooding the Radio Frequency channels with noise to disturb the messages being sent. The attacker might also conduct a focused energy attack to destroy the tags.
- *Physical attacks:* Physical attacks include manual removal of RFID tags from the tagged goods and destructing or washing out the stored information by radiation imprinting, circuit disruption etc.
- *Trace-ability:* An RFID reader at a place could track RFID tagged clothes, bank notes etc. carried by individuals passing by. Compiling data from numerous tag readers could trace the movement, social exchanges and financial transactions etc. of that person. This violates a person's location privacy.
- *Industrial Espionage:* Logistics and inventory data hold substantial monetary worth for commercial companies and their competitors. A company's tagged goods inventory may be examined by a competitor by conducting secret scans. By compiling the changes over time, competitor would be able to get sales data, rate of inventory turnover, shopping patterns of consumers and other inventory movement routine.
- *Side channel analysis:* This analysis is based on the difference in power consumption when the RFID tag receives incorrect or correct password. Attackers analyze this change in power consumption to crack the password.

Countermeasures

The disabling attack. In a disabling attack the attacker causes tags to assume a state from which they can no longer be identified by the back-end server. One way to prevent this is by having each tag share with the server a permanent (non-erasable) private identifying key k_{tag} (another way, which is however not suitable for low-cost tags, would be to use publickey cryptography). Then, when a tag is challenged by a reader, it will generate a response using this private key. Of course, it should be hard for an attacker to extract the private key from the tag's response. For this purpose a cryptographic one-way function should be used. This solution relies heavily on the assumption that the server is trusted and physically secured.

- *The cloning attack.* To defeat cloning attacks it should not be possible for an attacker to access a tag's identifying data. Such data should be kept private. However for authentication, it should be possible for the back-end server to verify a tag's response. The response must therefore corroborate (but not reveal!) the tag's identifying data. This can be achieved by having the server share a private key k_{tag} with each tag, as in the previous case.
- *The tracking attack.* Unauthorized tracking is based on tracing a tag responses to a particular tag. This can be prevented by making certain that the values of the responses appear to an attacker as random, uniformly distributed. In fact, since we are assuming that all entities of an RFID system have polynomially bounded resources, it is sufficient for these values to be pseudo-random.
- *Replay attacks.* To deal with replay attacks the tag's response must be unique for every server challenge. To achieve this, the values of the server challenges and the tag responses must be unpredictable. One way to achieve this is to enforce that the answers be (cryptographically) pseudo-random.

Non-Cryptographic counter measures

This measure does not include any cryptographic function. These measures are:

Destroy the tag measure: In order to protect consumer privacy, the best measure is to destroy the RFID tag before they goods are placed in the hands of customers. This can be done by detaching the antenna or short circuiting the tag coil. A tag with Auto-ID feature destroys itself upon getting a unique 8-bit password from the reader.

Selective Blocker Tag: Blocker tags create all its IDs from particular zone of ID standards and protect the specific zone from malicious readers.

Re-writable Memory: In this type of RFID tags, each tag is equipped with ROM and a re-writable RAM. A unique and permanent ID is set for the tag in the ROM by the manufacturer. In RAM, a temporary code is set by the holder of the RFID tag, The ROM mode offers unrestricted identification of items for any number of users and through RAM mode, the constraint of item identity to limited user is attained.

Cryptographic Measures

In these measures, data encryption, secret codes etc. are used to secure the RFID tags and its information from being leaked or modified. They are

Hash based entry regulator: This concept involves locking and unlocking the transponder to permit access. For this measure to function, the tag should invoke the hash function and manage keys at the back-end. The tag only reveals its stored information when the reader sends the correct key matching to the meta-ID.

Randomized Access Control: Randomized access control is a measure to improve traceability. Tags, besides having the hash feature, they also have a random digit generator. The tags works in a locked or unlocked state. An unlocked tag can be easily locked using simple instruction from the RFID reader. A tag answers to the RFID readers request by producing a random number, and then interpret its ID connected with and sending both the data to the RFID reader. A genuine RFID reader recognizes one of its tags by carrying out a search of its own IDs, interpreting each of them with the connected until it finds the match. This method is practical for owners of comparatively lesser number of tags.

XOR based One-Time Pad: Exclusive OR or XOR method. This technique only needs an XOR evaluation and therefore can be implemented at a very low cost. In this method, the RFID reader and the RFID tag shares the same list of random keys and they confirm that both has the same list in few exchanges. When the evaluation passes, the tag sends its ID. This technique involves several exchanges between the RFID reader and tag.

ADDRESSING PRIVACY CONCERNS

Data Protection and Privacy

In terms of data protection and privacy, RFID technology raises some concerns as it can be used to track and monitor the movement of individuals without their knowledge.

RFID technology cannot be easily switched off or logged off like other technologies, which can raise concerns about privacy and unauthorized access. One of the main concerns is that RFID tags can be read remotely, without the knowledge or consent of the individual or organization being tracked. This can make it difficult for individuals or organizations to control who has access to their information and how it is used.

Additionally, RFID technology can be vulnerable to hacking and other forms of unauthorized access, which can compromise the security of sensitive data. For example, an unauthorized person with the right equipment could potentially read the information stored on an RFID tag from a distance, or even alter the information stored on the tag.

RFID tags, particularly passive RFID tags, have limited memory and processing capabilities, which can make it difficult to implement encryption. Passive RFID tags rely on the energy from the reader to power the tag and communicate with the reader, which limits the amount of data that can be stored and processed on the tag.

PIA framework for RFID

A privacy impact assessment (PIA) enables organizations to anticipate and address likely data protection impacts of proposed initiatives and foresee problems. This process reflects measures taken to protect privacy of individuals about whom sensitive data are kept and addresses legal obligation to use appropriate security measures. Systems should be designed to avoid unnecessary privacy intrusion and with privacy-by-design features implemented to reduce possibility or effects of a security incident.

Individuals responsible for data protection (including their processing service provider) should be identified in the security policy. These documents identify roles, individual responsibilities, incident handling and reporting practices that have been put in place to protect personal data and their processing with appropriate technical and organizational measures to ensure, that at all times, integrity, confidentiality and availability of personal/sensitive data.

The PIA Framework for RFID of January 12, 2011 explains key concepts, internal procedures and classification criteria for RFID applications. For these criteria the PIA Framework provides a two phases approach. The initial analysis phase is used to determine if a PIA of RFID application is required. The decision, to which level an application belongs, has to be made after working through a decision tree where level 1 implies a small scale PIA while levels 2 and 3 require a full scale PIA. If an application is designed according to level 0 which means that no private data are concerned, there is no privacy threat given and further documentation is not needed. Level 2 applications may have controls to protect back-end data while level 3 applications may have controls to protect both back-end data and tag data. For level 1 applications, required controls and corresponding documentation in the PIA report are simplified.

The objective of the risk assessment phase is to document how risks are proactively mitigated through technical and organizational controls. The PIA process requires any RFID application operator to:

- Describe the RFID application;
- Identify and list how the RFID application under review could threaten privacy and estimate the magnitude and likelihood of those risks;
- Document current and proposed technical and organizational controls to mitigate identified risks;
- Document the resolution (results of the analysis) regarding the application.

The risk assessment requires evaluating the applicable risks from a privacy perspective. The RFID operator should consider:

- The significance of a risk and the likelihood of its occurrence.
- The magnitude of the impact should the risk occur.

The resulting risk level can then be classified as low, medium or high. A prime risk is that RFID tags could be used for profiling and/or tracking of individuals. In this case RFID tag's information – in particular its identifier(s) – would be used to re-identify a particular individual. Retailers who pass RFID tags on to customers without automatically deactivating or removing them at checkout *may* unintentionally enable this risk. A key question, though, is whether this risk is likely and actually materializes into an *undismissable* risk or not.

According to recommendation, retailers should deactivate or remove at the point of sale, tags used in their application unless consumers, after being informed of the policy in accordance with this framework, give their consent to keep tags operational. Retailers are not required to deactivate or remove tags if the PIA report concludes that tags that are used in a retail application and would remain operational after the point of sale do not represent a likely threat to privacy or protection of personal data.

The RFID operator should use categories below to indicate privacy and data protection implications of the RFID application:

- **Ready for deployment:** the RFID application as described provides for suitable practices, controls, and accountability.
- **Not ready for deployment:** the RFID application is not approved for operations in its current state. A specific corrective action plan has to be developed, and a new privacy impact assessment has to be performed and documented to determine if the application has reached an approvable state.

The PIA Framework provides only a generic scheme for the PIA and has to be complemented by more detailed schemes like roles, security targets, classes and templates reflecting the special aspects of industry-specific and individual applications.

Technical guidelines as templates for PIA

The approach of the European Commission suggests using so-called templates as extensions to the Framework document in order to reach the level of detail that is necessary to conduct a complete application-specific Privacy Impact Assessment. Such templates are specific to an application area and should provide a detailed guidance for the creation of a PIA report. This puts the "Technical Guidelines for the Secure Use of RFID" (TG RFID) into perspective which have been issued by Germany's Federal Office for Information Security (BSI).

The BSI launched this project which aims at providing technical recommendations for RFID systems that ensure secure implementations and protection of personal data but nevertheless support RFID operators' and service providers' business needs. The BSI achieved a consensus between supporters and critics. TG RFID are accepted by relevant parties and are now available for application areas: public transport, event ticketing, NFC-ticketing, retail & logistics and employee cards. First implementations proved practicality and viability of this approach.

A major goal of development for the TG RFID is to find a consensus and to gain acceptance of all relevant stakeholders. Therefore the BSI installed an intense review and alignment process and invited experts and relevant stakeholders from specific application area to participate. Representatives of RFID operators, service providers, customers, Data Protection Agencies (DPAs) and also critics of RFID have had the opportunity to comment early versions of the document and take part in review and alignment sessions. In this process, security goals, potential threats, security measures and especially remaining risks were identified, discussed and described.

This process provided information on potential impact and risks of RFID applications and generated transparency that is necessary to build trust and acceptance. So far Technical Guidelines for five application areas have been created. In all cases a consensus including acceptance from participating DPAs was achieved.

Unfortunately, TG RFID for logistics and retail have not been piloted so far, because progress with RFID in this sector is far behind former projections by retail stakeholders. RFID tags are actually mostly used on pallets and cartons. Products in supermarkets shelves are still only marked with traditional bar codes or with GS1 data bar, except cases like Gillette razors. Whereas in the sectors of ticketing, NFC (13.56MHz) and employee cards (125 kHz HID) a great progress with RFID is on its way.

TG RFID provide patterns for application specific templates which can be efficiently set up as required by PIA Framework.

Stakeholders of an application have individual and sometimes diverging requirements for a technical guideline. Data Protection Agencies (DPAs) want to protect data and privacy of citizens, customers and employees. TG RFID address their objectives by a detailed description of all relevant threats, appropriate safeguards and potentially remaining risks. Operators are focused on their business objectives. Their intention is on practicality, acceptance of their customers and a cost efficient and future proof solution. Balance between objectives of both parties is achieved by a scalable definition of safeguards. Minor threats are mitigated by simple, low-cost safeguards. Strong and costly controls are only applied in case of high protection demand and severe threats. This approach makes sure that cost of security measures and impact on usability are reduced to what is necessary.

Interoperability is an imperative for RFID implementations. Operators need to cooperate with business partners and customers want to use services from multiple service providers and across borders. This requires standardized and interoperable technical interfaces and security measures. In addition, comparability of security levels is of major importance. Operators can only cooperate if they can trust partner's system implementation. This includes a certain level of data protection, privacy and as well information security and safety. TG RFID support these fundamental requirements by two dedicated features:

- TG RFID include not only an assessment of privacy and data protection. In addition, a risk analysis and documentation of information security and safety is provided. The latter is mandatory to cover business requirements of operators.
- Risk assessment methodology and documentation of results comply with worldwide standard ISO27005. This makes it easy to compare PIA and security assessment reports of different implementations and systems.

Operators will refrain from investing in RFID applications if they can't determine the cost of security measures and their potential impact on services and usability. Both aspects have major influence on the overall business case. TG RFID define appropriate technical safeguards for specific scenarios of an application. This information builds a solid base for cost calculations and tenders. This feature of TG RFID counters a major roadblock for introduction of RFID.

The European Commission has identified lacking confidence in legal situation for RFID-implementations as one major roadblock for the broad adoption of RFID. Use of TG RFID is not mandatory in a legal sense. Nevertheless they will provide a solid basis for legal judgments of RFID applications because they are accepted by all stakeholders and represent the current state-of-the-art for implementations of RFID.

Description of structure and security methodology of TG RFID

TG RFID are created for specific application areas and consist of three major parts: description of the application area, assessments and recommendations. A detailed but generic description of all service and business models of an application area is given in the first part.

This is the foundation for assessments and recommendations and covers role models, services, products, business processes, use cases and any other information that may be relevant for security and privacy assessments. In order to ensure practicality and usability for all service providers and operators, this part is done in close cooperation and alignment with experts from the application domain.

The assessment part is based on description of application area and specific security targets. It covers all three domains of information security: security, privacy and safety. Security targets are defined and aligned with all stakeholders. Methodology of risk assessment is compliant with ISO 27005. Results of assessment are a list of relevant threats, appropriate safeguards that can mitigate these threats and a description of remaining risks.

The third part of guidelines document provides recommendations on how to implement a RFID-system in an appropriate way. Based on example scenarios from the application domain it is shown how findings of risk assessment are transformed into specific safeguards that should be applied to the relevant system components. This provides a clear and economically viable guidance for the design of system.

Organizations must be able to demonstrate that they have implemented a data protection management system (DPMS) using appropriate technology (PETs) and operational protective measures (OPMs) to protect personal data. PIAs incorporate tests of PETS and OPMs to prove data protection principles are met by the system. All personnel within the organization have a responsibility to ensure that they take steps to safeguard security of information that they are entrusted with and to use OPMs and PETs as established policy.

OASIS Privacy Management Reference Model (PMRM)

OASIS Privacy Management Reference Model (PMRM) Technical committee aims at achieving a standard-based framework that will help business process engineers, IT analysts, architects, and developers implement privacy and security policies in their operations. PMRM picks up where broad privacy policies leave off. Most policies describe fair information practices and principles but offer little insight into actual implementation. PMRM provides a guideline or template for developing operational solutions to privacy issues. It also serves as an analytical tool for assessing the completeness of proposed solutions and as the basis for establishing categories and groupings of privacy management controls.

This model is based on a service-based approach, describing them in three categories:

- **Core policy services :** agreements (with options and permissions), control (with policies and data management),
- **Presentation and lifecycle services:** interaction (manages data/ preferences/notice), agent (software that carries out processes), usage (data use, aggregation, anonymization), access (individual review/updates to personal information),

- **Privacy assurance services :** certification (credentials, trusted processes), audit (independent, verifiable accountability), validation (checks accuracy of personal information), enforcement (including redress for violations)

Personal information is stored in a container accessed by an agent (at entry point) for specific processing which must abide to privacy rules (referred to as agreement and control procedures). Assurance service guarantees conformity to these rules which can be a simple validation or a certification, leading eventually to an audit and an enforcement procedure.

Each use case invokes a sequence of service calls. Each service call executes a sequence of functions: define (operational requirements), select (input, process, and output) data and parameters, input (data and parameter values in accordance with select), process (data and parameter values within functions), output (data, parameter values and actions), link to other services, secure with appropriate security functions.

Open identity exchange trust framework

In the context of digital identity systems, a trust framework is a certification program that enables a party who accepts a digital identity credential (called the relying party) to trust the identity, security, and privacy policies of the party who issues the credential (called the identity service provider) and vice versa. In the Open Identity Trust Framework (OITF) model, an open identity trust framework provider can administer any trust framework that meets: 1) the principles of openness, and 2) any additional requirements imposed by the Trust Framework Provider (TFP).

The rules of every trust framework are defined for a particular set of participants in online (and possibly offline) interactions. The Open Identity Trust Framework Model defines six standard trust framework roles (in addition to the trust framework provider role played by OIX):

- Users
- Identity service providers
- Relying parties
- Assessors
- Auditors
- Dispute resolution service providers
- In addition, OIX has defined a seventh role, special assessor, which is an assessor responsible for assessing the qualifications of other assessors.

As defined in the Open Identity Trust Framework Model, a level of assurance (LOA) is a unit of measure for the degree of confidence a relying party can have in assertions for an identity credential from an identity provider. A level of protection (LOP) is a unit of measure for the degree of confidence: a) an identity provider can have in the protection provided by a relying party for the identity information disclosed in an identity credential, or b) a user can have in the protection provided by an identity provider and/or a relying party for the identity information disclosed in an identity credential.

Technical profiles

A technical profile is a specification of requirements for use of a specific technology, RFID in our case, in order to achieve technical interoperability in exchange of digital identity credentials that is consistent with associated LOA or LOP. Once an OIX trust framework is accepted for listing in the OIX Listing Service, participants may apply for certification.

For RFID open identity trust technical profile, four main functions have to be taken into consideration to provide appropriate tools for agents: anonymization and pseudonymization facilities, attributes management tools, identity management tools, security management tools.

Tag Privacy Protection Via Moisture-Dependent Contact and Other Sensors

Idea

Inclusion of RFID tags in clothing has been proposed as a means to support activities such as supply chain and retailer product management. However, including RFID tags in clothing raises privacy concerns to those that wear such garments. To enhance the privacy of users in this situation, a modified tag is proposed. The tag operates normally prior to sale. At the point of sale, the tag is disabled, e.g., by burning a ROM component or wire, which can be done by applying a large amount of power to the tag at the point of sale reader/terminal. Note that we do not completely kill the tag but rather disable its RF interface. Once in the disabled state, the tag can still function but only if enough conducting moisture is present.

This can be done by means of a switch (put in a strategic location such as the tag's antenna) that can only make electric contact if conducting liquid is present. Therefore, the tag is effectively disabled in the street (as long as it stays dry) and can be finally re-enabled when the washing machine pumps water onto the clothes. One may worry that tag readout is hampered by large volumes of water absorbing RF radiation. However, studies have shown that this is not a problem. In particular, it is well known that at low frequencies (in the 10–20 MHz range) water is transparent to an RF signal.

At higher frequencies, the attenuation is significant and it is highly frequency dependent. For example, the study shows that the attenuation of the signal traveling a distance of 6 cm varies between 7 and 23.5 dB for frequencies between 100 and 950 MHz. Note, however, that there are solutions starting to appear that can perform well in the presence of water and metals at high frequencies.

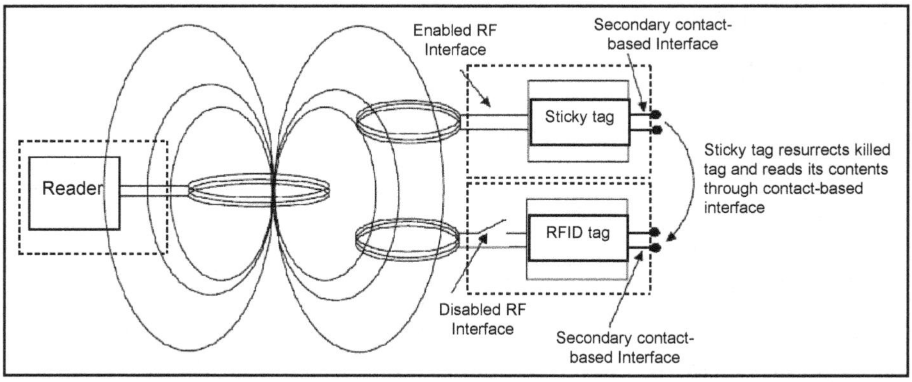

Fig. 1 Sticky tag in the presence of a reader with a secondary contact-based interface

Finally, for the particular case of an RFID-tag operating in the 13.56-MHz band, a weakening of the signal by 10 dB is deemed acceptable. It can be shown experimentally that at frequencies around 10 MHz the RF signal penetrates 25 cm into salty liquid, which is more than sufficient for the washing machine example.

Discussion

In addition to supporting activities such as supply chain and retailer product management, RFID tags associated with clothing items could also support other applications such as smart washing machines. Smart washing machines could be equipped with an RFID reader, which allows the machine to access clothing information. Therefore, the machine could autonomously select a washing program based on that information or it could advise the user to remove an item that needs a different washing program via an alarm.

A second example of a sensor used to enhance privacy is a temperature sensor for a smart refrigerator application. In this setting, RFID tags could be allowed to be read-only in certain temperature ranges. Thus, when the groceries are in the refrigerator at a certain temperature range, the RFID tags associated with the groceries would be readable and otherwise not. Such an RFID tag would enable applications as diverse as checking whether a product has been at the correct temperature during the whole supply chain or placing an automatic order when the user has run out of certain food items. On the other hand, one can argue that whenever the temperature outside was also in the range of the refrigerator temperature, the RFID tag would be allowed to transmit and thus, the user would be traceable.

However, the ability that an attacker has to trace someone would be highly dependent on weather conditions and not on the attacker's choice. This diminishes the attacker's tracing abilities or forces him to change environmental conditions around his target. In this case, security is also highly dependent on how close the attacker can get to his target and stay there for extended periods of time. Clearly the closer the attacker is to his target, the easier it is for him to be discovered but also the more successful he will be in cheating the system. Finally, note that a single sensor will probably not be applicable to all scenarios, with the possible exception of the light sensor.

For example, a humidity sensor might be suitable for clothing but not for electronic items, and similarly temperature sensors might work well with food but not with clothing. Light sensors, on the other hand, seem to allow a wide range of applications.

Sticky Tags and Privacy

Current privacy preserving solutions for RFID are such that they either add cost to the tag by including additional hardware to perform cryptographic functions or require the modification of current tag specifications to perform additional operations. On the other hand, the most widely available (standardized) solution for privacy concerns is the kill command that permanently disables the tag.

This solves the privacy problem but it gives up the advantages that RFID tags can provide in other applications. Thus, the idea proposed in this section can be seen as middle ground between the two extremes of rendering tags completely useless with the kill command or having additional costs added to current RFID tags. It can also be seen as yet another instantiation (with different properties and characteristics) of a privacy sentinel or watchdog tag.

Idea

The basic idea is to allow the kill command to completely disable the RF functionality of the RFID tag but to allow access to the information in the tag via a second interface, which requires proximity to the tag. This second interface could take different forms. The simplest instantiation of the second interface would be a contact-based interface. In this case, proximity means "as close as it is physically possible," i.e., touching the disabled tag. We emphasize that adding a contact interface to an RFID tag is not new.

However, to the authors' knowledge the idea that a second interface can be used in combination with a second (more powerful) tag to "resurrect" the functionality of the killed tag and guarantee privacy (and security) for the user is novel. Note that the resurrecting functionality is different from the resurrecting duckling security policy of Stajano and Anderson, where a node in an ad hoc network establishes a secure channel after being "resurrected" by an adjacent node. A second possibility is a modified antenna system which upon receiving the kill command changes its configuration. For example, the read-range could be limited by the kill command to 1 mm.

By a modified antenna system, we mean both an antenna which changes its range or simply a system consisting of two antennas. The first antenna has a normal range and it gets disabled upon the tag receiving the kill command whereas the second antenna has a very short range and it is not affected by the kill command. Note that this instantiation might succumb to relay attacks.

The second interface can then be used by another device, presumably a more powerful RFID tag both in terms of computational power and security, to access the data in the original RFID tag and communicate in a secure manner with RFID readers. We will refer to this device in what follows as a sticky tag to illustrate the fact that we expect such devices to be implemented as a sticky label that adheres to objects whose original RFID tags have been killed. "Sticking" our new more powerful tag on the less powerful tag has the effect of "resurrecting" the tag.

Figure 1 depicts an illustration of the system. In particular, a standard reader powers up both antennas, the sticky tag's antenna and the original RFID tag's antenna. Since the RFID tag's antenna has been disabled, only if the sticky tag is present will the reader obtain a response from the RFID tag. Note that the sticky tag acts as a bridge between the disabled RFID tag and the RFID reader.

As such, the sticky tag, when queried, forwards the information residing in the original RFID tag to the reader. Also the sticky tag must not have an identifier (e.g., EPC) of its own. In addition, the sticky tags do not necessarily have to be more powerful devices. A sticky tag could simply be a much cheaper device without memory or functionality other than reviving the killed RF interface of the original tag. This instantiation would have the advantage of extremely low cost. Finally, an added advantage of sticky tags is that they could be used to resurrect RFID tags with a defective RF interface.

Discussion

As usual, at check-out the RFID tag is disabled. However, by attaching a sticky tag to the killed tag now the user is able to take advantage of the information stored in the killed tag just as if the tag in the object had never been killed. This has the added advantage that the identifier is transmitted to the readers in a secure manner (if the sticky tag is equipped with cryptographic functionality) or in a more secure environment, since it is the user that decides where and when to resurrect the killed tag. The sticky tag is also envisioned to be reusable, i.e., users could have a bag of such sticky tags and attach them to objects whose RFID tags have been killed.

Once the object's usable life has expired, the user could simply detach the tag and store it for future use after discarding the object. The manufacturer who would also like to check an object's information once the object is in the recycling phase, could similarly resurrect the originally embedded RFID tag by using a sticky tag as well. A final usage case is the scenario in which a user returns a product to the shop because of regular maintenance, repair, or malfunction. In this case, the shop can use a sticky tag to read the product information available in the original tag associated with the object. Admittedly, a main issue with the sticky tags is usability.

Can we expect that users will tag their groceries so that they can make use of their smart refrigerator? Note that owning a smart appliance implies that the user has an interest in using the intelligence features in the refrigerator, otherwise he would not have bought it in the first place. In addition, attaching a sticky tag both at home and at the repair shop scenarios does not need to be a cumbersome activity. It could be similar to the customary practice of detaching antitheft tags at clothing stores once an item has been sold or to adding a pricing tag to an item as it had been done for years (and in some places it is still done) before the widespread adoption of bar codes. On the other hand, a main advantage of the sticky tags is that they are an opt-in solution. By default, we are safeguarding individual's privacy and if they desire they can regain many of the advantages that RFID offers. Sticky tags would be best suited to objects that are meant for home use once they have bought (e.g., groceries, TVs, DVD players, etc.). Similarly, using sticky tags for clothing for example, would imply that the user needs to remember to detach the sticky tag from his clothing before going out. Otherwise, he could risk traceability. This seems a burden not likely to be accepted by most people.

PART IV: RFID SYSTEM MANAGEMENT

CHAPTER-12

RFID DATA CAPTURE AND PROCESSING

RFID belongs to a group of technologies referred to as Automatic Identification and Data Capture (AIDC). AIDC methods automatically identify objects, collect data about them, and enter those data directly into computer systems with little or no human intervention. RFID methods utilize radio waves to accomplish this. At a simple level, RFID systems consist of three components: an RFID tag or smart label, an RFID reader, and an antenna. RFID tags contain an integrated circuit and an antenna, which are used to transmit data to the RFID reader (also called an interrogator). The reader then converts the radio waves to a more usable form of data. Information collected from the tags is then transferred through a communications interface to a host computer system, where the data can be stored in a database and analyzed at a later time.

Think of RFID as the next generation or an "enhanced" bar code. Like bar codes, it is an essential element of an enterprise mobility system, offering even greater access to information across your systems. With RFID, data capture takes a quantum leap forward, with much higher information capacity, non-contact information transmission, and always-on identification with limited or no human intervention. It takes capturing, moving, and managing information to the next level, and it allows companies to:

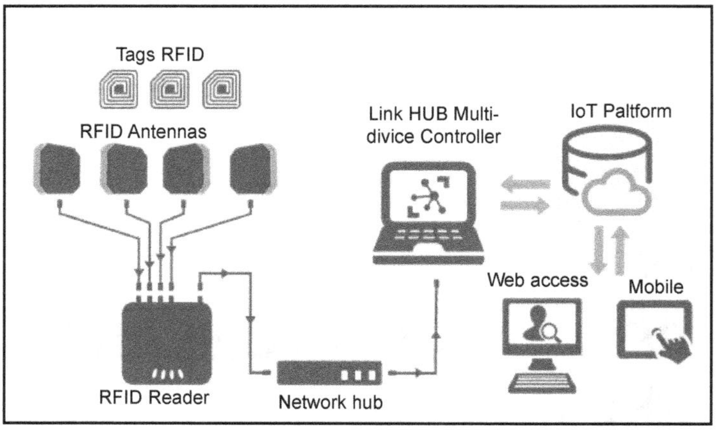

Fig. 1. Automatic Identification and Data Capture

- Increase visibility into their supply chain operations
- Increased visibility of asset status and location
- Reduce errors and labor costs through increased automation
- Increased utilization — improvements in asset visibility and utilization reduce the need to purchase or lease spare parts and equipment
- Increase speed and accuracy of item counting
- Reduced asset loss
- Validated deliveries and pick-ups at customer locations
- Automated, instant data entry without hand counts, manual tabulations or reporting
- Deliver powerful insights into traffic patterns
- Increase customer service, satisfaction and loyalty
- RFID technology is a natural fit for some applications offering incremental benefits and works in a complementary fashion or partners with bar codes in others. Although RFID tags and bar codes provide similar data capture functionality, there are several differences:

RFID tags

The tag, also known as the transponder, is at the heart of any RFID system. Two types of tags and their variants - active and passive - dominate the marketplace and are designed for specific applications. Active tags are battery-powered with onboard battery power sources, contain up to hundreds of kilobytes of memory, and can communicate data over longer ranges than passive tags. The tags are always on and always talking.

Fig. 2. RFID tags

Active tags, mainly because of the built-in batteries, are far more expensive than passive tags. Active tags have been used for years and are typically used in long-range tracking applications to track high-value inventory.

Companies managing their supply chains primarily focus on passive UHF RFID tags. Because of their low cost and relatively long read ranges (up to 25 feet), these passive tags offer the best performance/value ratio across the supply chain.

Passive tags communicate with readers leveraging backscatter technology and are "beam powered," meaning they derive all of their operational power from the RF environment. The RFID reader generates a radio signal and broadcasts it via the connected antenna configured in a radio frequency (RF) field. A tag with an onboard antenna senses the radio signal and is energized, releasing its preprogrammed data and reflecting it to the reader via a modulated radio signal. The reader then decodes the reflected signal, aggregates the data, and passes the data to the host system. It all happens in an instant.

Readers and Antennas

There are various types of readers, including mobile handheld devices, fixed-mounted readers, and vehicle-mounted readers — and form-factor variations. The environment, application, and a customer's supply chain requirements will determine the reader's choice. Choosing the best reader for the job will optimize performance, and it is not a one-tool-fits-all equation.

Fig. 3. Readers and Antennas

A reader that is right for a high-speed conveyor in a factory might not be the best tool for a chilly, 1.2 million square foot warehouse densely filled with RFID-tagged cartons and pallets.

A fixed reader would more likely be deployed for applications at the dock door, such as shipping/ receiving, or aligned along a conveyor belt as part of a work-in-process application.

Handheld RFID readers are typically used where the most flexibility is required. For example, exception processing, stock picking, price audits, or price changes are typical applications for a handheld RFID reader. A handheld makes sense when it is more convenient to bring the reader to the item. Multi-protocol readers provide the capability to read Gen 2 tags. Advanced RFID readers will provide a firmware upgrade capability to Gen 2 and be dense-reader mode certified by EPCglobal.

Read ranges between tags and readers vary, and the user should look for readers that offer longer read ranges, higher yield quality, and flexible orientation. A reader offering a more industrial design is better prepared to face the challenges of actual-world use; in addition, look for readers that offer multi-reader modes, particularly dense reader modes, if the work environment is operating a large number of readers in a small area.

Readers are also offered as reader systems or packaged systems that deploy readers in multiple form factors, including portal systems, conveyor systems, and vehicle-mounted (e.g., forklift) readers. Packaged systems provide turnkey solutions which are designed for rapid enterprise deployment. Point product solution offerings are characteristic of early market technology. For RFID to reach broad, mainstream deployment, RFID solution vendors must offer packaged solutions to minimize the deployment complexity.

Software Platform

SmartX HUB is a next-generation RFID software platform for data collection.

It is a cloud-based asset tracking platform that leverages various AIDC technologies for data collection and analysis. The technologies include RFID, Barcodes, and more. SmartX HUB improves asset tracking and eliminates manual entry errors using RFID or Barcode technologies. It keeps track of your assets' complete life cycle (Receiving to Consumed / Disposed of), including scheduled maintenance or repair.

Fig. 4 Software Platform

LinkHUB is at the heart of the platform, an RFID Middleware software component that includes extensive reader management and enterprise-grade integration capabilities. In conjunction, there is a business suite of software applications to solve everyday business needs with vertical-based workflows, reporting, analytical and dashboard capabilities.

REAL-TIME DATA CAPTURE AND PROCESSING

Multi-agent based RFID Middleware (MARM) is designed using the concept of Agent Oriented Software Engineering (AOSE) which is a new paradigm in software engineering and currently being practiced in a wide variety of applications. The main motivation behind designing MARM was to design a middleware for processing and managing data produced by RFID systems for an asset management application used by Central University of Technology (CUT) in South Africa. MARM uses SMURF for smoothing the unreliable data captured by RFID readers and a temporal data to facilitate application event processing. MARM architecture was implemented using PASSI methodology, which is one of the AOSE methodologies for designing and developing MAS (Multi Agent Systems).

The architecture is divided mainly in three layers which are device management layer, data management layer and interface layer. The client applications at the interface level specify the data they wish to receive and the kind of data they want to be reported by communicating with the data management agents such as ECReport-Request manager and ECReportSpec Manager respectively. Data management agents in turn communicate with the appropriate reader agents in the device layer, collect the raw data, process it, generate the requested reports and send them all back to the client application.

Two ontology class diagrams have been modeled to achieve the objective of successful and timely coordination among agents, one of them is Domain Ontology Description (DOD) and the other is Communication Ontology Description (COD). DOD describes the ontology of middleware design by representing predicates of the domain and some agent actions. COD describes the ontology about the knowledge of agents and the association between the communicating agents. MARM is designed to provide not only the functionalities such as data capturing, smoothing and event processing but also the processing of application level events within the middleware.

Accada

Accada which has been renamed Fosstrak is an open source RFID platform. Its implementation is based on EPCglobal Network Specifications. Fosstrak is developed after an extensive research work done at ETH Zurich. It provides an RFID infrastructure to the RFID Community benefiting the researchers and application developers with the implementation of lowlevel message bindings with EPC Network components. This fosters the use of EPC Network and availability of modifiable software components according to their requirements rather developing them from scratch.

Fosstrak platform consists of three modules: reader, filtering and collection middleware, and EPC Information Services (EPCIS). Reader module performs filtering, synchronous/asynchronous data dissemination as specified in EPCglobal reader protocol and reader management. It can be used in three different modes. In the first mode it wraps a proprietary RFID reader protocol and runs on a separate server. In the second mode, Fosstrak reader is used in simulation mode in which it will make use of its built in simulated RFID readers belonging to different vendors. This can be handy especially in the case no physical RFID reader is available. In the third mode, Fosstrak reader implementation is deployed on the RFID reader itself to provide data filtering and dissemination capabilities. Once the readers capture the relevant tag data, they notify the Fosstrak filtering and collection middleware, which combines the data arriving from different readers in a report that is sent to the subscribed applications according to a predetermined schedule.

The interface between filtering and collection middleware and a host application is based on EPCglobal Application Level Events (ALE) specification [14]. Since it also provides the aggregation functionality, it can omit the redundant read events from different readers originating from the same location. EPC Information Services (EPCIS) is a component responsible for receiving the RFID data from the filtering and collection middleware, translating them into business events and making them available to the application.

It comprises of three different modules: EPCIS repository, EPCIS capture module which receives the RFID data and EPCIS query module which provides the facility to retrieve events from the repository. The current Fosstrak implementation does not provide persistence for RFID data in the filtering and collection middleware module and it provides limited support for proprietary reader protocols.

WinRFID

WinRFID is an RFID middleware, designed and developed at The University of California, United States. Its architecture is based on five layers: RFID hardware layer, protocol layer, Data processing layer, XML framework, and Data presentation layer. The RFID hardware layer handles the deployment, configuration and communication related issues with readers, tags and the I/O module of its readers. There are three components in this layer: reader, tag and I/O. The protocol layer abstracts the most common readertag protocols such as ISO 15693, ICode, EPC Class 0 and EPC Class 1.

It runs a protocol engine whose responsibility is to parse and process the tagged data in the raw format as per any of the standard protocols mentioned earlier. The data processing layer implements the rules to process the raw data coming from the protocol layer by ways of removing the duplicate reads and verifying the tag reads.

Any abnormality at this layer is handled through different forms of alerts such as emails, messages and user defined triggers.

The clean and formatted tag data then gets forwarded to the xml framework layer to be presented in xml format to pave the way for this data to be used by variety of different enterprise applications as well as warehouse management and supply chain management systems.

The data presentation layer is an application layer which uses the data supplied from the xml framework layer for visualization and decision making. WinRFID is designed using the .NET Framework which facilitates adding functionality to the applications by means of runtime plug-ins. To reap this benefit, WinRFID has an adaptable rule engine therefore end users can easily add their own rules by way of plug-ins.

Hybrid Middleware

Hybrid middleware is a middleware based on group communication in peer-to-peer (P2P) networks. It is purely designed for an electronic parking management system (EPMS) in a University campus. Hybrid middleware architecture consists of overlay groups of peer nodes such as peer group membership manager, group communication coordinator, parking event manager and service connectors. Group membership management such as create or destroy or change group membership is handled by the group membership manager node. The group communication coordinator node ensures the affective and timely coordination among the member nodes so that any change in the parking status gets detected with minimum delay. Forwarding all parking events to the database service is the job of the parking event manager node. Service connectors perform the management control of individual nodes. Hybrid middleware is currently designed to handle two type of parking events: ENTERING and LEAVING which occur when a vehicle enters the parking slot and when it leaves the parking slot respectively.

RF^{2}ID

RF^{2}ID (Reliable Framework for Radio Frequency Identification) is designed and implemented with the aspiration of providing a middleware with traits such as reliability, load balancing, high throughput, scalability and data organization. The architecture of the middleware is built on the concept of virtual reader (VR) and virtual path (VP). Each VR is associated with a set of physical RFID readers (PR) in its geographical region. The main responsibilities of each VR are the following: filtering the data coming from the connected PRs and from other VRs, timestamping the data, virtual path management and query management. Virtual Paths (VPs) are logical channels dynamically created by VRs in order to provide functionalities like high scale reliability of the data, efficient query responses and load balancing among the readers.

LIT Middleware

Logistics Information Technology (LIT) is a middleware addressing both application needs and the constraints of RFID technology. It is designed using the concepts of Application Level Events (ALE) and EPC Information Services (EPCIS) proposed by EPCglobal. ALE software architecture of the middleware consists of four layers: Application Abstraction, State-based Execution, Continuous Query and Reader Abstraction Layers. In order to achieve high performance the state-based execution model has been used in this architecture. The EPCIS software architecture consists of three layers: Query Service Layer, Repository Layer and Capturing Service Layer. The Data Source Access Component at the repository layer has been designed to provide persistence and connections to different databases such as Oracle, MS SQL Server, and MySQL etc.

REFiLL

REFiLL is a light weight filtering and collection middleware platform based on EPCglobal network architecture. It is designed as a programmable environment, which provides flexibility to the developers of RFID applications in the presence of heterogeneous hardware platforms and anecdotal requirements. REFiLL is positioned between the reader virtualization layer and the Application Level Events (ALE). REFiLL engine comprises of filters and output managers. Filters are used to receive input from the readers or other filters. Each filter has the following attributes: input ports, out put ports and event processors. Filters are defined and interconnected with the help of editable XML-based markup files which are then compiled into java code to provide the functionality of collection and filtration of RFID events. Output managers provide the functionality of receiving the processed data from the filters and abstractions to the output systems such as RDBMS, Files, Sockets and Web Services.

DATA FILTERING AND VALIDATION

Overview of RFID Data Filtering Techniques

Sliding Windows Technique

The main objective of this approach is reducing the noisy readings. Researchers proposed a sliding window technique. This method uses the FIFO queue “win-buffer" to solve the problem and store the data. The win-buffer holds the sliding windows. Win-Buffer contains two main parameters before adding the incoming tag queue to it. It includes win-size and time that is described in the model of [t1, t1+win-size], after a period T, the model will become [t1+T, t1+win-size+T].

RFID reader reads the data rows that have entered into the sliding windows queue with a count Threshold of EPC values to reduce noise. If the count of readings with the same tag EPC value is equal to or bigger than the threshold, then the EPC value is not noise. It continues to be forwarded to further processing. Otherwise, the reading is ignored. They used two parameters: win-size of a sliding time and threshold to detection the noise.

The RFID reader uses three parameters: header id, tag id, timestamp. Every parameter has a particular task, the tag id refers to the EPC of tag, and header id refers to EPC of the reader and timestamp. In their algorithm, it is possible to consider the pair of keys (header id, tag id) for reading. It uses multiple readers to observe same tags by tag id.

Merge Baseline Technique

RFID system used a network sensor for reading and transferring data. The reader, can read the data from time to another via the network several times. Researchers proposed the algorithm that has been named Marge Baseline. The goal of this algorithm is deleting or minimizing the redundancies. It is noted that the algorithm has one parameter: max-distance.

The reader compares between the current and previous readings. If a reading is within max-distance in time, have the same key, then the reading is found as a duplicate. The algorithm presented in compares between the tag id key that exists in the winbuffer queue and the same id tag key that is existing in the incoming queue.

If nothing is found, that means, not duplicate has been found, and it is output as a new reading, and then the reader has added the data from incoming queue to the win-buffer queue. Otherwise, the reader deletes the id tag and his data from income queue and adds the rest of the tags to the win-buffer queue.

De-noising Technique

The de-noising technique has been implemented for processing and detection of noisy readings. The technique works under two conditions. The first condition is checking for every reading from the tag. If the reading is not found in the list, then add the reading to the list and store detection time: the initial and latest time of reading the tag. The second condition is calculating the number of repeated readings of the tag in the RFID reader. If the count of repeated readings is greater than or equal a count-threshold and time length of repeat reading the tag is less than or equal timethreshold, then reading is correct. Otherwise, the reading is noise.

Multiple Readers Filtering Technique

This Technique addresses one of the false readings problems which occurs by of misreading between the reader and Tags. There is a lot of reasons for this problem such as jamming signals, pressure on readers to read more than his capacity at the same time. In addition to the security problems and penetration. It is necessary to control multiples readings through orientation of the signals. The signals are visible to some readers and invisible to another. Identification of the tagged object is necessary to be confirmed if it gets the positive reading. Otherwise, the reader uses the probabilities P for identifying the tagged object.

Other Techniques

Researchers proposed a new method that has named a sliding window for denoising. This method has a low occurrence rate. It used the FIFO queue "win-buffer" to solve the problem and stored the data. The win-buffer holds the sliding windows of reading the size of sliding windows that pass with the times. The method used Threshold of EPC values to reduce noise. The performance of this proposed has been studied under different noise ratios. Each tag is repeated ten times, with 200 milliseconds, the overall tag arrival rate is 1/sec. The results indicated noise ratios between 1, to 50%. The output readings of their method are not in the correct time order.

Researchers proposed a de-noising algorithm that used the count-threshold and time-threshold parameters to indicate the number of frequent reading and time is set for the number of frequent reading that should be achieved in order correct reading respectively. The proposed technique keeps the recent readings of the tags in the list and calculates the length of time by the difference between the initial time and the latest time of reading the tag. The performance of the proposed technique is reducing the processing of time reading from 0.308 to 0.125, and the algorithm is performed under different arrival rate. Every tag reading has been repeated for ten times. The applied noise ratio varied between 10 to 50%. Therefore, the noise ratio is very high.

An element can be tested whether it is already in the array by hashing it using the same set of hash functions. An element is said to be a member of the array if all positions are set to 1. The Count Bloom Filter (CBF) approach filters duplicate RFID data stream at reader level. The Time Bloom Filters (TBF) and Time Interval Bloom Filters (TIBF) are approaches for removing RFID duplicate filtering. TBF is a simple extension of the conventional Bloom Filters while TIBF need more spaces to reduce errors. However, these approaches suffer from error rates while the number of tuples increases.

The Chain-Linked Counting Bloom Filter (CCBF) attempts to reduce filtering processing rate according to the hashing times. This approach combines Counting Bloom Filters with dynamic chain lists to reduce errors. But this approach is complex and consumes a lot of time. It also relates dynamic setting with the object arrival rate and not the departure rate which indicates readings that can be removed from the filter. d-Left Time Bloom Filter (DLTBF) is an extension of d-Left Counting Bloom Filter (DLCBF). The DLTBF approach needs to compute the least loaded bucket before insertion. However, it is able to store the detected time of an element into one counter. The common denominator of the existing BF-based RFID duplicate data filtering approaches is that they use multiple hash functions. Table 1 provides a summary of the duplicate RFID data filtering approaches.

Table 1. Summary of existing duplicate RFID data filtering approaches.

Approaches	Weaknesses
DLTBF	Needs to compute the least loaded bucket before insertion. Also, it uses a number of hash functions.
CBF	Filters duplicate readings only at a reader level. It also uses a number of hash functions.
BF	The filter is easily becoming full since it does not allow deletion and therefore generates a higher rate of false positive.
TBF, TIBF	Not memory efficient because multiple time counters are needed to store the reading time.
Sliding windows	Inefficient since it has to scan along the sliding window every time new reading is coming in which it scans almost the same data. Besides that, sliding windows can overlap but disjoint the first items.
Landmark windows	Size of the window can be very big to provide more accommodation and accurate results. Besides that landmark windows can overlap in any way.
CCBF	Delay process because when it gets to identify probability of duplicate, it has to search the double-linked list to check whether the intersection of all time intervals corresponding to each hash function is empty so that the tag did not arrive within time. Just related dynamic setting with the object's arrival rate and not the departure rate which indicates readings that can be removed from the filter.

Removing Duplicate RFID Data Stream

In this section, the proposed multilevel duplicate RFID data stream filtering approach is presented. The overall filtering approach is illustrated in Figure 5. Generally, RFID reading vicinities are divided into major and minor areas. All tag readings will be first filtered at the reader itself (local filter) and the readings among the readers will then be filtered at the middleware before the data is sent to the database and subsequently to the application for processing.

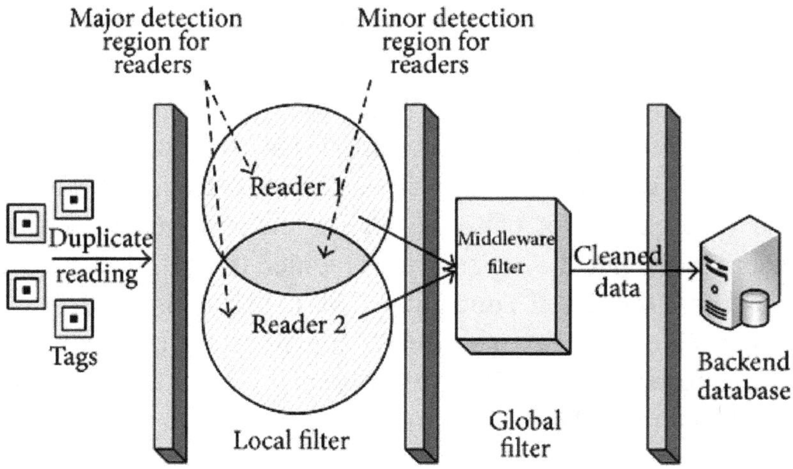

Fig. 5 Multilevel duplicate RFID data stream filtering approach.

We assume that the readers probe the tags every 5 seconds. Algorithm 1 shows the pseudocode of the proposed RFID duplicate data filtering approach which we refer to as a Duplicate Filter Hash (DFH). The algorithm maintains two arrays. As in [19], the landmark window is used in the proposed filtering approach because movement of the tagged object cannot easily be predicted and it may sometimes stay longer in the same area. Besides that, landmark window also naturally suits the Bloom Filter and it will remove all data when specific point is met.

Algorithm 1

DFH.

INPUT: TID

BEGIN

(1) **IF** (Time ==

True) **THEN**

//initialize the

arrays

(2) array1 =

array2 =

(3) **ENDIF**

(4) **FOREACH TID DO**

(5)

Pos

! Hash(TID)

//get hash value for TID

(6)

IF ((array1[pos] ==

TID) (array2[pos]

== TID))

THEN

(7) Duplicate read
(8) **ELSEIF** (array1[Pos] ==) **THEN**
(9) array1[Pos] ! TID //store in array1
(10) **ELSEIF** (array2[pos] ==) **THEN**
(11) array2[pos] ! TID //store in array2
(12) **ELSE**
(13) False Positive
(14) **ENDIF**
(15) **ENDFOR**END DFH

DFH will first check the time to remove all the readings at lines 1–3. If the time is met, all the counters will be reset to zero. This is related to the storage management of large volume RFID data. Each incoming reading will be hashed with a single hash function (line 5) and the output is considered as the counter position into the two arrays. The algorithm first checks to see if the reading is duplicated and if so the reading is discarded (lines 6 and 7). Otherwise, if array1 position at the counter is empty, then the tag ID is stored there, or else, if the array2 position at that counter is empty, then the tag ID is stored there. If not, the reading is reported as a false positive. We now illustrate DFH using the read data shown in Tables 2 and 3.

Table 2 Reading on tags by multiple readers.

Time	Reader ID	Tag ID
5	R1	7
5	R2	9
10	R2	15
10	R1	9
15	R1	15
15	R2	20

Figure 6 shows the sequences of read data mappings. Figure 3(a) shows the state of DFH before the arrival of tag reading. The first read is tag TID = 7 (see Table

3). Let us say that the hash value of TID = 7 is 3. Therefore, we store 7 at position 3 in array1 (Figure 6(b)). For the new tag reading 9, its hash value is 7. This reading is stored in array1 since it is still empty (Figure 3(c)). For tag reading 15 and hash value 3, we cannot store it in array1 as that position is already occupied. However, the counter value of array2 at this position is not occupied; thus 15 is placed there (Figure 3(d)). The next reading is 9 and the hash value is 7. This reading is considered duplicate in array1 since previously tag ID 9 has been stored. Similarly, the next for tag ID 15 with hash value 3 is considered duplicate in array2. Finally reading 20 with hash value 3 will be considered as false positive since both arrays at position 3 are not empty.

Table 3 Reading on tags by single reader.

Time	Tag ID
5	7
5	9
10	15
10	9
15	15
15	20

Initial

	Array1		Array2
[0]	0	[0]	0
[1]	0	[1]	0
[2]	0	[2]	0
[3]	0	[3]	0
[4]	0	[4]	0
[5]	0	[5]	0
[6]	0	[6]	0
[7]	0	[7]	0
[8]	0	[8]	0
[9]	0	[9]	0

Figure 6 The state of DFH before and after insertion of x.

CHAPTER-13

RFID MIDDLEWARE AND SOFTWARE SOLUTIONS

RFID middleware is a layer of software created between RFID readers and the enterprise/business applications, it is used to process all information and streams from the RFID readers. The middleware not only manages RFID readers and communicates between these devices and the business applications but also manages, filters, aggregates and makes sense of the data coming from the RFID tags.

In the actual application, the RFID middleware completes the data processing, transmission and parameter management of the RFID readers, monitoring working status of RFID device, manage and process the data flow between the RFID tag and the reader, and provide application program interfaces(APIs) between the RFID devices and the business application. It's good and fast solution for system integrators who are not familiar with RFID development.

RFID MIDDLEWARE ENGINE

RFID middleware engine is a radio-frequency identification, management software which positioned between the RFID reader and the enterprise application or database. There are many RFID reader manufacturers and each of them has their own firmware, software development kit, or APIs. These SDK provides ways to program and configure the readers based on the device's functionality and parameters. These manufacturers have different types of readers and upgrading or introducing RFID readers with new functionalities. HexaRFID software tracks these changes and updates the middleware engine. Hence, you will have a play & play RFID system.

Basic Edition

HexaRFID Software Basic Edition offers entry-level RFID tracking for business use cases such as RFID based employee attendance, material inventory tracking, and asset tracking. Customers opt for the basic edition can start using the software immediately without any hassles. We provide options to transfer the data directly to your application URL or database.

Professional Edition

This version of the software provides more sophisticated features to the client. Customers can use any number of readers in this version. Device management is part of this solution as a customer can manage all the readers and antenna from one application. This also included zones and sub-zone creation and allocation of reader and antenna for the same.

Enterprise Edition

This version of the RFID software allows an organization to have a customized algorithm as per the business use case requirement. Every business is not same. Hence, if a customer requires business logic implementation and behavior of RFID readers with a different perspective are the possibilities in this edition. We will work closely with customers in this version.

Functions

- **Collect, integrate data** According application requirement, the middleware is able to set system tag reading interval, reader reconnection time, each reader reading time etc, after configuration collect data from readers connected, and process it and then send it to where it needs to go (applications like warehouse management, internal database and some other destination).
- **Manage RFID Devices** The RFID Middleware is able to control the networking and settings of RFID readers (and other similar devices) and provides a simple way to update any changes that need to be made, for example, add/deduct readers, configure antenna ports, connection type etc.
- **Filter data** RFID middleware can be used to filter out the RFID tag reads deemed most important and remove redundant or repetitive reads. In some applications, RFID tagged items are read over and over again by the same RFID reader depending on how long the equipment is stagnant in the read field. RFID Middleware can assist by filtering out hundreds of identical reads so that the user only receives the data important to the application, such as a timestamp of when the equipment was placed inside of and removed from the read field. Filtering out excess data can be extremely helpful for

users because massive amounts of tag data can slow down networks and fill up databases quickly.

- **Monitor RFID readers states** With middleware user can monitor/check reader connection, reading states at any time
- **Records and log** User can view the real-time log of the middleware operation, such as the connection status of the reader, the RFID tags information read, or you can close the log.

Advantages

- Fullfill most applications requirement
- Support multiple readers work at the same time
- Data filter rules configurable
- Real time collecting and processing mass data
- Flexible and diverse interface(database, socket, Webservice etc)
- Friendly operation interface
- Other customized functions

Case pictures

Middleware server

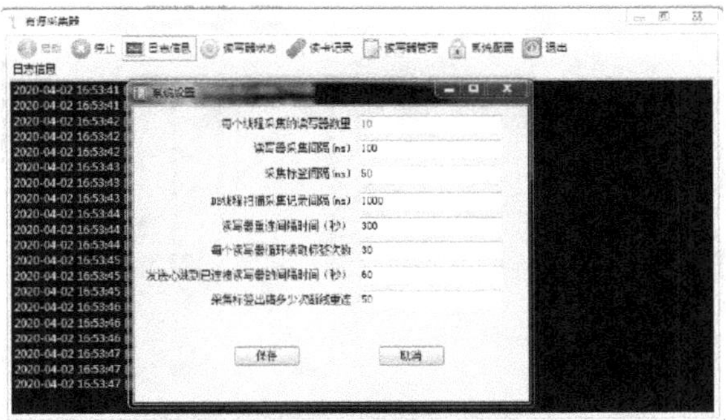

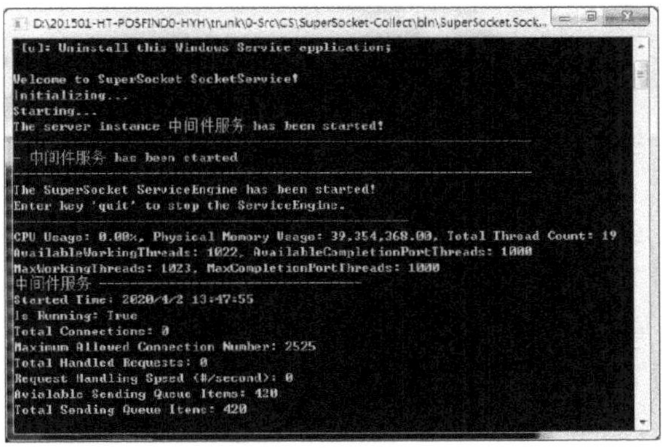

Final application software

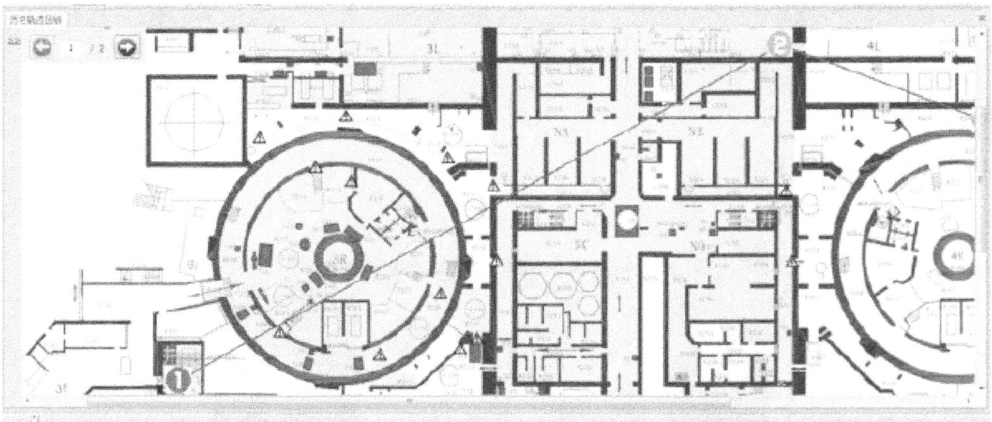

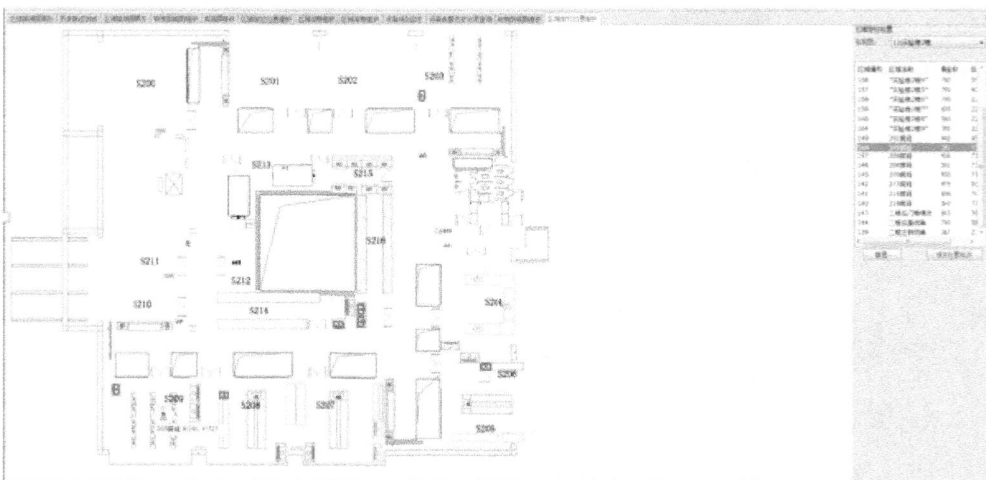

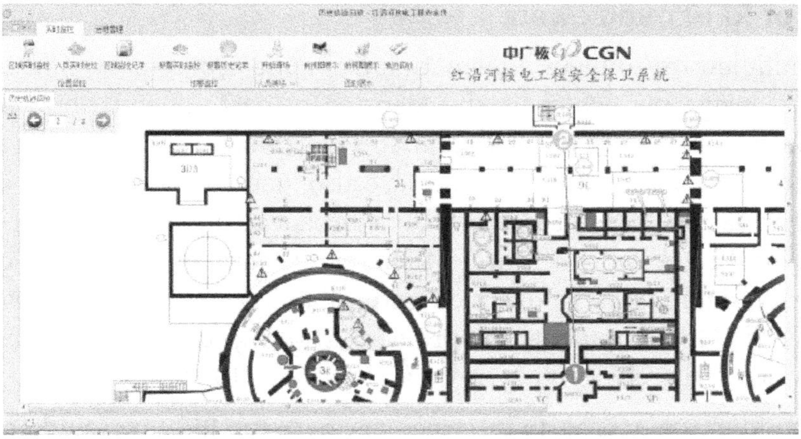

ROLE OF MIDDLEWARE IN RFID SYSTEMS

RFID Middleware is a radio-frequency identification (RFID) software, that sits between the readers and the enterprise/business applications. The middleware has several functions and plays a major role in RFID system operation and management. The middleware not only manages RFID readers and printers and communicates between these devices and your business applications but also manages, filters, aggregates and makes sense of the data coming from the RFID tags.

Due to the sheer amount of data coming from the RFID tags (imagine hundreds or thousands of tags read at virtually the same time thousands of times, radio-frequency identification (RFID) systems require a new kind of middleware, as well as conventional integration middleware. Conventional middleware is used primarily to link disparate applications, both internally and externally, to the enterprise for:

- Routing data using different transport protocols
- Translating data into different formats
- Web services

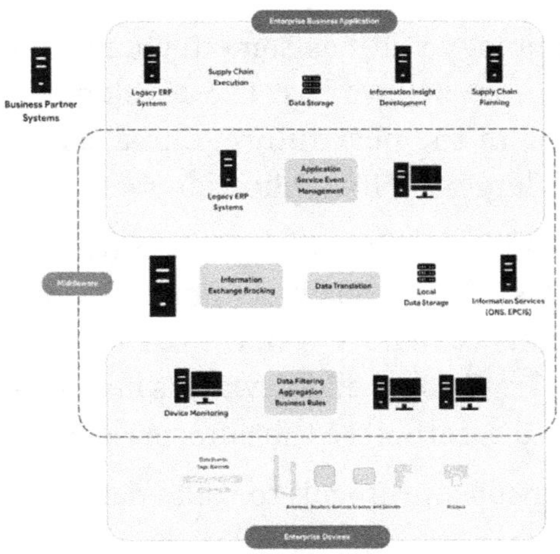

The role of RFID middleware

RFID middleware conveys information from one program to another program or multiple programs, which is the transfer of data information between the application system and the RFID system. It is worth mentioning that in addition to transmitting information, RFID middleware also includes services such as security, data interpretation, error recovery, data broadcasting, finding cost-compliant paths, and locating network resources. RFID middleware solves the problems of RFID data security, data format conversion and reliability. It shields the diversity and complexity of RFID equipment, and provides a strong support for the background business system, thereby driving wider and richer RFID applications.

RFID middleware acts as an intermediary between RFID tags and applications, and directly calls the standard general interface given by the RFID middleware framework from the application side to operate on tag data within the scanning range. One end of the middleware is connected to the reader data interface, and the other end is connected to the application program data interface. It effectively realizes the data transfer between the application program and the RFID electronic tag, and reduces the difficulty of data transfer and data reading. It not only reduces the complexity and development difficulty of the application program, but also makes the system more convenient for optimization, improvement and system maintenance.

Therefore, even if the database software or back-end application program storing RFID tag information is added or replaced by other software, or even when the types of RFID readers increase, the application side does not need to be modified. This not only effectively solves the problem of data read rate, but also saves other problems such as the maintenance complexity of many-to-many connections. In the future, RFID middleware will have a very good development prospect in the application of service-oriented architecture and business information security issues.

Although RFID technology still has some technical and application problems such as low reading rate, we believe that the development of RFID will be better and better in the future. In the near future, China, as the global manufacturing base, will be the world's largest RFID application market in the future.

Due to the large amount of data from RFID tags (think thousands or thousands of tags are read almost simultaneously at thousands of times), radio frequency identification (RFID) systems require a new kind of middleware and traditional integrated middleware. Traditional middleware is mainly used to connect different applications (internal and external) to the enterprise in order to:

- Use different transport protocols to route data
- Translate data to different formats

- Web Services

Here are the key roles and functions of RFID middleware:

- **Hardware Abstraction:** RFID middleware provides a standardized interface to communicate with different RFID hardware components. It abstracts the complexities of various hardware devices and protocols, allowing business applications to interact with RFID systems in a consistent and vendor-agnostic manner. This abstraction layer simplifies the integration process and provides flexibility in choosing and changing RFID hardware components.
- **Data Collection and Filtering:** RFID middleware captures and filters RFID data from readers, including tag reads, sensor data, and event triggers. It aggregates data from multiple readers and filters out irrelevant or duplicate reads, ensuring that only accurate and meaningful data is passed on to the business applications. Data filtering and normalization capabilities help improve the quality and relevance of RFID data for further processing.
- **Data Transformation and Enrichment:** Middleware can perform data transformation tasks, converting raw RFID data into a standardized format that is compatible with existing business systems or applications. It can enrich RFID data by adding additional contextual information, such as time stamps, location data, or business-specific metadata. This transformation and enrichment process helps to make RFID data more meaningful and actionable for downstream applications.
- **Event Management and Notifications:** RFID middleware enables the definition and management of events and triggers based on RFID data. It can generate real-time notifications, alerts, or triggers based on predefined rules or business logic. For example, it can trigger an alert when a specific tag is detected in a restricted area or send notifications when inventory levels reach a certain threshold. This functionality allows businesses to respond quickly to events and take proactive actions.
- **Integration with Business Applications:** One of the key roles of RFID middleware is to seamlessly integrate RFID data with existing business applications or systems, such as enterprise resource planning (ERP), warehouse management systems (WMS), or inventory management systems. Middleware provides APIs, web services, or connectors that facilitate the bidirectional exchange of data between RFID systems and business applications, enabling real-time visibility and automation of business processes.
- **Analytics and Reporting:** RFID middleware often includes analytical and reporting capabilities. It can generate reports, dashboards, or visualizations

based on RFID data, allowing users to gain insights into operations, track key performance indicators (KPIs), and make data-driven decisions. Analytics and reporting features help organizations optimize processes, improve efficiency, and identify trends or anomalies in RFID data.

RFID MIDDLEWARE EPCGLOBAL SPECIFICATION

The EPCglobal community, which includes many technology vendors and end-users who design and deploy RFID technology and develop RFID middleware, has developed specifications for the interface between standardized RFID tags, RFID readers, and enterprise systems. There are four main criteria: Low-Level Reader Protocol (LLRP), Discovery Configuration and Initialization (DCI), Reader Management (RM), and Application-Level Event (ALE) standards.

LLRP

The LLRP standard specifies the interface between the RFID reader and the client. This protocol is called a low-level protocol because it controls RFID air protocol operation timing and access to air protocol command parameters.

DCI

The DCI standard specifies the interface between the RFID reader and the access controller and its operating network. The standard is designed to specify the operation of the reader and the client so that the reader and the client can use the network to which they are connected to communicate with other devices, exchange configuration information and initialize the operation of each reader.

RM

The current RM standard describes the wired protocol used by the management software to monitor the operating status and health of RFID readers that comply with EPCglobal standards. The reader management protocol specifies the interaction between the device that can interface with the tag and the management software.

ALE

The ALE standard states that for customers to specify, in a high-level, declarative way, what kind of electronic product code (a means of EPC) data they are interested in is that there is no governing implementation. It provides a standardized format for reporting cumulative, filtered EPC data that is largely independent of the source or processing of EPC data.

RFID technology is classified as a wireless automatic identification and data capture (AIDC). A basic RFID system is composed of a tag containing a microprocessor, a reader and its antennas, and a computer equipped with a middleware program, in which business rules are configured (Asif and Mandviwalla, 2005). The tag generally attached to a product communicates through radio frequencies with the reader's antennas. The reader sends the location and unique identification of the product to a computer. On the basis of preconfigured rules, the middleware can adjust or initiate business processes automatically.

RFID middleware is considered as one essential intelligence-added component of any RFID system and could be linked with other firm information systems. More precisely, the middleware consists of the operating system, the data repository, and the processing algorithms that convert multiple tag inputs into visible tracking or identification data. The middleware could provide the following:

- multiple reader configuration, control and monitoring;
- access coordination to an environment with multiple applications;
- receiving events generated by a reader;
- data filtering, smoothing, and aggregating; and

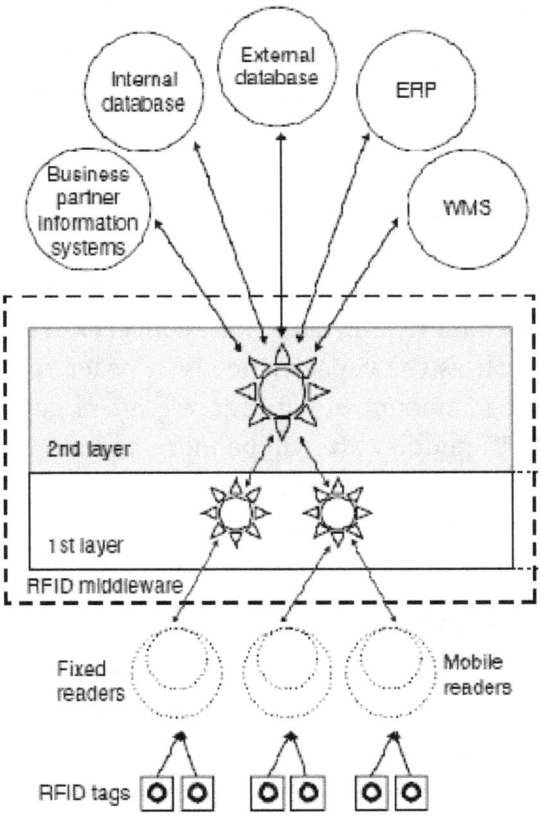

Positioning RFID middleware in an RFID system.

- data routing to enterprise applications such as a Warehouse Management System (WMS), Enterprise Resource Planning (ERP), Transport Management System (TMS), or a Manufacturing Execution System (MES).

Driven by the rising number of RFID applications and by mandates from important players such as Wal-Mart, the U.S. Department of Defense, Tesco, Target and Metro AG, and from their own major suppliers, the market for RFID middleware has grown rapidly in recent years. O'Connor (2006) estimates that the global market for RFID middleware had expanded from 2004 to 2005 by almost 162%.

Although the market for RFID middleware is estimated to reach for $135 million in 2007 or roughly 3% of RFID systems revenues, it is projected to grow to almost $1,557.5 million in 2011. The RFID middleware offering is characterized by the presence of numerous firms, ranging from

- Pure-play vendors such as GlobeRanger and OATSystems;
- application vendors such as Manhattan Associates, RedPrairie, Oracle, and SAP; and
- integration specialists such as TIBCO Software and Ascential Software,
- platform giants like Sun Microsystems, IBM, Oracle, and Microsoft.

Some of the major obstacles to widespread RFID adoption tend to disappear. First, the costs of an RFID middleware have decreased drastically, moving from about $125,000 per installed site a few years ago to $5,000 to $20,000 today. This downward trend positions RFID technology in a more affordable spectrum of potential investments and will eventually facilitate its adoption. Second, the current correct tags reading has reached 100% at the pallet level and is constantly improving at the item level. Third, chip technology has improved to a point where tags have become much more affordable. The concerns are now more focussed on middleware issues such as the capacity needs in order to manage large number of readers and the huge amount of data these readers generate. In addition, the next trends in the RFID middleware will be more and more integrated with other technologies. For example, the integration with wireless technologies, such as Local Area Network (LAN), General Packet Radio Service (GPRS), and Global Positioning System (GPS), could enable real-time tracking and tracing.

Evaluating and Selecting RFID Software

RFID systems can be made up of many different components, standards and differing RFID technology; any combination of which can have different performance, cost and implementation implications. So the correct choice of technology/components is crucial if the RFID system selected is to meet the needs that it is intended to meet.

In the fast-paced and demanding world of enterprise operations, tracking and managing assets efficiently is the key to success. As companies grow, so does the complexity of managing their valuable assets. This is where asset tracking software can play a significant role.

In this comprehensive guide, we will explore the process of choosing the perfect asset tracking software for your organization. We'll also learn why RFID asset tracking is highly recommended for all your asset tracking needs.

Steps to Choose the Best Asset Tracking Software

Assess Your Needs

- **Define Your Objectives** – To start your journey towards choosing the right asset tracking software, it's crucial to define your objectives clearly. What are your specific goals for implementing an asset tracking system? Are you looking to gain visibility into your assets spread through the Enterprise, locate assets easily, improve operational efficiency, or ensure compliance with industry regulations? Understanding your objectives is the first step toward making the right choice.
- **Identify Your Assets** – If you want to track your assets effectively, you need to know exactly what you're tracking. Create a comprehensive inventory of all the assets you intend to track. This includes equipment, machinery, vehicles, IT assets, and more. A clear understanding of your assets will help you select the software that aligns with your needs.
- **Determine Tracking Methods** – Asset tracking can be done through various methods, including RFID, barcodes, GPS, or a combination of these technologies. Evaluate which tracking method suits your assets and operational processes the best. For many enterprises, RFID stands out as a powerful and versatile option, offering real-time asset tracking capabilities.

Consider Integration

- **Compatibility with Existing Systems** – Efficiency is the key in enterprise operations. When choosing asset tracking software, consider how well it integrates with your existing systems. Seamless integration ensures that your new software won't disrupt your workflow but rather enhance it. RFID asset tracking software, in particular, can be integrated with a wide range of systems.
- **Scalability** – Your enterprise will likely grow over time. Therefore, it's crucial to choose software that can scale with your business. Opt for software that can accommodate the increasing demands of a growing enterprise without significant disruptions.
- **User-Friendly Interface** – Simplicity is elegance when it comes to software interfaces. Evaluate the user-friendliness of the software. A straightforward interface ensures that your team can quickly adapt to the new system and maximize its benefits.

Evaluate Features

- **Real-Time Tracking** – One of the defining features of asset tracking software is the ability to provide real-time information about your assets. Assess whether the software can offer live updates on asset locations and statuses. RFID asset tracking software excels in this regard, offering instantaneous insights into your assets' movements.
- **Customization** – Asset tracking needs may not be alike for all companies/ industries. Therefore, your asset tracking needs may be unique. Look for software that can be customized to suit your specific requirements. RFID technology allows for extensive customization, making it an **ideal choice for tailored solutions.**
- **Reporting and Analytics** – The ability to generate detailed reports and analyze asset data is invaluable. Consider software that offers robust reporting and analytics capabilities. These insights will empower you to make data-driven decisions and optimize your asset management processes.

Budget Wisely

- **Total Cost of Ownership** – When evaluating asset tracking software, consider not only the initial purchase cost but also the total cost of ownership (TCO). This includes ongoing subscription fees, maintenance expenses, and any additional costs associated with the software. An RFID asset tracking solution may have an initial investment, but its long-term benefits often outweigh the **RFID implementation costs.**
- **ROI Analysis** – Calculate the potential return on investment (ROI) that the software can deliver. ROI is a critical factor in determining the value of your asset tracking solution. By reducing losses, improving efficiency, and ensuring compliance, RFID asset tracking software often proves to be a sound investment.

Security and Compliance

- **Data Security** – Protecting your asset data is paramount. Ensure that the software offers robust data security features, including encryption and access controls. Security breaches can be costly, so it's essential to invest in a solution that safeguards your sensitive information.
- **Compliance** – Different industries have various regulations and standards that must be adhered to. Verify that the asset tracking software aligns with these industry-specific compliance requirements. RFID asset tracking software has a strong track record of meeting industry standards.

Vendor Selection

- **Reputation** – Selecting a reputed vendor is crucial to the success of your asset tracking implementation. Research the vendor's track record and seek out customer testimonials. A vendor with a solid reputation is more likely to provide reliable software and support.
- **Support and Training** – Adequate support ensures that you can address any issues promptly. Training is essential to ensure that your team can utilize the software effectively. **RFID asset tracking solution providers** often offer comprehensive support and training packages.
- **Scalability** – Just as your enterprise grows, your vendor should be capable of accommodating your expanding needs. Confirm that the vendor can scale its services to meet your future requirements. RFID asset tracking software providers are well-equipped to handle the scalability requirements of growing enterprises.

Implementation Plan

- **Pilot Testing** – Before implementing asset tracking software on a large scale, consider conducting a pilot test. Starting with a small-scale pilot allows you to identify and address any potential issues or challenges. This phased approach can lead to a smoother transition.
- **Data Migration** – If you're transitioning from an existing system, plan for the smooth transfer of your asset data. Data migration is a critical step to ensure that historical asset information is preserved and seamlessly integrated into the new software.
- **User Training** – Comprehensive user training is vital for the successful adoption of asset tracking software. Ensure that your team is well-trained on how to use the new system effectively. RFID asset tracking software providers often offer thorough training programs to equip the users.

Selecting the Right WMS Solution Integrated with RFID for Your Warehouse

Choosing a suitable WMS solution integrated with RFID for your warehouse needs is important. Here are some valuable tips to help you in selecting the right one:

Identify Warehouse Requirements

Finding the appropriate WMS system that is connected with RFID requires first determining your warehouse's needs. Since each warehouse is different, the WMS system you select should be tailored to meet your particular requirements. Assessing your warehouse's picking, packing, and shipping methods, as well as inventory management, should be your first step.

Look for RFID Integration

Warehouses can track and manage inventory in real-time with RFID, which lowers the possibility of human mistakes and boosts overall productivity. Making sure a WMS system has RFID integration capabilities is crucial when choosing one. Implementing an RFID integrated ERP system allows warehouses to not only effectively manage their inventory in real-time but also streamline various processes such as order fulfillment, procurement, and supply chain management.

Consider Scalability & Flexibility

Your warehousing operations will expand along with your business. Choosing a WMS system that can grow and change with your warehouse's demands is essential. As your company grows, look for a WMS that is flexible enough to integrate new technologies and procedures. By doing this, you'll save the trouble and expense of eventually transferring to a new WMS.

RFID Enhances Inventory Management In Warehouses

RFID technology plays a pivotal role in enhancing inventory management in warehouses through real-time inventory tracking, improved accuracy and efficiency, and streamlined receiving and shipping processes. Discussed below are the advantages of RFID in detail:

Real-time Inventory Tracking

RFID technology enables real-time inventory tracking by using radio waves to identify and track tags attached to inventory items. Unlike traditional barcode systems, RFID does not require line-of-sight scanning, allowing for multiple items to be scanned simultaneously. This results in a more efficient and accurate inventory tracking process.

With RFID, warehouse managers can monitor the movement of inventory items in real-time, enabling them to make informed decisions about inventory levels, stock replenishment, and order fulfillment. Real-time inventory tracking also facilitates better visibility and control over inventory, reducing the risk of stockouts and overstocking.

Improved Accuracy & Efficiency

RFID technology enhances the accuracy and efficiency of inventory management in warehouses in several ways. Firstly, RFID tags can store more data than traditional barcodes, including product details, batch numbers, expiration dates, and other relevant information. This comprehensive data storage capability minimizes the likelihood of errors and inaccuracies in inventory records. Additionally, the automated nature of RFID scanning reduces the need for manual data entry, which is prone to human error. This automation not only improves the accuracy of inventory records but also increases the efficiency of inventory management processes, allowing warehouse staff to focus on more value-added tasks.

Furthermore, RFID technology facilitates faster and more frequent inventory counts, as items can be scanned and counted in bulk without the need for physical handling. This frequent and accurate inventory counting capability enables warehouses to conduct cycle counts and spot checks more regularly, leading to better inventory accuracy and reduced discrepancies. Overall, the improved accuracy and efficiency resulting from RFID technology contribute to better inventory control and operational productivity in warehouses.

Streamlined Receiving & Shipping Processes

RFID technology streamlines receiving and shipping processes in warehouses by expediting the identification, verification, and tracking of incoming and outgoing inventory. When goods arrive at the warehouse, RFID tags attached to the items are automatically scanned as they pass through RFID readers at receiving docks. This automated identification process accelerates the receiving and put-away of inventory, reducing the time and labor required for manual data entry and inspection. Similarly, when fulfilling customer orders for shipping, RFID technology enables quick and accurate picking, packing, and shipping processes.

Moreover, RFID facilitates the verification of outbound shipments, ensuring that the correct items are being sent to the right destinations. This verification capability minimizes shipping errors and reduces the occurrence of mis-shipments, ultimately enhancing customer satisfaction and loyalty. By streamlining receiving and shipping processes, RFID technology contributes to the overall efficiency and effectiveness of warehouse operations, enabling faster order fulfillment and improved supply chain performance.

CHAPTER-14

TROUBLESHOOTING AND MAINTENANCE

After you have designed and installed your RFID system, what will inevitably come next? The answer to this question is problems, all kinds of problems, including reader failure, tag failure, network connectivity problems, and so on. This is where monitoring and troubleshooting enter the scene.

An RFID system is made of three components: hardware, software, and data. The hardware consists of tags, readers, and antennas. The software largely consists of middleware that manages to take the data from the reader to the enterprise applications; it comprises the nervous system of the EPCglobal network. Monitoring your RFID system involves status monitoring and performance monitoring. Performance monitoring involves measuring some performance metrics. To find the causes for the problems identified during monitoring, you will need to troubleshoot the system.

So, the core question addressed in this chapter is how to monitor and troubleshoot an RFID system. In search of an answer, we will explore three avenues: monitoring, measuring performance metrics, and troubleshooting.

There are many parts to an RFID system and a lengthy list of factors that may influence their performance. Often, a system malfunction can create a chain of blame that extends from end-user to manufacturer, the assumption being that if a problem is not immediately solvable, the reader is simply defective. In reality, many RFID failures are caused not by the reader itself but by issues with system design, hardware, setup, environment, and other influences that are entirely within the end user's control. Yet, with so many potential sources to choose from, it can be near impossible to decide where to start your search, especially if you are unfamiliar with the details of RFID systems and operations.

Hardware and Interference

A good starting point when troubleshooting read failures is at the system's basic hardware, as improper and/or misplaced components are a common cause. Luckily, they are also typically simple to address.

The first step in determining if the hardware is the root of your malfunction is checking the level of electrical noise interfering with any HF system using either the tools provided by the manufacturer or some other noise measurement devices.

Cables

Cable length and type are a common concern of those utilizing RFID systems as well as a common site of errors. While 50-ohm antenna cables are the standard, not all are equal. Close attention must be paid to ensure that the ones you select are capable of supplying the desired signal and installed to do so as efficiently as possible.

With HF antennas, the cable length is instrumental; while it is common to assume that a shorter cable will provide a better performance, cables in an HF application suffer higher losses as they shrink. Rather, they should exactly match the recommendation given by your manufacturer.

In contrast, UHF antenna cables do perform best with as short a cable as possible but require a specific type of cable carefully selected based on its attenuation. Cables at the lower end of the market have far more attenuation, causing huge portions of your signal to be lost.

Antennas

With RFID, the antenna's primary responsibility is communicating with the transponder, thereby, determining the range in which tags can be detected. It is very important to select the size and type of transponder that fulfills the needs of the system.

All HF systems utilize loop antennas, which generate a symmetrical magnetic field whose size can be adjusted based on signal strength and size of the antenna. Meanwhile, UHF systems use antennas that produce a directional field whose specifications vary based on their individual design. Of the two, UHF environments are more likely to be the source of poor antenna performance, as directional fields can be easily disrupted by objects within their beam angles, causing reflections as well as reading holes and islands.

Frequency

The frequency a reader operates on forms the foundation of its capabilities. HF and UHF, the two most common passive RFID frequencies, each have a unique mechanism to transfer energy and perform couplings between the reader and transponder. HF, at 13.56 megahertz, utilizes a magnetic field or inductive coupling to perform these tasks, while UHF, sitting between 860 and 960 megahertz for FCC countries, employs an electrical field known as backscatter coupling. Although it may seem simple to select the correct frequency for your application, the fact is that many are unaware of the intricacies where failures can occur.

To determine if you've chosen the ideal frequency for your application, consider the following:

Material Density

RFID reception is heavily influenced by the materials a frequency must pass through to deliver information to the reader; particularly, their density is an important determining factor in which frequency is best suited to your application. When using an incorrect frequency, materials like water, human bodies, and metal can cause reflections and absorptions that can be construed as poor reader performance.

Applications that involve high-density materials are best served by lower frequencies that use magnetic coupling, such as HF and nearfield UHF.

Tag Density

In the same vein, tag density is a major determining factor of the proper frequency one should use. If your application requires reading a large number of tags bundled close together (such as a stack of documents or poker chips) that are collected in a single, small area, using an improper frequency can cause antennas to detune, rendering the reader unable to detect any tags at all.

In these cases, an ISO18000-3M3 HF transponder will provide the best performance.

Reading Speed

Although the reading speeds of various RFID frequencies can be found listed from various sources throughout the market, they are often far off from the results observed in real-life settings. For instance, ISO 18000-3M3 transponders are presented as reading as many as 800 tags per second. In UHF, the same can be said of EPC Class 1 Gen 2 transponders, which are often said to read up to 1,000 tags per second. In testing, we've found each to perform far below these estimates in real world environments.

Reading Distance

When purchasing RFID readers, people often ask for a straightforward answer on the distance capabilities of particular readers. Yet, it is near impossible to provide an accurate estimate without testing the reader in its intended application first. This is because reading distance is subject to an extreme number of influences:

environmental factors, densities at play, sensitivity, tag type, size, and location, plus many more.

For example, in a case where multiple tags in a low density are collected in a small space, HF and nearfield UHF each appear as options. However, if unrelated tags are nearby, HF will prove the most appropriate; unlike UHF antennas, the range of HF antennas can be precisely controlled.

Security

One place perhaps underlooked when attempting to trace and resolve RFID malfunctions is system security. While this may not be a problem in applications such as inventory tracking, where no private data is recorded, there are many in which choosing the proper protection for your system is a crucial concern.

Several security strategies are available for use with RFID systems, the least of which is password protection on data collected by the transponder. Above that, encryption keys can be used to lock down user memory or data; however, these keys must be carefully kept to prevent a compromise of the entire system. Cryptographic authentication is the highest level of security available, utilizing transponders running either a cryptographic engine or processor that allows each reader to transponder interaction to be uniquely encrypted.

In most cases, failures in RFID systems are not due to misunderstanding the technology, misstepping in your setup, or overlooking important factors, but the result of not realizing the wide variety of options available on the market, particularly when many companies offer only one flavor of RFID technology. If you continue to have reader failures that your manufacturer cannot resolve, it may be that they simply do not offer the best solution for your needs. At the end of the day, gathering the specifics of your application and using them to guide your decisions will always be the best route to optimal RFID performance.

COMMON ISSUES IN RFID IMPLEMENTATIONS

Cost of RFID Technology

The major challenge is the price and return on investment (ROI) in the implementation of RFID technology. Companies have to bear the cost of all RFID elements; RFID tags, readers, hardware, software along with the routine maintenance.

Furthermore, manufacturing companies can't shut the existing business of barcodes as customers preferred barcodes over RFID tags. Thus, companies are bearing the cost of both barcodes and RFID to meet customer's demands.

The cost of passive tags was decreased to 20 cents per tag from 100 cents per tag in the year 2000, but firms must explore other opportunities to make passive, semi-passive and active tags a cost-effective solution.

Standards of RFID Technology

Supply chain stores can reveal maximum benefits of RFID technology if they share common standards, protocols, transmission frequency and bandwidth.

Presence of conflict across the world-wide partners increases the cost of RFID technology. If the supply chain retailers agree on a single standard, the cost of RFID deployment will fall and force the manufacturers to build only compatible RFID tags, readers, microchip, hardware and application for all sectors.

Currently, several standards of RFID technology are present in the market such as ISO 11785, ISO/IEC 14443or ISO/IEC 15693, ISO/IEC 18000-6 associated with low-frequency, medium frequency, and ultra-high frequency respectively.

Selection of RFID Tags and Reader

Antenna design of tag, an operating frequency of tag, antenna shape of the reader are all the important factors that affect the performance the RFID tags and reader.

Challenges of Low-Frequency RFID Tags

The size and cost of low-frequency RFID tags are elevated as they need a large dimension of antenna design. Moreover, these LF tags are resistive towards metal presence and non-ferrous metallic nature.

Challenges of High-Frequency RFID Tags

The size and cost of high-frequency RFID tags are limited as they need the miniature size of antenna design; however, expensive readers are needed to transmit RF signals. Though at high frequencies, it is easy for RFID readers to transfer data and maintain speed, yet it is hard to protect the human body from RF radiation. In contrast to the above, HF tags are impacted by the presence of metals, water, glass surface and moist atmosphere.

Polarization of Reader Antenna

It is recommended to use a circularly polarized antenna for the reader if the position of the tag is unknown in the RF field, but it can't provide promising results for longer ranges and enhanced penetration. Nevertheless, the use of linear polarized reader antenna can solve this problem.

Security of RFID Tags

Security of passive RFID tags is also considered as one of the major challenges in RFID field. There are many unguarded passive tags that can be exposed to malevolent and spiteful attacks, including spoofing, eavesdropping, denial of service. As a result, hackers can exploit this data for misleading customers and similar illegal activities.

Wrapping Up

RFID technology offers potential benefits, but to take advantage of these benefits, one has to overcome limitations and challenges. Among all, cost and security of RFID technology are of major concern. Manufacturing industries must explore new solutions to limit the cost and to boost the security of RFID tags. In this way, supply chain stores and retailing companies would experience seamless integration in the coming years.

Interference

RFID technology operates on radio waves, which can be affected by interference from other radio-frequency devices. The interference can cause data loss, errors, or incomplete readings, which can compromise the accuracy of the data captured by RFID tags.

To overcome interference challenges, businesses should select RFID tags and readers that operate on a frequency that is less susceptible to interference. Additionally, they should ensure that the RFID infrastructure is installed correctly and away from other radio-frequency devices.

Tag placement

RFID tags must be placed in the correct location on the item being tracked for the technology to work effectively. If the tag is placed in the wrong location or is obscured by other items, the RFID reader may not be able to read the tag, resulting in inaccurate data capture.

To overcome tag placement challenges, businesses should develop a standard for where RFID tags should be placed on each item type. Additionally, they can use RFID readers with built-in sensors that can detect if a tag is not in the correct location and alert employees to reposition it.

Integration with existing systems

Many businesses already have existing inventory management systems that they rely on, and integrating RFID technology with these systems can be challenging. The integration process may require changes to the existing infrastructure and software, which can be time-consuming and costly.

To overcome integration challenges, businesses should work with RFID technology vendors that provide software and hardware solutions that can be easily integrated with their existing systems. Additionally, they can work with experienced system integrators who can assist in the integration process.

Privacy concerns

RFID technology raises privacy concerns, especially when it comes to tracking people or sensitive items. For example, RFID tags embedded in passports, credit cards, and other personal items can be scanned by unauthorized individuals, compromising personal data.

To overcome privacy concerns, businesses should implement privacy policies that protect the data captured by RFID tags. Additionally, they can use RFID tags with built-in encryption and limit access to the RFID infrastructure to authorized personnel only.

RFID Education and Training

Another opportunity that RFID professionals face is the education and training of themselves and others in RFID technology and skills. RFID education and training can help RFID professionals to update and enhance their knowledge and competencies in RFID technology and practices, as well as to share their expertise and experience with others who are interested or involved in RFID projects. RFID education and training can take various forms, such as courses, workshops, webinars, certifications, publications, and mentorships. RFID professionals need to seek and participate in RFID education and training opportunities, to advance their careers and contribute to the development of the RFID field.

RFID Networking and Collaboration

One more opportunity that RFID professionals face is the networking and collaboration with other RFID professionals and stakeholders in the RFID community. RFID networking and collaboration can help RFID professionals to expand their connections, learn from others, exchange ideas, discover opportunities, and create partnerships. RFID networking and collaboration can occur through various channels, such as events, conferences, forums, associations, and platforms.

RFID professionals need to engage and interact with other RFID professionals and stakeholders in the RFID community, to foster a culture of mutual support, innovation, and excellence.

RFID Professional Networks and Associations

One of the ways that RFID professionals can network and collaborate with other RFID professionals and stakeholders is by joining and participating in RFID professional networks and associations. RFID professional networks and associations are organizations that aim to promote, support, and represent the interests and needs of RFID professionals and the RFID industry.

Some examples of RFID professional networks and associations are the Association for Automatic Identification and Mobility (AIM), the International Association for Radio Frequency Identification (RFIDIA), the RFID Journal Network, and the RFID Professional Institute. These organizations offer various benefits and services to their members, such as education, certification, events, publications, advocacy, and recognition.

RFID professionals can benefit from joining and participating in RFID professional networks and associations, by accessing valuable resources, enhancing their visibility and credibility, and influencing the direction and growth of the RFID field.

MAINTENANCE STRATEGIES FOR RFID SYSTEMS

By attaching RFID sensors to the tools in your factory, you can track relevant data such as temperature, vibrations, or rotations to ensure that the sensors operate accordingly at all times. Smart factory management systems use this data in conjunction with advanced prediction models and analytical tools to predict failures and address them proactively.

Instead of waiting for the tools to fall into disrepair, or planning unnecessary maintenance, the models will accurately predict how well it's functioning. This takes the guesswork out of maintenance and saves you time and money in the long run.

Maintenance management is very important subject special in construction lab. To manage related information of equipments and instruments plays an important role in the view of construction lab management. Those equipments and instruments need high standard and requirement in precision and accuracy of tests. Managing maintenance work effectively is extremely difficult in construction lab owing to various equipments and instruments with different specification.

Furthermore, it will take high cost to maintain those instruments in the good conditions for the test correctness. With the advent of the Internet, web-based information management solutions enable information dissemination and information sharing among related maintenance staff members. Generally, maintenance managers and staffs require access to the equipments and instruments location to handle inspection and maintenance work in construction lab. Usually, maintenance staffs generally use sheets of paper to handle various types of maintenance information, including checklists, specification, and maintenance procedure.

Consequently, there is serious rework progress regarding the data capture and entry in maintenance progress. In order to enhance the effectiveness of inspection and maintenance work in construction lab, this study presents a novel system called Mobile RFID-based Maintenance Management (M-RFIDMM) system for the acquisition and tracing of lab equipments and instruments maintenance information on locations and providing an equipments and instruments maintains information sharing platform among all participants using web technology and RFID-enabled PDAs.

Integrating promising information technologies such as RFID-enabled PDAs, Radio Frequency Identification (RFID) scanning and data entry mechanisms, can help improve the effectiveness and convenience of information flow in the maintenance management. The primary objectives of this study include:

- applying such a system that integrates RFID technology with RFID-enabled PDAs to increase the efficiency of equipments and instruments inspection and maintenance data collection, and
- designing a web-based portal for equipments and instruments management and control, providing real-time information and wireless communication between offices and instruments locations.

The main purposes of this study include:

- developing a framework for a mobile maintenance management system for instruments in the lab;
- applying such a system that integrates RFID technology with PDA technology to increase the efficiency of instruments inspection and maintenance data collection in the lab;
- designing a web-based portal for maintenance management and control, providing real-time information and wireless communication between offices and instruments locations, and
- Evaluating the effectiveness of the proposed system in construction lab.

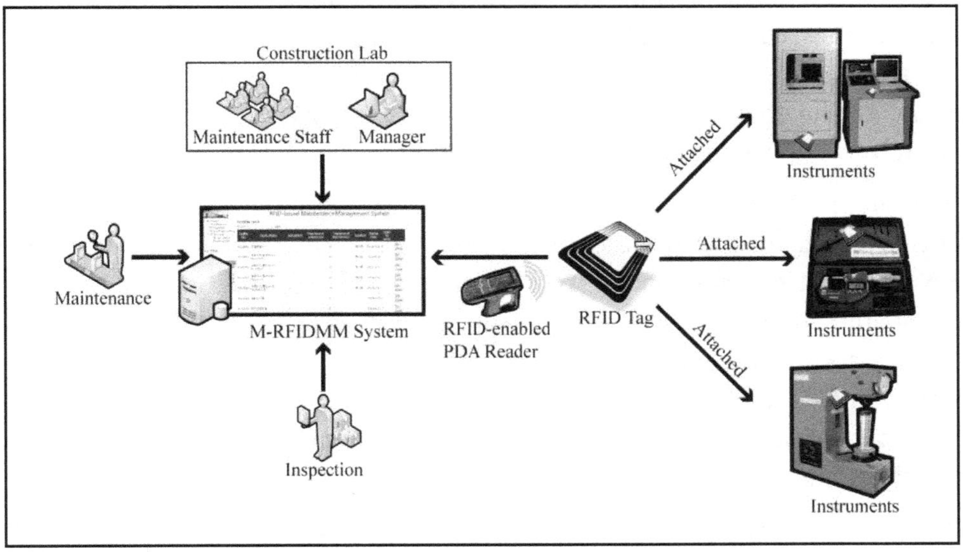

Fig. 1. M-RFIDMM System Framework Overview

Figure 1 illustrates solutions used in a real case utilized M-RFIDMM system in Taiwan construction lab. With appropriate modifications, the M-RFIDMM system can be utilized at any instruments inspection and maintenance service for maintenance management divisions or managers in support of the M-RFIDMM system.

The use of technology to improve delivery process control is not a novel concept. Many industries have applied barcodes to track materials for many years. Construction companies began to examine the use of barcodes for tool management in the early 1990s. Although barcode is an established and affordable technology, it has presented problems in the construction industry due to the short read range and poor durability of barcodes — a barcode requires a line of sight, and becomes unreadable when scratched or dirty.

An RFID system is composed of an RFID tag and an RFID reader. The RFID tag comprises a small microchip and an antenna. Data are stored in the tag, generally as a unique serial number. The RFID tags can be either passive (no battery) or active (battery present). Active tags are more expensive than passive tags and have a read range of 10–100 meters. Passive tags have a read range of 10mm to approximately 5m (Manish and Shahram, 2005). The vast majority of RFID tags applied in the construction industries are passive.

The RFID reader functions as a transmitter/receiver. The reader transmits an electromagnetic field that "wakes up" the tag and provides the power required for it to operate (Lahiri, 2005). The tag then transfers data to the reader via the antenna. This data are then read by the RFID reader, and transferred to a Pocket PC or computer. Unlike barcodes, RFID tags do not require line-of-sight to be read; they only need to be within the reader's radio range. Additionally, RFID tags, unlike barcodes, can be read through most materials. RFID tags are shrinking, with some measuring only 0.33mm across. Although RFID systems can apply different frequencies, the most common frequencies are low (125KHz), high (13.56MHz) and ultra-high (UHF) (850–900MHz) (Lahiri, 2005).

Notably, RFID systems are one of the most anticipated technologies that will potentially transform processes in the engineering and construction industries. In the construction industry, RFID technology can be utilized with PDAs, thereby allowing staff members to integrate seamlessly work processes at labs and sites, due to the ability to capture and carry data. With a RFID scanner plugged into a PDA, the RFID-enabled PDA is a powerful portable data collection tool. Additionally, RFID readings increase the accuracy and speed of information communication, indirectly enhancing performance and productivity.

The advantages of using mobile devices in the construction industry are well documented. Moreover, mobile devices have been applied in numerous construction industries, to provide the following support:

- Providing wearable field inspection systems;
- Supporting pen-based computer data acquisition for recording construction surveys;

- Supporting collaborative and information-sharing platforms;
- Using mobile computers to capture data for piling work, and
- Utilizing mobile devices in construction supply chain management systems.

System Development

Application Scenario and Requirements

RFID technology is employed to improve the efficiency of traditional building maintenance solutions. The first step in system development is the scenario design. The maintenance staff carries a tablet PC while executing maintenance activities. A portable RFID reader/writer is attached to the tablet PC. The staff can implement maintenance jobs using a web-based application through an Internet browser. Using the web-based software, staff can read/write information from/into tags. Information related to maintenance jobs are accessed from a single database through the Internet in real-time. As a result, multiple users can maintain various kinds of objects at the same time. To further improve working efficiency, staff can setup maintenance periods for each item. The software can remind users about which items require attention and automatically arrange maintenance sequences. Maintenance preparation and effort can therefore be reduced. Three modules i.e. management, statistical, and scheduling are obtained according to this scenario.

System Development Process

The web-based RFID building management system development process is illustrated in Fig. 2. Each activity is explained as follows.

- **Determine hardware and software:** System hardware and software that conform to application requirements are investigated in the first step. ASP.NET is chosen as the development platform to establish the web-based application. ASP.NET is a new technology developed by Microsoft. It supports browsers that execute on various kinds of platforms including personal computer, cell phone, personal digital assistant (PDA) etc. A portable RFID reader/writer, namely UHF-Block, manufactured by Ensyc Technology is selected. This device is compatible with the GEN2 protocol and can be connected using USB interface.

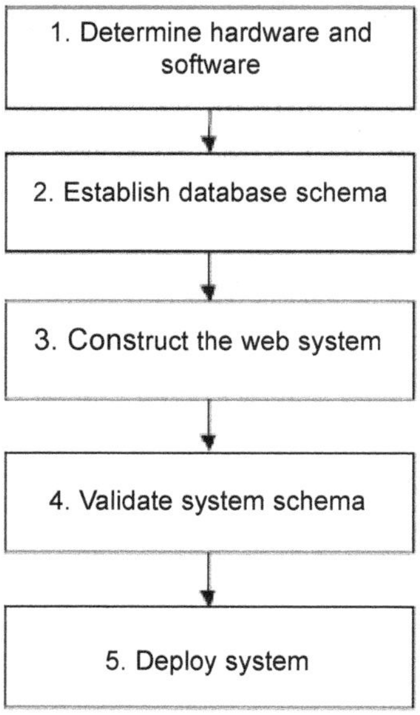

Fig. 2. System Development Process.

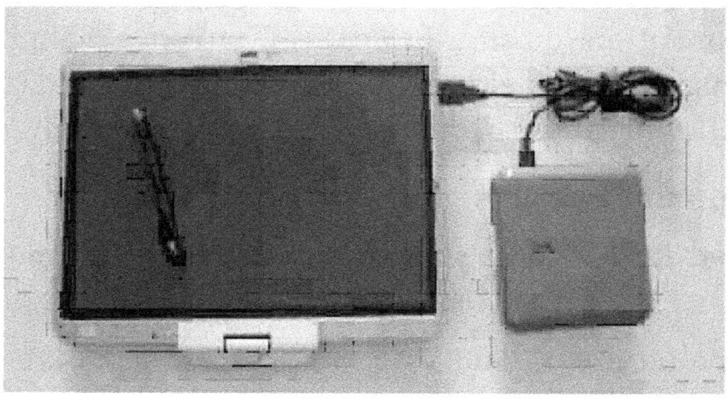

Fig. 3. Maintenance Kit.

Figure 3 represents devices for the staff to implement maintenance work. The system hardware and software used for system development are summarized as follows:

- Web and database server: Dell enterprise personal computer.
- Integrated development environment: Visual Studio.NET (C#.NET).
- Operation system: Windows XP professional.
- Database format: Microsoft Access.
- Tablet PC: HP 2710P.
- RFID device: UHF-Block.
- RFID tag: UHF G2.
- **Establish database schema:** Building maintenance induces numerous records. For managerial convenience, information is stored in a single

database. The database is designed using third normal form of the relational model.

- **Construct the web system:** This web-based system is programmed using C#.NET and transferred through Http/Https protocols.
- **Validate system:** System applicability is validated using a real case. Deploy system: The developed web system is implemented in a real building.

Data Management Module

The data management module is designed to allow manipulating the data stored in the system database. Functions provided by this module are summarized in Table 1. A maintenance object contains the following information: category, item, name, safety degree, durability, frequency of use, purchasing cost, purchasing date, part list, warranty period, seller, holder, location, etc. Users can fill out the information by entering values or selecting a proper description from a list. Each object is identified using RFID code that is a unique identification number written onto the RFID tag. The RFID code structure is shown in Fig. 4.

The codification is designed for building maintenance using four sections. The first section, category, is used to store equipment or facility. The second item stores types of equipment or facility, such as universal test machine and electron microscope. Third part involving four cells is used to store serial number. The final area is designed for future extension. RFID code is automatically generated by the module and can be written onto a tag using the RFID device.

1	2	3	4	5	6	7	8	9	10	11	12
Category		Item			Serial number				Extension		

Fig. 4. RFID Codification Structure. For searching for information about a specific maintenance object, users can queryC by its category, name, RFID code, or identify it using RFID device.

Table 1. Functions of Data Management Module

Function	Explanation
Login	Users enter username and password to log onto the web-based system. Two kinds of authorization are provided in the system: manager and administrator.
Manage user	Only administrative users can add/edit/remove system users.
Manage category	Users can add/edit/remove categories that are served as the highest level of maintenance object classification.
Manage item	Users can add/edit/remove items that are served as the second level of maintenance object classification.
Manage parts	Users can add/edit/remove parts for each maintenance item.

Function	Explanation
Manage object	Users can add/edit/remove a maintenance object and generate its RFID code.
Manage space	Users can add/edit/remove a space for maintenance object.
View history	Users can view maintenance record history for each object. Object can be identified using a RFID reader.
Manage seller	Users can add/edit/remove the seller information for maintenance objects.

The main form of data management module is shown in Figure 5.

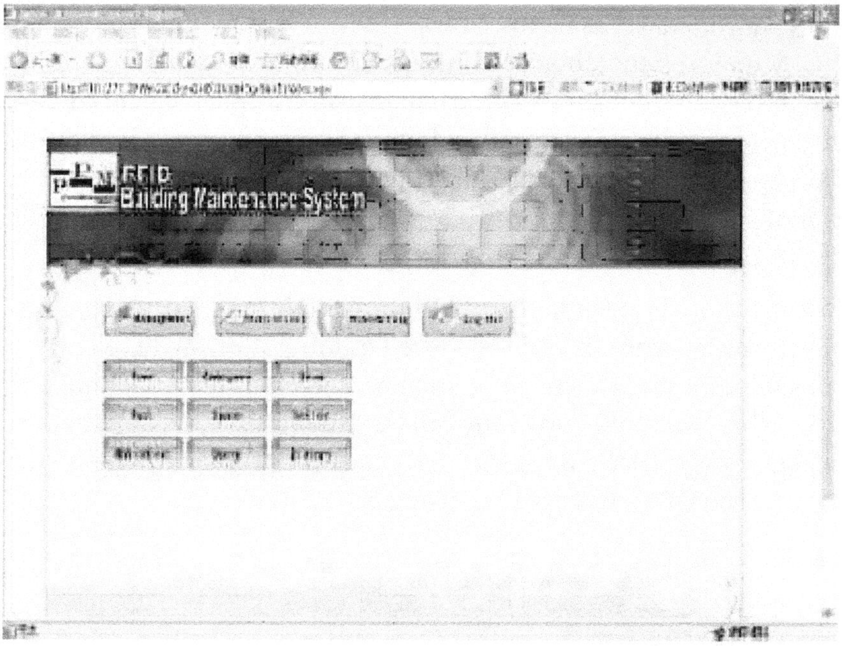

Fig. 5. Main Form of Data Management Module.

Statistical Module

This study collected numerous data while implementing maintenance jobs stored in the system database. However, this data row is meaningless to users. The objective of the module is to represent the system database using statistical charts allowing users to understand the data distribution and properties. This module provides four charts for users to observe the data, i.e. circle graph, ogive, bar chart and line chart.

Statistical graphs can help users understand maintenance status. A recommendation table is proposed to assist users making decisions according to the graphs, as explained in Table 2. An example of demonstrating purchasing costs using line chart is depicted in Figure 6.

Table 2. Decision Support for Statistical Graph

Statistical group	Decision support
Maintenance object amount	Number of objects located in an individual space can be identified. Therefore, users can understand the status of maintenance objects such as missing and broken.
Repair frequency	According to the graphs, users can recognize the durability of maintenance objects. The information can be fed back to the procurement department, repair partners, and property holder for preventive analysis.
Repair cost	The information can be used to determine whether the maintenance objects should be replaced or not. The procumbent department can also use the information as purchasing reference.
Object life time	Maintenance efficiency effects life time of property. It can also be used as another index for property durability.
Breakdown causes	Graphs about breakdown causes are ideal for breakdown causes analysis. The information can be used for troubleshooting

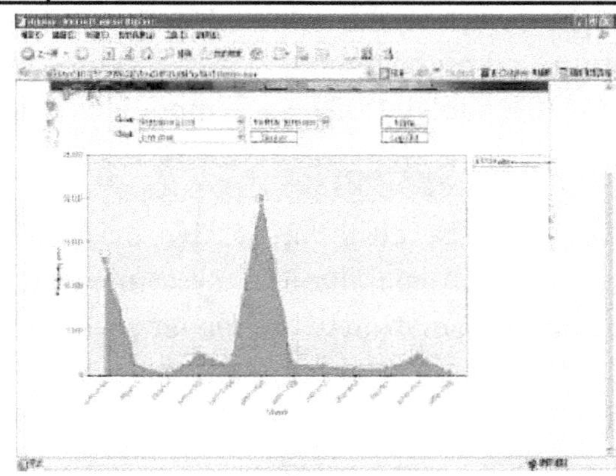

Fig. 6. Line Chart of Purchasing Costs.

Scheduling Module

Scheduling involves tasks of making decisions regarding the allocation of available capacity or resources to jobs, activities, tasks, or customers over time. It thus results what is to be done, when, by whom, and with what equipment.

Building functions rely on periodic maintenance. Parts wearing out can induce malfunctions. Worn out parts can be identified and replaced by regular maintenance. However, diverse maintenance objects involve various kinds of parts, which increase the maintenance complexity. A proper maintenance schedule is thus needed to effectively accomplish jobs.

The scheduling module developed in this study focuses on arranging maintenance sequences. Two strategies are proposed to enhance maintenance efficiency:

System implementation

System architecture

The M-RFIDMM system has three main components, a PDA, RFID and a portal. Significantly, both the PDA and RFID components are located on the client side, while the portal is on the server side. All instruments-related information acquired by maintenance staff members within the M-RFIDMM system is recorded in a centralized M-RFIDMM system database. All staff members can access required information via the portal based on their access privileges. Moreover, the portal is limited by design to thirty persons logging in when all participants acquire the same case information at same time. The M-RFIDMM system extends the RFID-based instruments management system from the office to instruments locations to assist with inspection and maintenance services, while the M-RFIDMM system primarily deals with data transactions in all departments or systems integration. When the data are updated on the M-RFIDMM system, e-mails are automatically sent from the server to the maintenance managers of the management division and to staff members involved in the relevant activity. The M-RFIDMM system consists of an inspection and management portal integrated with mobile devices and RFID technology (RFID-enabled PDA). Each module is briefly described below.

RFID Module of M-RFIDMM System

The RFID technology can be either a passive or active system. The major difference between an active and a passive RFID system is that an active tag contains a battery, and can transmit information to the reader without the reader generating an electromagnetic field. The case study uses UHF passive RFID technology due to budget restrictions and long distance read range requirement.

Mobile Device (PDA) Module of M-RFIDMM System

The M-RFIDMM system adopts a Unitech RH676 with an UHF RFID Reader as the RFID-enabled PDA hardware. Unitech RH676 PDA is operated on Windows CE. All data files in the PDA module are transmitted to the server directly through the web. The Internet explorer 6 was chosen as web browser in the RFID-enabled PDA hardware system.

Web Portal Module of M-RFIDMM System

The web portal is an information hub in the M-RFIDMM system for an instruments management. The web portal enables all participants to log onto a single portal, and immediately obtain information required for planning. The users can access different information and services via a single front-end on the Internet. For example, a customer can log onto the portal, enter an assigned security password, and access real-time inspection schedule information. A general contractor can check the test or inspection status, availability of reports and various other case-related data. The web portal of M-RFIDMM system is based on the Microsoft Windows 2000 operating system with Internet Information Server (IIS) as the web server. The prototype was developed using ASP.NET, which are easily combined with HTML and JavaScript technologies to transform an Internet browser into a user-friendly interface. The web portal provides a solution involving a single, unified database linked to all functional systems with different levels of access to information, based on user role, both within an organization and across organizations and other members.

Modules of system functions

This section describes the implementation of each module in the M-RFIDMM system.

Test Report Module

The report module provides maintenance staff members with a complete record of inspection and maintenance performed in the maintenance management.

Inspection and Maintenance Module

Maintenance staff members can download the most up-to-date maintenance schedule from the Internet, and enter instrument maintenance results directly via a PDA. Additionally, PDAs display the checklist for every instrument maintenance task. Maintenance staff members can record instrument information for dates, conditions, inspection result, descriptions of problems and suggestions that have arisen during maintenance. Furthermore, maintenance staff members can also mark unacceptable tasks, and select relevant tasks from lists in the PDA. The module has the benefit that maintenance staff members can enter/edit inspection and maintenance test results, and all test records can be transferred between the PDA and portal by real-time synchronization, eliminating the need to enter the same data repeatedly.

Progress Monitor Module

This module is designed to enable maintenance staff members to monitor the progress of inspections and maintenance. Additionally, maintenance managers and staff members can access the progress or condition of inspection and maintenance tasks. The progress monitor module provides an easily accessed and portable environment where maintenance staff members can trace and record all information regarding the status of inspections delivered to the maintenance or scheduled for repair.

E-Documents Module

This module allows maintenance staff members to download manuals and specifications in advance, and reference them during inspection. This module also has a search function that enables the information to be found and retrieved easily, which is a valuable feature in dynamic environments. Moreover, maintenance staff members who do not need paper-based manuals or specifications can download e-manuals or e-specifications and access them directly using their PDAs.

PART V: CASE STUDIES AND BEST PRACTICES

CHAPTER-15

RFID SUCCESS STORIES

RFID, or radio frequency identification, is a technology that allows unique tags placed on products to be read by a compatible reader. Generally, the reader can read the tag from up to a few feet away and does not need to be in the direct path of the tag.

RFID is used to help locate items in the shipping or storage process, so they can be easily found and accessed by shippers, manufactures, or people in retail stores. The reader is able to read the special information unique to each tag and relay that information back to a computer program designed to collect and interpret the information. That information can then be read by a human and they can use said information for whatever purpose they need.

Although this may seem like a new type of technology, it has actually been in use as far back as the 1970's. However, with all of the advances in our technology, it has improved and changed over the years to become more precise, efficient, and complex.

Today, we see many success stories of companies who have implemented RFID into more of their processes that have help reduce lost items, loss of money, and much more. We will take a look at some examples below and explore how RFID technology has improved the lives of workers and consumers alike.

Success Story #1

A manufacturer that produces doors for storage facilities would have an average of fifty to sixty loads of doors shipped out every day. These doors were moved with contract trucks and many of the doors would never make it to their final destination because the truck drivers would sell the doors to contractors illegally in an effort to make a profit. Because the doors were not arriving at the storage facilities, customers were left unhappy and the company would have to shell out millions of dollars per year to make replacements and ship them out again.

In order to combat this issue, the door company began to place FRID tags on all of the pallets that contained the doors before they were shipped out in the contract trucks. With the tag, they were able to track the shipments/door in real-time, so they could always see where their products were. They were able to not only tell the precise location they were, but if the shipment was on time, if they were delays, or any damages to the items.

Customers were not just getting their doors as promised, but the company could even provide shipping updates for the customers, so they could see when the doors were scheduled to arrive. Once the items were delivered properly, the tags were removed and then sent back to the company.

The introduction of the RFID tags prevented the company from losing any more doors due to theft and allowed them to save millions of dollars per year.

Success Story #2

Salvatore Ferragamo, a high-end Italian shoe and fashion designer, began to use RFID technology in his products in an effort to halt counterfeit fashion pieces from being sold as authentic Ferragamo designs. With billions of dollars of counterfeit fashion being sold just in Europe alone, it is a major issue that many brands have been aiming to correct for many years.

Ferragamo ad his team began to use RFID tech to help solve the counterfeiting issue and crack down on fakes circulating throughout the world. Essentially, the company insert tiny microchips into all of their fashion products and have been doing so since 2014. They can scan to make sure a product is authentic, but they can also track all of their items to gather information.

For customers, they are able to scan any product they buy from the brand to check for its authenticity and to find out more information about the product the recently purchased as well.

Success Story #3

Dole, the major fruit and vegetable grower and supplier, has found much success with RFID tags and packaging. Quite a few years ago, Dole experienced a major E. coli outbreak the made hundreds of customers sick from eating contaminated food. In 2006, the company began the experiment with RFID tags to track their food supply chain. The introduction of the tags were meant to improve the ability to trace their products and to make sure the food remained safe and uncontaminated.

Dole would use the RFID tags and GPS to track the fruits and veggies from the harvesting processing to packaging to shipment to stores all around the world.

CASE STUDIES HIGHLIGHTING SUCCESSFUL RFID IMPLEMENTATIONS

Taiwan construction lab

This study is applied in Taiwan construction lab for the case study. This study utilizes an M-RFIDMM system in the instruments maintenance management in construction lab. Existing approaches for tracking and managing instruments maintenance adopt manually updated paper-based records. The most of inspection in maintenance work were paper-based work by manual entry although instruments maintenance management system was developed for information management. However, information collected by staff members using such labor-intensive methods is rework and ineffective in the maintenance results entry. Therefore, maintenance management division and maintenance staff used in the case study. After the critical instruments were selected, each UHF RFID tag for the instruments was made, and the unique ID of the instrument was entered into the M-RFIDMM system database. After the instrument was assigned to be monitored for maintenance, the instrument was scanned with a RFID tag to enter the M-RFIDMM system.

During the setup phase, all the ID of instrument in the RFID tag had been determined and entered the database for system, and then the RFID tag was attached in the instrument. Finally, the tag will be scanned and checked before the maintenance work. Furthermore, the tag suggested to be attached on the non-metal surface (like wooden box) or placed a formcore (about 5 mm) for the interface for decreasing the influence because the RFID tag will be influenced by metal facilities (see Fig. 1-Fig. 3).

Fig. 1. Displayed the UHF RFID tags using in the case study.

Fig. 2. Displayed the instrument attached UHF RFID tag in the case study.

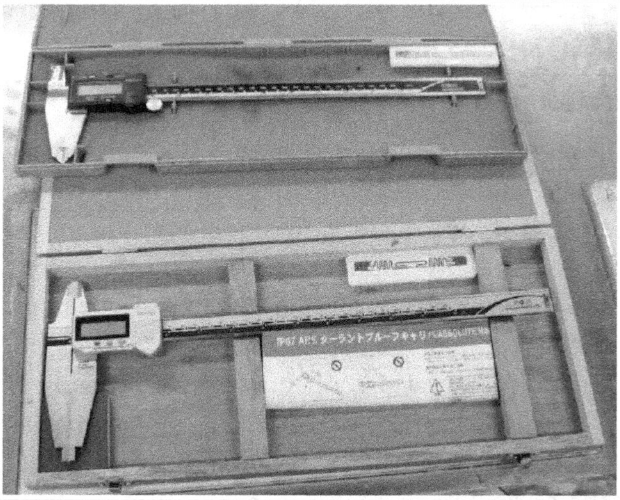

Fig. 3. Displayed the instrument attached UHF RFID tag in the case study (2).

Before the inspection/maintenance work, the instruments staff members can check the instrument list from PDA, refer the relative information and can make the preparation work without printing any paper document. During the inspection/ maintenance progress, the instruments staff member scanned the RFID tag first and to confirm the instrument, then checked the further detail information like maintain procedure, notification, and fittings (see Fig. 4 and 5). The system would support any information of instrument via browser under wireless circumstance.

Fig. 4. Displayed maintenance staff member used RFID-enabled PDA to scan RFID tags (1).

Fig. 5. Displayed maintenance staff member used RFID-enabled PDA to scan RFID tags (2).

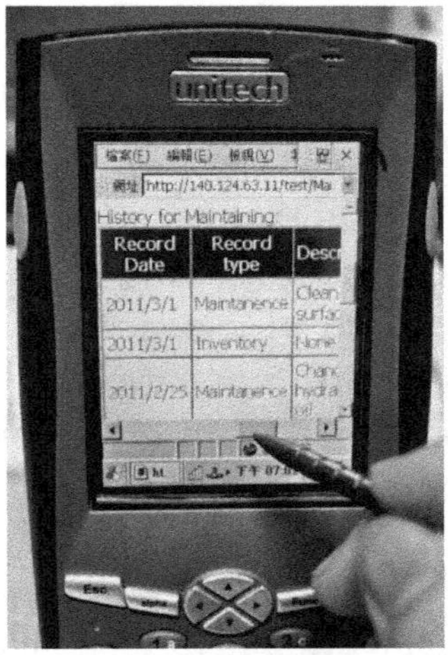

Fig. 6. Displayed maintenance staff member entered the result of inspection, edited the description in the PDA.

After the instruments were inspected, staff members recorded the status and execute the work by procedure. After the operation, instruments staff member entered the result of inspection, edited the description in the PDA, and provided the updated information to the system (see Fig. 6). Once the instrument was break and need to be repaired, the system also can provide the supplier information and handle the problem immediately. Finally, the instruments manager and the authorized staff members accessed the updated information from office synchronously.

Successful RFID Implementation in Logistics

Case studies play a crucial role in understanding the practical applications of RFID technology in logistics. They provide real-life examples of successful implementations, showcasing how businesses have optimized their warehouse operations through the use of RFID. By analyzing these case studies, we can gain valuable insights from different perspectives and learn about the challenges faced, the solutions adopted, and the benefits achieved. In this section, we will delve into some notable case studies that highlight the successful implementation of RFID in logistics.

retail Inventory management

One of the most common applications of RFID in logistics is retail inventory management. A large retail chain implemented RFID tags on their products to automate the inventory tracking process. This allowed them to accurately monitor stock levels in real-time, reducing out-of-stock situations and improving overall inventory accuracy. As a result, the company experienced a significant reduction in stockouts, leading to increased sales and customer satisfaction.

Supply Chain Visibility

RFID technology has been instrumental in **enhancing supply chain visibility**, enabling organizations to track and trace goods throughout the entire logistics process. A global logistics provider integrated RFID tags into their shipments, allowing them to monitor the location and condition of goods in transit. This improved visibility enabled them to proactively address any potential delays or issues, ensuring timely deliveries and enhancing customer trust.

Warehouse Efficiency

Implementing RFID technology in warehouse operations can greatly enhance efficiency and productivity. A distribution center adopted RFID-enabled pallets and shelves, enabling automated inventory management and location tracking. By eliminating manual processes and reducing search times, the company achieved significant time and cost savings. Additionally, the RFID system provided accurate data on inventory levels, enabling better demand forecasting and optimizing *warehouse space utilization*.

Returnable Asset Tracking

Returnable assets, such as pallets, containers, and totes, are prone to loss or misplacement, resulting in additional costs for businesses. A logistics company employed *RFID tags* on their returnable assets to track their movement within the supply chain. This allowed them to accurately monitor asset utilization, reduce losses, and streamline the return process. As a result, the company experienced *improved asset visibility*, reduced operational costs, and *enhanced customer satisfaction*.

Comparing these case studies, it becomes evident that the implementation of RFID technology in logistics offers numerous benefits. The ability to track and monitor inventory in real-time improves overall supply chain visibility, reduces stockouts, and enhances customer satisfaction. Additionally, RFID enables automation and streamlining of warehouse operations, leading to improved efficiency and cost savings. Moreover, the utilization of RFID for returnable asset tracking minimizes losses and optimizes asset utilization, further enhancing operational efficiency.

These case studies demonstrate the successful implementation of RFID technology in logistics, showcasing the tangible benefits it brings to businesses. From retail inventory management to supply chain visibility, warehouse efficiency, and returnable asset tracking, RFID has proven to be a valuable tool for optimizing warehouse operations. By leveraging the insights gained from these case studies, businesses can make informed decisions about implementing RFID in their own logistics operations, thereby reaping the rewards of increased efficiency, improved customer satisfaction, and *reduced costs*.

Audi cars

German premium automaker Audi has deployed an RFID-based system for tracking assembled vehicles at its Hungarian facility. Utilizing Avery Dennison Smartrac's Dogbone UHF tags, the system provides information about each car's position in the finishing, storage and shipping processes. This results in reduced labor for drivers who locate and transport the vehicles, as well as increased visibility for production management.

Automobile manufacturer Audi is preparing to install a radio frequency identification solution for tracking its newly manufactured vehicles through finish work and shipping, at multiple global factories, based on a template installation in use at its new Hungarian plant. The EPC Gen 2 ultrahigh-frequency (UHF) RFID system, provided by German RFID company noFilis, was taken live when Audi Hungaria Motor Kft. launched the production in GyQr, Hungary, in June 2013. The system is now being used to track the finishing and inspection of the A3 sedans and A3 cabriolets that the plant produces, as well as the vehicles' outbound preparation and shipping.

The car company chose to create a template system at its new plant, where implementation would be easier than at factories that already have operational procedures in place for tracking vehicles. The manual systems typically employed at other plants require that drivers use paperwork to direct them through the finishing process, and that they exit the cars and scan bar codes at some locations as well, in order to create a record of their movements.

Once an assembled vehicle has its wheels in place, it begins moving through what is called finishing work. A driver actually drives the car to each appropriate station, to the storage yard, and then onto a truck or train. At the GyQr plant, 160,000 vehicles are currently being produced annually, though that number is expected to increase. The cars are stored within one of two lots: one dedicated to shipping by truck and another dedicated to train shipment. A third yard contains additional spaces intended for use as production increases and new models are launched.

Audi sought to eliminate paperwork and make the finishing, outbound-preparation and subsequent shipping processes more transparent and leaner.

Once a vehicle has been assembled, a UHF Avery Dennison Smartrac Dogbone tag with an Impinj Monza 4QT inlay is attached to the inside of the front bumper.

An automated tag-commissioning process in the production line writes the vehicle identification number (VIN) to the tag, as well as another ID number used by assembly stations. In this way, even if the computer system or local network goes down, workers can continue to identify each vehicle in front of them via an RFID reader.

The company installed approximately 50 Sick RFU 630 fixed readers within its assembly areas, as well as at gates leading into and out of storage yards. It also equipped workers with a Nordic ID Merlin or Agillox AGX DOT 300 handheld reader.

After a vehicle completes the assembly process and is tagged, a driver moves that car past an RFID reader, which forwards the tag's ID number to the back-end system. noFilis CrossTalk Agent software, residing on each reader, interprets the reads, filters out unnecessary data or false-positive read events and forwards the relevant information to Audi's business middleware, which identifies the vehicle and transmits that data to Audi's back-end system. The driver passes through a series of finishing and inspection stations, and with each read event, a record is created of which steps have been carried out. At the same time, the CrossTalk software manages and monitors the health of the RFID hardware and software. In the event that it identifies a problem, the system then issues an alert to the assigned recipient.

Once the finishing work is concluded, the driver moves the vehicle to the storage lot and parks it in one of the open parking spaces displayed on an LED screen. According to Patrick Hartmann, noFilis' global sales director, tags are attached not only to vehicles, but also to some of the storage yard parking spaces, in order to create a record of that space in Audi's management system and the CrossTalk software. Once the car is parked, the driver uses a handheld reader to interrogate the UHF RFID tag affixed to that space, as well as the tag on the car's bumper, thereby creating a record of which space the vehicle is in. CrossTalk Mobile Agent software, installed on the handheld device, sends the data to Audi's management system via a Wi-Fi connection. If there is a Wi-Fi problem, the data is stored until the network connection is resumed"

Chipotle deploys RFID for traceability and food safety

Chipotle Mexican Grill has become one of the first restaurant companies to announce that it is piloting Avery Dennison RFID solutions to optimize their operations and trace ingredients at its distribution center and approximately 200 restaurants in the Chicago area. The spotlight is on the restaurant sector as food safety along with better supply chain and inventory management becomes ever more critical. To address these market needs, Avery Dennison is leading a number of initiatives to drive digital transformation in this field.

Scott Boatwright, Chief Restaurant Officer at Chipotle remarked: "RFID labels transform inventory management into an automatic, digital function that optimizes restaurant operations and gives our Restaurant Support Centers access to inventory data in real-time. This integrated technology is improving our employee experience in participating restaurants while also benefiting our supply partners."

Chipotle will be using serialized RFID case labels to track ingredients from suppliers to restaurants. Ingredients arrive at Chipotle restaurants affixed with Ultra High Frequency (UHF) RFID enabled case labels and are scanned by staff using RFID readers. The RFID system does not require line of sight and reads hundreds of tagged items in seconds. The tech-enabled traceability system is designed to allow the company to act on food safety and quality concerns swiftly, efficiently, and precisely.

Avery Dennison has partnered with RFID software provider Mojix, plus scanning and printing hardware provider Zebra Technologies on the pilot.

"We have been developing our RFID program for two years and see this innovation as the next evolution of traceability and food safety. We are excited to test this innovation in the field with our suppliers and restaurants to enhance our robust traceability program," added Laurie Schalow, Chipotle's Chief Corporate Affairs and Food Safety Officer.

Francisco Melo, vice president and general manager at Avery Dennison Avery Dennison Smartrac, highlighted the drivers for the project: "Food safety and inventory efficiencies are paramount for the food industry. RFID plays a critical role in solving these challenges by enabling accurate inventory visibility, operational improvements in labor, and end to end traceability. We are pleased to be working with Chipotle on this game changing initiative."

At Avery Dennison we believe that traceability across the food supply chain is critical to optimizing operations. Digital ID solutions offer the opportunity for businesses to avoid overproduction by gaining better visibility into inventory and products' expiration dates—reducing spoilage and waste.

Implementing RFID now also sets the foundation to drive future sustainability initiatives: We are confident that, over time, the data collected through RFID-enabled supply chains will enable Chipotle to optimize food supply to meet consumer demand.

RFID at Galeria Kaufhof

Kaufhof Warenhaus AG operates 126 department stores in Germany, 113 of them under the brand name "Galeria Kaufhof", and 15 in Belgium. Galeria Kaufhof is a subsidiary of Metro Group, the fifth largest retailer worldwide (Deloitte 2008). It is visited – as one of Europe's leading department store chains – by more than two million customers each day and has a total sales floor of 1.5 million square meters. Its assortment primarily consists of international brands of middle to upper price level. The company employs about 25,000 people and generated €3.6 billion in sales in 2007

Kaufhof's first RFID activities – a collaboration with the fashion merchandise manufacturer Gerry Weber (Loebbecke and Palmer 2006a; Loebbecke 2007) - date back to 2003. The main objective of this first project was to examine to what extent RFID can contribute to the acceleration and simplification of supply chain operations under real-world conditions (Metro 2005), including the assessment of achievable read rates and time-savings due to automatic object identification, and to investigate the technology's suitability for replacing conventional Electronic Article Surveillance (EAS) systems, a topic that has traditionally been of particular interest in fashion retailing.

The project team also considered the idea of utilizing RFID to realize novel customer applications and to change in-store processes. However, these scenarios remained in the abstract and were not part of the trial itself. The quantitative business case analysis concentrated on time and labor cost savings due to process automation at various points in the supply chain. The overall evaluation of the RFID business potential, including the many qualitative results gathered by the project team, was very positive.

This experience motivated Kaufhof to join the consortium of "Building Radio Frequency Identification Solutions for the Global Environment" (BRIDGE), an R&D project funded by the European Commission in July 2006 for a duration of 36 months. BRIDGE is a 13 million Euro RFID research project running over 3 years and partly funded by the European Union. The objective of the BRIDGE project is to address ways to resolve barriers to the implementation of the EPCglobal Network in Europe by conducting research and by developing and implementing tools that enable the deployment of EPCglobal applications in Europe (BRIDGE 2009). The project comprises several chapters composed of working packages, in which thirty interdisciplinary partners from 12 countries (Europe and Asia) work together on hardware development, serial look-up service, security, anti-counterfeiting, supply chain management, manufacturing process, reusable asset management, item-level tagging for non-food items as well as policy recommendations (BRIDGE 2007), for example. The company's main interest in BRIDGE was to implement RFID in its own processes, to speed up RFID adoption in the textile sector, and to share its experiences with industry organizations and standardization bodies. As part of the project, Galeria Kaufhof implemented an RFID infrastructure in the menswear department on the third floor of its store in Essen, Germany, with a total of 2,000 square meters in September 2007.

RFID Applications

Customer Applications

For an improved customer experience and for the improvement of customer service, Galeria Kaufhof developed based on the described infrastructure various RFID customer applications and installed them on the sales floor. The goal of these applications was to practically demonstrate and evaluate the customer value of RFID.

Smart Monitor: RFID readers in the fitting rooms recognize the product codes of clothing that is brought in. A screen inside each fitting room at the Gardeur shop displays additional information on the product and other available sizes and colors. Depending on the set of detected items, the system offers recommendations regarding alternative or complementary products (Fig. 7a).

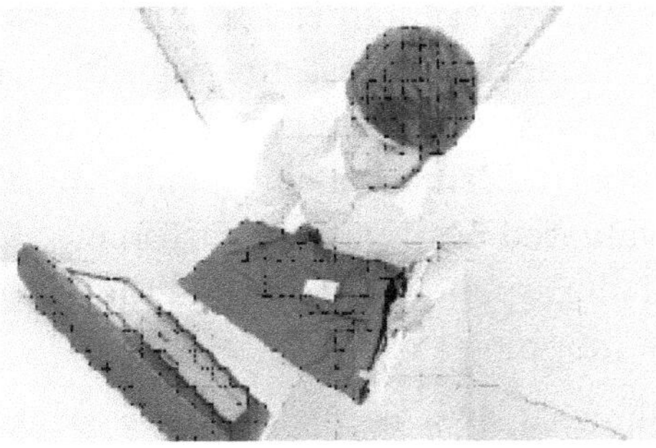

a) Smart Monitor in the fitting rooms

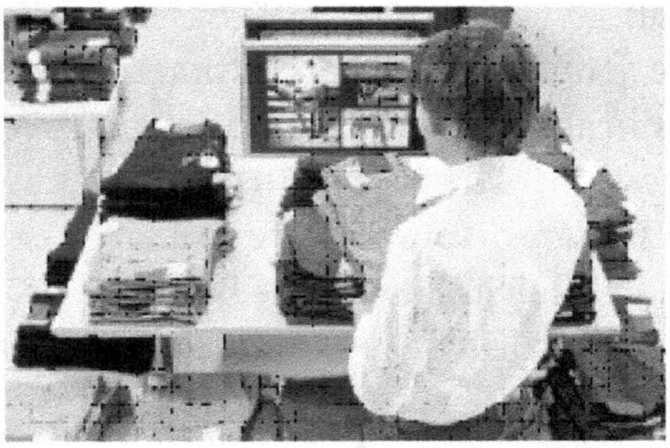

b) Smart Shelf in the Gardeur-Shop

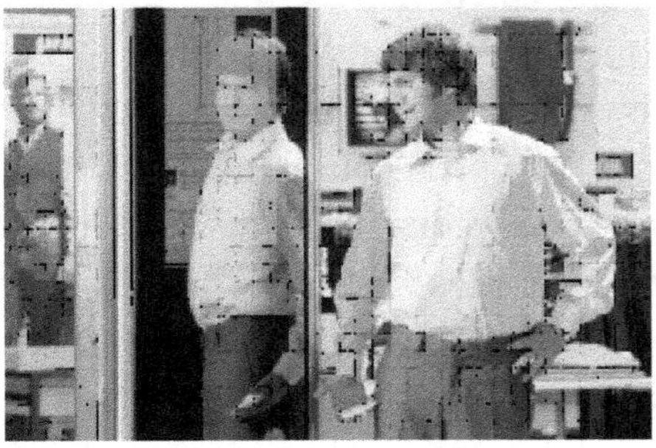

c) Smart Mirror in the Gardeur Shop

d) Mobile Handheld Device

Fig. 7. RFID Customer Applications on the Sales Floor of the Galeria Kaufhof Essen Department Store

Smart Shelf: Several shelves in the Gardeur shop are equipped with RFID readers and screens. A screen of each shelf shows the current availability of items on the particular shelf. Thus, customers looking for a specific item do not need to check the entire shelf to know which sizes and colors are available (see Fig. 7b).

Smart Mirror: A large mirror with a built-in screen on the sales floor offers product information. Once a customer approaches the so-called "Magic Mirror" with a tagged item receive information about materials, care instructions, available sizes, and colors (see Fig. 7c).

Mobile Handheld Devices: Using mobile handheld devices ("MDE"), store employees can scan the item's RFID tag in order to send a query to the RFID system regarding the availability (e.g., different size and color) and location of other items in the same category on the sales floor or in the backroom. Furthermore, MDE devices are also used for goods receipt and inventory counting to accelerate the process beyond what is possible when manually counting each item using a mobile barcode reader (see Fig. 7d).

Customer and Employee Surveys

For the evaluation of customer attitudes towards the RFID-based applications, Galeria Kaufhof conducted a survey among 250 customers (50% women, 50% younger than 40 years). The RFID-based applications were presented to the customers on the front store. The customers were asked to answer questions regarding the applications using a fully structured interview guideline with primarily open questions. The three RFID customer applications (i.e., smart shelves, magic mirror, and smart displays) were to a large extent evaluated positively by customers, with smart shelves having the best ratings. 56% of all respondents regarded these items as constituting a great improvement in their shopping experience.

Smart displays were equally successful, with 49% recording very positive answers. The customers appreciated the detailed information on product availability in particular. Customers were also asked if they had perceived any negative aspects of either application. This question was answered in the negative by 83% and 79% of the respondents, respectively. In the contrast, the magic mirror was seen as an improvement by only 33%. As some of the comments indicated, this can be attributed to the limited usefulness of the information displayed and the position of the display in the mirror area. Privacy issues were not considered in the survey, but Kaufhof informed their customers about the presence of RFID readers and prepared their employees to answer specific questions. Perhaps as a result, only three privacy-related customer complaints were observed during the whole trial period.

Kaufhof also conducted interviews with their sales employees. They were asked to report on their experiences with RFID. The respondents appreciated most of all the use of the mobile devices for inventory counting and the search functionality, which allows them to easily locate items on the sales floor. The interviews clearly showed that the employees' attitude towards RFID was dependent on its benefits in the completion of everyday processes. Moreover, a number of suggestions for improvement were gathered – e.g., regarding the available search criteria.

From a technical perspective, the project has been highly innovative regarding the use of the newest transponder technology (UHF) and interface standards for the realization of integrated RFID systems. Read rates of virtually 100% were possible even at chokepoints such as in the transition between backroom and sales floor. The Galeria Kaufhof RFID project in Essen offered Kaufhof a unique possibility to empirically investigate different relationships between RFID investments and the effects on operational and management processes, thus improving the understanding of the business value of RFID in retail.

Various possibilities for improvements of logistical in-store processes, as well as of customer processes, could be demonstrated in the course of the project. These include, for example, RFID-enabled inventory counting, accelerated goods receipt processes, or sales support through mobile devices. Besides automational effects on the operational level, however, the project surpassed earlier trials by illustrating the relevance of the technology for the department store management. RFID as a fully automated measurement and control instrument provides information about inventory level developments on the sales floor, the time cycle and the quality of replenishment activities, the number of try-ons (on the item level and on the level of the whole category), and the types of tried on articles, respectively. Additionally, the trial showed that by providing more transparency, RFID can help to close the "data void" which exists between the goods receipt and the POS of the department store. The technology can thus help to discover process inefficiencies, which were so far intransparent and to help to control effective countermeasures accordingly. Furthermore, RFID technology not only helps to cut costs, but also improves the service quality and the quality of service processes on the sales floor.

Transponders were only removed from the products on request to allow for the identification of returned items. The company nevertheless experienced virtually no negative reactions during the whole trial period. Whether this is a consequence of their open communications policy or the consumers' perception of RFID benefits cannot be ascertained for certain at this point in time. Another conceivable explanation could be that the privacy debate in recent years, despite its presentation in the media, never really resonated with the broader public. However, the implementation of integrated RFID systems might trigger a second wave of anti-RFID activities and re-intensify the discussion around privacy risks.

LESSONS LEARNED FROM REAL-WORLD APPLICATIONS

Store level inventory process and data improvements

- **Improvement in overall accuracy** – RFID can transform the in-store inventory accuracy to upwards of 98%, approaching that of warehouses. The typical retail inventory process is very manual, time-consuming, and only done at predetermined intervals. Historical data shows that for every

~3% improvement in in-store inventory accuracy, you can expect a ~1% increase in sales. Typical retailers operate at ~70% accuracy by year-end (2–3% reduction in accuracy per month), leaving significant opportunity for positive impact on sales.

- **Receiving** — Because RFID antennas and wands do not require line of sight to scan RFID tags, shipments to the store can be instantly and accurately received into inventory. This is a huge win compared to time-sucking individual carton and item scanning, or even worse, blind receipts.
- **Finding items** — Handheld RFID wands typically have the ability to track items in the store using a system akin to metal detectors, beeping faster as the wand approaches a given item. More complex systems of fixed antennas throughout a store can also be set up to pinpoint a specific tag's location.
- **Cycle count time** — Since line of sight is not necessary and RFID antennas can work at a distance, a cycle count can be done significantly faster and more accurately than any traditional processes.
- **Removal of formal inventory counts** — RFID readers are accurate enough such that RFID-based inventory counts may be allowed by your auditor after showing a history of accuracy.
- **Auto reorders at safety stock levels** — Because your overall accuracy is improved, the rules that are set up for replenishment orders can be set and forgotten in-lieu of manual spot checking or ensuring replenishments are needed.

Store operations

- **Spread breadth of available products while reducing depth** — thinking about a product like men's jeans, one style may have 10 different widths, 10 different lengths, and 10 different colors. It will be impossible to keep any significant amount of inventory for all variations displayed. Inevitably many will stock out on the floor and others will have no movement. This may change on a day-to-day basis with some trends, but not enough to make impactful floor inventory decisions. With RFID in place, employees can be notified when a specific combination is no longer available on the floor (or has low inventory), where to find it in the backroom, and exactly how many to pull, on a nearly instantaneous and continuous basis.
- **BOPIS and ship from store** — Both buy-online-pick-up-in-store and ship from store are customer expectations approaching a must-have capability for retailers. If the business cannot trust their inventory accuracy, they cannot consistently deliver these capabilities. In simplest terms, without accurate, real-time inventory counts, a retailer could be selling an item for pickup that doesn't actually exist in the store.

In-store traffic patterns

- **Customer and product flow** – By aggregating and plotting RFID item movement throughout a store, retailers can begin to draw conclusions about how people and products navigate the physical confines of the space. Benefits could include: monetizing high-traffic endcaps, tracking in-store cart or product abandonment, removing physical pinch points, understanding how certain product categories or items correlate to different paths in the store at different times of day, days of the week, etc.
- **Associate flow** — Whether for training purposes or data collection, RFID tags could be used to track employee movement throughout a store.
- **Equipment flow** — Whether it's forklifts at a home improvement retailer or a restocking cart at a clothing store, valuable data can be gleaned from seeing how equipment flows through a store's physical space.

Fitting room

- **Magic mirror** – Imagine a fitting room that uses touch screen monitors in place of mirrors. By geo-locating specific RFID tags, this fitting room tracks the item that is being tried on, shows other available colors and what those might look like on you, shows available complementary clothes, and could provide relevant product information such as the fabric technology.
- **Tracking pickup/try-on vs. purchased** – As items are tried on and not purchased, that information can be tracked for either internal analysis or to remarket to the individual who didn't purchase later.

Checkout process

- RFID can speed up and potentially eliminate the traditional checkout process altogether. Items could pass on a conveyor through scanners that read on-the-fly rather than individual bar code scans. Items in a bag or cart could be tagged to a pre-loaded customer loyalty account to aid in creating a frictionless checkout experience where a customer simply walks through an RFID gate on their way out of the store.

Security

- **Theft** – RFID movement tracking can be paired with sales data and video data to determine if items left the store in larger quantities than were purchased at that specific time. With this data aggregated, retailers can see systematically which exact items were stolen, which door they exited through, at what exact time, and have HD video of the specific perpetrator. This data can be actioned real-time through alerts to associates, used for monitoring of general trends, or as evidence to work with authorities creating criminal cases.

Post-purchase enablement

- Another use case is linking product usage to marketing to create future sales. For instance, if a retailer's app could track activities or read from other apps, it could enable unique capabilities. For one specific example, if running shoes were RFID enabled (the item itself, not the packaging), your phone or watch could recognize when you are wearing those shoes on a run. When the shoes approach expected end-of-life (based on miles run, user weight, user speeds) the retailer could trigger a coupon to replace that shoe with the newest iteration.

Considerations

- **Physical or financial incompatibility** — Not all products make sense with RFID. This could be because an item is low value and doesn't justify any additional cost, or it could be because the product itself is incompatible with RFID. Very dense products or metal items will have radio penetration problems and will not allow for the full benefits of RFID.
- **System integrations** — RFID and RFID software can exist as a stand-alone solution for some in-store problems. However, at some point decisions will need to be made as to the overall direction of RFID within the company, and whether it makes sense to integrate fully into inventory, allocation, master data, point of sale, digital asset management, and other systems.
- **RFID tag applications** — RFID tags (specifically external tags vs. embedded) can be applied anywhere in the supply chain — at the supplier, distribution center, or retail store — each with different costs, control, accuracy, and benefits. Depending on corporate goals, you must have a strategy for this.
- **Edge vs. Cloud** — An integrated RFID solution at all retail stores could lead to an astronomical increase in data and calls to central systems and thus, cost. Cost-benefit analysis should be done to decide whether companies must bring in new data processing capabilities as their RFID solution advances, such as Edge networks to control these costs.
- **Shielding** — Storefront operations need to be radio shielded from back-of-store operations for RFID to function properly (so systems don't accidentally mix inventory). The most effective way is with the addition of physical shielding, or even better, physical shielding installed during store construction. Many RFID software providers are now seeing success with virtual shielding, using algorithms to identify front-of-store vs. back-of-store location. As these algorithms advance, it could become completely unnecessary to have physical shielding, making potential adoption even quicker.

- **Privacy** – If RFID is embedded into products itself, complications with user privacy could emerge, and must be considered during the product design phase on a country-by-country basis. What is significant is that unlike GPS, RFID can't be tracked or pinpointed over large distances.
- **Supply chain ripple** – RFID can quickly expose larger supply chain issues such as supplier relationships, store allocation accuracy, distribution channel on time in full, supply chain visibility, store inventory practices, shrinkage, returns/repairs, and overall agility. To see additional company-wide benefits after initial RFID adoption, going down supply chain improvement paths may be necessary.

CHAPTER-16

BEST PRACTICES FOR RFID DEPLOYMENT

RFID technology has revolutionized inventory management and asset tracking for industries across the globe. However, when it comes to tracking items on metal surfaces, traditional RFID systems can often fall short. That's where metal mount RFID comes in. Brands like Invengo offer highly durable and reliable metal mount RFID solutions that are specifically designed to overcome the challenges of tracking metal-based assets. In this blog post, we will explore the best practices for installing and deploying metal mount RFID systems to ensure optimal performance and efficiency.

Understanding the Challenges of Tracking Metal Assets

Metal surfaces can interfere with traditional RFID signals, causing read errors and inaccurate data collection. Metal mount RFID systems use specialized tags and antennas that are designed to work effectively on metal surfaces. Before installing a metal mount RFID system, it's crucial to understand the specific challenges posed by metal assets and how metal mount RFID technology can address them.

Proper Tag Placement and Orientation

When installing metal mount RFID tags on metal assets, proper positioning and orientation are key. Unlike standard RFID tags, which can be placed on any surface, metal mount RFID tags need to be placed strategically to ensure optimal read performance. Tags should be affixed to the asset in a way that minimizes interference from the metal surface. Additionally, the orientation of the tag in relation to the RFID reader plays a significant role in read accuracy. Careful placement and orientation of metal mount RFID tags are essential for achieving reliable and consistent tracking results.

Choosing the Right RFID Reader and Antenna Setup

In addition to selecting the appropriate metal mount RFID tags, it's important to choose the right RFID reader and antenna setup for your specific tracking needs. Metal mount RFID systems typically require specialized readers and antennas that are optimized for use on metal surfaces. By selecting the right combination of reader and antenna, you can ensure seamless communication between the tags and the reader, resulting in accurate and reliable data collection.

Conducting Thorough Testing and Optimization

Once your metal mount RFID system is installed, it's essential to conduct thorough testing and optimization to ensure optimal performance. This includes testing read range, read accuracy, and data capture speed in real-world conditions. By testing the system in different environments and scenarios, you can identify any potential issues and make adjustments as needed to optimize performance. Regular maintenance and calibration of the system are also important to ensure long-term reliability and efficiency.

Metal mount RFID technology from brands like Invengo offers a robust solution for tracking assets on metal surfaces. By following these best practices for installing and deploying metal mount RFID systems, you can maximize the benefits of RFID technology and achieve accurate and efficient asset tracking. With proper tag placement, the right reader and antenna setup, and thorough testing and optimization, you can ensure the successful implementation of a metal mount RFID system in your organization.

In conclusion, metal mount RFID technology provides a reliable and effective solution for tracking assets on metal surfaces. By following best practices for installation and deployment, you can overcome the challenges of tracking metal assets and achieve optimal performance. Brands like Invengo offer cutting-edge metal mount RFID solutions that can help streamline inventory management and asset tracking processes. Embracing metal mount RFID technology is a smart investment for businesses looking to improve efficiency and accuracy in asset tracking.

KEY STRATEGIES FOR SUCCESSFUL RFID INTEGRATION

Introduction:

In today's rapidly evolving retail landscape, implementing an effective RFID (Radio Frequency Identification) strategy has become a strategic imperative for many businesses. RFID technology offers tremendous potential to streamline operations, improve inventory accuracy, enhance customer experiences, and drive overall business growth. However, successful RFID implementation requires careful planning and consideration of various factors to maximise its benefits and ensure a seamless transition. In this article, we will delve into the main considerations when implementing an RFID strategy for retail, helping you navigate the path to success.

Define Your Objectives:

Before embarking on an RFID implementation, it is crucial to define your objectives clearly. Identify the specific pain points you aim to address, such as inventory visibility, stockouts, or theft prevention. Determine your desired outcomes, such as improved inventory accuracy, enhanced supply chain efficiency, or personalised customer experiences. Clearly articulating your objectives will guide your RFID strategy and help measure its success.

Conduct a Pilot Study

To mitigate risks and ensure a smooth transition, it is advisable to conduct a pilot study before full-scale deployment. Select a few stores or departments to test the RFID technology, allowing you to fine-tune processes, identify challenges, and assess the potential impact on your operations. The pilot study will enable you to gather valuable insights, identify any necessary adjustments, and build confidence among stakeholders.

Establish a Scalable Infrastructure

Implementing RFID requires a robust and scalable infrastructure to support the technology's operations. This includes strategically positioning RFID readers and antennas, investing in RFID tags and printers, and integrating RFID software with existing systems like inventory management, point of sale (POS), and customer relationship management (CRM). Designing an infrastructure that can accommodate future growth and changing business needs is critical to maximising the long-term benefits of RFID.

Optimise Inventory Management Processes

RFID technology empowers retailers with real-time, accurate inventory data, enabling better visibility and control over stock levels. However, to fully leverage this potential, it is essential to optimise your inventory management processes. This includes redefining workflows, retraining staff, and implementing new procedures to capitalise on RFID's capabilities. By aligning processes with RFID technology, you can reduce stockouts, improve replenishment cycles, and enhance overall inventory accuracy.

Ensure Data Security and Privacy

As with any technology implementation, data security and privacy are paramount. RFID systems involve the collection and transmission of sensitive information, such as product details, customer data, and employee information. Implement robust security measures to safeguard the RFID network, including encryption, access controls, and regular audits. Additionally, comply with relevant privacy regulations, ensuring transparency and obtaining explicit consent when handling customer data.

Educate and Engage Employees

Employee buy-in and understanding are crucial for the successful adoption of RFID technology. Invest in comprehensive training programs to educate employees on the benefits of RFID, how to use the technology effectively, and how it enhances their roles. Encourage open communication channels, address concerns, and foster a culture of innovation. Engaged and empowered employees will drive the success of your RFID strategy.

Continuously Monitor and Optimise

RFID implementation is not a one-time event but an ongoing process. Establish metrics to track the performance of your RFID strategy, such as inventory accuracy, operational efficiency, and customer satisfaction. Regularly monitor the system's effectiveness, identify areas for improvement, and fine-tune your strategy accordingly. Embrace a culture of continuous improvement to optimise your RFID implementation continuously.

Assess your business needs and your goals with RFID

Never start an RFID installation project without first defining your business goals. You should specify your intentions whether you're implementing RFID to satisfy your business's asset tracking requirements or the retailer's obligation. It helps in the formation of a framework that enables more informed decision-making. Setting defined objectives rooted in your business needs can keep your team concentrated on the most important tasks and help you isolate the primary goals from the secondary and tertiary objectives.

An RFID system is used, for instance, in a manufacturing plant to improve raw material inventory management, have better visibility on the floor, and streamline production procedures. Reducing stockout conditions, increasing customer satisfaction, and streamlining inventory management are possible objectives in a retail setting. Knowing your needs before setting up an RFID system is crucial because these objectives require completely different setups.

Choose the Right RFID Tags

In the case of RFID technology or system, selecting the right tag, reader and software is important too.

There are three types of RFID tags. Since each type has benefits and drawbacks, it's important to select the one that best suits your company. The cost of each RFID tag depends upon their specific feature and uses cases.

- **Passive RFID Tags:** UHF Passive RFID tags are the most widely used because they come at a low cost and don't support any power backup. To transfer data, they rely on the energy released by a reader. Passive tags are therefore only effective when placed a short distance, up to 15m, from the reader.
- **Active RFID Tags:** Active RFID tags are self-sufficient, they can track objects across extended distances, going up to 100m. They are perfect for large-scale logistics since they have a far longer data transmission range than passive tags. But compared to passive tags, active tags cost more and need more upkeep.
- **Semi-passive Tags:** Semi-passive tags rely on the reader's energy for communication, but they have a battery to power their circuitry. They are an excellent balance for various applications because they are less expensive than active tags and give a longer range than passive tags.

RFID Readers

The equipment that scans and reads the data encoded in the RFID tags is called an RFID reader. The range you require, the frequency of the tags, and the surrounding conditions will all influence the kind of reader you select. Let's look into the types of readers:

- **Fixed RFID Readers:** RFID Fixed Mount Readers are widely used to track the movement of items through the supply chain and keep an eye on inventory levels in manufacturing facilities, warehouses, and retail establishments. For tracking goods in a specified location, fixed readers work well. These are fixed gadgets that you can put on ceilings, walls, or other surfaces.
- **Handheld Readers:** Handheld RFID Readers are mobile readers, frequently used to track assets across a wide area in the logistics and transportation industry. When field service and maintenance professionals need to keep track of the location and conditions of tools and equipment, handheld readers come in handy. Handheld readers are more flexible to use than fixed readers.

Focus on the Software Requirements

A platform or procedure of some kind is required by your company to handle all of the data captured by an RFID technology. All the data related to your supply chain and inventory management software, as well as your ERP (Enterprise Resource Planning) and WMS (Warehouse Management System), should be compatible with the software you select.

Therefore, find a software program that can produce reports and extract useful analytics. You can use your software to make better decisions about your assets if the reporting is better and provides deeper insights.

Software for inventory management, asset, tool, and equipment tracking, and supply chain tracking with auto-generated reports and insights are all included in our end-to-end RFID solutions that we provide at EnCstore.com.

Cost Estimation on your RFID Implementation

Before proceeding, one must calculate the costs of RFID system implementation. The cost estimates will differ depending on whether RFID is used to track valuable assets in a warehouse, a retail environment, or a healthcare facility. Each business will incur different costs due to distinct operational needs. As a result, estimating the total capital expenditure for RFID technology implementation will be critical. Most importantly, this will provide an outline of the investment's ROI.

Validate and test Your Software System

RFID performance varies between tags and devices, so thoroughly test and validate your system before deploying it. If you're applying to metal containers, curved surfaces, or certain types of packaging materials, you may need specialized tags designed to RFID tags to adhere to your surface type. To ensure that your proposed system produces the best results, test it in your environment or a simulated environment that replicates your RFID operating conditions. This will assist you in identifying any specialized requirements and selecting the appropriate tags and hardware configuration before embarking on a full-fledged implementation.

Train the staff

Another important thing for businesses is to train the workers on all RFID features in addition to implementing RFID. They should be knowledgeable about it beyond the bare minimum. The essential project workers should also be more knowledgeable about the involved technology. The technology will be more efficient if people understand how it operates better. RFID technology cannot be successfully implemented without the input of various departments, such as manufacturing, supply chain, maintenance, sales, IT, and so on.

Check the accuracy and performance of your RFID

Even with RFID, errors might still happen, therefore constant development and optimization may be required if you want to achieve 100% accuracy. You need a procedure for keeping track, auditing, and logging your RFID results to accomplish this. You can assume results that are at or almost at 100 percent accuracy with adequate tuning and monitoring of system accuracy. Different tools and reports will show you how accurate your RFID scanning and tracking are and where you might need to align your RFID solution to get the outcomes you want.

In conclusion, implementing RFID technology offers numerous benefits to businesses, including improved efficiency, enhanced inventory management, and streamlined operations. However, to ensure successful integration and maximize the potential benefits, several important factors must be considered. From understanding the specific goals of the RFID implementation and selecting the right RFID tags and readers to choosing the appropriate software to manage RFID data, Cost estimation, and ROI analysis to justify the investment, you must think in advance for better results. Thorough testing, validation, and staff training are also critical to efficiently utilize the RFID technology. Finally, ongoing monitoring and performance evaluation are necessary to identify and address any issues and continuously improve the accuracy and effectiveness of the RFID system.

AVOIDING COMMON PITFALLS

At the time of starting an RFID project, selecting an RFID tag is usually one of the first tasks. However, common mistakes at this stage of the project can cause issues down the line. With thousands of RFID tags to choose from, it's important to avoid these common mistakes.

Incorrect Frequency

Radio Frequency Identification (RFID), is actually not a single technology but a group of technologies. Each of these of technologies , explained in detail here, have their own use cases and applications. Choosing the wrong frequency, can lead to issues where the RFID tags may not have the appropriate read ranges.

In addition, as each of these technologies operate on different frequencies, they often have their own protocols and standards, thus having mismatching frequencies between the RFID tags and their respective hardware may lead to a mismatched system.

A simple way to avoid this mistake is cross reference the frequency, protocols and standards between the RFID tags and the desired RFID hardware that is to be used in the project.

Incorrect Formfactor

These are certain materials out that that work really well with RFID such as cardboard and most plastics. However, other material such as metal or items that have liquid inside of them may play an impact on the performance of the system. This doesn't mean that RFID doesn't work with this material but instead means that the correct RFID tags should be chosen for the job. For example, with UHF (RAIN) RFID, metal reflects RFID so special on-metal RFID tags and labels should be used.

Durability

It's important to consider the entire lifecycle that the item which is being RFID tagged is going to go through, as the RFID tag is itself will need to have the same robustness. For example, if the item will go through extreme temperature or moisture, it's important to cross check the RFID tag to ensure it's rated for the same environment.

Scalability

When starting off, it's really easy to make decisions in regards to how or where an RFID tag will be attached to an item. However, consider the long term. When the project scales across the company, will you still be able to manually attach the tag to the asset or would it be easier to have a vendor attach it during manufacturing?

In addition, consider the data you are placing onto the RFID tag - will this scale when the asset or item moves through its lifecycle. If other entities wanted to leverage the data (assuming you'd want to have interoperability), it is easy to share the data?

How about where you are attaching the RFID tag on the product. Will this cause issues to others down the line?

Considering these common mistakes may help you avoid a pitfall and lead to success with your RFID project. Do you need help with your RFID implementation? Please reach out and we'd be happy to help.

PART VI: FUTURE TRENDS AND INNOVATIONS

CHAPTER-17

EMERGING TRENDS IN RFID TECHNOLOGY

Future trends in RFID include the integration of sensors and IoT (Internet of Things) capabilities, enabling companies to monitor various parameters such as temperature, humidity, and pressure during transportation and storage. This enhanced visibility not only improves efficiency but also ensures compliance with regulatory requirements and quality control standards.

RFID FUTURE TRENDS

As we witness ongoing developments in RFID and barcoding, there's an anticipation for an array of additional applications to emerge in the near future. The landscape is evolving, and we eagerly anticipate the realization of these solutions, adding further excitement to the already dynamic realm of RFID and barcoding advancements.

Let's look at some future trends in RFID:

Increased Sustainability Measures

RFID technology will align with sustainability goals, with a focus on developing eco-friendly tags and solutions. The industry will explore materials and manufacturing processes that reduce environmental impact. Sustainable RFID applications will contribute to a more responsible and environmentally conscious use of technology.

Flexible Printing Options

Harnessing high-performance thin-film transistor technology, today's RFID tags are remarkably thinner and more flexible than previously envisioned. This innovation allows them to seamlessly adhere to diverse surfaces.

Integrating RFID into a bend-resistant, flexible substrate expands its applications, overcoming previous limitations in settings with physical constraints.

Integrations with Other Technologies

Today's RFID tags boast versatility and emerging integrations propel them to new heights. Current warehouse management systems leverage RFID for enhanced traceability, precision in picking, and efficient delivery.

Looking ahead, the integration of smart-sensing RFID into the Internet of Things (IoT) will revolutionize warehouses by tracking various factors, including temperature, for optimized supply chain operations.

Cloud-Based Data Storage

RFID's enduring advantage lies in mobility, a facet set to evolve with the integration of cloud-based data storage into future systems. Storing real-time data in the cloud enhances accessibility, optimizing stock accuracy, product availability, and replenishment. This streamlining benefits supply chain processes, boosting productivity and accuracy across teams.

More Innovative Applications

Beyond the highlighted materials and technologies, RFID trends will advance as industry leaders innovate for optimal solutions. These systems are increasingly recognized as interconnected solutions, encompassing various applications and readers.

Future accessibility extends beyond warehouses and healthcare, envisioning consumers installing personal RFID readers at home for seamless integration with management systems and IoT devices.

Market Outlook

- **Growing Adoption Across Industries:** RFID technology is gaining prominence as an alternative identification system, particularly in challenging environments. Industries are increasingly recognizing its potential for diverse applications.
- **Innovative Tamper-Proof RFID Labels:** Identiv's creation of a Tamper-Proof RFID label showcases advancements in security. The label's data carrier erases information upon removal, addressing security concerns and preventing unauthorized access to company data.
- **Printed Sensors Integration:** Integration of printed sensors onto RFID smart labels marks a significant development. The inkjet-printed multi-sensing platform on flexible substrates, incorporated into high-frequency RFID smart labels, offers capabilities like humidity, ammonia, and temperature detection simultaneously.
- **Cost-Effective Manufacturing:** The inkjet printing technology allows flexible plastic surfaces, reducing manufacturing costs. RFID smart

labels deliver information gathered by readers from integrated sensors, enhancing environmental monitoring in the supply chain, especially in the food industry.

In a Nutshell, here are the latest innovations in RFID Technology

Explore how these developments revolutionize asset management across industries, from innovative tag manufacturing to enhanced antenna designs.

- **Innovative Tag Manufacturing:** Thin, flexible RFID tags integrate with printed sensors and batteries, enabling potential on-site chipless tag production.
- **Enhanced Antenna Designs:** New antenna designs offer increased range and versatility, crucial for enhancing tag performance.
- **Smart Tag Evolution:** Increasing memory capacities facilitate "smart asset" applications, particularly benefiting high-value assets and security-sensitive industries.
- **Integration with Sensor Technology:** RFID seamlessly integrates with sensors, enabling comprehensive asset monitoring and enhancing capabilities in IoT applications.
- **Cloud-based Data Management:** Cloud solutions simplify RFID data management, facilitating real-time inventory updates and just-in-time production.
- **Flexible Printing Options:** On-site printing allows customization to meet durability and application requirements, utilizing various materials and technologies.
- **Technological Integrations:** RFID integrates with existing business technologies, enabling real-time tracking and inventory management.
- **Environmental Responsibility:** Manufacturers develop sustainable RFID options to comply with waste management standards, promoting environmental sustainability.

IOT INTEGRATION AND RFID

The terms RFID and IoT are sometimes used synonymously to describe approaches for automatically tracking products, pallets and containers across the supply chain, and users often combine the two technologies. However, RFID and IoT are different in important ways.

RFID generally refers to a technology through which users read data from special RFID tags affixed to items. IoT generally refers to a broader array of technology for the communication and control of smart devices.

Differences between RFID and IoT

RFID and IoT have some important differences. These include the following:

- IoT can support any network, while RFID requires a specific radio technology.
- IoT can work over short-, medium- and long-range networks, while RFID only works over a few inches or feet.
- IoT can support any kind of data communications, while RFID is only suited for brief tags or authentication tokens.
- IoT is better for capturing real-time sensor data, while RFID is better suited for recording objects' proximity.
- IoT devices tend to be more complex and expensive, while RFID tags are generally optimized for low cost and simplicity.
- IoT can exchange data across wireless and wired networks, while RFID reads data in one direction from nearby tags.

In addition, less common types of RFID with more expensive active tags can support longer ranges and two-way communication in some use cases.

Use Cases for RFID and IoT in Asset Tracking

In an era where information is the lifeblood of business operations, the ability to track and manage assets efficiently and accurately holds paramount importance. This challenge has given rise to the convergence of two groundbreaking technologies: Radio-Frequency Identification (RFID) and the Internet of Things (IoT).

These powerful systems, individually impactful in their own right, have joined forces to revolutionize asset tracking across a multitude of industries.

In this exploration, we venture into the realm of RFID and IoT, focusing specifically on their remarkable applications in asset tracking. We will uncover how these technologies, with their ability to capture, transmit, and analyze data in real-time, are reshaping the way organizations safeguard and optimize their valuable resources.

From manufacturing floors and healthcare facilities to logistics hubs and smart cities, RFID and IoT offer a dynamic duo of solutions that provide unparalleled visibility, control, and efficiency.

Whether you're an industry professional seeking to enhance your asset management strategies or simply intrigued by the transformative potential of these technologies, this guide will illuminate the diverse use cases, benefits, and future prospects of RFID and IoT in the dynamic landscape of asset tracking.

Join us on this journey as we explore how RFID and IoT are driving innovation and reshaping the way we manage our most valuable assets.

Asset Tracking

In a manufacturing facility, IoT and RFID technologies are seamlessly integrated for efficient asset tracking. RFID tags with unique identification information are affixed to assets, while strategically placed IoT devices, including RFID readers and sensors, continuously monitor and transmit data over the internet.

This real-time tracking provides precise asset location information and enables real-time monitoring of conditions like temperature and humidity. The facility benefits from accurate inventory management, optimization of asset utilization, enhanced security, and loss prevention, as well as predictive maintenance scheduling based on historical data.

The combination of IoT and RFID technology streamlines asset tracking, reducing costs and enhancing overall operational efficiency.

Cold Chain Monitoring

RFID and IoT play a critical role in cold chain monitoring, ensuring the safe and efficient transportation of temperature-sensitive goods, such as pharmaceuticals, vaccines, and perishable foods. RFID tags and IoT sensors can continuously monitor and transmit temperature and humidity data, allowing for real-time tracking and management of cold chain logistics.

If temperature deviations occur, automated alerts can be triggered, enabling immediate corrective actions to prevent spoilage or compromised product quality. This technology also offers comprehensive data logging and analytics, helping companies meet regulatory compliance requirements and maintain the integrity of their cold chain, ensuring that products reach consumers in optimal condition.

Supply Chain Visibility

IoT technology complements the supply chain visibility offered by RFID, creating a robust ecosystem for efficient and transparent logistics. In this integrated approach, IoT sensors are incorporated into the RFID system to provide real-time data and insights throughout the supply chain.

These sensors monitor factors such as temperature, humidity, and environmental conditions, ensuring the integrity of sensitive products.

This combination enables proactive decision-making by alerting stakeholders to any deviations from ideal conditions, guaranteeing product quality and safety. Additionally, IoT extends the benefits of RFID technology to route optimization through data analytics, offering insights into traffic patterns, weather conditions, and delivery schedules.

Together, IoT and RFID empower organizations to achieve end-to-end visibility, improve efficiency, reduce waste, enhance product safety, and ensure timely and secure delivery of goods across the supply chain.

Predictive Maintenance

RFID and IoT technologies provide powerful tools for predictive maintenance across various industries. By embedding RFID tags and IoT sensors in critical equipment, companies can continuously monitor the condition and performance of assets in real time. This data is then processed and analyzed, allowing for the early detection of potential issues or anomalies.

Predictive maintenance enables proactive and scheduled repairs or replacements, reducing downtime, extending asset lifecycles, and ultimately saving on maintenance costs. Whether in manufacturing, healthcare, or transportation, this technology-driven approach ensures that equipment remains in optimal working condition, enhancing operational efficiency and reliability.

Quality Control

RFID and IoT technologies play a significant role in quality control processes across various industries. In manufacturing, RFID tags can be attached to individual components or products, while IoT sensors collect data on environmental conditions and equipment performance. This real-time information is then analyzed to identify deviations from quality standards. Automated alerts can trigger immediate corrective actions, helping prevent defects and ensuring consistent product quality.

In addition, RFID and IoT data can be used to track and trace products throughout the supply chain, aiding in identifying the source of quality issues and streamlining recalls. This technology-driven approach enhances quality control, reduces waste, and improves overall product quality and customer satisfaction.

Benefits of Combining RFID and IoT for Asset

The convergence of Radio-Frequency Identification (RFID) and the Internet of Things (IoT) has opened a gateway to a new era of asset tracking and management. Together, these technologies offer a dynamic synergy that empowers organizations to achieve unprecedented levels of visibility, efficiency, and control over their valuable assets.

Real-Time Visibility

The amalgamation of RFID and IoT ushers in the era of real-time asset visibility. RFID tags constantly broadcast their data, and IoT devices efficiently capture and transmit this information to a centralized management system. This immediate access to asset whereabouts and status empowers organizations to make informed decisions and promptly address asset-related issues.

Enhanced Accuracy

RFID technology excels in asset identification and tracking accuracy. When paired with IoT, the data collected not only remains accurate but is also delivered promptly. This precision in asset management reduces errors, enhances accountability, and ensures that assets are effectively utilized.

Improved Efficiency

Efficiency gains represent a major boon of RFID and IoT asset tracking. Automated data collection and reporting streamline processes, thereby reducing the time and effort required for manual tracking and reporting. This empowers employees to redirect their focus towards more strategic tasks.

Cost Reduction

Mitigating asset loss or theft and optimizing asset utilization through RFID and IoT can result in significant cost savings. The ability to identify underutilized or surplus assets empowers organizations to make data-driven decisions regarding asset allocation, retirement, or reallocation.

Compliance and Security

Several industries, such as healthcare, logistics, and finance, are subject to stringent regulatory requirements governing asset tracking and security. RFID and IoT solutions not only provide robust tracking capabilities but also enhance security measures, ensuring organizations remain compliant and secure.

ADVANCES IN RFID HARDWARE AND TAGGING TECHNOLOGIES

RFID-enabled supply chains improved inventory visibility, reduced out-of-stock incidents, and enhanced supply chain efficiency. In the healthcare sector, RFID systems played a vital role in patient monitoring, asset management, and medication authentication.

The continuous advancements in RFID technology have revolutionized our perception of the Internet of Things. The concept of IoT often remained in the realm of imagination. However, with the aid of RFID technology, we can now connect the physical and virtual worlds, creating intelligent and highly efficient environments. Several key aspects of the latest progress in RFID technology are noteworthy.

Smaller-sized tags

With technological advancements, RFID tags have significantly reduced in size, transitioning from traditional centimeters to miniature tags measuring just a few millimeters. These miniature tags can be more easily embedded in various objects such as goods, devices, and even the human body. They not only provide unique identification for items but can also carry additional information such as location, temperature, humidity, etc., thereby offering greater possibilities for IoT applications.

Broader application areas

RFID technology has already achieved tremendous success in supply chain management and logistics tracking. However, recent advancements have expanded its role into several other domains. For instance, in healthcare, RFID technology can be used for patient authentication, medication management, and medical equipment tracking. In smart cities, RFID tags can contribute to intelligent transportation systems, public infrastructure management, and urban surveillance. The emergence of these applications will bring greater convenience and security to our lives.

Integration with other technologies

RFID technology's integration with other technologies is driving its further development. When combined with sensor technology, RFID enables real-time monitoring of environmental conditions, thereby enhancing production efficiency and resource utilization. When integrated with cloud computing and big data analytics, RFID enables the collection and processing of large-scale data, providing more accurate information for business decision-making. When combined with artificial intelligence and machine learning, RFID facilitates intelligent recognition and prediction of items, further advancing automation levels.

Future prospects

Despite the significant progress RFID technology has made in the past few decades, its potential for development remains vast. In the future, we can expect even smaller and more intelligent RFID tags, as well as broader application areas such as smart homes and smart agriculture. Additionally, RFID technology will continue to integrate with other emerging technologies like 5G, blockchain, etc., further propelling the development of the Internet of Things.

The latest advances in RFID technology provide strong support for realizing a smarter Internet of Things. Smaller-sized tags, broader application areas, and integration with other technologies demonstrate the ongoing evolution and innovation in RFID technology. It is reasonable to believe that over time, RFID technology will become one of the key driving forces behind the development of the Internet of Things, ushering in a future that is more convenient and intelligent.

Advancements in RFID Tags

RFID tags have improved with time. Here is how these tags have improvised.

- **Compact size** – The size of RFID tags has significantly decreased over time. They have become thinner and lightweight.

- **Sensitivity** – The sensitivity of tags has increased over time. Previously, the tags could not be read in specific orientations that we use today. Nowadays, even if the tag is present under ten layers of clothing, it can still be sensed by the reader. This was not possible a few years ago.
- **Lower Cost** – previously, tags were not as cheap as they are today. Buying ten tags would often be heavy on the pocket for people.
- **Types of tags** – The kinds of RFID tags we have today were impossible to imagine a decade ago. Unique tags for metals and liquids have made RFID technology much more user-friendly.

Advancements in RFID Antennas

- *Lower costs* – antennas available today are much cheaper as compared to their prices a few years ago.
- *Wide variety* – today, you can choose from a wide variety of RFID antennas available in the market. In 2010, there were only a few types available.
- *Smaller size* – The weight and size of antennas has decreased over time, making it easy for users to carry handheld RFID readers.

Advancements in RFID Readers

- *Increased Sensitivity* – The sensitivity of RFID readers has also improved along with the sensitivity of tags.
- *Increased Read Rate* – Previously, the number of tags an RFID reader can scan simultaneously was not as much as it is today. Nowadays, RFID readers can read up to 1200 tags per second. That's insane!
- *Increased Power* – The power at which the radio frequency signal is transmitted depicts how far the signal will travel. Readers these days produce enough transmit power to overcome losses and make sure the signal reaches its destination.
- *More Connectivity Options* – Previously, it wasn't possible to connect the RFID device to the Wi-Fi or cellular network. The only connectivity option available was USB or ethernet cable.
- *More Types* – Nowadays, you can get readers in a wide variety of options, including handheld devices, walkthrough gates, and wristbands.
- *Lower Costs* – The overall Cost of an RFID reader has decreased with time. Previously, it wasn't possible to get an RFID reader for under $1000.

CHAPTER-18

RFID AND INDUSTRY 4.0

It is increasingly important for internal processes in industry to be better optimised and more efficient. Industry 4.0 promotes new production techniques using data and information provided by new technologies that complement company organisation, workers and assets.

Having access to precise information exactly when you need it is essential for industry development. This is why the fourth industrial evolution has transformed industry. The value offered by these data and how they are processed can give companies in these sectors greater production power and the ability to transform physical information into digital information.

RFID Technology for the Revolution 4.0

RFID technology is the perfect solution for automating processes in any industry. With radiofrequency identification, we can identify anything we want. It quickly and automatically retrieves all the related data, such as what or who has interacted with it, when, where, etc.

As previously mentioned, Industry 4.0 is made up of multiple pillars from different sectors. Let us explain some of the new technologies that are driving this new industry 4.0:

- **Internet of Things (IoT)**: The Internet of Things (IoT) refers to the connection of physical devices, vehicles, buildings and other objects to the internet, allowing them to send and receive data and connect them all together. IoT is used in industry to improve efficiency, cut costs and boost productivity. For example, IoT sensors can monitor computer performance, process control systems can automate production and device connectivity can automate inventory management. Introducing RFID technology with IoT allows you to better monitor and analyse data, which in turn helps you make decisions based on such data and improve quality and efficiency.

- **Big Data:** aims to gather all of the data produced in a company's industrial process. Big Data provides raw data, which then needs to be analysed to retrieve the most important information for the company. Software programmes are used to process this huge amount of data, analyse them in real time and present it in a practical format to be studied. All of this information can then be used to optimise processes within the company or factory.
- **Cobots:** Robots were one of the great advances of Logistics 4.0, and thus Industry 4.0. They can perform a wide range of tasks, including sorting and transporting heavy loads. Cobots (collaborative robots) are especially designed to interact in environments where they must work with humans. They are very useful as they optimise production and take monotonous or dangerous tasks off the hands of employees.
- **The Cloud:** is one of the pillars of the new Industry 4.0. It allows you to store a large amount of data and acts as a link between different sectors of the same company (engineering, supply chain, production, sales, distribution and services). It makes information analysis and processing more efficient and profitable. Well-managed cloud computing could also help to reduce startup expenses for small- and medium-sized companies. They can adjust it to their needs and expand as the business grows.
- **Artificial Intelligence (AI):** the fact that machines can "think for themselves" is an unprecedented level of technological independence. AI and machine learning enable companies to make use of all the data that the machines can retrieve from production plants and all of their business units (including from its partners and third-party stories).

THE ROLE OF RFID IN THE FOURTH INDUSTRIAL REVOLUTION

One of the fundamental aspects of Industry 4.0 functionalities is the data transferred using RFID technology. Using this tried-and-tested technology, not only is it possible to transfer information and localise objects, but it is also possible to establish a globally unique object identification system. Although until recently the use of RFID was still restricted to discrete production, the approach is now moving into a growing number of processes and industries. As a consequence of the growing demand for automation, RFID technology is gaining a new tail wind. The reason? Industry 4.0 requires the digital identification of workpieces, tools, containers, machinery and equipment. These objects also need to be able to exchange information with each other. There are RFID solutions available for virtually every range of distance.

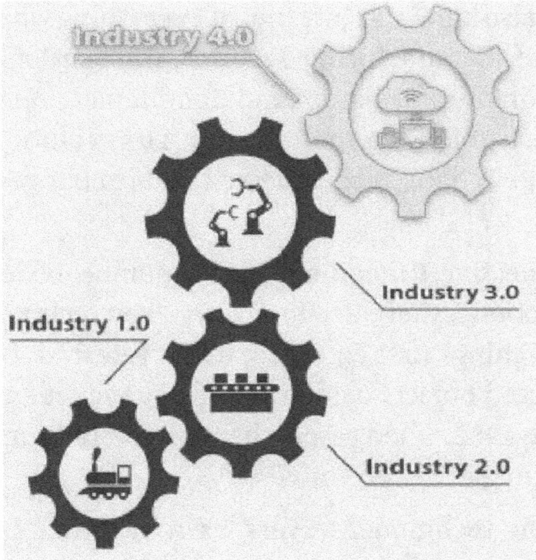

Fig. 1. Digitisation make it possible: Cross-industry, Cross-technology integration of processes and systems linked together

The RFID transponder can also remain on a product, thereby providing traceability - an asset that is currently very much in demand in the production and process industry. With the aid of RFID transponders, up-to-date machine data can be read out and then automated status messages sent to defined recipients. Overall, it is becoming clear that with their expertise in the field of RFID technology, smart-TEC is supporting one of the key goals of Industry 4.0. Optimised digital communication between man and machine.

Industry 4.0 concepts

There were nine pillars of Industry 4.0 when it was first announced: cyber-physical systems, Internet of Things, Big data, 3D printing, robotics, simulation, augmented reality, cloud computing and cyber security. As the world keeps exploring the concepts of Industry 4.0 and their practicalities, we see from many literature, to name a few, that some of the concepts have been shifted around. Whether it is a better-fitting name or some further clarifications, we see an increasing individualization in our understanding of the Industry 4.0 itself.

Internet of Things

In simple terms, the Internet of Things consists of physical devices that are embedded with electronic sensors, actuators, and digital devices with specific software enabling communications. All of them are connected to an internetworking world, typically through the Internet. Typical example of these devices may include almost all suitable home appliance such as kettles and light switches, as well as industrial machines like pumps and motors. Some literature refers to the industrial section as Industrial Internet of Things.

Additionally, it is also known as Internet of Everything which consists of Internet of Service, Internet of Manufacturing Services, Internet of People, an embedded system and Integration of Information and Communication technology. Although the connectivity is not unique to the Industry 4.0 revolution, the integration via Internet of Things allows data to be collected and exchanged on a unprecedented scale.

On a detailed perspective, to handle a gigantic number of devices and dynamically manage these connections, there are innovative key techniques required. In fact, when the Internet of Things first emerged, it was referred to uniquely identifiable interoperable connected objects using radio-frequency identification technology. One may trace back to 1982, when researchers connected a modified Coke Machine to the Internet at Carnegie Mellon University.

This identification technique servers as a tag that is uniquely identified and allows tracking in real-time. Later on, this technique is expanded to cooperating via wireless network, Bluetooth, cellular networks or near field communication. Researcher defines the Internet of Things as "a dynamic global network infrastructure with self-configuring capabilities based on standard and interoperable communication protocols where physical and virtual 'Things' have identities, physical attributes, and virtual personalities and use intelligent interfaces, and are seamlessly integrated into the information network."

A large number of Internet of Things application have already been applied, for example, monitoring in fields of industries, environments, transportation, and healthcare [96– 100]. However, we note that to connect billions of devices, some standard protocols must be followed by all players in the new ear of Industry 4.0. This can cause new issues such as privacy, security as well as proprietary ownership. Thus, innovative interdisciplinary research is ever paramount to address news problems from new solutions.

Big data and data analytics

Imaging the amount of information we have created from the dawn of civilisation to 2003, we now create as much every 2 days, this is according to a former executive chairman of Google Eric Schmidt. That is approximately five exabytes a day (around 5 million TBs). Initially, storage and handling of the data were at the centre of research and development. Then we worried about the quality of the data. Now it is clear that data has become a commodity. In general, Industry 4.0 generates data from a large various channels, such as sensor readings, log files, video/audio, network traffics, transactions, social media feeds.

Industries such as big technology companies have already tasted success at analysing big data and mining valuable information from it. Those information could give companies insights into the business market and get ahead of its competition. For example, with shop-floor data from all across a large region, advanced algorithm can find patterns and correlations identify future market trends and customer preferences. According to researchers, research has shown an increase of 15-20% in return on investment by introducing big data analysis. Big data visualisation is another research trend to tackle the difficulties of making senses from a gigantic dataset.

Cloud and information technology

Industry 4.0 is based upon the changes from advanced information technologies and cloud has become a major part of the this paradigm. It is clear cloud has become a mainstream in communication and hub of information exchange. Cloud, or cloud computing, is a general term referring to computational services that offers scalable resources for various activities over the Internet. Some literature such as considers it as "the fifth utility", alongside with electricity, gas, water and telephone.

Cloud serves as remote servers that is generally available around the clock. Its high-performance and low-cost feature suits perfectly for information storage, and over the recent years, rapid resource sharing, dynamic allocation, flexible extension have expanded its influence to our day to day life. Researchers reports from a survey that 88% of companies participated stated cloud yields positive outcomes, and often allows access to new markets and new customers.

According to a chief officer of Facebook, Sheryl Sandberg, more than 50 million business using Facebook Pages to communicate with customers. One third of customers now have an expectation to receive an response from a business within half an hour and over 40% expect within an hour.

With the increasing use of cloud, the idea of cloud manufacturing has emerged that allows modularization and service-orientation. For example, design from cloud manufacturing enables a large number of participants from all stages of the production process. Therefore, customer suggestions and engineer concerns can all be included into the design phase, largely reduce its turnaround time. Apart from the design, there are aspects of cloud manufacturing such as software as a service, customer relationship management, platforms for data analytics, collaboration and business planning.

Robots and automated machinery

Robots play an important role in Industry 4.0. Depending on different requirements, it can be robotics arms, a whole assembly line, vehicle-type rover, android or legged patrol robots. Many can already be seen in the fields of chemical processing, pharmaceutical manufacturing, food and beverage productions. Here are some examples. KUKA iiwa is a lightweight robot for sensitive industrial tasks, developed by KUKA Robotics. Baxter from Rethink Robotics is an interactive production robot for packaging purpose. BioRob Arm can be used in close proximity with humans. Automated machinery is aimed to perform repeated actions with high speed and precision as well as be able to work where human workers are restricted. Researchers illustrates an interface that controls industrial robots with augmented reality.

3D printing

3D printing, officially known as additive manufacturing in the Industry 4.0 terminology, enables construction of various complex geometries of structures using metal or plastic. In the recent years, it has attracted increasing investment. The 3D printing market is estimated to be worth $80.78 billion. The growth is believed in customised products and 3D printing is the ideal way of reducing overall manufacturing costs, flexible and extremely fast at producing small quantity. It also helps to reduce component weight and minimise waste, thus is of particular benefit to the automotive and aerospace industries. In other cases, 3D printing allows flexible production locations, reduced transportation and stock on hand.

3D printing shows the way forwards as decentralised manufacturing as it makes production faster and cheaper. With increasing digitisation and the demand to decrease product life cycles, more areas find its benefits. Associated technologies have also been focused, such as fused deposition method, selective laser melting and selective laser sintering. As product individualization becomes the trends, we are expecting to see ever more customised 3D printing services in the coming years.

Simulation

Simulation is the combination of isolation and recreation. It first identifies variables within a situation and makes hypothesises, then comparing the simulation results to observation. After repeated testing, when the results are satisfactory, we can then make predictions with a given set of variables and conditions.

Simulation requires extensive work and is very important in areas like plant operations. For example, while monitoring real-time data, any oscillations or intended changes can be put into a well-studied simulation to predicted the real-world outcomes. Simulation can be used to ensure the quality of the product, as well as minimising costs from market price changes. When errors occur, simulations can be used to shorten the down times. If possible outcomes can be predicted, it can also help decision-making.

SMART MANUFACTURING AND RFID INTEGRATION

Since the popularization of RFID technology, RFID has been used in a wide range of applications. Initially, it was mainly used in logistics. However, since its development, RFID applications can be seen in retail, logistics, transportation, medical care, manufacturing, etc. Although RFID technology is no longer a new technology, with the advent of the smart era, the industry has continued to develop various RFID application scenarios based on market demand in recent years. In the case of smart manufacturing, in view of the demand for resources and improved cost efficiency, manufacturers have also begun to adopt RFID technology to achieve applications such as real-time location tracking, asset or personnel monitoring, process control on production lines, and supply chain management.

Application of RFID technology in smart products

RFID technology combined with smart boards can realize full-cycle information management from design, production, sales, inspection, diagnosis and maintenance, information statistics, scrapping, operation information record feedback, diagnosis and analysis. It is of great value to enhance the intelligent image of products and realize the intelligentization of products throughout their life cycle.

Application of RFID technology in smart logistics

Supply chain vehicle guidance and unloading management

Through RFID technology, combined with the material supply needs of the factory area, it can realize the reservation, queuing, identification of factory supplier vehicles, and intelligent allocation of unloading resources in the factory area. Just like the bus ticket booking system, before arriving at the station (factory), the supplier makes an appointment and queues (purchases tickets) through the online appointment system. After arriving at the factory (station), follow the signs to the reserved unloading space to unload (wait and get on the bus)).

Currently, the Malong base of a well-known domestic brand of microwave ovens has implemented a material-pull supply chain model by deploying and implementing a supply chain vehicle guidance and unloading management system. Through the RFID system, we can understand the status of logistics resources in the entire factory area, channelize the logistics resources in the factory area, realize the entry time of supply chain vehicles into the factory, unloading resource arrangement guidance and time control, and improve the utilization rate of logistics resources in the factory area. Through the unified deployment and guidance of vehicles and unloading resources in the factory area, the factory has increased the utilization rate of logistics resources to more than 30%, and the delivery accuracy has increased to more than 15%.

Material distribution turnover box management

The application of RFID technology to logistics turnover box management can greatly improve the operating efficiency of the logistics system and realize digital warehousing management (warehousing location management, rapid real-time inventory), etc., making management more scientific, timely and effective, and ensuring high-quality data exchange in the supply chain. This will bring about a significant improvement in logistics efficiency, thereby reducing the overall cost of the system.

In Factory Building No. 18 of a state-owned enterprise, Honglu RFID readers are installed at all material distribution outlets, and RFID pickers are installed beside the assembly line. All material incoming and outgoing and line-side picking information will be collected in a timely manner and fed back to the backend system. The intelligent identification system for palletizing warehouses can realize transparency and intelligent guidance of the distribution process through intelligent components such as automatic warehouses, RFID smart trolleys, and RFID pallets, and improve the efficiency and accuracy of assembly material distribution.

Application of RFID technology in smart workshops

Tool life cycle management and control

As we all know, the purpose of tool management and control is to realize the information management of the tool life cycle and to understand the use and inventory status and location of the tool in a timely manner. Before the tools are purchased and stored in the warehouse, RFID electronic tags are installed on the tools as the unique identification information of the tools. During the scheduling and use of tools, by collecting tool information in a timely manner through RFID reading and writing equipment, you can clearly understand in the system whether the tool has been loaded, the specific corresponding machine tool, and the cycle and duration of use. By tracking the position and usage status of the cutting tools in a timely manner, companies can promptly understand the wear and tear of the cutting tools and replace them to ensure the safety of the cutting tools.

A domestic heavy-duty machine tool company uses an RFID reader to promptly collect machine tool RFID tag information to understand tool usage status data, and promptly replaces tools based on the tool wear status feedback system. Improve the safety of tool use and ensure that machine tool processing production efficiency is at its most efficient state.

Production line mixed flow manufacturing

With the growth of users' personalized needs, selection and customization have gradually become a trend in the industrial production of manufacturing companies.

The mixed assembly line production model of mixed flow manufacturing can well meet the personalized customized selection production needs. Mixed flow manufacturing is a production method in which enterprises produce multiple products on one assembly line within a certain period of time.

Several product varieties with basically the same process flow and production operation methods are scientifically arranged and put into production on an assembly line in a rhythmic and proportional manner. Mixed continuous flow production is based on a comprehensive balance of variety, output, working hours, and equipment load.

By installing RFID electronic tags on complex parts and pallets, and installing RFID industrial readers and writers on processing equipment and lines, intelligent communication between products and equipment is achieved, effectively avoiding many problems such as chaotic process management caused by untimely data collection. Provide data support for MES through timely collection of work-in-progress status and production process status, ensuring that MES can timely produce and schedule each workstation. Keep each workstation busy in a cycle to complete the maximum amount of operations, thereby reducing idle time and improving productivity.

At present, an automobile company has installed RFID tags on the cylinder block and head processing production line to achieve the mixed-flow production of more than 6 types of cylinder blocks. The quality data and process data of the entire production line are effectively collected.

A certain brand of home air conditioners installed RFID tags on the factory's flexible assembly lines, processes, and work boards to automatically collect data during the home appliance assembly process, increasing the data collection rate to 99%. Manual barcode scanning events are reduced by 5 minutes for a single product on each line, and the MES data accuracy rate is increased to 90%.

Intelligent mold maintenance management

A company in Dongguan that focuses on the production of electrode tubes has improved CNC processing efficiency, reduced warehouse personnel, reduced measuring personnel, and increased EDM utilization by more than 20% by opening up the information flow and manufacturing flow from mold design to manufacturing.

Intelligent and integrated RFID (II-RFID) system

With the development of the RFID technique, it becomes increasing possible to acquire real-time production data. However, it is far from sufficient for the company only to collect the massive amounts of RFID data and do the track and query. RFID data-based decision-making provides more value to the company and improves the production efficiency. Thus, an II-RFID system is proposed, which combines the RFID data acquisition with decision support based on DM.

II-RFID system architecture

As a highly automated data acquisition and decision support system, the II-RFID system comprises six levels as:

- assets level, which contains products (from materials to finished goods), conveyor belts, machines, pallets, packages and shelves, etc.,
- data acquisition level, which consists of RFID tags, antennas, readers and middleware,
- control level, which consists of PCs, middleware and other network devices used to connect the equipment,
- database level, which combines RFID database and other high level databases,
- decision support level, which involves DM approaches or computational intelligence for decision making, and
- management level, which is the intended final endpoint for the construction of an II-RFID system.

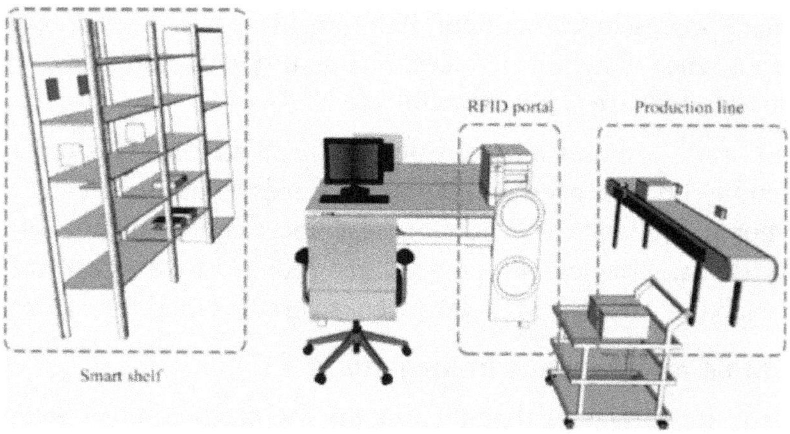

Fig. 2 RFID lab layout

Functions of the II-RFID system

The II-RFID system works on the foundation of the realtime collected RFID tag information. The following tasks based on RFID data acquisition can be achieved: online part information collection, online processing progress statistics, daily processing capacity statistics per station, total processing time for a batch of product and processing time of each working process, production progress visualization and remaining processing time prediction, and quality statistics (including scrap and recall).

Considering production management in the II-RFID system for instance, the main functions of the RFID production management system include WIP management, processing station management, manufacturing process management, production task management, personnel management and tool/fixture management. Typical data collection and reporting include the following.

- **WIP management:** WIP registration, WIP inspection registration, quality query, product positioning and tracking, prediction of the remaining processing time.
- **Processing station management:** processing station registration, WIP of processing station query, processing station output query, process information query.
- **Manufacturing process management:** manufacturing process registration and query. Manufacturing process management is the basis of production task schedule query.
- **Production task management:** production task registration and query, production task schedule query.
- **Personnel management:** personnel registration, personnel productivity and production query.
- **Tool and fixture management:** tools/fixtures registration, tool position allocation, maintaining proper maintenance schedule.

Implementation of II-RFID system

The II-RFID system has a multiple level system structure. In the KDL, the II-RFID system is implemented with both RFID hardware and software. The experiment equipment comprises infrastructure of a warehouse and production line, RFID data acquisition system and production management software. The layout of the RFID lab is shown in Fig. 2

The RFID lab comprises three functional areas, which are the production line, the RFID portal and the smart shelf. Referring to the proposed II-RFID system architecture, the implementation of each system level is shown in Table 1.

Table 1 II-RFID system implementation

System level	Implementation
Asset level	Assembly line, pallet, portal, trolley, shelf
Data acquisition level	RFID tag, RFID antenna, RFID reader, handheld reader, router/ switch
Control level	Middleware, computer, software
Database level	Local RFID database
Decision support level	Program on the basis of computational intelligence
Management level	Manager, expert

Each functional area is installed with a variety of RFID antennas. One or multiple antennas are set to be one read point, to represent the location of the business step. For instance, the conveyor belt is used to represent the production line. Two antennas are assigned along the conveyor belt representing two working stations. The portal area consists of an entrance and an exit. Each portal is installed with two antennas to monitor the tagged goods passing by. The warehouse area comprises three shelves, where shelf 1 and shelf 2 are monitored by layer separately, while shelf 3 is monitored completely.

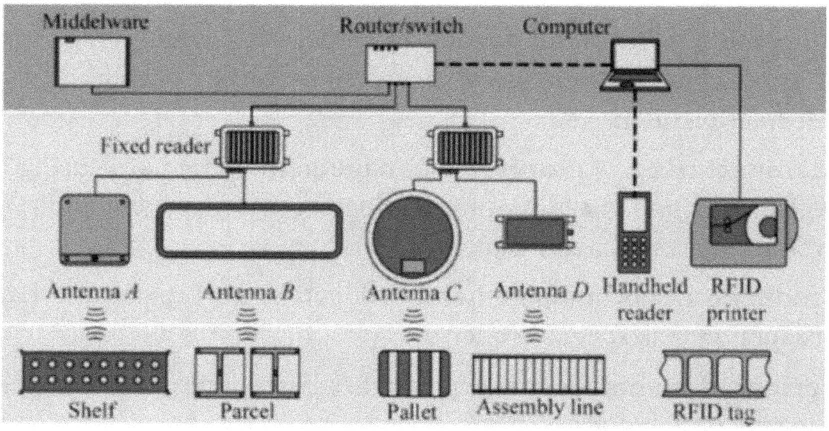

Fig. 3 Six types of RFID antennas are used in the II-RFID system implementation

GLOSSARY OF RFID TERMS

Access Code: A tag's Access Code/Access Passcode is a password that can be used to lock and unlock a tag's reading and writing capabilities and is stored in the Reserved Memory Bank.

Access Control: A security technique that allows a company to control who or what enters a place or an area. This can be achieved by using RFID technology to allow or restrict access to buildings, rooms, areas, lots, roads, garages, and other contained areas.

Active: "Active" means that the RFID transponder/tag has its own power source. It broadcasts its signal and typically has a longer read range than passive transponders/tags. Read more about how Active RFID Systems apply to your RFID application.

Active Tag: An RFID tag that has its own power source that sends signals to the readers and antennas. Usually has a battery life of 5-10 years.

Agile Reader: An RFID reader that can read tags operating at different frequencies or use multiple means of communication between the tags and readers.

Air Interface Protocol: A set of rules governing how tags and readers communicate.

Antenna (RFID): An RFID Antenna is a device that connects to an RFID Reader via an Antenna Cable. An RFID Antenna takes the AC current sent by the RFID Reader through the Cable, builds an electromagnetic field, and then releases the energy as Electromagnetic waves in the direction dictated by the Antenna's radiation pattern. An RFID Antenna also collects modulated RF energy that is sent back from RFID tags in the read area.

Antenna Cable: An Antenna Cable, also called a Coax Cable or Coaxial Cable, is an electrical cable surrounded by a layer of insulation that helps contain the conducted energy within the Cable. An Antenna Cable is used to connect an RFID Reader and RFID Antenna in an RFID System.

Antenna Gain: The antenna's ability to direct scattered radio frequency into a more direct and effective plane. Antenna gain increases the signal, which enables antennas with higher gain to read tags from a greater distance. Read more about how Antenna Gain applies to your RFID application.

Antenna (Tag): The component that allows the transponder/tag to send and receive data. The tag antenna connects to the tag's IC and powers the IC with the RF energy it collects and takes the IC's modulated data and sends it back out into the read area.

Anti-Collision: Describes the various methods of preventing interference between the radio waves of multiple devices. Ideal feature for reading more than one tag in a crowded read zone. Read more about how Anti-Collision applies to your RFID application.

Application Programming Interface (API): Application Programming Interface, called API is the interface implemented by an application that allows communication with other applications. API is set in a certain programming language that explains how data will be remembered.

ASCII Code: ASCII, or American Standard Code for Information Interchange, is an encoding method that uses 128 specific characters, each represented by two strings of four bits. ASCII can represent the entire alphabet (lower case and upper case), numbers 0-9, as well as some special characters, such as asterisks, question marks, and parenthesis.

ASIC: An ASIC is also known as an application specific integrated circuit (IC) and is basically an integrated circuit that was manufactured for or customized for a specific application. Customization usually includes adhering to a unique set of standards for a specific application industry.

Asset Tracking: One of the most common applications for RFID. Companies can quickly locate high-value assets and/or transport containers by placing RFID transponders/tags on or in them. By implementing an Asset Tracking system, companies can increase the usage of individual assets, track and maintain asset usage history, strategically plan future asset usage, and reduce costs associated with losing and replacing lost assets.

Attenuation: Attenuation is the reduction of amplitude of a signal, electric current, or other oscillation. Attenuation is typically discussed when referring to RFID antenna cables and the RF energy that can be lost within the cable between the RFID Reader and RFID Antenna.

Authentication: Authentication is the act or process of proving that something is genuine, true, or valid. Authentication of a product or item can be done using RFID technology, making RFID Authentication an RFID application.

Backscatter: A method of communication between passive tags and readers. RFID tags using backscatter technology receive radio waves from a reader and reflect those waves back to a reader, usually at the same carrier frequency. The reflected signal is then modulated to transmit data.

Barcode: A Barcode is a number that is coded in the form of varying patterned lines that is printed on a product or item and read by machines like scanners, phones, and other devices. The lines are read, decoded, and the code is then used to identify the product or item it has been printed on.

Barcode Scanner: A device, also known as an optical scanner, that uses a light source (typically a laser) to scan and decode barcodes.

Battery-Assisted Passive Tags (BAP Tags): Battery-Assisted Passive Tags, also called BAP tags, Semi-Passive Tags, or Semi-Active Tags, Battery-Assisted Passive (BAP) tags are essentially passive RFID tags with an internal battery. Because these tags wait for a signal from an RFID reader before they respond, they function similarly to active transponder tags.

Binary Code: Binary Code is a coding system using the binary digits 0 and 1 to represent a letter, digit, or other character in a computer or other electronic device.

Bistatic: Bistatic refers to a system that uses two separate devices to communicate – one to transmit a signal, and one to receive a signal. Most RFID systems are Monostatic, which means they use one RFID Antenna to both transmit and receive a signal. However, bistatic systems can be created that use one RFID antenna to transmit signals and a different RFID antenna to receive signals.

Bits: Bits are basic units of information that can either be a "0" or a "1". Strings of bits can be converted into hexadecimal coding or ASCII coding depending on the exact placements of "0" and "1". Read more about how Bits apply to your RFID application.

BLE Beacons: A BLE Beacon is a radio transmitter that continually broadcasts specific data via Bluetooth low-energy signals to BLE devices that can receive the data within a specific area.

Cable Bend Radius: Cable Bend Radius is the smallest allowed radius the cable can be bent around in order to not cause stress on the cable. If the cable is bent further than the appropriate bend radius, it can damage and degrade its performance and generate interference in data transmission.

Central Processing Unit (CPU): The "brains" of the computer. The CPU controls all other parts of the computer and is responsible for executing operations.

Circular-Polarized Antenna: A circular-polarized antenna sends its radio waves in a circular pattern to make it easier to read tags in which the direction cannot be controlled. The circular pattern emitted from the antenna increases the wave's chance of reaching the antenna; however, their read range is shorter than that of a linear-polarized antenna.

Commissioning (Tag): Commissioning generally refers to writing or programming an RFID tag with a specific EPC number or Data.

Compatibility: Two RFID systems must use the same protocols, frequencies, and voltage levels to be considered compatible. Being compatible allows two systems to operate together within the same overall application.

Constructive Interference: Constructive Interference is when two electromagnetic waves sent out by the RF antenna intersect at the same phase, which strengthens the wavelength. The strengthened wavelength makes it possible to read well outside of normal read ranges thanks to constructive interference.

Data Retention: The ability of a microchip to maintain the information stored in read-only memory. RFID tags can usually retain data for 10 years or more depending on temperature, humidity, and other factors.

dBi: Defines the gain of an antenna relative to an isotropic antenna. Read more about how dBi applies to your RFID application.

dBm: dBm is a unit of measurement to indicate that a power level is expressed in decibels (dB) with reference to one milliwatt (mW) and is commonly used to express RFID Reader Transmit Power.

dBw: dBw is a unit of measurement of the strength of a signal expressed in decibels relative to one Watt.

Deactivation (Tag): Deactivation generally refers to making the RFID tag unusable, which can be done via a Kill Command or physically destroying the tag. Deactivation can also be done in a system or database to indicate that the tag is no longer in use or no longer available. Usually system deactivated tags can still be read, but are no longer registered in a company's database or associated with any relevant information.

Dead Tag: An RFID Tag that can no longer be read.

Decibel: A unit of measurement that represents the difference in the intensity of an emitted signal or level of power when 0 dB is used as the reference. dB is used to measure antenna gain, cable losses, and reader power output.

Encryption: A way of scrambling data in which only intended users are able to unscramble and read the data. Used as a security measure to protect the information stored on a transponder's microchip and to prevent communications between the tag and reader from being intercepted. Read more about how Encryption applies to your RFID application.

Electronic Product Code: The Electronic Product Code (EPC) uses a series of unique digits to universally identify an item's manufacturer, product category, and the individual item.

EPC Gen 2: The standard air-interface protocol approved by EPC global for the second generation of EPC technologies. Read more about how EPC Gen2 applies to your RFID application.

EPC Memory Bank: The Electronic Product Code (EPC) Memory Bank on standard Gen2 RFID Tags is one of four memory banks, and it holds the EPC number, also known as the Electronic Product Code. The EPC number can be reprogrammed by an RFID Reader and usually varies in length from 96 bits to 496 bits; however, the most common EPC lengths are 96 and 128 bits. Read more about how EPC Memory Banks apply to your RFID application.

EPC Global: A non-profit organization set up by the Uniform Code Council and EAN International to commercialize EPC technology. Read more about EPCglobal.

Faraday Cage: A Faraday Cage or Shield is an enclosure used specifically to block electromagnetic fields and RF energy from entering or exiting a specific area. In RFID applications, Faraday Cages can be used to contain RF energy and create a custom read zone or block RF energy.

Far-Field Communication: An RFID tag is considered to be in the "far-field" if it is outside of one full wavelength of the reader. Passive RFID systems that rely on far-field communication have a longer read range than those using near-field communication. Read more about how Far-Field Communication applies to your application.

Fixed Readers: A Fixed RFID Reader is an high-performance RFID reader that is typically affixed to a wall, shelf, or other fixed position and does not need to be mobile.

Form Factor: The various types of packaging a transponder can be put in, such as thermal transfer labels, plastic cards, key fobs, etc. Read more about how Form Factor applies to your RFID application.

Frequency: The rate at which cycles of waves occur in a single second. Frequency is measured in Hertz and 1 Hz is equal to one wave cycle per second. There are several levels of frequencies in RFID tags that are beneficial for different applications. The four frequencies that RFID Tags use are low (135 kHz), high (13.56 MHz), ultra-high (860 – 960 MHz), and microwave (2.4 GHz).

Frequency Hopping: Frequency hopping is a technique that RFID Readers use to prevent reader collisions that allow them to 'hop' to different frequencies within a set range. Readers stay and transmit on one frequency (also called a channel) for no more than 0.4 seconds and then hop to another frequency to avoid transmitting on the same frequency as another reader - which would cause a collision.

Gen 2v2: Gen2v2 is the second version of the Gen2 protocol, set by GS1 and ratified in 2015.

GIS Software: GIS Software, or Geographic Information System Software, is software that 'is designed to store retrieve, manage, display, and analyze all types of geographic and spatial data.'

Global Positioning System (GPS): A satellite-based radio navigation system owned by the United States Government that can send and receive location data.

GPIO: A GPIO device is a device that plugs into an RFID Reader's GPIO port and performs actions based upon triggers sent by the RFID reader. GPIO devices provide additional functionality like audio or visual signals to RFID applications.

Hexadecimal (Hex): Hex, or hexadecimal coding (also called base 16), is a coding method that utilizes only 16 types of characters - letters A-F and numbers 0-9. Each hexadecimal character represents a string of four bits. Read more about how Hexadecimal coding applies to your RFID application.

High-Frequency: High-frequency is a frequency measurement that is between 3 MHz and 30 MHz. High-frequency tags can transmit data faster than low-frequency tags, but they use more power than low-frequency tags. For RFID, the typical operating frequency is 13.56 MHz.

Inductive Coupling: In an RFID system that uses inductive coupling, the coil on the reader antenna and the coil on the tag antenna form a magnetic field. The tag draws energy from the field and that energy is used by the microchip to change the electrical load on the tag antenna. The reader antenna picks up the electrical changes and translates them into a unique serial number.

Inlay: Composed of just an Integrated Circuit and an aluminum, copper, or silver antenna. They can be classified as "wet" or "dry" depending on if the inlay has an adhesive liner or not. Inlays can also be converted into smart labels.

Input/Output Ports: Ports on an RFID reader that allow external devices to be connected for the unique needs of a user's application.

Integrated Circuit (IC): An Integrated circuit is a microchip/chip that is a small wafer made of silicon that can hold transistors, resistors, and capacitors, that store usage data and algorithms. In an RFID tag, the Integrated Circuit holds four memory banks and performance information like communication modes and frequency protocols.

Interrogation Zone: An Interrogation zone is very similar to a read zone and is an area of space that an RFID reader can successfully read an RFID tag.

Isotropic: Identical in all directions. An antenna that releases equal amounts of energy in every direction is an isotropic antenna.

Kill Command: Also called Kill Code, when sent to a tag, a kill command will deactivate the tag and will make any data on the tag unreadable.

License Plate Tag: A license plate tag is an RFID tag that contains specific information for identifying the automobile or machine to which it is attached.

Linear-Polarized Antenna: An antenna that sends its radio waves out in a specific alignment. Linear polarization increases read distance and allows better penetration through dense materials. Tags must be aligned with the reader antenna in order to be read.

Locking (Tag): Locking an RFID Tag is essentially locking the tag's memory from being read. Locking a Gen2 RFID Tag can be accomplished by using the Access Password in the Reserved Memory Bank.

Low-Frequency: Low-frequency is a frequency measurement that is between 30 kHz and 300 kHz. Low-frequency tags are not as prone to interference as ultra-high frequency tags. However, data is sent at a slower rate, and they must be read from three feet or closer.

Memory: Memory is the total data that can be stored in a specific microchip. A microchip can hold between 64 bits and 32 kilobytes of memory. On an RFID tag, there are typically four memory banks - EPC, User, Reserved, and TID.

Memory Banks: Groups of Memory that are partitioned separately according to Gen2 protocols – four banks are available on Gen2 RFID tags, EPC, Reserved, User, and TID.

Memory Block: A Memory Block is essentially a grouping of memory bits in a tag's memory bank that typically can be operated on independently from other banks.

Microcontroller: A Microcontroller is a small computer on a single integrated circuit chip that contains CPU's, memory, and input/output peripherals.

Middleware: Middleware is a layer of software that is created to connect two other software pieces – typically connecting two software programs or a software program and a device's firmware. Middleware allows communication and data flow between programs so that each component in a system doesn't have to be managed separately.

Mobile Computer: A Mobile Computer is a handheld device that is small, lightweight, and portable. Mobile Computers have operating systems, which mean that they have similar capabilities to a PC, with the addition of the ability to scan barcodes and capture data.

Modulation: The various methods of changing the radio waves between a reader and an RFID tag to enable the transmission of information.

Monostatic: Monostatic refers to any system that uses one device to communicate – both to transmit and receive message. A Monostatic RFID system is a system that uses one antenna to both transmit and receive tag data. Monostatic RFID systems are the most common type of RFID system.

Multiplexer: In RFID systems, a multiplexer is a device that allows an RFID reader to connect to more RFID antennas than possible on it's own. Multiplexers allow for readers to double or triple the number of antennas per reader, which cuts costs and needed space for RFID applications.

Near-Field Antennas: Generally, passive UHF RFID antennas have two segments broken up by how they communicate with tags, the near-field communication portion that uses magnetic coupling and the far-field communication portion that can communicate via backscatter. Near-Field RFID Antennas are antennas that only have, and use near-field coupling to communicate with RFID tags up to one wavelength away (a few inches).

Near-Field Communication: Near-field communication is the term used to describe the communication between an RFID tag and RFID reader within one wavelength (a few inches). Within the short vicinity, the tag uses magnetic/ inductive coupling in order to communicate and not backscatter, like in Far-Field Communication. This type of communication and coupling is most often used with NFC/HF RFID tags, but can still be used in UHF tags within a close range.

NFC RFID Tags: NFC Tags, or Near-Field Communication Tags operate within the HF Frequency on a single frequency of 13.56 MHz. NFC tags are incredibly standardized and operate via ISO 14443 A and B, making them easily adoptable, globally. NFC tags use Near-Field communication (magnetic coupling) to send and receive data at short distances - on a few centimeters or inches. Read more about NFC RFID and popular applications.

Noise: Unwanted electrical signals or electromagnetic energy found in the immediate surrounding of operating RFID equipment.

Non-Volatile Memory: A long-term form of storage that remains after the power to a system is turned off.

Null Spot: The area in a reader's field that does not pick up radio waves. Read more about how Null Spots can affect your RFID application.

Orientation: The location of a tag antenna position relative to a reader antenna. Linear-polarized antennas need to be aligned with the tag antenna for the tag to be read. If the tag's alignment is not oriented correctly, the tag antenna will only receive a fraction of the energy.

Passive: An RFID passive tag does not have an internal battery; therefore, it does not have an individual power source or transmitter. Radio waves sent from the reader to the chip's antenna are converted into energy to power the microchip.

Penetration: The ability of radio frequencies to go through non-metallic materials.

Permalock: Permalock is a feature available on RFID tags, such as some Monza R6 tags, which permanently locks a memory bank so that the data on the bank cannot be changed.

Printer (RFID Printer): RFID Printers are devices that simultaneously print and encode information on RFID inlays or labels. These devices are the only way to print on labels, and they also save time by automating the manual process of encoding each tag. RFID Printers have embedded RFID Reader Modules that allow them to read and write RFID inlays.

Protocol: A set of rules that regulate the communication between RFID systems.

Q Algorithm: Also called Q-Protocol, or adaptive Q Algorithm, the Q Algorithm is the most commonly used Anti-Collision protocol for Class 1 Gen2 UHF RFID Readers and Tags. It is a derivative of one of the main algorithms, Slotted Aloha. The Q-Algorithm is used during an inventory count, the interrogator (reader) breaks up the inventory into rounds (also called frames) and then asks the tags to pick a number between a certain set, 0-15 for example. The interrogator then starts to count down from the highest number of the set and each number it counts is considered a 'slot'. The tags, meanwhile, select a random 16-bit number and use the last digit(s) as its Q-value or number between 0-15. When the tag hears the reader respond with its selected random number or Q-value, it responds with its 16-bit random number.

Radio Frequency Identification (RFID): Describes the various methods of using radio waves to identify unique objects. Typically, this interaction happens when a reader communicates with a transponder to retrieve information stored on its microchip.

Random Access Memory (RAM): A type of memory used to temporarily store data on a device. When the device's power is cut off, all data stored in the RAM is cleared.

Read Accuracy: The percentage of tags that are successfully picked up by a reader in an RFID system. If 98 out of 100 tags are read in the operating environment, the read accuracy is 98 percent.

Reader: An RFID reader is the brain of the RFID system and is necessary for any system to function. Readers, also called interrogators, are devices that transmit and receive radio waves in order to communicate with RFID tags.

Reader Collision: Reader Collision is when two readers in the same read area on the same frequency interfere with each other's signals. Reader Collisions can be mitigated by using Dense Reader Mode and Frequency Hopping and RF shielding.

Read-Only: Data stored on a RFID tag's microchip that cannot be altered without reprogramming the microchip.

Read Range: Read Range describes how far away a reader can successfully communicate with a tag. Active tags and passive tags have different read ranges. Because active tags have a battery, their read range is longer than passive tags. The read range of a passive tag is based on frequency, reader output power, antenna type, and the way the tag powers up.

Read Rate: The number of times a specific tag can be read in a period of time.

Read Sensitivity: Read Sensitivity is a value determined and assigned to RFID tags by the manufacturer during testing that quantifies the lowest amount, or minimum amount of power required by the RFID reader for a successful tag read.

Read-Write: Data stored on an RFID tag's microchip that can be rewritten as needed.

Reserved Memory: The Reserved Memory Bank stores the kill password and the access password (each are 32 bits).

RSSI (Received Signal Strength Indicator): RSSI, or Received Signal Strength Indicator, is a measurement of the power received from the returned signal from an RFID tag when interrogated by a reader.

Singulation: A method that an RFID reader uses to be able to identify the unique identification number on a specific tag and distinguish it from the other tags in the same area.

Skimming: The act of reading an RFID tag on someone without their knowledge or consent. Also called Eavesdropping, read more about Eavesdropping and how it could affect your RFID system.

Slotted Aloha: Slotted Aloha is an Anti-Collision protocol that reduces the number of collisions from happening that result from two tags sending data to the same reader at the same time. With a true Slotted Aloha protocol, RFID tags can answer at the beginning of a randomly selected time slot to prevent answering at the same exact time. Most Class 1 Gen2 UHF Tags and Readers use the Q algorithm, based on Slotted Aloha as their Anti-Collision protocol. Read more about Slotted Aloha and how it could affect your RFID application.

Synchronization: Timing readers or reader antennas in the same operating environment to avoid interference.

Tag (RFID Tag): An RFID tag is the microchip/antenna combination that receives signals from and then returns signals to an RFID reader. With a unique encrypted serial number, an RFID tag can communicate specific information about the item that it is applied to. Tags can be active, passive, or semi-passive and can come in many shapes and sizes to fit the application.

TID Memory (Tag Identifier): The TID Memory Bank is part of Gen2 UHF RFID tags and it stands for "Tag Identifier". TID numbers are usually 32 -80 bits in length, contain the chipset's type and manufacturer, and are a read-only memory bank. Read more about TID Memory Banks and how they can affect your RFID application.

Transceiver: A device with the ability to send and receive radio waves.

Transponder: Transponder is another name for an RFID tag. Transponders receive signals from and then send signals to an RFID reader.

Ultra-High Frequency (UHF): A frequency measurement that between 300 MHz and 3 GHz. Ultra-high frequency tags can transmit information farther and faster than high and low-frequency tags. However, their electrical waves have a difficult time passing through items with a high concentration of water.

Ultra-WideBand (UWB): Ulta-WideBand is a for of Radio Frequency communication that uses low-energy, very high frequency range (3.1 to 10.6 GHz), short transmissions to communicate. It is similar to Wi-Fi and Bluetooth in that it its main purpose is location discovery and device communication, but it is more accurate and uses less power than the other methods.

Unique Identifier (UID): A unique encoded number that identifies the RFID tag. Also called TID.

Universal Product Code: The 12-digit data structure used in UCC barcodes.

User Memory: The User Memory Bank is the second writable memory bank for user-defined data on Gen 2 RFID Tags. The User Memory Bank is typically used to store more information if the EPC Memory Bank runs out of space. Not all UHF RFID tags have User Memory Banks, and some have extended User Memory Banks. Read more about how the User Memory Bank can affect your RFID application.

WORM (Write Once, Read Many): A tag that can only be written to one time, but can be read repeatedly.

Write Rate: Describes how quickly information is transferred to a tag, stored into the tag's memory, and confirmed to be correct.

Write Sensitivity: Read Sensitivity is a value determined and assigned to RFID tags by the manufacturer during testing that quantifies the lowest amount, or minimum amount of power required by the RFID reader for a successful tag read.

RFID STANDARDS AND REGULATIONS

There are a number of industry standards that are used to define the different elements of RFID. These RFID standards enable manufacturers to make the same products for a variety of markets and in this way gain the economies of scale.

The RFID standards, like standards for any other technology, enable products from different manufacturers to operate together. It enables, for example tags that may be required in very large quantities to be bought from a large scale manufacturer, whilst obtaining the reader, writer or transceiver from another manufacturer. Having RFID standards in place means that these two elements will operate properly together.

RFID STANDARDS ORGANISATIONS

There are two main international RFID standards organisations or bodies that govern RFID:

- ISO - International Standards Organisation
- EPCglobal - Electronics Product Code Global Incorporated

Although these two organisations provide the main RFID standards organisations, there is also a plethora of other standards that apply to niche areas of RFID.

In terms of the standardisation organisations ISO is the longest established. In 1996 it set up a joint committee with IEC to look at standardisation for RFID technology.

The ISO RFID standards fall into a number of categories according to the aspect of RFID that they are addressing. These include: air interface and associated protocols; data content and the formatting; conformance testing; applications; and various other smaller areas.

In addition to the ISO RFID standards, there are also the standards from EPC Global. In 1999 a number of industrial companies with MIT set an consortium known as the Auto-ID consortium with the aim of researching and standardising RFID technology.

In 2003 this organisation was split with the majority of the standardisation activities coming under a new entity called EPCglobal. The Auto-ID Center retained its activities associated with the research into RFID technologies.

Auto-ID tag standards

In order to be able to standardise the RFID tags, the Auto-ID Center devised a series of classes for RFID tags. was generated and these still form the basis for a developed system of RFID tag classes seen today:

- *Class 0:* Basic read-only passive tag using backscatter where the tag was programmed at the time the tag chip was made.
- *Class 1:* Basic read-only passive tag using backscatter with one-time non-volatile programme capability.
- *Class 2:* Passive backscatter tag with up to 65k of read-write memory.
- *Class 3:* Semi-passive tag with up to 65 k read-write memory and a battery incorporated to provide increased range.
- *Class 4:* Active tag using a with battery to enable extra functionality within the tag and also to provide power for the transmitter.
- *Class 5:* An active tag that provides additional circuitry to communicate with other class 5 tags.

The responsibilities for Class 0 and Class 1 RFID tag definitions and standards was handed on to EPC Global in 2003.

Although other newer RFID tag standards and now available, reference is still made to these original tag classes.

RFID standards tabulation

Some of the main RFID standards are summarised in the table below.

	RFID STANDARDS
RFID STANDARD	DETAILS
ISO 10536	ISO RFID standard for close coupled cards
ISO 11784	ISO RFID standard that defines the way in which data is structured on an RFID tag.
ISO 11785	ISO RFID standard that defines the air interface protocol.
ISO 14443	ISO RFID standard that provides the definitions for air interface protocol for RFID tags used in proximity systems - aimed for use with payment systems

RFID STANDARDS	
RFID STANDARD	DETAILS
ISO 15459	Unique identifiers for transport units (used in supply chain management)
ISO 15693	ISO RFID standard for use with what are termed vicinity cards
ISO 15961	ISO RFID standard for Item Management (includes application interface (part 1), registration of RFID data constructs (part 2), and RFID data constructs (part 3).
ISO 15962	ISO RFID standard for item management - data encoding rules and logical memory functions.
ISO 16963	ISO RFID standard for item management - unique identifier of RF tag.
ISO 18000	ISO RFID standard for the air interface for RFID frequencies around the globe
ISO 18001	RFID for item management - application requirements profiles.
ISO 18046	RFID tag and interrogator performance test methods.
ISO 18047	The ISO RFID standard that defines the testing including conformance testing of RFID tags and readers. This is split into several parts that mirror the parts for ISO 18000.
ISO 24710	Information technology, automatic identification and data capture techniques - RFID for item management - Elementary tag license plate functionality for ISO 18000 air interface.
ISO 24729	RFID implementation guidelines - part : RFID enabled labels; part 2: recyclability of RF tags; part 3: RFID interrogator / antenna installation.
ISO 24730	RFID real time locating system: Part 1: Application Programming Interface (API); Part 2: 2.4 GHz; Part 3: 433 MHz; Part 4: Global Locating Systems
ISO 24752	System management protocol for automatic identification and data capture using RFID
ISO 24753	Air interface commands for battery assist and sensor functionality
ISO 24769	Real Time Locating System (RTLS) device conformance test methods
ISO 24770	Real Time Locating System (RTLS) device performance test methods

ISO 18000 series RFID standards

The ISO 18000 series standards is a series of standards that define the air interface for the different RFID frequencies in use around the globe. There is a total of seven standards withn the ISO 18000 series as outlined in the table below:

ISO 18000 SERIES RFID STANDARDS	
ISO 18000 STANDARD	**DETAILS OF THE PARTICULAR ISO 18000 SERIES STANDARD**
ISO 18000-V1	Generic parameters for air interfaces for globally accepted frequencies
ISO 18000-V2	Air interface for 135 KHz
ISO 18000-V3	Air interface for 13.56 MHz
ISO 18000-V4	Air interface for 2.45 GHz
ISO 18000-V5	Air interface for 5.8 GHz
ISO 18000-V6	Air interface for 860 MHz to 930 MHz
ISO 18000-V7	Air interface at 433.92 MHz

RFID standards, like standards for other system provide a real impetus to the overall RFID eco system. A variety of manufacturers can enter the same market and equipment purchasers are able to buy from one of a variety of vendors knowing that different parts will interoperate. This grows the whole market and enable all participants to benefit.

As such the RFID standards have enabled the technology to the major technology in this market area, although many manufacturers can supply equipment. The presence of standards has enabled the system to flourish and grow.

BIBLIOGRAPHY

1. Abad E, Palacio F, Nuin M et al (2009) RFID smart tag for traceability and cold chain monitoring of foods: demonstration in an intercontinental fresh fish logistic chain. J Food Eng 93(4):394–399

2. Al-Kassab, J., Lehtonen, M., Michahelles, F. (2008). D5.4. Anti- Counterfeiting Prototype Report, Deliverable of the EU-BRIDGE project, Project no. 033546, 1-63.

3. Amini, M., Otondo, R. F., Janz, B. D., Pitts, M. G (2007). Simulation Modeling and Analysis: A Collateral Application and Exposition of RFID Technology. Production and Operations Management, 16(5), 586-598.

4. Angeles, R. (2005). RFID Technologies: Applications and Implementation Issues. Information Systems Management, 22(1), 51-65.

5. Asif, Z. & Mandviwalla, M. (2005). Integrating the Supply Chain with RFID: A technical and business analysis. Communications of the Association for Information Systems (AIS), 15(24), 1-57.

6. Auto-ID Labs (2003). White Paper: Beyond the EPC™ – Making Sense of the Data Proposals for Engineering the Next Generation Intelligent Data Network. http://www.autoidlabs.org/uploads/media/MIT-AUTOID-WH024.pdf. Accessed on 10 February 2010.

7. Bamfield, J. (2004). Shrinkage, Shoplifting and the Cost of retail Crimes in Europe: A Cross-Sectional Analysis of Major Retailers in 16 European Countries. International Journal of Retail and Distribution Management, 32(5), 235-241.

8. Barney, J. B. (1991). Firm Resources and Sustained Competitive Advantage. Journal of Management, 17(1), 99-120.

9. Barratt, M. & Choi, T. (2007). Mandated RFID and institutional responses: cases of decentralized business units. Production and Operations Management, 16(5), 569-585.

10. Bharadwaj, A. (2000). A Resource-Based Perspective on Information Capability and Firm Performance: An Empirical Investigation. MIS Quarterly, 24(1), 169-196.

11. Bhatt, G. D. & Grover, V. (2005). Types of Information Technology Capabilities and their Role in Competitive Advantage: An Empirical Study. Journal of Management Information Systems, 22(2), 253–277.
12. Bridge (2007). D7.1 – Supply Chain Management in the European Textile Industry, deliverable D7.1 of the EU-funded research project "Building Radio frequency Identification solutions for the Global Environment" (BRIDGE). Project no. 033546, August 2007.
13. Bridge (2009). BRIDGE Overview Brochure of the EU-funded research project "Building Radio frequency Identification solutions for the Global Environment" (BRIDGE). Project no. 033546, September 2009.
14. Brintrup A, Ranasinghe D, McFarlane D (2010) RFID opportunity analysis for leaner manufacturing. Int J Product Res 48(9): 2745–2764
15. Brown, S. A. (1997). Revolution at the Checkout Counter. Harvard Business Review Press, Cambridge, MA.
16. Cabanes G, Bennani Y, Chartagnat C et al (2008) Topographic connectionist unsupervised learning for RFID behavior data mining. In: Proceedings of the 2nd international workshop on RFID technology—concepts, applications, challenges, IWRT 2008, pp 63–72
17. Chryssolouris G et al (2009) Digital manufacturing: history, perspectives, and outlook. J Eng Manuf 223(5):451–462
18. El-Sobky H, AbdelAzeim M (2011) A novel model for capturing and analyzing customers' references for ceramic tiles, secondary a novel model for capturing and analyzing customers' references for ceramic tiles, pp 460–465
19. Emond JP, Nicometo M (2006) Shelf-life prediction and FEFO inventory management with RFID. In: The cool chain association workshop: temperature measurements when, where and how? Knivsta, Sweden.
20. Gunther O, Kletti W, Kubach U (2008) RFID in manufacturing. Springer, Berlin
21. Haberman, A. L. (2001). 17 Billion Reasons to Say Thanks. In A. L. Habermann (Ed.) Twenty-Five Years Behind Bars (pp. 113-151), Harvard University Press, Cambridge, MA.
22. Heese, H. S. (2007). Inventory Record Inaccuracy, Double Marginalization, and RFID Adoption. Production and Operations Management, 16(5), 542- 553.
23. Heim, G. R., William, R. W. Jr., Peng, D. X. (2009). The Value to the Customer of RFID in Service Applications. Decision Sciences, 40(3), 477-512.
24. Hicks, L. E. (1975). The Universal Product Code. AMACOM, New York, NY.
25. Ho GTS, Choy KL, Poon TC (2010) Providing decision support functionality in warehouse management using the RFID-based fuzzy association rule mining

approach. In: Proceedings of 2010 8th international conference on supply chain management and information systems (SCMIS), Hong Kong, China

26. Hou, J.-L. & Huang C.-H. (2006). Quantitative performance evaluation of RFID applications in the supply chain of the printing industry. Industrial Management and Data Systems, 106(1), 96-120.
27. Hozak, K. & Collier, D. A. (2008). RFID as an enabler of improved manufacturing performance, Decision Sciences, 39(4), 859-881.
28. Huang GQ et al (2008) RFID-enabled real-time wireless manufacturing for adaptive assembly planning and control. J Intell Manuf 19(6):701–713
29. Huang GQ, Wright PK, Newman ST (2009) Wireless manufacturing: a literature review, recent developments, and case studies. Int J Comput Integr Manuf 22(7):579–594
30. IDTechEx (2005). RFID progress at Wal-Mart. http://www.idtechex.com/products/en/articles/00000161.asp. Accessed 5 February 2009. Karaer, Ö. & Lee H. L. (2007). Managing the Reverse Channel with RFIDEnabled Negative Demand Information. Production and Operations Management, 16(5), 625-645.
31. Kärkkäinen, M. (2003). Increasing efficiency in the supply chain fort short shelf life goods using RFID tagging. International Journal of Retail & Distribution Management, 31(10), 329-336.
32. Kaufhof (2009). Kurzporträit. http://www.galeria-kaufhof.de/sales/coco/co_unternehmen_011_kurzp_1033.asp?FLEXID=0. Accessed on 9 November 2009.
33. Kelly, E. P. & Erickson, G. S. (2005). RFID tags: commercial applications v. privacy rights. Industrial Management & Data Systems, 105(6), 703-713.
34. Koutsoumanis K, Taoukis PS, Nychas GJE (2005) Development of a safety monitoring and assurance system for chilled food products. Int J Food Microbiol 100(1–3):253–260
35. KPMG (2005). Vertikalisierung im Handel. Auswirkungen auf die zukünftige Absatzwegestruktur.
36. Langer, N., Forman, C., Kekre, S., Scheller-Wolf, A. (2007). Assessing the Impact on RFID on Return Center Logistics, Interfaces, 37(6), 501-514.
37. Laniel M, Emond JP, Altunbas AE (2008) RFID behavior study in enclosed trailer/container for real time temperature tracking. In: Food processing automation conference, Providence, Rhode Island, USA
38. Lee, H. L. & Özer, Ö. (2007). Unlocking the Value of RFID. Production and Operations Management, 16(1), 40-64.

39. Lehtonen, M., Al-Kassab, J., Michahelles, F., Kasten, O. (2008). D5.3. Anti-Counterfeiting Business Case Report, Deliverable of the EU-BRIDGE project. Project no. 033546, 1-79.
40. Lehtonen, M., Michahelles, F., Fleisch, E. (2007). Trust and Security in RFID-based Product Authentication Systems. IEEE Systems Journal, Special Issue on RFID Technology: Opportunities and Challenges, 1(2), 129-144.
41. Lewis S (2004) A basic introduction to RFID technology and its use in the supply chain. Laran RFID, White Paper
42. Library, 25(1), 54-64.
43. Masciari E (2011) Trajectory outlier detection using an analytical approach. In: 23rd IEEE international conference on tools with artificial intelligence (ICTAI), 2011, pp 377–384
44. McAfee, A., Sjoman, A., Dessain, V. (2004). Zara: IT for Fast Fashion. Harvard: Harvard Business Publishing.
45. Metro AG (2005). RFID im Praxiseinsatz: Ein Pilotprojekt von Kaufhof und Gerry Weber. Metro Group Future Store Initiative, 1-43.
46. Michael, K. & McCathie, L. (2005). The Pros and Cons of RFID in Supply Chain Management. Proceedings of the International Conference on Mobile Business (ICMB'05), 623-629.
47. Mo JPT et al (2009) Directional discrimination in radio frequency identification system for materials flow control in manufacturing and supply chain. Proc Inst Mech Eng B 223(7):875–883
48. Moon, K. L. & Ngai, E. W. T. (2008). The adoption of RFID in fashion retailing: a business value-added framework. Industrial Management & Data Systems, 108(5), 596-612.
49. Quirk RE (Jr) (2007) RFID's new challenge. Traffic World 271(12):19–21
50. Ren Z, Anumba CJ, Tah J (2010) RFID-facilitated construction materials management (RFID-CMM)—a case study of watersupply project. Adv Eng Inf 25(2):198–207
51. Rockwell Automation (2004) RFID in manufacturing—a practical guide on extracting measureable value from RFID implementations in plant and warehouse operation.
52. Saygin C, Sarangapani J, Grasman SE (2007) A systems approach to viable RFID implementation in the supply chain. Springer series in advanced manufacturing, pp 3–27
53. Thiesse, F. & Fleisch, E. (2008). On the value of location information to lot scheduling in complex manufacturing processes. International Journal of Production Economics, 112(2), 532-547.

54. Thiesse, F., Al-Kassab, J., Fleisch, E. (2009). Understanding the value of integrated RFID systems: a case study from apparel retail. European Journal of Information Systems, 18, 592–614.

55. Tzeng, S. F., Chen, W. H., Pai, F. Y. (2008). Evaluating the business value of RFID: Evidence from five case studies. International Journal of Production Economics, 112(2), 601-613.

56. Venables, M. (2005). Analysis: RFID - Don't believe the hype. IEE Manufacturing Engineer, October/November 2005, 8-9.

57. Wang K, Yu Q, Ricke K (2013) Feasibility study of RFID (radio frequency identification) for Hansen protection AS. SINTEF report, No. A24703, ISBN: 9788214056105, Trondheim

58. Wang K, Yu Q, Wang Y (2013) RFID based data mining for E-logistics. In: ICE-B 2013 (intentional conference of e-business), 29–31 July, 2013, Reykevik, Iceland

59. Wang, L.-C. (2007). Enhancing construction quality inspection and management using RFID technology, Automation in Construction, 17(4), 467-479.

60. Wang, S. W., Chen, W. H., Ong, C. S., Liu, L., Chuang, Y. W. (2006). RFID applications in hospitals: A case study on a demonstration RFID project in a Taiwan hospital. Proceedings of the 39th Hawaii international conference on systems science, Los Alamitos, CA, 1-10.

61. Wessel, R. (2007). Metro Group's Galeria Kaufhof Launches UHF Item- Level Pilot, RFID Journal. www.rfidjournal.com/article/articleprint/3624/-1/1. Accessed on 10 February 2010.

62. Wheatley, M. (2008). Learning to track ROI, Data collection technologies offer true business value – if you know where to look. Manufacturing Business Technology, 26(9), 28- 30.

63. Wyld, D. C. (2006). RFID 101: the next big thing for management. Management Research News, 29(4), 154-173. 87. Yu, S.-C. (2007). RFID implementation and benefits in libraries. The Electronic

64. Wyld, D. C. (2008). Death sticks and taxes: RFID tagging of cigarettes. International Journal of Retail & Management, 35(7), 571-582.

65. Yu Q, Wang Y, Wang K (2012) Extracting associative rules for RFID data. In: Proceedings of IWAMA 2012 (international workshop of advanced manufacturing and automation). Tapir Academic Publisher, Trondheim, pp 467–474

66. Zhu, K. (2004). The Complementarity of Information Technology Infrastructure and E-Commerce Capability: A Resource-Based Assessment of Their Business Value. Journal of Management Information Systems, 21(1), 167-202.

Index

www.ingramcontent.com/pod-product-compliance
Lightning Source LLC
LaVergne TN
LVHW062113200926
848484LV00007B/1661